Managed Care Services

Managed Care Services

Policy, Programs, and Research

Nancy W. Veeder
Boston College

Wilma Peebles-Wilkins
Boston University

New York Oxford
OXFORD UNIVERSITY PRESS
2001

Oxford University Press

Oxford New York
Athens Auckland Bangkok Bogotá Buenos Aires Calcutta
Cape Town Chennai Dar es Salaam Delhi Florence Hong Kong Istanbul
Karachi Kuala Lumpur Madrid Melbourne Mexico City Mumbai
Nairobi Paris São Paulo Shanghai Singapore Taipei Tokyo Toronto Warsaw

and associated companies in
Berlin Ibadan

Published by Oxford University Press, Inc.
198 Madison Avenue, New York, New York, 10016
http://www.oup-usa.org

Library of Congress Cataloging-in-Publication Data

Veeder, Nancy W.
Managed care services : policy, programs, and research / Nancy W. Veeder,
Wilma Peebles-Wilkins.
p. cm.
Includes bibliographical references and index.
ISBN 0-19-513429-X (alk. paper)—ISBN 0-19-513430-3 (pbk. : alk. paper)
1. Managed mental health care. 2. Managed care plans (Medical care)
3. Community mental health services. I. Peebles-Wilkins, Wilma
II. Title.
RA413.V44 2000
362.2'0425—dc21

00-037471

Printing (last digit): 10 9 8 7 6 5 4 3 2 1

Printed in the United States of America
on acid-free paper

◆ CONTENTS

◆ FOREWORD

There was a time when I thought I understood the concept of managed care. That was in 1971–72 when, as director of the Massachusetts Medicaid program, I signed a contract with the Harvard Community Health Plan (HCHP) to provide services to 1,200 families living on Mission Hill in Boston. HCHP would receive a monthly per capita payment for each family in the enrolled population, thus providing an incentive to keep the enrollees healthy. All services would be provided by or through HCHP to assure accountability and quality. Medicaid expenditures would be fixed at the number of enrollees multiplied by the per capita, thus giving me some control over the Medicaid budget. Today, as the editors note in the concluding chapter of this book, HCHP is in receivership and the care of 1.1 million enrollees is threatened. What happened to this relatively simple idea over the last twenty-five years?

The simple answer is that HMOs and Managed Care Organizations (MCOs) evolved to find a special niche and to survive in the changing health care market. The demand to control costs, the need to improve quality, and the opportunity to make money all contributed to this evolution. This process resulted in a range of managed care models. The Institute of Medicine (IOM) has identified ten types of managed care organizations. These include: Health Maintenance Organizations (HMOs) [staff model, group model, network model, individual practice association model, mixed model], Preferred Provider Organizations (PPOs), Point of Service (POS) plans, Management Service Organizations (MOSs), Employee Assistance Programs (EAPs), and, Managed Behavioral Health Care Organizations (MBHCOs) (Institute of Medicine, 1997). Each of these models affect payer, provider, and consumer behavior in different ways.

The only valid conclusion from the IOM study, for me, is that the concept of managed care is in need of serious refinement. Do the simple incentives of the early HCHP work in an MCO where every provider in the network is also in the network of every other MCO in the area? Can an MCO guarantee accountability and quality when there is nothing distinguishing about its providers? Why invest in the health of your enrollees when, as an organization or provider, you may lose your contract and not be around to reap the benefits? Will a POS produce the same consumer results as a staff-model HMO?

Policy-makers and practitioners need a road map to find their way among the confusing varieties of reimbursement and organizational arrangements that now characterize managed care. It is not possible to understand program outcomes without knowing the specific incentives built into the program design. I no longer discuss "managed care" unless the specific form has been stated in operational terms. "Operationalize it," then I will discuss it. To remind myself of this I have developed an acronym—Reimbursement and Organizational Arrangement Design (ROAD).

This volume provides the information and critical evaluations that will be useful to the reader in making her/his own ROAD map. The various chapters cover macroeconomic effects, biotechnology, multicultural issues, ethics, special populations, training needs, and research. Each section introduction presents a cogent overview of each of the upcoming chapters and knits together their common themes. I do not intend to duplicate these here, but rather focus on a few items of interest.

Managed care usually has been associated with health care, but as noted by Jackson, McCullough, and McCarthy (Chapter 6), increasingly is being used in child welfare services. This is not surprising since total public spending on child welfare was over $19 billion in 1998, with an additional $13.8 billion spent on children's mental health, substance abuse, and juvenile justice (*Open Minds,* 2000a, p. 7). One source estimates that about $500 million public dollars for these services were offered for managed care–type contracts in 1999 (*Open Minds,* 2000b, p. 6). States are taking advantage of federal waivers to institute managed care programs. "Nineteen states have currently been granted Title IV-E waivers that will allow them to use federal dollars to finance services not initially included in the original intent of Title IV-E funding (non-categorical services), and in reimbursement arrangements different than fee-for-service" (*Open Minds,* 2000a, p. 4). These developments mean that social workers in many sectors of human services will have to understand managed care if they are to be influential in program design and effective as advocates for their clients. They will need to develop their personal ROAD map.

Managed care, however it is defined, has numerous critics who point to its perverse incentives to reduce care, to skim a healthy population, and to devalue professional labor. While there is empirical support for these concerns, critics often fail to recognize the shortcomings of the nonmanaged human services world: Services were provided to reach the limit of insurance coverage, providers had no incentives to integrate services, and rigid service definitions limited flexibility. A substantial body of research in health and mental health show that consumers are not worse off after managed care and in some cases are better off. Some child welfare specialists see managed care as a way to expand the range of services and integrate them across jealous agency jurisdictions. The success or failure of any particular effort may all depend on the nature of the reimbursement and organizational arrangements (ROAD).

The chapters discussing special populations highlight the importance of taking account of population characteristics in designing systems of care. Older persons are the most heterogeneous of any age group and a managed care program that fails to realize this does so at its own peril. While some Medicare HMOs cite low reimbursement rates as the reason for dropping the Medicare option, it is likely that they did not understand the type and range of needs of older persons. Children, adolescents, cultural minority persons, and individuals with severe mental illness or chronic chemical dependency all have unique characteristics that will not be accommodated by a one-size-fits-all model. These characteristics need to be understood and incorporated into system design.

The current state of managed care calls for more research across a variety of dimensions. These needs are laid out in the final chapter. Practitioners, however, must take action whether or not the research has been done. They must rely on their ethical sense, their state of knowledge, and the immediate facts. The articles in this book will increase their knowledge base substantially, and help them make their own ROAD map.

James J. Callahan Jr., Ph.D.

REFERENCES

Child welfare title IV-E waivers and beyond. (2000). *Open Minds, 11*(10), 3–6.

Edmunds, M. et al. (Eds.). (1997). *Managing managed care.* Washington, DC: National Academy Press.

Sloves, H. (2000a). Federal and state spending for children exceeds $62 billion." *Open Minds, 11*(10), 6–7.

Sloves, H. (2000b). Public sector bidding opportunities in B.H.S.S. exceed $4 billion in 1999." *Open Minds, 11*(11), 6–7.

◆ CONTRIBUTORS

Barbara Berkman, Ph.D., is Helen Rehr/Ruth Fizdale Professor of Health and Mental Health at Columbia University School of Social Work and Adjunct Professor, Department of Community and Preventative Medicine, Mount Sinai School of Medicine in New York City. Her professional contribution to the knowledge base of social work in geriatric health care is evidenced in her publications, which include books, chapters, and over one hundred articles.

James J. Callahan Jr., Ph.D., is Professor and Director of Mental Health Training at the Heller School, Brandeis University, Waltham, MA. He is a former commissioner of the Massachusetts Department of Mental Health.

Susan M. Chandler, Ph.D., is Professor of Social Work at the University of Hawaii. She is currently serving as the state Director of Human Services and oversees the welfare, food stamps, child welfare, and Medicaid programs for the state.

King Davis, Ph.D., is Robert Lee Sutherland Chair in Mental Health and Social Policy at the School of Social Work, University of Texas at Austin. He previously served as Commissioner of Mental Health, Mental Retardation and Substance Abuse Services for the Commonwealth of Virginia.

Scott Miyake Geron, Ph.D., is Associate Professor of Social Welfare Policy and Research at Boston University School of Social Work. His research interests include long-term care policy and financing; home care; care management and managed care for the elderly and other high-risk and medically complex populations; and the measurement of quality and performance. He is coauthor of the recently published *Assessing Satisfaction in Health and Long-Term Care: Practical Approaches to Hearing the Voices of Consumers.*

Roberta R. Greene, Ph.D., is currently Professor at the Indiana University School of Social Work and has broad experience in direct practice, teaching, and social work administration. She has written extensively in the areas of human behavior, gerontology, and diversity.

Vivian H. Jackson, LICSW, ACSW, is Co-Principal of Jackson Mental Health and Addictions Consultants, Inc. She served as Child Welfare Advisor for the National Resource Network for Child and Family Mental Health Services at the Washington Business Group on Health. She is coeditor of *Cultural Competency in Managed Behavioral Health Services.*

Jan McCarthy, M.S.W., is a director of child welfare policy at the Georgetown University Child Development Center, where she coordinates the child welfare component of the Health Care Reform Tracking Project, which examines the impact of managed care in the public system on children with emotional problems and their families. She has coauthored several publications related to managed care in the health, mental health, and child welfare systems; welfare reform; health care considerations for children in foster care; and the 1997 Adoption and Safe Families Act.

Charlotte McCullough, M.Ed., worked for 15 years in the behavioral health field, in both public and private settings, before joining the Child Welfare League of America 13 years ago. In January of 1996, she created and became Director of the CWLA Managed Care Institute. In the fall of 1997, she also became Director of the newly created Mental Health Division of CWLA.

Wilma Peebles-Wilkins, Ph.D., ACSW, is Professor and Dean of Social Work at Boston University. She has almost thirty years of experience as an African American practitioner and educator. She has worked both in public and private sectors, as well as in an acute care hospital in pediatrics. While her publications cover a range of issues associated with services to families and children and curriculum development, her more recent scholarship focus has been on the contributions of black women to American social welfare historical developments, as well as research needs in managed health and behavioral health care.

Elizabeth Pearson Philp, M.S.W., received her M.S.W. from Boston College in 1993 and is currently a doctoral candidate at Columbia University School of Social Work. Her primary research interest is in the neurocognitive effects of violent trauma. She has worked in managed health care for eight years.

Fredric G. Reamer, Ph.D., is Professor in the graduate program of the School of Social Work, Rhode Island College. He is the author of many books and articles on professional and social work ethics and served as chair of the committee that wrote the NASW *Code of Ethics.*

Susan Saunders, CSW, ACSW, is Director of Continuity of Care and Case Management at the University of Rochester Medical Center, Director of Social Work for the Strong Health System, and Assistant Professor of Community and Preventative Medicine at the University of Rochester School of

Medicine and Dentistry. In addition, she serves as a consultant and lecturer in the field of health system care management.

Wes Shera, Ph.D., is Dean of the Faculty of Social Work at the University of Toronto. His major research interests include mental health, community development, social policy, and multicultural and international social work. His most recent work has focused on operationalizing and testing concepts of empowerment with individuals, organizations, and communities and has led to a book entitled *Empowerment Practice in Social Work: Developing Richer Conceptual Frameworks* (Canadian Scholars Press, 1999).

Judith Shindul-Rothschild, Ph.D., R.N., C.S., is Associate Professor at Boston College School of Nursing and is co-author of the book *Aging and Public Policy: Social Control or Social Justice?*. Her research and writings have focused on the relationships between health care financing, nurses? working conditions, and nursing practice. She is best known for her national survey of almost 10,000 nurses about the quality of health care services in the United States published in the *American Journal of Nursing*.

Susan Stern, Ph.D., is Associate Professor and Director of the Family Therapy Certificate Program at Boston University School of Social Work. She is known for her research on family context, family processes, and adolescent mental health and delinquency from the longitudinal Rochester Study "A Panel Study of a Reciprocal Causal Model of Delinquency," funded by the Office of Juvenile Justice and Delinquency Prevention. In addition, she has published in the areas of family therapy, anger management, child abuse, and dissemination of empirically validated interventions. Her most recent work focuses on contextually responsive treatment for disadvantaged urban families and on moving evidence-based practices into the field with fidelity.

W. Patrick Sullivan, Ph.D., is Professor at Indiana University School of Social Work and is the former Director of Indiana Division of Mental Health. He has written extensively in the areas of mental health, alcohol and drug treatment, human service policy, and strengths-based practice.

Nancy W. Veeder, M.B.A, Ph.D., has been engaged in health and mental health services, planning, program development, marketing, and research for over 30 years in the United States, Jamaica, West Indies, and Mauritius, Indian Ocean. In addition to her academic teaching and research, she has carried out extensive services utilization research and health and mental health services delivery outcomes studies. She is Associate Professor at the Boston College Graduate School of Social Work, where she teaches research and management.

INTRODUCTION

Managed Health and Behavioral Health Care Services Delivery: A Complex, Interrelated System of Policies, Programs, and Research

Managed care is a complex health and behavioral health care services delivery system. This system has evolved over a lengthy period of time and the current managed care "revolution" is, therefore, more appropriately termed an evolution.

The currently evolving managed care systems encompass wide-ranging policies and programs affecting many diverse service-delivery domains and populations at-risk in need of services. In addition, research efforts in managed care range from individual consumer, group, community, and organizational needs assessments to programmatic and services outcome evaluations based on qualitative and quantitative data.

The structural complexity of managed care services is further complicated by the potential for its two stated goals of cost-efficiency and services delivery effectiveness to be either working at cross purposes or to be in direct competition for scarce resource allocation. The most "efficient" cost-controlled methods of delivering services (e.g., least costly in time, personnel, and financial resources) may in fact not be the most "effective" in terms of providing quality service solutions to severe and persistent health and behavioral health problems. Efficiency as a concept may also be at odds with professionally defined "quality of life" outcomes variables for special populations, which may, in fact, be more expensive to deliver. For example, some psychosocial behavioral health problems need the input of more resources, over a longer period of time, with more intensity of human contact, thus making them more costly (by definition, inefficient) in order to be effective.

How can we conceptualize managed care? Mechanic (1999) has proposed that "managed care is simply a framework. What takes place within this framework will continue to be affected by our economic and social philosophies and values, and by our conceptions about the nature of [health,] mental health, and mental illness" (p. xii). Others have defined managed care as a system designed to control costs while maintaining quality services delivery (Wernet, 1999; Veeder and Peebles-Wilkins, 1998).

Regardless of the definition of managed care, most of the managed care systems literature has focused on the delivery of individual services and issues attendant to micro-level clinical services delivery. This book, on the other hand, addresses managed care at the broader systemic level in terms of policy issues, programmatic issues, and research issues related to service delivery domains and special populations.

A significant emphasis in this book is on the accountability-research area. Both policy and programmatic areas must be evaluated and modified by research in order to assess the crucial area of services delivery effectiveness. Efficiency is necessary but never sufficient to assess a product's viability. In this book we focus throughout on the crucial variables that produce effectively delivered services, especially to at-risk and vulnerable groups in society, such as children, the elderly, the poor, disabled, minorities of color, unemployed persons, substance abusers, and the mentally ill.

In order to lay the groundwork for the delineation of issues in managed care that follows, salient features of the historical evolution of managed care will be described in the next section.

THE EVOLUTION OF MANAGED HEALTH AND BEHAVIORAL HEALTH CARE

Concepts and practices contained in current managed care systems are not new (Hawkins, Veeder, and Pearce, 1998). As far back as the 13th and 16th centuries, organizations mutualized costs and delivered health care to certain trade professionals. However, the first formal funding of managed care came about in 1929 with the Ross-Loos Clinic in Los Angeles and the Elk City Farmers Cooperative Association in Elk City, Oklahoma. Ross-Loos contracted with the city of Los Angeles to provide prepaid health care for the city's water workers. The Elk City Cooperative, a consumer farmer-driven and -controlled health plan, fought for autonomy from county and state medical societies for twenty years.

In California in the 1930s, Kaiser was established as a west coast leader in managed care; in the 1940s, the Health Insurance Plan of New York brought managed care east. However, government involvement in health and behavioral health care services delivery was minimal until the 1965 passage of Titles XVIII and XIX of the Social Security Act, part of Lyndon Johnson's Great Society program. Designed solely as an antipoverty program, the passage of the two titles had the unanticipated effect of tremendous increases in medical services utilization and costs.

Health care costs skyrocketed due to the explosion of new products and pharmaceuticals and a hospital building boom. In addition, the public began to view health care delivery as free and a "right." Under these arrangements, employers paid for health insurance for their own employees, and the government paid for the elderly and the poor.

Means for cost-cutting were sought. These high costs were attributed to a fee-for-service system in which the professional provider, especially doctors and hospitals, charged whatever fees they deemed appropriate, with minimal to no governmental controls. Under the Nixon administration, managed care was endorsed and promoted under the Part C addition to Titles XVIII and XIX of the Social Security Act. Federal endorsement of the concept of Health Maintenance Organizations (HMOs) came with the 1973 passage of Public Law No. 93-222, which authorized the use of federal loans and grants funds to aid in the development of HMOs. The Tax Equity and Fiscal Responsibility Act of 1982 enabled Medicare patients to enroll in HMOs. Preferred Provider Organizations (PPOs) have had a parallel growth history to HMOs since the early 1900s (Hawkins, Veeder, & Pearce, 1998, pp. 9–11).

In a review of the evolution of managed care with a somewhat different set of emphases, Wernet (1999) notes that managed care began with industry's wish to contain health care expenditures. Three health care cost-containment approaches emerged over time: (1) decreasing the extent of health care coverage provided by employers to employees; (2) decreasing the amount paid by employers for health care while increasing copayment costs for employees; and (3) developing a third managed care solution, which necessitated a cost-effective match between the service needed or desired by the consumer and the service provided by the health care professional or system.

The first two cost-containment solutions failed to contain health care costs for industry, but the third managed care solution had several goals to improve cost containment: constraint of autonomous medical practitioner decision-making; use of generic treatments; redesign of the health care delivery system away from institutional-based care (largely hospital) and services delivery toward community-based care and delivery of health and behavioral health care services (Wernet, 1999, pp. 2–3).

This history of the evolution of managed care does not address whether or not these managed health care services delivery arrangements have successfully met either of the primary two goals of efficiency and effectiveness. These issues will be discussed in the section on the structure of managed care systems which follows.

THE STRUCTURE OF MANAGED CARE SYSTEMS

Wernet (1999) posits a managed care levels model that is similar to the categories used in this book. He observes that all managed care systems have three levels: the policy making, system design and implementation, and service provider levels. Wernet's model does not include an overarching accountability, research or policy, and programmatic outcome evaluation level. The focus of this book adds this fourth level to the Wernet scheme.

At the policy-making level, general guidelines for achieving cost containment and high-quality services are generated in both the private and public sectors. At the second level, system design and implementation activities such as designing service systems, establishing treatment protocols, implementing gatekeeping operations, and implementing utilization review and quality-assurance mechanisms take place. The major activity at the third (or service provider) network level involves selecting and certifying, or qualifying, providers for the network (Wernet, 1999, pp. 4–7).

The five essential elements in the implementation of all managed care systems regardless of structural and organizational differences are: (1) capitation and performance contracting; (2) deflection of consumers to less expensive substitute care; (3) preauthorization; (4) utilization review; and (5) case management of higher volume users (Wernet, 1999, pp. 7–13). Capitation and performance contracting are based on both sophisticated historical service utilization and predictive statistical future demand forecasting databases. Essentially, in a capitation system, a provider receives a set, predetermined dollar amount per actual or potential participant in either (or both) a catchment area or targeted population; the rate of dollars per person is not based on an individual's use of services but is based on a group formula or projection. Performance contracting is also based on complicated cost-risk formulas, complicated data on historical services use patterns and historical costs, and sophisticated use-cost projections or forecasting. These all require a comprehensive management information database.

Underlying the capitation aspect of managed care is the concept of risk assumption. The assumption of risk has been shifted rather dramatically from the individual payer and health insurers in a fee-for-service system to the provider sector. In other words, if services actually rendered cost more than the capitation payment rate, the provider absorbs those costs. If the a priori performance target is not achieved, the final payment on the contract is withheld from the provider.

The second element of managed care implementation—deflection of consumers to less expensive substitute care—mandates that certain treatments, services, and programs must be used in lieu of other services because these substitute services will produce outcomes as good as or better than the original services at lower cost. Cost efficiency is, again, the focus.

Another important aspect of managed care systems is preauthorization, frequently described as precertification or gatekeeping. The goal of gatekeeping is to match the need of the client, given the major problem constellation, with the most appropriate and least costly service in the system. Here again, cost containment is the major focus. Cost containment is aimed at limiting consumer access to the most costly treatments, adhering to services substitutability factors, and balancing medical necessity with clinical appropriateness.

The fourth aspect of managed care is utilization review, an assessment of services delivery effectiveness by the managed care system itself. Important aspects are treatment efficacy (or effectiveness) and the viability of the treatment protocols. The fifth element of managed care—case management of high-end users—is an intervention used primarily in public sector managed care efforts. Case management has been utilized extensively in other systems, currently and in the past, with considerable success.

CRITICAL POLICY, PROGRAMMATIC, AND RESEARCH ISSUES IN THE DELIVERY OF MANAGED HEALTH AND BEHAVIORAL HEALTH CARE SERVICES

The numerous critical policy, programmatic, and research issues of concern to us, all of which will be discussed in subsequent chapters in this book, will be briefly addressed here and in more detail in the overview introducing each section of the book.

The change in control of services allocation, in terms of both cost and appropriateness, has radically shifted from those trained in the delivery of health and behavioral health services to those trained in the fiscal bottom line. It was clear to most health and behavioral health care services policy generators and services designers that efforts had to be mounted to stem the breathtaking escalation of health care costs (among the most costly and least accountable of which are mental health services). However, in the efficiency-effectiveness equation, efficiency was the clear winner in the managed care redesign, thus producing many unresolved issues involving all of the stakeholders in managed care systems: consumers, providers, and funding systems.

Policy and Programmatic Issues

Health Care as a Commodity As one of our chapter authors observes, our system of health care delivery has been transformed by managed care from an essential social good into a commodity, a commodity totally dependent upon the vicissitudes of the marketplace. The locus of decision-making and power has clearly been transferred from the professional provider level (physicians, nurses, social workers, and other essential health care personnel) to the business-management level. This transfer of power encompasses both the services cost area and the substance of clinical decision-making and care.

Cost of Care In the cost area, cost-cutting is the overriding services delivery concept. This is precisely why the two major goals of managed care—efficiency (less cost) and effectiveness (quality service, as measured by controlled outcome studies)—are seen by many providers and consumers as an oxymoron. The first concern in managed care is cost control. It stands to reason that if this is the primary concern, more expensive (but frequently better in terms of outcome data) treatments and interventions will always be the managed care non-reimbursable choice. If managed care will not reimburse providers then providers will not provide and consumers will be denied some services regardless of at-risk status and compelling need.

On the other hand, because of the potentially vast resources of managed health care systems, they offer hope for the provision of both preventive and acute crisis services not available in previous fee-for-service arrangements. In those past fee-for-service systems, those most at-risk (children, mentally ill, elderly, disabled, poor, under- and unemployed, people of color) could not afford to buy services, and government support was inadequate.

Access to Care Through a variety of means such as capitation and performance contracting, gatekeeping and preauthorization, mental health and substance abuse carve-outs, substitution of less costly services, termination of service, and a variety of other cost shifting schemes, access to health and behavioral health care services may be severely curtailed, especially to at-risk groups most in need of these services. Lack of access to needed services is a major issue in managed care, one that is a recurrent theme in the chapters that follow.

Parity of Behavioral Health Services Reimbursement A major factor in lack of access to behavioral health services is the common failure of states to pay for treatment of mental health disorders at rates that are in parity with health. This flies in the face of a recent U.S. Surgeon General's Report on mental health (*Surgeon General's Report on Mental Health,* 2000), which noted that one in five Americans have a mental disorder in any given year. Currently only twenty-eight states have some, not necessarily full, parity in payments for mental health services. Of these twenty-eight, only four have comprehensive mental illness parity laws. The other twenty-four have only partial parity laws for mental illness.

Utilization of the Health and Behavioral Health Care System If equitable access to services is denied, utilization of services is curtailed. It is not possible to separate access-utilization in managed health and behavioral health discussions. The above-mentioned Surgeon General's Report on mental health in the United States cites lack of access to, and utilization of, mental health services as major deterrents to seeking services, particularly among those most at-risk for mental illness. The report points out that mental illness is second only to heart disease in industrialized countries as a cause of years lost to premature death or years spent suffering from severe disability.

Services Design and Delivery The overriding emphasis on cost containment leads to pared-down services delivery programs, narrow definitions of eligibility, and least-cost services substitution. This minimalist approach to services design can fail to produce services sufficient in breadth and complexity to ameliorate both acute and chronic illnesses, particularly among special needs and at-risk groups.

Education of Health Care Professionals and Professional Autonomy The single most important criterion for a professional is autonomy of practice. There is widespread feeling among health and mental health professionals that resources are being allocated by persons in managed care organizations who are not trained sufficiently in diagnostic categories and appropriate treatments. It is thought by many, if not most, health care professionals that managers who are cost- and resource-controlling decision-makers in managed care companies are focused on cutting costs and denying services, rather than on professional intervention factors based on the nature of problems.

Services Delivered to the Most At-Risk Populations Services for the most vulnerable populations must not only be accessible and appropriate, they must also be delivered in a culturally competent manner. This is another major point in the *Surgeon General's Report on Mental Health* (2000) and throughout the chapters in this book.

Systems Design and Case/Care Management Case management—or care management as it is more currently known—is at the programmatic, operational care-giving level. Care management has been recently described as an advanced clinical intervention mode which combines disposition planning, service referral, and follow-up with assessment, planning, linking, monitoring, and advocacy, to which is added client engagement, consultation, individual counseling, psychoeducation, crisis intervention, and collaboration with other treating clinicians in both inpatient and community outpatient settings (Hawkins, Veeder & Pearce, 1998).

Care management has been rightly described as an extremely complex intervention technique, necessitating high-level, sophisticated clinical and research skills that require "appreciation of general medical and psychiatric needs and care; and sophistication about such varied issues as housing, disability, and welfare benefits, psychosocial rehabilitation, sheltered and competitive work programs, and issues relating to the legal and criminal justice system" (Mechanic, 1999, p. 199).

Advanced levels of practice such as care management must be designed as an integral part of a system-wide care management model. This model must have a strong empirical database in all of its components, from top management to line interventions.

Ethics Ethics is the area where the greatest dissonance between the ethos of the professional caregiver and the ethos of the "bottom-liners" is most apparent and troublesome. The major ethical issues revolve around access to care and issues associated with privacy, carve-outs of mental health and substance abuse services, termination of services, parity for mental health services, and avoidance of the most at-risk populations.

A major issue is that of access to care for those most in-need and at-risk, and those who by culture, ethnicity, race, and gender are most likely both to underutilize services and to be denied free and easy access to them. That managed care has recently shown a trend to pull away from support of Medicaid programs, and has severely curtailed support of elder Medicare patients (especially in relation to drug subsidies) are disturbing signs of withdrawal from "costly" consumers. Many private clinicians continue to complain about confidentiality-related issues in information disclosures associated with reimbursement. Continued concern exists which is associated with legislative threats to allow more extensive disclosure without patient consent in medical records privacy provisions.

The managed care program of mental health carve-outs further reinforces that system's lack of dedication to the most chronic and needy populations. In order to cut mental health services delivery expenses, managed care companies mandate that mental health treatment for consumers be delivered at a not necessarily convenient "central site," or be decentralized entirely, rather than integrated into a coordinated, convenient, and highly accessible on-site health and mental health package.

Research Issues

Empirical data underlay the generation of all public policy, which, in turn, guides the design and development of health and behavioral health care programs and interventions to address consumer need. Research provides the primary basis for accountability on both major managed care goals of efficiency and effectiveness. Outcomes research in relation to managed care policies and programs is currently insufficient, a point made by all of the chapter authors in this book.

One reason for the inadequacy of empirical outcome data is that managed care systems themselves rely almost exclusively on consumer satisfaction surveys to assess the viability of services delivery. However, consumer satisfaction forms are carefully designed to control any expressions of dissatisfaction.

In addition, most consumer satisfaction forms do not link satisfaction with the specific problem for which service was requested, or with the type or complexity of service received. Such consumer satisfaction forms are interested in "your most recent encounter" with a managed care–affiliated health care facility, without providing any place to note whether that encounter was for a routine blood test or a diagnostic work-up for diabetes, cancer, or heart disease. Finally, researchers know that most clients will be "satisfied" when asked for their opinions by the source of the service they have received.

Client satisfaction measures are at best a minimal outcome measure precisely because clients should be satisfied with services delivered, especially with populations such as the elderly, disabled, and severely mentally ill, where need is great and any intervention or expression of caring is seen as a plus. Hence, managed care systems report positive client outcome satisfaction data, and use these data to generate their "report cards" for provider services and organizations as a basis for future reimbursement. Clients are usually not cognizant of the specific effectiveness, or completeness, or appropriateness of the service delivered, particularly in addressing intervention goals generated by providers at the beginning of service delivery.

To assess the accountability of managed care policies and services delivery, controlled empirical studies are needed that examine differential services delivery outcomes, with different target groups, with diverse health and behavioral health problems. Data gathered must be analyzed through the equally important filters of initially set behavioral goals achievement, time spent, nature of problem in terms of severity and chronicity, and cost to deliver the particular services. Data gathering must be both quantitative and qualitative, with particular attention paid to ecological and psychosocial quality-of-life factors. Only then will we be able to factor out which problems need increased resources to cure, ameliorate, or simply to maintain an adequate quality-of-life functional level throughout the life span.

ORGANIZATION OF THE BOOK

This book is organized into two parts: (1) The Context of Human Service Practice in Managed Care Environments, and (2) Managed Care: Services Delivery Domains for Special Needs and At-Risk Populations. Each part has a brief overview delineating themes and summarizing major points of the chapter authors in the respective part.

REFERENCES

Hawkins, J. W., Veeder, N. W., & Pearce, C. W. (1998). *Nurse-social worker collaboration in managed care: A model of community case management*. New York: Springer Publishing Company.

Mechanic, D. (1999). *Mental health and social policy: The emergence of managed care*. Boston: Allyn and Bacon.

Surgeon General's report on mental health. (2000). Washington, DC: Office of the Surgeon General of the United States.

Veeder, N. W., & Peebles-Wilkins, W. (1998). Research needs in managed behavioral health care. In G. Schamess & A. Lightburn (Eds.), *Humane managed care?* Washington, DC: NASW Press.

Wernet, S. P. (1999). *Managed care in human services*. Chicago: Lyceum Books.

◆ PART ONE ◆

THE CONTEXT OF HUMAN SERVICE PRACTICE IN MANAGED CARE ENVIRONMENTS

The five chapters in this part focus on the macroeconomic impact of managed care; the impacts of biotechnology on managed care in terms of health care cost, clinical practice, and education of health care professionals; the implications of fee-for-service, managed health care, and cultural competence for health care policy and services for people of color; the broader ethical issues pertaining to managed care policy formation and implementation; and a centralized systemic model for the implementation of care management.

The general themes in these five chapters all revolve around lack of focus on, primarily, the consumers of health and behavioral health care services, and, secondarily, the providers of these services. All stress the failure or potential failure of managed care systems to address the substantial needs of those most at-risk and vulnerable populations, such as the poor, elderly, children, the disabled, the un- and under-employed, persons of color, and the mentally ill. These target groups provide a theme for both parts of this book.

In "The Macroeconomic Impact of Managed Care," Judith Shindul-Rothschild discusses the realignment of power in managed care systems from practitioners to corporations; in short, she describes how health and behavioral health care services delivery was apparently swiftly transformed from an essential social good to a commodity bought and sold on Wall Street or on the Internet. The fear expressed is that profits supersede the needs of patients, a fear well taken in view of managed care systems' overriding obsession with the efficiency (or cost cutting) aspects of services delivery.

The point is also made that "consumers" in U.S. managed health care are now corporations. Numerous examples are given, such as shifting financial risk to providers by means of capitation and selective contracting, withholding physicians' salaries for exceeding projected expenses, bonuses and incentives for cost savings, and withdrawal from unprofitable Medicaid and Medicare business lines.

Shindul-Rothschild calls for needed research in such areas as fee-for-service models versus managed care costing models in terms of services outcomes from both the provider and consumer vantage points (and makes the point that there exist clear research findings showing that consumer satisfaction is much higher among not-for-profit than for-profit insurance plans); analysis of quality indicators; and empirical assessments of health care financing models in terms of cost, quality, and access efficacy. Direct care providers must always be equal partners in research, in order for clinical impacts to be correctly and adequately measured. Finally, Shindul-Rothschild calls for health and behavioral health care professionals to work together in interdisciplinary teams to restore humanistic values as an essential feature of the U.S. health care system.

Elizabeth Pearson Philp and Barbara Berkman, "Biotechnology and Managed Care: Effects on Health Care Cost, Clinical Practice, and Education of Health Care Professionals," begin by observing that managed care challenged traditional medical care hierarchies by inserting non-medical financial decision-makers and market forces into the whole services-delivery process. The shift to a market-driven health care system, coupled with advances in health care technological knowledge, led to rapid changes in health care services delivery, impacting the system in five areas: the cost of care, access to care, utilization of the system by consumers as well as providers, service delivery, and the education of health care professionals.

Cost-cutting efforts of managed care have made it unlikely that health care will ever return to a fee-for-service system. Cost reduction coupled with interest in quality of care is a complicated duality, providing ethical struggles to reconcile competing, if not mutually exclusive goals. Capitation systems, prominent in managed care, necessitate contributions from multiple disciplines in order to attain adequate understanding of psychosocial factors in health behaviors and the social implications of illnesses like HIV/AIDS, tuberculosis, or trauma. Attempts to regulate and cut costs in relation to access to health care may generate societal costs such as greater dependence on the support and assistance of informal caregivers, lost wages, increased caregiver strain, and individual financing of private homecare assistance.

Common to all managed care mental health service delivery models are biopsychosocial assessments, brief interventions, and the use of standardized treatment protocols to attain functional outcomes. The common system of mental health and substance abuse carve-outs poses many problems, among which is the lack of mental health training among generalist physician gatekeepers in the carve-out system.

Impacts of managed care on education of health professionals are many, including erosion of the current system of training and research for health professionals caused by financial constraints coupled with decreasing patient populations, the need for multidisciplinary collaborative teaching models, updated curricula to include managed care, and updated substantive areas in educating health care professionals to be more in line with widespread changes in services delivery. Philp and Berkman urge a shift to greater accountability through research in such areas as comparisons in terms of treatment outcome viability between integrating versus carving out mental health services.

In "The Intersection of Fee-for-Service, Managed Health Care, and Cultural Competence: Implications for National Health Care Policy and Services to People of Color," King Davis presents data which show that people of color have mental health problems misdiagnosed more frequently, are diagnosed more severely than the symptoms warranted, and are treated less frequently than whites with current medical procedures, even when there were no differences between the two groups in ability to pay for services. Davis maintains that the key variable in this inequity of racial treatment is absence of equitable access. Further, added to the access issue is demonstrated differential response by health care providers to the race and gender of the patient, which influences health care decisions that are made.

Davis asserts that "monoculturalism" is a way specifically designed to not understand, and, hence, to improperly treat, people of color. He notes that if the costs of serving people of color are perceived to be higher than for other populations, there will be few incentives for managed care plans, stimulated by profit and cost savings, to voluntarily seek to cover people of color without additional consideration. Davis further points out that the costs of serving people of color may, in fact, be artificially inflated by diagnostic and treatment errors stemming from a monocultural frame of reference that results in higher utilization rates of more expensive inpatient care.

Davis asserts that previous American health policies (including fee-for-service, Medicaid, and Medicare) have failed to solve problems of marked differences in access to quality health care, years of living, risk and vulnerability to illness and, disproportionately high death rates of America's poor, severely mentally ill, unemployed, and underemployed populations as well as populations of color considered medically underserved. On the other hand, managed care contains several potential virtues, including increasing both access and quality for low income consumers.

Davis suggests the use of culturally competent practice and policy. By cultural competency he means practices and policies which integrate and transform attitudes, behaviors, knowledge, information, facts, patterns, history, and data about individuals, groups, and communities of color into goals, policy, change strategies, desired outcomes, organizational structures, and service standards and locations that match the individual's culture.

The key to all of the above is good data. Davis raises ten critical public policy questions that must be subjected to empirical research in relation to issues of linkages between race, health status, and the cost of managed health and behavioral health care services.

Frederic G. Reamer, "Ethics and Managed Care Policy," focuses on broader ethical issues as they relate to managed care policy formation and implementation. Reamer points out that ethical dilemmas (moral right or wrong and duty and obligation choices) arise when professionals face conflicting values or moral duties, obligations, or responsibilities. Managed health and behavioral health care services delivery, because of its potentially conflicting goals of cost containment and the delivery of quality services, provides fertile ground for ethical dilemmas among professional caregivers.

Reamer suggests the development of a specialty within managed care called *ethical risk prevention and risk management.* Three major ethical issues to be addressed include the individual's access to services, the delivery of services, and the termination of services. Guidelines for ethical managed care are suggested, all of which may include multiple and frequently conflicting goals: meeting clients' needs; enhancing client freedom of choice for providers and services; enhancing professionals' autonomy and ability to meet clients' needs consistent with their best judgment; and allocating limited resources in a fair, just, and cost-effective manner consistent with social workers' obligation to be "diligent stewards" of resources.

Like the other authors in this section, Reamer asserts that the major challenge is to establish empirical outcome criteria in order to assess quality of care. This requires four important components: a variety of levels of outcome data (including tentative or suggestive evidence, promising or interesting evidence, probable effectiveness, and established effectiveness); adherence to practice guidelines or protocols; client satisfaction; and judgments of professional peers.

Susan Saunders, "System Care Management: Purpose, Structure, and Function" provides a model for care management in large, complex health and behavioral health care settings. She describes trends which have, and will continue to, lead to six transformations shifting health care delivery from person as customer to population as customer; illness care to wellness care; revenue management to cost management; professional autonomy to professional interdependence; continuity of provider to continuity of information; and patient as non-consumer to consumer of cost and quality information.

Saunders outlines several means by which health systems will achieve cost-efficiency, including continued channeling of care to lower-cost ambulatory environments; further reduction in staff-to-patient ratios; group purchasing and tightly controlled supply consumption; care standardization to cap clinical resource utilization; elimination of cost-leader programs; and continued system consolidation to achieve greater cost control across the continuum of care.

High levels of consumer satisfaction and positive clinical outcomes are crucial to any managed health and behavioral health care system. Saunders focuses on case management, within the larger care management model, as a crucial health service delivery modality. She outlines ten core objectives of case management: consumer empowerment; improved health; managed disease; managed utilization; managed risks; case continuity; managed cost; enhanced satisfaction; improved quality; and demonstrable outcomes. Finally, Saunders outlines a systemic model for centralized care management and the empirical assessment of its outcomes.

In conclusion, all of the chapter authors in this section stress both the complexity of managed health and behavioral health care services-delivery systems, and the need for multidisciplinary research to provide baseline data in every aspect of these complex systems.

◆ CHAPTER 1 ◆

The Macroeconomic Impact of Managed Care

JUDITH SHINDUL-ROTHSCHILD

The financing of health care services has historically been complicated by a patchwork of providers and insurers whose interests often conflict with those of the public. Over the past decade, payers and consumers did reach accord that aggressive measures were needed to bring the spiraling costs of health care under control. For years, policy makers and insurers recognized that the "blank check" form of financing had rewarded providers for charging and doing more. Regulations promulgated at the state and federal level had slowed health care costs in some states and for some services, but overall, reports of unnecessary or inappropriate surgical procedures, tests, and specialist referrals continued virtually unchecked.

Managed care offered several innovations in financing that theoretically would force providers and patients to become more cost conscious through competition, not regulation. Capitation and other risk-sharing arrangements were among the novel reimbursement schemes proposed by managed care insurers. Under the old cost-based form of reimbursement, providers billed insurers for services rendered and received a payment based on their charges. The incentive was to drive up volume, which in turn drove up costs. In capitation, providers are paid a lump sum for each patient enrolled in the provider's organization. Under capitation, financial risk is shared jointly by the provider and the insurer. These risk-sharing arrangements give providers an incentive to control utilization through health promotion and careful case management.

Managed care also promised to rid the health care system of redundant or unnecessary services through consolidation and gatekeeping. Hospitals became "vertically integrated," adding an array of ambulatory and long-term care services. The integration of community-based services with acute care was driven by the need to deliver "seamless care" in which patients moved quickly from more expensive to less costly care centers. A common refrain became "the right level of care, at the right time, for the right patient." Referrals to specialists, admissions to hospitals, tests, and even emergency care could not be accessed unless nurses and physicians hired by managed care organizations first give patients and their physicians approval.

Given the high expectations that managed care would rein in costs and improve quality through such innovations, it's not surprising that a majority of Americans are now receiving health care benefits through a managed care provider. As managed care has proliferated, so too has the debate on whether managed care has helped or hurt patients. Some facts are indisputable: There has been a realignment of power from practitioners to corporations that has had a profound impact on the nature of caregiving.

What disturbs many health care practitioners is that a singular focus on the bottom line has resulted in a delivery system in which profits supercede the needs of patients. How health care delivery was so swiftly transformed from an essential social good to a commodity bought and sold on Wall Street is the focus of this chapter. We will look at the broad macroeconomic forces that set the stage for free-market reforms. We will examine the sweeping role of government both on the state and federal level to mediate some of the untoward effects of managed care. And finally, we will ask how practitioners may work together to restore humanistic values as an essential feature of the U.S. health care system.

A BRIEF OVERVIEW OF MACROECONOMIC THEORIES

In a capitalist economy, costs can be controlled either by market forces or government regulation. In health care, competition and regulation have been used simultaneously to control costs, maintain quality, and assure access to care. Health care economists such as Samuelson (1954) originally proposed that by measuring the social value of public goods, economists could advise nations about allocating capital resources to embody the ideals of equity and fairness. Gradually, these social welfare models were replaced with economic models that relied on market forces, not government, to efficiently distribute health care goods. Pauly (1971) and Feldstein (1973) were among the first health care economists to develop economic models where fairness or equity was secondary to considerations of market efficiency.

Attempts to purify health care economics by formulating alleged "value-free" models ignored the fact that by omission these models implied the market was preferable to government in allocating health care resources (Melhando, 1998). Further complicating economic prescriptions and government planning was the confusing, contradictory, or at times totally absent data on effectiveness of treatment—an essential prerequisite for determining health care need (Melhando, 1998). If economists and policy experts were daunted by the elusiveness of macroeconomic analyses of health care, then, by default, the task for determining the proper allocation of health care services largely fell to the political process.

The public would debate how much of every tax dollar should be spent on health care, education, national defense, or other essential social goods.

Government budgets would mirror the social values of the electorate and budgets planned accordingly. Empiric evidence suggests that despite the shortcomings of this system, nations, and even states within the United States, have been successful at regulating costs while simultaneously fulfilling their social responsibility to broad segments of the population (Shindul-Rothschild & Gordon, 1994). However, beginning in the 1980s, the appeal of the market mounted as budgetary impasses grew and political wrangling stalled any meaningful health care reform.

Another critical factor contributing to abandonment of regulation and the growing appeal of market-based reforms was the behavior of providers. In every other industrialized country, providers have agreed to budgetary limits on their income in exchange for retaining control over allocation of health care services (Brown, 1998). To date, U.S. providers, in particular physicians, have been unwilling to make such a concession. American physicians and hospitals have presumed that their own economic self-interest would be better served if health care was distributed as a commodity in the market, not as an essential social good by government.

Against this backdrop came an initiative in Clinton's first term as president to increase government's role in health care financing. Precisely why the Clinton health care plan failed is the source of endless academic debate. Some political scientists fault the intellectual or health policy elites for their inability to reach consensus (Patel & Rushefsky, 1998), or even when they did, to effectively influence the political process (Wilensky, 1997). Other political scientists cite the opposition of corporate interest groups—especially the private insurance industry, which wields enormous clout in Congress (Weissert & Weissert, 1996). Journalists found fault with the media and its inability to effectively communicate to the public the essential features of the Clinton health care plan (Johnson & Broder, 1996), which in turn led health care economists to conclude that the public simply didn't have the will to enact reforms (Brodie & Blendon, 1995).

Whatever the cause, the outcome was the same. Private industry won over government as the preferred arbitrator of health care services. At the time, no one could have predicted how the possibility of a larger federal presence in health care would spur the intervention of corporate America. Thus the stage was set for the rapid proliferation of financial reimbursement schemes under the rubric of managed care. The latest data does suggest that managed care has delivered on its promise of lowering health care costs. The question now has become, which costs and for whom?

INTERNATIONAL COMPARISON OF MACROECONOMIC POLICIES

Economists have used sophisticated statistical analyses to demonstrate that there is a linear relationship between health care spending and gross domestic product (GDP) across a wide array of countries, financing schemes, and delivery systems (Pheleps, 1997). In other words, the wealthier the country, the more it will spend on health care. Therefore it's not surprising that the United States, the wealthiest country in the world, would spend the most on health care services for its citizens.

In the aggregate, health care costs in the United States do exceed the expenditures of other countries either as a percentage of GDP or as a ratio to per capita costs. But statistics cannot answer the complicated question of how much health care consumption in American society is too much. Or, restated, when does the percentage of GDP for health care become "inefficient" or a drain on the U.S. economy?

If one examines the rate of growth of health care from 1993 to 1996, health care costs have declined as a percentage of GDP in Canada and flattened in the United States. In the 1990s, the share of GDP devoted to health care in the United States has remained stable at about 12% (*Health Care Financing Review,* 1998). While some might attribute this slowing to the effectiveness of the market, in Canada even greater savings were achieved during a comparable period under a single-payer national health insurance plan.

Gross comparisons of aggregated costs also do not explain which part of the health care delivery system contributes the most to rising costs. Economists credit both a deceleration of health care spending and a growing economy with keeping national health spending unchanged as a share of the nation's GDP (Levit, Lazenby & Braden, 1998). The general health of the economy—specifically, economic inflation—accounted for over half (52%) of the rise in health care costs in 1996. Thus, the single most effective way to lower health care costs is, first and foremost, to have a robust economy.

After overall economic inflation, other factors contributing to rising costs are population growth (21%), a rise in the intensity of services (19%), and overall medical inflation (4%) (*Health Care Financing Review,* 1998). It is commonly assumed that the rise in "intensity of health care services" is a function of American's overuse or inappropriate use of health care services. However, when economy-wide and medical price inflation are taken into account, the real services purchased per person increased a mere 0.8% in 1996 (*Health Care Financing Review,* 1997).

In 1996, hospital expenditures as a percent of total personal health care expenditures decreased to 39.5% (*Health Care Financing Review,* 1998). Spending for physician services experienced the slowest rate of growth since the 1960s, dropping to 22.3% of all personal health care costs (*Health Care Financing Review,* 1998). The annual growth of spending decreased in both home health care and in nursing homes by 9.5% and 5.3%, respectively (*Health Care Financing Review,* 1997). And finally, between 1990 and 1996 the annual rate of growth in personal health expenditures was slower than at any time in recorded history. Remarkably, all of these decreases in the growth of spending are occurring at a time when the numbers of the aged and the uninsured are on the rise.

In practical terms, Americans are seeing their doctors less, spending less time in hospitals, and if they do go home, are receiving fewer home care visits. In 1993, Americans visited physicians slightly less often a year (6 visits) than citizens in Canada (6.8 visits), and when Americans were hospitalized they remained in the hospital on average four less days than Canadians did (OECD, 1997). Is this prudent rationing of services, or are Americans being denied necessary services? And what is the effect of these practices on the quality of health care?

If one compares morbidity and mortality statistics across industrialized countries, the cost of health care does not appear to be associated with the health status of U.S. citizens. In 1995, out of twenty-seven industrialized countries only six countries (Czech Republic, Hungary, Korea, Mexico, Poland, and Portugal) had a life expectancy for men lower than the United States (72.5 years). During the same period, the same six countries plus Ireland and Denmark had a life expectancy for women lower than that of the United States (79.2 years). Only six countries (Greece, Hungary, Korea, Mexico, Poland, and Turkey) had infant mortality rates per one hundred live births higher than the United States (0.80) in 1995 (OECD, 1997).

With the noted exception of the United States, there is a strong statistical relationship between medical spending, per capita income, and mortality (Pheleps, 1997). How can we account for such discrepancy between what the United States pays for health care in the aggregate, and the overall health status of its citizenry? The answer lies in how the U.S. health care market allocates its health care resources.

THE IMPACT OF MACROECONOMIC POLICIES ON MEDICARE AND MEDICAID

Since the 1970s, states have experimented with managed care as a way of slowing the escalating costs of Medicaid. By 1997, almost half of all Medicaid beneficiaries were receiving care through a managed care program (Gold, 1999). Logic would say that taking care of poor or chronically ill elderly patients is not likely to be profitable. A series of reports from the federal agencies and researchers has found that competitive financing presents a myriad of problems for vulnerable populations.

Almost a decade ago, the General Accounting Office (GAO) documented that the incentive to underserve was a major problem with Medicaid managed care programs (GAO, 1990). A subsequent GAO report released in 1996 found that allowing Medicaid managed care insurers to market their programs directly to Medicaid recipients had also resulted in numerous abuses and outright fraud (GAO, 1996). The GAO attributed the incentive to underserve Medicaid clients to capitation and other financial arrangements used by managed care organizations that shifted the financial risk from the insurer to individual providers (Medicaid Managed Care, 1992). The GAO recommended a number of safeguards including capping financial bonuses to providers for coming in under the capitated rate and limiting providers' financial risk.

In addition to capitation, competitive bidding to select plans for participation in managed care programs became a significant trend in the mid-1990s. In New York, competitive bidding for Medicaid business has had the perverse effect of discouraging new managed care plans from entering the market and triggering an exodus of existing managed care providers (Sparer, Brown & Kovner, 1999). Undeterred by the experience of state-administered Medicaid programs, the Clinton administration's Medicare reform proposal plans to save $8 billion through a "Competitive Defined Benefit" financing scheme. Skeptics, such as former HCFA administrator Gail Wilensky, cannot "imagine" how the federal government can realistically implement competitive bidding as a way to reign in Medicare costs (Weschler, 1999).

By 1996, only 35% of HMOs were profitable compared to 90% in 1994 (Levit et al., 1997). HMOs with the highest number of Medicaid subscribers had the worse financial performance (McCue, Hurley, Draper & Jurgensen, 1999). Industry representatives attribute lower profit performances in 1998 to the Balanced Budget Act of 1997, which tightened the payments to Medicare managed care providers. In 1998, one hundred health plans exited the Medicare managed care markets, and observers believe that Medicaid managed care insurers are not far behind (Saphir & Rauber, 1999).

Recent estimates from the Health Care Financing Administration are that 327,000 Medicare beneficiaries will lose coverage in the Medicare managed care programs by the year 2000 (Fisher, 1999). The GAO disputes industry claims that low reimbursement and excessive regulation are the culprits behind the exodus of Medicare managed care plans. Instead, the GAO attributes the loss of Medicare managed care plans to "the normal reaction of plans to market competition and conditions" (*Business & Health*, 1999:14). While industry and government officials may disagree on the semantics, HMOs clearly have "pulled back from unprofitable business lines like Medicare and Medicaid" (Walker, 1999, p. 8).

The use of competitive financing schemes to slow rising costs in Medicare and Medicaid is also being felt by populations not directly covered under either program. Prior to the advent of managed care, capitation, and competitive bidding, providers often relied on revenues from private insurers to cross-subsidize care for the uninsured or underinsured. With selective contracting, providers are now forced to compete on the basis of price and can no longer rely on the capital surplus from private insurers to cover their losses due to uncompensated care.

Cunningham (1999) used data from the Community Tracking Study to examine the effects of managed care penetration and uninsurance on access to care for low-income individuals. The study concluded that an "access gap" exists in areas characterized by high managed care penetration because financial "incentives limit the cross-subsidization of care to the medically indigent."

THE IMPACT OF MACROECONOMIC POLICIES ON PRIVATE HEALTH INSURANCE

One distinguishing characteristic of the U.S. health care system is that apart from Medicare and Medicaid, the main purchasers of health insurance are American businesses that provide health care coverage as a benefit of employment. To appreciate recent macroeconomic trends in health care, one must first recognize that American industries, as a major purchaser of health care services, exert enormous influence over every aspect of health care financing and delivery. It is American businesses who have actively sanctioned or promoted many of the practices imposed by managed care insurers to rein in escalating health care costs.

In every international measure of health care utilization—preventative services, physician visits, hospital stays, and home health care visits—the United States lags behind other comparable industrialized countries. Yet, managed care insurers convinced American businesses that one of the primary reasons premiums were rising was due to excess demand by consumers. Managed care proponents successfully persuaded American businesses that usurping consumers' freedom to access health care was critical to slowing the rise of health insurance premiums.

Under managed care, efficient allocation of services was to be left to a managed care gatekeeper or to the patient's primary care provider, who would authorize access to health care services—even emergency care. Access to health care providers or institutions would be limited to those providers chosen by the insurer. Of all the macroeconomic policies imposed by managed care, the loss of freedom to choose one's health care provider has unquestionably had the most far-reaching impact on access to care in the United States. Ironically, American businesses actively colluded with managed care insurers to eliminate one of the cornerstones of a free or unfettered market.

American businesses view health care costs as a social debt to employees. Every dollar spent on an employee's health insurance benefit package is one less dollar available to reinvest or to pass on to shareholders in the form of dividends. Given these financial tradeoffs, growing numbers of businesses have reneged on their social responsibility to provide health insurance for their employees. In 1997, the U.S. Census Bureau estimated that 41.7 million Americans had no health insurance, an increase of 1.7 million Americans from the previous year (Carrasquillo, Himmelstein, Woolhandler & Bor, 1999).

Varying explanations have been proposed for the paradoxical rise in the number of uninsured working Americans during a period of relative prosperity. The income group that had the largest increase in uninsurance between 1994 and 1996 was middle-income families. Researchers have attributed the decline to employers' dropping health insurance as a benefit of employment, or discouraging employees from using their health insurance benefit (Carrasquillo, Himmelstein & Woolhandler, 1999).

Theoretically, a free market operates most efficiently when consumers have complete information about goods or services so they can make informed purchasing decisions. Complete information alone is not useful unless consumers have unrestricted access to providers. Complete information and purchasing freedom are considered key elements to lowering costs and maintaining quality in a free market. Lack of access to information on quality of care has been repeatedly associated with the failure of managed care to deliver on its promise of controlling costs while simultaneously improving quality.

MACROECONOMIC POLICIES AND THE IMPACT ON QUALITY

Any discussion about a complicated concept such as quality must be prefaced with a few caveats. There is no consensus about what connotes quality health care, let alone how to objectively measure it. Essential to a discussion on quality is agreement on benchmarks. What yardstick is used to judge if outcomes are exceptional, acceptable, or unacceptable? Is it acceptable for the United States to have one of the worst infant mortality rates of all industrialized countries? Or, given the country's level of health care expenditures, is it a reasonable expectation that the United States should have the *lowest* rate of infant mortality? Even if quality-assurance experts were able to reach broad agreement on preferred outcomes, benchmarks, and risk-adjustments to make legitimate comparisons across providers, there remains the daunting task of determining who will pay for the collection and dissemination of information to the primary stakeholders.

The question of who the primary stakeholders are is important because the target audience for quality information will have a significant influence on who participates in the process, what information will be collected, and who is likely to receive it. Possible stakeholders include businesses that purchase health insurance on behalf of their employees; employees and their dependents, who are the beneficiaries; state, federal, or local governments, which may be major purchasers, regulators, or both; direct care providers; and, of course, the managed care industry.

The health insurance industry has an enormous financial self-interest in assuring that whatever information is released, it does not adversely affect their bottom line. These questions may seem elementary, but it is crucial to recognize that, to date, some of these stakeholders have had access to outcome data while others have not. Some stakeholders have willingly shared outcome data and others have not. Each stakeholder has some bias about what kinds of information about quality and outcomes is most relevant, and each will use their leverage to influence the analysis and dissemination of information measuring quality.

The disinterest in quality among businesses and insurers is another deterrent to improving the health status of Americans. Washington Business Group on Health found that while almost all businesses (91%) considered cost when selecting a health insurance plan for their employees, less than a third (31%) considered quality. A survey of seventy-seven businesses by the National Commission on Quality Assurance (NCQA) found that information from the Health Care Employer Data and Information Set (HEDIS) was made available to employees by only four of the businesses (Born & Geckler, 1998). The usefulness of the HEDIS information is limited to the 329 insurers who voluntarily participated in 1996. Pressure is growing on insurers to participate in HEDIS and it is anticipated there will be a 50% increase in respondents when the data is released in the fall of 1998 (Meltsner, 1998). But, some for-profit health insurers view quality evaluations as proprietary and flatly refuse to release the information at all (Emanuel & Goldman, 1998).

A common concern among beneficiaries is whether there is a measurable difference in quality between managed care insurers and fee-for-service indemnity plans. A meta-analysis of forty-eight studies found no consistent pattern of differences in quality between managed care and fee-for-service (Dudley, Miller, Kornbrot & Luft, 1998). Although differences in clinical outcomes may not be apparent between managed care insurers and fee-for-service plans, a 1997 national survey of consumer satisfaction conducted by the National Research Corporation strongly suggests that consumers are much more satisfied with their overall care in fee-for-service plans than in managed care.

A study of managed care utilization review companies did find that nonprofit companies were more likely than proprietary companies to provide more public goods and to be more community-oriented (Schlesinger, Gray & Bradley, 1996). Not-for-profit insurer plans also allocate significantly more services to prevention than their for-profit counterparts. The higher quality not-for-profit plans had, on average, one additional physician visit per year when compared to inferior plans.

One possible explanation offered by the researchers for this difference is that not-for-profits spend significantly less of every premium dollar on administrative overhead and more on medical expenses (Born & Geckler, 1998). The percentage of each premium dollar that is expended on administrative overhead versus direct medical care is termed the medical loss ratio (MLR).

Consumer surveys conducted by a wide range of organizations from private foundations (Kaiser Family Foundation) to quality assurance organizations (NCQA) to popular magazines (*US News and World Report*) all reach the same conclusion: Consumer satisfaction is much higher among respondents covered by the not-for-profit insurance plans than among those covered by the for-profit plans. Although there is not clear empirical evidence that for-profits provide inferior quality care compared to not-for-profits, there is an unmistakable pattern in consumer satisfaction surveys where the highest ranked plans are consistently the not-for-profits, which also have higher MLRs (Meltsner, 1998).

Lower MLRs make for-profit managed care insurers more attractive to investors and in 1997 the MLRs for for-profits averaged 87.2% compared to 91.5% among the not-for-profits (Meltsner, 1998). But aggregate differences in MLRs between investor-owned and not-for-profit insurers may be illusory. Eventually, as for-profits increase their market penetration, cuts to medical services initiated by for-profits are mimicked by their not-for-profit counterparts as they compete head to head on costs.

MACROECONOMIC POLICIES AND THE IMPACT ON ADMINISTRATIVE COSTS

Unlike Canada, the United States has some 1,500 different private health insurers, all with varying rules and regulations, some nonprofit, others for-profit, some private, and others public. As a result, in 1994 the United States spent $187 per capita on administrative costs while Canada spent a mere $42 per capita, adjusted for purchasing power parity (PPP) rates (OECD, 1997). The Congressional Budget Office estimated that under a single-payer system, the decrease in overhead costs would range from a net decrease of $18.2 to $58.3 billion—enough to cover the costs of health care insurance for all uninsured Americans (Congressional Budget Office, 1991).

In August 1996, Congress signed into law the Health Insurance Portability and Accountability Act, which contained a provision to standardize health claims data by all U.S. health insurance payers and providers. The electronic data interchange (EDI) was expected to save $9 billion per year in administrative costs (Lewis, 1998). When EDI was conceived, capitated models of financing were rare. Now, each capitated provider must upgrade its claims processing to meet the EDI standard. Some experts anticipate that projected fines and penalties for noncompliance with EDI could quickly exceed the net worth of many medical practices (Moynihan, 1997). A recent study of capitated providers did find that their administrative costs rose steeply as they assumed more administrative functions previously performed by managed care insurers (VanderLaan, de la Houssaye, Jaqnousek & Derus, 1998).

Since the early 1990s, there has been a rapid corporatization of medical practices into physician practice management companies (PPMCs). It is estimated that over the past decade the number of group practices formed each year has nearly doubled, reaching nearly 20,000 groups in 1995 (Burns, 1997). PPMCs are attractive to practitioners because they provide sophisticated administrative support crucial to managing medical risk in capitated modes of reimbursement. While proponents of PPMCs claim that they are crucial for economic survival, critics see PPMCs as just another clever financial incentive that enables physicians to liquidate their practices for staggering sums of capital.

At every step, health care providers must add clerical staff to compile and submit claims to public and private insurers. As a result, American hospitals spend twice as much on administrative overhead as their Canadian counterparts (Himmelstein and Woolhandler, 1993). The highest administrative costs are in private for-profit hospitals, where slightly over one-third of the hospitals' total budget (34%) covers overhead expenses, compared to less than a quarter (22.9%) in public hospitals. Charges per discharge are also almost $1,000 greater in for-profit hospitals that in their nonprofit counterparts (Woolhandler & Himmelstein, 1997).

Clearly, the most inefficient aspect of the U.S. health care system is administrative overhead. But, paradoxically, the very remedy for improving efficiency—managed care—has significantly higher administrative costs than the traditional fee-for-service or indemnity insurance plans. Administrative costs of managed care companies range from between 18% and 25% of total revenues, compared to 14% for traditional indemnity plans (Himmelstein & Woolhandler, 1993).

THE CORPORATIZATION OF THE AMERICAN HEALTH CARE SYSTEM

The lucrativeness of the health care industry has accelerated the trend toward conversions of both nonprofit insurers and providers to for-profit status. The number of publicly traded health companies increased from 33 in 1992 to 144 in 1996, with total capital increasing from $36 billion to $140 billion (Friedman & Savage, 1998). Between 1981 and 1997 the number of for-profit insurers tripled and for-profit HMOs now cover two-thirds of all managed care enrollees. In a ten-year period (from 1987 to 1997), the net worth of for-profit HMOs increased thirteen-fold from $3 billion to $39 billion. For the average investor this meant that an investment of $100 grew to $492, while a $100 investment in a for-profit HMO grew to $821 (Friedman & Savage, 1998).

In 1997, on average, CEOs at for-profit HMOs made annual salaries equaling $2 million. The CEO with the largest unexercised stock option package was William McGuire of United Health Care at $61.2 million (Fischer, 1998). The highest paid executive was Stephen Wiggins of Oxford Health Plan, who netted $30.7 million in salary and $8.7 million in stock options. In an interesting twist to corporate incentives for top executives, Wiggins's salary was increased in 1997 by $10 million even though Oxford lost more than $80 million. Such clear disregard for fiduciary accountability forced insurance regulators to intercede and dismantle Wiggins's salary package, but not before he received an additional $3.6 million (Meltzner, 1998).

In addition to financial windfalls, the merger/conversion/corporatization frenzy has spawned colossal financial debacles as well as outright fraud. Columbia-HCA, the nation's largest hospital chain, reported its net earnings were up 51% even as it was the subject of the largest Medicare fraud case in history (Limbacher, 1998). The country's second largest hospital chain, Tenet Healthcare, agreed to pay $100 million to former patients who charged the hospital illegally committed them to obtain their insurance benefits

(Blouche, 1998). In yet another case of lost corporate accountability, Allegheny Health Foundation, the corporate parent of Pennsylvania's largest nonprofit health system, went bankrupt, owing creditors more that $1.5 billion (Bilchik, 1999).

To prevent the squandering of valuable community assets, twenty-five states have passed legislation overseeing the conversion process of not-for-profit providers to for-profit status. Most state regulators can do little more than force nonprofits to transfer the value of their assets to a new charitable foundation. Without minimal safeguards, there is a genuine possibility that social debts to the community will be circumvented and assets will be redirected into the hands of trustees, CEOs, and investors. But, as can be seen in the Pennsylvania case, even charitable foundations are no guarantee that financial assets will be protected. Undeterred by either financial disaster or the threat of government oversight, the number of conversions of nonprofit hospitals and insurers to for-profit corporations shows no sign of abating (Fox & Kelly, 1998).

THE IMPACT OF MACROECONOMIC POLICIES ON PRACTITIONERS

Health care insurers have long recognized that controlling physician decision-making is key to controlling health care costs. The professional prerogatives of physicians seemed inviolable until the advent of managed care. Once managed care insurers convinced businesses and consumers that the only way insurers could control costs was to control access to physicians, insurers had the leverage they needed to extract significant concessions from medical providers.

In the early days of managed care, gatekeepers second-guessed physician decision-making and acted as intermediaries to ration care. As managed care evolved, the cost of these invisible diagnosticians grew and the savings they extracted reached a plateau. Managed care insurers began experimenting with alternative cost-containment strategies that shifted more of the financial risk to providers.

A 1995 survey by the Physician Payment Review Commission found that almost two-thirds of managed care providers penalize physicians by withholding portions of their salary for exceeding projected expenses. Another one-third of managed care providers offer physicians bonuses and financial incentives for cost savings. It is estimated that these financial inducements can vary a physician's annual salary by as much as 30% to 50%. Surveys of registered nurses (Shindul-Rothschild, Berry & Long-Middleton, 1996), physicians (Kerr, 1997), psychologists and social workers (Chambliss, Pinto & McGuigan, 1997) all found high rates of dissatisfaction due to the encroachments by managed care insurers on their professional practice. Despite the obvious ethical conflicts they raise for health care professionals, these models have become an essential cost-savings innovation from the point of view of managed care executives.

POLICIES TO CORRECT IMPERFECTIONS IN THE MANAGED CARE MARKETPLACE

In hindsight, its shocking that the purchasing power of American industries remained acquiescent as long as it did and that the concessions imposed upon consumers by businesses and insurers went unchallenged for so long. Alan Enthovan (1980) is credited with first proposing that such purchasing power could be harnessed to force greater efficiency through novel financing arrangements. Now that this power has been unleashed, there is little likelihood of putting the genie back in the bottle. Even if employer-based health insurance is scrapped altogether in favor of a government-financed single-payer plan, it is unlikely government regulation would be substituted for selective contracting or capitation, two of the cornerstones of managed care.

One popular rationale for relying on market forces rather than government regulation is the assumption that in a free market there would be less government oversight. But savvy students of economics recognize that heightened competition often necessitates more government regulation, not less. In free market economies, an important function of government is to intercede and correct market imperfections that inhibit competition and cause untoward effects on consumers.

A staggering number of laws and regulations have been promulgated at both the state and federal level to protect health care consumers. The Patients Bill of Rights Act of 1998 recently passed by Congress contains provisions that would address problems with access to care, access to information about benefits, quality assurance, grievance appeals, and professional relationships between practitioners and patients. The Health Care Financing Administration (HCFA) has also promulgated regulations requiring managed care plans participating in Medicare to use HEDIS measures and the Consumer Assessment of Health Plans Survey (CAHPS).

New York and New Jersey have enacted similar sweeping managed care reform initiatives. Most states are proceeding with very narrow reform efforts aimed at addressing specific issues affecting access (such as mandated stays for certain surgical procedures) and professional relationships (such as prohibiting "gag clauses"). The number of bills introduced at the state level to regulate managed care is in the thousands. Whether these reforms will have a meaningful effect on access and quality of care is unclear. However, there is little question that the degree to which federal and state governments are micromanaging health care in response to some of the egregious practices of managed care insurers is unprecedented.

CONCLUSIONS: IMPLICATIONS FOR RESEARCH AND PUBLIC POLICY

The area of research offering the most immediate benefits to patients and practitioners is the analysis of quality indicators. At the moment, both private industry and the government are actively involved in developing measures of quality. Direct care providers must be equal partners in such research efforts to insure that outcome measures are not merely hospitality indices. The input of health care practitioners is crucial if benchmarks are to be established that meet, or exceed, professional standards of care.

Capitation as a model of health care financing is in its infancy. The factors practitioners most consider when evaluating risk and negotiating contracts with managed care providers need careful elucidation through empirical research. As practitioners assume greater financial risk, they must be wary not to become narrowly preoccupied with cost. Any investigation of emerging models of health care financing must measure efficacy on the basis of cost, quality, and access.

The macroeconomics of the U.S. health care system is deceivingly simple to comprehend. Corporate health care has enriched a few at the expense of millions of uninsured and underinsured Americans. State and federal governments have attempted to fashion a safety net with piecemeal initiatives. But marginal reforms that tinker with an array of incentives or penalties will never correct the true inefficiencies in the U.S. health care system. Those who know the most about health care economics are those at the bedside, not those in the boardroom. In December 1997 a group of nurses and physicians gathered at Faneuil Hall in Boston to spearhead a national movement against the corporatization of health care services (Shindul-Rothschild, 1998; *JAMA*, 1997). Market imperfections can be corrected if we have the political will to put patients ahead of profits and supplant the values of corporate self-interest with those of social justice.

REFERENCES

Bilchik, G. S. (1999). The eyes have it. *Hospitals and Health Networks, 73,* 62–66.

Bloche, M. G. (1998). Should government intervene to protect nonprofits? *Health Affairs, 17,* 7–25.

Born, P., & Geckler, C. (1998). HMO quality and financial performance: Is there a connection? *Journal of Health Care Finance, 24,* 65–77.

Brodie, M., & Blendon, R. J. (1995). The public's contribution to congressional gridlock on health care reform. *Journal of Health Politics, Policy and Law, 20,* 403–10.

Brown, L. D. (1998). Exceptionalism as the rule? U.S. health policy innovation and cross-national learning. *Journal of Health Politics, Policy and Law, 23,* 35–51.

Burns, L. R. (1997). Physician practice management companies. *Health Care Management Review, 22,* 32–46.

Business & Health (1999). Dissecting the Medicare HMO pullout, 17,13–14.

Carrasquillo, O., Himmelstein, D. U., Woolhandler, S., & Bor, D. H. (1999). Going bare: Trends in health insurance coverage, 1989 through 1996. *American Journal of Public Health, 89,* 36–42.

Chambliss, C., Pinto, D., & McGuigan, J. (1997). Reactions to managed care among psychologists and social workers. *Psychological Reports, 80,* 147–154.

Congressional Budget Office (1991). *Universal health insurance coverage using Medicare's payment rates* [brochure]. Washington: U.S. Government Printing Office.

Cunningham, P. J. (1999). Pressures on safety net access: The level of managed care penetration and uninsurance rate in a community. *Health Services Research, 34,* 255–270.

Dudley, R. A., Miller, R. H., Korenbrot, T. Y., & Luft, H. S. (1998). The impact of financial incentive on quality of health care. *The Milbank Quarterly, 76,* 649–660.

Emanuel, E. J., & Goldman, L. (1998). Protecting patient welfare in managed care: Six safeguards. *Journal of Health Politics, Policy and Law, 23,* 635–659.

Enthoven, A. C. (1980). *Health plan: The only practical solution to the soaring cost of medical care.* Reading, MA: Addison-Wesley.

Feldstein, M. (1973). The welfare loss of excess health insurance. *Journal of Political Economy, 81,* 251–280.

Fischer, M. J. (1998). Analysis of HMO CEO pay released. *National Underwriter, 102,* 45.

Fischer, M. J. (1999). Medicare + Choice losing more members than earlier thought. *National Underwriter, 103,* 1, 39.

Fox, C. D. & Kelly, C. (1998). Sales of not-for-profit to for-profit corporations. *Trusts & Estates, 137,* 38–46.

Friedman, L. H., & Savage, G. T. (1998). Can ethical management and managed care coexist? *Health Care Management Review, 23,* 56–62.

General Accounting Office (August 27, 1990). *Medicaid: oversight of health maintenance organizations in the Chicago area.* Washington, DC: Author.

General Accounting Office (1996). *Medicaid: States' efforts to educate and enroll beneficiaries in managed care.* Washington, DC: Author.

Gold, M. (1999). Making Medicaid managed care research relevant. *Health Services Research, 33,* 1639–1650.

Himmelstein, D. U., & Woolhandler, S. (1993). *Health policy in the Clinton era: The national health program chartbook.* (Vol. 2.) Cambridge, MA: The Center for National Health Program Studies.

Journal of the American Medical Association. (1997). Policy perspectives. For our patients, not for profits. *Journal of the American Medical Association, 278,* 1733–1738.

Johnson, H., & Broder, D. S. (1996). *The system: The American way of politics at the breaking point.* Boston: Little, Brown & Co.

Kerr, E. A., Hays, R. D., Mittman, B. S., Siu, A. L., Leake, B., & Brook, R. H. (1997). Primary care physicians' satisfaction with quality of car in California capitated medical groups. *Journal of the American Medical Association, 278,* 308–312.

Levit, K. R., Lazenby, H. C., & Braden, B. R. (1998). National health spending trends in 1996. *Health Affairs, 17,* 35–51.

Levit, K. R., Lazenby, H. C., & Braden, B. R., et al. (1998). Personal health care expenditures: CYs 1990–2005. *Health Care Financing Review, Statistical Supplement,* 20–43.

Levit, K. R., Lazenby, H. C., & Braden, B.R., et al. (1997). National health expenditures, 1996. *Health Care Financing Review, 19,* 161–249.

Lewis, A. (1998). 1998 delivers health care industry new rules and regulations. *Remington Report, 6,* 22–23.

Limbacher, P. B. (1998). A taste of profit. *Modern Healthcare, 28,* 6.

McCue, M. J., Hurley, R. E., Draper, D. A., & Jurgensen, M. (1999). Reversal of fortune: Commercial HMOs in the Medicaid market. *Health Affairs, 18,* 223–230.

Medicaid managed care: Hearing before the Subcommittee on Health for Families and the Uninsured of the Senate Committee on Finance, 102nd Congress, 2nd session on S. 2077 (April 10, 1992) (testimony of Janet Shirkles).

Melhado, E. M. (1998). Economists, public provision and the market: Changing values in policy debate. *Journal of Health Politics, Policy and Law, 23,* 215–263.

Meltsner, S. (1998). For-profit or not: Where's the best care. *Business & Health, 16,* 46–52.

Moynihan, J. J. (1997). The administrative cost of health care: 1997 and beyond. *Healthcare Financial Management, 51,* 102.

Organization for Economic Cooperation and Development (1997). Health Data 1997 [Software]. Paris: CREDES.

Patel, K., & Rushefsky, M. E. (1998). The health policy community and health-care reform in the US. *Health, 2,* 459–484.

Pauley, M.V. (1971). *Medical care at public expense: A study in applied welfare economics.* New York: Praeger.

Phelps, C. E. (1997). *Health economics.* Reading, MA: Addison-Wesley.

Physician Payment Review Commission (PPRC). (1995). *Arrangements between managed care plans and physicians: Results from a 1994 survey of managed care plans.* Washington, DC: Author.

Physician Payment Review Commission (PPRC). (1997). *Annual Report to Congress. Chapter 20, Medicaid: spending trends and the move to managed care.* Washington, DC: Author.

Samuelson, P. A. (1954). The pure theory of public expenditure. *Review of Economics and Statistics, 36,* 387–389.

Saphir, A., & Rauber, C. (1999, June 21). Medicaid HMOs exit markets. *Modern Healthcare, 29,* 46–48.

Schlesinger, M., Gray, B., & Bradley, E. (1996). Charity and community: The role of nonprofit ownership in a managed health care system. *Journal of Health Politics, Policy and Law, 21,* 697–751.

Shindul-Rothschild, J. (1998). Nurses week tribute: A nursing call to action. *American Journal of Nursing, 98,* 36.

Shindul-Rothschild, J., Berry, D., & Long-Middleton, E. (1996). Where have all the nurses gone? *American Journal of Nursing, 96,* 25–39.

Shindul-Rothschild, J., & Gordon, S. (1994). Single-payer versus managed competition: Implications for nurses. *Journal of Nursing Education, 33,* 198–207.

Sparer, M., Brown, L. D., & Kovner, A. R. (1999). Implementing Medicaid managed care: The New York story. *Journal of Health Care Finance, 26,* 1–17.

VanderLaan, B. F., de la Houssaye, M. Janousek, K., & Derus, C. (1998). Performance under capitation: The true cost of infrastructure. *Journal of Health Care Finance, 24,* 27–38.

Walker, T. (1999). Higher premiums fuel solid profits for HMOs. *Managed Healthcare, 9,* 8 & 11.

Weschler, J. (1999). Clinton plan jeopardized Medicare managed care. *Managed Healthcare, 9,* 16.

Weissert, C. S., & Weissert, W. G. (1996). *Governing health: The politics of health policy.* Baltimore: Johns Hopkins University Press.

Wilensky, H. L. (1997). Social science and the public agenda: Reflections on the relation of knowledge to policy in the United States and abroad. *Journal of Health Politics, Policy and Law, 22,* 1241–1265.

Woolhandler, S., & Himmelstein, D. U. (1997). Costs of care and administration at for-profit and other hospitals in the United States. *New England Journal of Medicine, 336,* 769–74.

◆ CHAPTER 2 ◆

Biotechnology and Managed Care:

Effects on Health Care Cost, Clinical Practice, and Education of Health Care Professionals

ELIZABETH PEARSON PHILP AND BARBARA BERKMAN

Health and mental health care have evolved into increasingly complex service systems. This complexity derives from a number of factors, but the combined effects of biotechnological advances and managed care strategies are having an unprecedented impact on consumers as well as health care providers.

Biotechnological advances have increased treatment options across patient populations. These advances have changed the demographics of the health care consumer population. We are increasingly able to push back mortality at both ends of the age spectrum, sustaining life in the youngest as well as in older adults and the elderly. Biotechnological research has led to an expanding array of diagnostic and treatment tools as well as methods of health improvement and disease prevention. Illnesses that were once inevitable are now preventable and diseases that were once fatal are now treatable, shifting the focus of care from acute intervention to prevention and chronic disease management (Berkman, 1996; Pardes, Manton, Lander, & Tolley, 1999). Along with technological changes in our society, the characteristics of our society are also changing rapidly. Our population is becoming older. The percentage of the population over age 65 is expected to increase to 69 million between 2010 and 2030, resulting in fewer people under age 18 than over age 65 (Mechanic, 1999). Currently, chronically disabled individuals over age 65 have health costs seven times those of healthy individuals (Pardes et al., 1999). Between 1982 and 1994, the age-adjusted chronic disability prevalence rate declined 1.3% annually (Manton, Corder & Stallard, 1997). Expanding knowledge of human biology, neurophysiology, and the interdependence of physical and psychosocial health will continue to alter the health status and behavior of the population (Shine, 1998). Increased technological capability to sustain life has created a population of patients with complex chronic medical and mental health needs. Concomitantly, these technological advances have increased medical expenditures due to increased health care utilization. We are confronted with the dilemma of containing costs while maintaining quality of care.

Issues around the financing of health care have been with us since the formation of organized medicine. Funding models remarkably similar to such current models as capitation and the use of primary care gatekeepers appear in conference archives as early as 1888 (Ancker, 1888). Although the issues around funding for adequate medical treatment are not new, these issues have changed and grown significantly under managed care, challenging traditional approaches to health care practice. Currently, managed care as a means of cost containment is generating a flurry of academic discussion (Baker, Chiverton & Hines, 1998; Bloomgarden, 1996; Carpinello, Felton, Pease, DeMasi & Donahue, 1998; Colone, 1993; Costello, Connors & Beavan, 1996; Davidson & Davidson, 1995; Donelan, Blendon, Benson, Leitman & Taylor, 1996; French, Dunlap, Galinis, Rachal & Zarkin, 1996; Holahan, Zuckerman, Evans & Rangarajan, 1998; Krop et al., 1998; Miller & Luft, 1997; Robinson, 1996). Although the fundamental purpose of managed care is to contain skyrocketing costs, managed care strategies, in their various forms, aim to restructure the health and mental health care delivery and financing system (Stuart & Weinrich, 1998).

Restructuring can imply destructive as well as constructive change. Borrowing from systems theory, it is understandable that many providers as well as patients have been reluctant to embrace managed care, seeing it primarily as destructive (Carpenter & Platt, 1997; Cerminara, 1998; Chang et al., 1998; Colenda, Banazak & Mickus, 1998; Davidson & Davidson, 1996). Prior to wide-scale adoption of managed care strategies, the system, or culture, of health care was primarily a closed system consisting of a physician-driven hierarchy of health care providers functioning as autonomous fee-for-service decision-makers. Managed care challenged the traditional hierarchies within medical care by inserting non-medical financial decision-makers and market forces into the process. This shift to a market-driven health care system, along with advances in health care technological knowledge, has led to rapid changes in health care service delivery, impacting the cost of care, access to care, utilization of the system by consumers as well as providers, service delivery, and the education of health care professionals. Biotechnology, managed care, and new financial strategies have important implications for each of these arenas.

IMPACT ON COST OF HEALTH CARE

Prior to 1996, the cost of health care in the United States was increasing at an estimated rate of 10% per year, comprising 15% of the Gross National Product (GNP) (Scutchfield, Lee & Patton, 1997; Shortell, Gillies & Devers, 1995). Medicaid spending growth outstripped all other health care spending with an increase of 28% per year between 1990 and 1992. Widespread implementation of managed care strategies has dramatically reduced the rate of Medicaid cost increase among Medicaid managed care enrollees (Holahan et al., 1998). Concomitantly, approximately 37 million people are covered by Medicare (Moon, 1996). Approximately 17% of current Medicare beneficiaries are enrolled in some type of managed care plan (HCFA, 1999). Sampling limitations make it difficult to accurately measure the cost effects of managed care within this population. The health status of current Medicare managed care enrollees is not representative of the total population of Medicare beneficiaries. Managed care enrollees have been relatively healthy and suffer fewer chronic illnesses or other complicating medical conditions than the general beneficiary population (Miller, Weissert & Chernew, 1998). The 1997 Balanced Budget Act restructured reimbursement rates, and managed care penetration within the Medicare population is expected to rise (Lee, Eng, Fox & Etienne, 1998; Scutchfield et al., 1997). Given the combination of rising costs and an aging population, it is easy to envision the growing crisis of health care financing.

In response to these escalating cost increases, the health care system is changing rapidly. What began as cost-containment strategies have developed into an assortment of financing systems aggregately referred to as managed care. Many types of managed care organizations are currently operating in the United States. All managed care involves some form of prepayment of health care costs, limited panels of providers, and assumption of financial risk on the part of the providers. Consumer and provider behavior is modified through financial incentives. For the consumer, these incentives may include co-payments and reduction or denial of coverage outside a designated network. For the provider, these incentives could include risk sharing in the form of capitation, risk pools, and withholds. With capitation the physician is paid a per-member, per-month fee regardless of whether the patient uses the service. Risk pools distribute financial risk among a group of providers; for example, the primary physician shares the financial risk with specialists. A *withhold* is a percentage of fee-for-service payments that is withheld during a set period of service and returned to the provider based on his/her practice patterns. The percentage of the withhold that is returned to the provider is based on the costs he/she generates. In effect, the provider is penalized for costly practices that fall outside the mean of other contracted providers. In the United States, public and private insurance plans are turning to managed care as a method to control health care expenditures. Given the dramatic decline in costs attributable to managed care, it is unlikely that our health care system will return to the fee-for-service structure that had previously dominated the market.

Hospital mergers and reduction of provider service redundancy are major strategies for operational cost containment (Globerman & Bogo, 1995). These strategies are expected to increase efficiency while maintaining expertise and quality of care. Cost reduction and quality of care is a complicated duality and the literature reflects the ethical struggle to merge competing, if not mutually exclusive, goals (Colone, 1993; Davidson &

Davidson, 1996; McDaniel & Erlen, 1996; Reamer, 1997; White, Wimmons & Bixby, 1993). Early attempts to resolve this struggle resulted in managed care strategies that focused on reducing costs by lowering the amount paid to a network of approved providers through negotiated contracts, or by staff-model group practices that employed salaried health care providers and restricted members from using outside providers. These early managed care strategies provided little financial incentive for providers to participate and required providers to negotiate a complicated system of utilization review, which could involve prospective, concurrent, or retrospective reviews of medical treatment, and could include preapproval or denial of claims and procedures.

Managed care continues to evolve and the evolving funding model is capitation. Capitation shifts the focus of practice from patient-provider to population-provider and this model is frequently referred to as *population-based care.* In a population-based care system, a per-member, per-month fee is paid to the provider and the provider assumes responsibility, and financial risk, for all care within that defined population of enrollees. Under capitation arrangements, providers of health services are required to negotiate with managed care organizations for adequate capitation rates. Assessment of the rate of payment requires an accurate prediction of the risk present in the insured population and projection of aggregate costs (Broyles, Brandt & Biard-Holmes, 1998). Capitation shifts the focus from the individual patient to aggregate cost-benefit decision-making. Forecasting health care needs within a population requires in-depth knowledge of the health status of that population. Demographic and diagnostic information provide necessary but insufficient information for providers negotiating payment rates within a capitated fee structure (Grimaldi, 1998b). Contribution of expertise from multiple disciplines is necessary to attain an adequate understanding of the psychosocial factors in health behavior and the social implications of illnesses such as presented by AIDS, tuberculosis, or in trauma cases (Volland, 1996).

No reimbursement system is inherently good or bad. Proponents have argued that capitation models encourage preventive care, coordination of service, and collaboration among medical specialists (Chandler, Meisel, Hu, McGowen & Madison, 1998; Haugh, 1998). Opponents of capitation have argued that this system poses serious ethical dilemmas for the provider (Davidson & Davidson, 1996; McDaniel & Erlen, 1996; Reamer, 1997) and substantial risk of inadequate care for the most vulnerable members of our society—i.e., the elderly, the poor, the disabled, and children.

As Medicaid and Medicare are privatized through managed care organizations, the potential to underserve vulnerable groups who are the primary recipients of Medicaid and Medicare increases (Perloff, 1996). Initially, state Medicaid capitation rates were inadequate for the higher costs of services to disabled patients. Despite dramatic growth in enrollment during the past decade, few states are enrolling older chronically ill or disabled individuals—the most expensive beneficiaries—primarily because these populations are excluded from mandated managed care enrollment in most states (Holahan et al., 1998; Mechanic, 1999). Managed care organizations that chose to participate in Medicaid were able to exclude enrollees in these high-cost categories. These exclusionary practices are also evident within the Medicare population. A national comparison of traditional and managed care Medicare expenditures determined that Medicare managed care enrollment is associated with significant increases in hospital, skilled nursing facility, home health care, and hospice expenditures among fee-for-service Medicare enrollees (Baker, 1999). Managed care market share increases from 10% to 20% are positively correlated with a 9.4% increase in costs per beneficiary within the traditional Medicare population. As healthier individuals move into managed care plans, there is an aggregate increase in utilization within the traditional Medicare group. Capitation distribution strategies have changed and new methods have different levels of financial incentive to provide services (Schmalzried & Luck, 1998). One such method involves strategies to identify financial risk factors within a given population and to adjust capitation fees based on those risk factors. This method is commonly referred to as risk adjustment. Without risk adjustment, health plans do not have an incentive to enroll persons with the heaviest care needs (Grimaldi, 1998b). Risk adjustment is intended to minimize selection of low-risk patients or enrollees in health plans (Newhouse, 1998, p. 122) but there is tremendous variability in the way individual managed care organizations incorporate risk adjustment strategies into their capitation rates. The most effective means of risk adjustment have yet to be determined.

Previous attempts to predict health care needs within a given population have included estimates based on past service utilization (Roth, Snapp, Lauber & Clark, 1998). This strategy has had limited success. Patient populations are not static and significant changes within any given patient population can occur quickly as members move in and out of the population. These changes have been shown to significantly effect the aggregate population profile (Roth et al., 1998). For example, Medicare has historically used factors of age and male gender to set payment rates, yet those factors have been shown to be inadequate predictive variables of health care costs (Krop et al., 1998). Thus, past health care utilization of any one population is not sufficiently predictive of future utilization.

This lack of predictability was clearly reported in a national study of Medicare beneficiaries with a primary diagnosis of diabetes. This study found that, on average, individuals with diabetes (n = 188,470) were 1.5 times as expensive as all Medicare beneficiaries (n = 1,371,960). There were wide cost variations within the defined sample. Within the total sample of Medicare beneficiaries with diabetes, the most expensive 10% of beneficiaries accounted for 56% of expenditures and the least expensive 50% of beneficiaries accounted for 4% of expenditures. "Acute care hospitalizations accounted for the majority (60%) of total expenditures, whereas outpatient and physician services accounted for 7% and 33%, respectively" (Krop et al., 1998, p. 747). Among older adults with diabetes, the average number of hospitalizations was 1.6 times higher and the average length of stay was two days longer. Although age, male gender, and number of diabetic complications were positively related to costs, they had minimal predictive power (R2 = 0.0006) (Krop et al., 1998). The addition of psychosocial and medical comorbidity factors explained 20% of the variation in total health care expenditures within the population (R2 = 0.196), supporting the need for multidisciplinary collaboration within a capitated managed care system.

The cost impact of comorbidity factors was also revealed in a Maryland study of Medicaid expenditures. This study found that 88% of high-cost patients (top 10% of annual expenditures) are under Medicaid categories of elderly or disabled (Stuart & Weinrich, 1998, p. 253). The remaining high-cost patients are children with special needs and/or mental health problems. Within the total high-cost population there were significant variations of expenditures depending on comorbidity factors. Comparison between expenditure and utilization patterns of Medicare patients with chronic obstructive respiratory disease (COPD) (n = 42,472) and all Medicare beneficiaries (n = 1,221,615) revealed that expenditures for patients with COPD were 2.4 times the per capita expenditures for all Medicare beneficiaries. Using a 5% nationally representative sample of older Medicare beneficiaries, the most expensive 10% of Medicare beneficiaries with COPD accounted for nearly half of total expenditures for this population. Again, comorbidity factors were associated with higher expenditures. Additional analytic studies are needed to more specifically identify psychosocial and medical characteristics associated with these individuals (Grasso, Weller, Shaffer, Diette & Anderson, 1998).

Medicaid and Medicare beneficiaries with chronic conditions, multiple problems, and limited resources are at higher risk of inadequate health care when appropriate risk-adjustment strategies are not incorporated into capitation funding. Because patients with complex chronic medical conditions such as diabetes or COPD are more expensive than the average older adult, previous Medicare capitation rates were inadequate. The method used to determine capitation rates for Medicare risk-bearing health plans changed on January 1, 1998. Minimum rates that are substantially higher than the amounts Medicare previously paid in most of the nation's counties reduce the volatility in the rates, and guarantee all participating health plans at least a 2% annual rate increase for the next several years. These changes aim to decrease exclusionary enrollment practices and motivate more health plans to become Medicare contractors in rural areas where managed care plans have been reluctant to participate (Grimaldi, 1998a).

Given the significant changes in Medicare and Medicaid reimbursement, cost-benefit analysis of managed Medicare and Medicaid is still in the early stages. Managed care could provide an environment conducive to better care for chronically ill patients. A review of the performance of managed care organizations in relation to quality-of-care found both positive and negative results when compared with traditional plans. However, in several instances, Medicare managed care enrollees with chronic conditions showed worse quality of care. Evidence comparing hospital and physician resource use showed no clear pattern, whereas evidence on enrollee satisfaction varied by measure and enrollee type (Miller & Luft, 1997). Claims that managed care improves overall quality also were not supported, in part because of inadequate quality measurement and reporting. Two major changes necessary to improve care of the chronically ill were identified. First, chronic care management must become more aggressive, with an emphasis on maintaining optimal functioning; second, an information infrastructure is needed to help focus clinicians' attention on treatment outcomes (Kane, 1998). These changes may occur as population-based practice expands, changing the financing structure as well as the access to, and utilization of, health care services. As the market continues to evolve, outcome research will be needed to assess the benefits of managed care services for these vulnerable populations.

IMPACT ON, ACCESS TO, AND UTILIZATION OF CARE

Access to services is a concern of both consumers and providers of health care. All managed care models restrict professional access to their provider roster as a method of cost containment. Limiting the number of providers within a network and monitoring their practices are common management strategies. If providers are not directly involved in capitated risk sharing, their contract will specify the level of pay for service and will restrict the numbers of patients to be included in their practice. Practice methods are monitored for aggregate comparison. Usage patterns that fall outside the mean of similar providers must be justified or the provider may be penalized financially or removed from the network. Exclusionary provider networks limit the numbers and locations of professional providers. These restrictions are designed to decrease duplication of services and costly technology.

Credentialing is the primary means of limiting provider access to a managed care network. This may include several strategies such as board certification for medical specialties, a designated number of years of post-degree experience, and a demonstrated expertise in a specific diagnostic category or field of practice. Credentialing is time-limited and performance reviews may be required for recredentialing. Managed care organizations can establish their own credentialing rules but most companies follow the criteria of the National Committee for Quality Assurance (NCQA), an organization that establishes standards of accreditation for managed care organizations. Established in 1990, NCQA is a nonprofit, nongovernmental agency whose mission is to evaluate and report on the quality of managed care organizations (Sennett, 1997, p. 35). To receive accreditation, a managed care organization must provide evidence that it meets NCQA standards. Approximately 15% of organizations that apply are denied accreditation (p. 42). NCQA accreditation is voluntary but many large corporations and other bulk-purchasers of health care require contracted plans to undergo NCQA review (p. 43). NCQA provides information to consumers as well as providers about the quality of managed care organizations.

A study of patients' perceptions of managed care found that patients' specific concerns were access to specialists and advanced diagnostic tests, waiting times, and quality of some services (Donelan et al., 1996). Access to care is a particular concern among elderly Medicaid and Medicare managed care enrollees (Miller et al., 1998). Medicaid managed care enrollees are more likely than low-income, privately insured managed care enrollees to be poorer, have health problems, and experience access problems (Donelan et al., 1996; Lillie-Blanton & Lyons, 1998; Perloff, 1996; Wholey, Burns & Lavizzo-Mourey, 1998). Compared with low-income populations in fee-for-service care, managed care enrollees—whether in Medicaid or privately insured—report more problems in obtaining care and are more likely to be dissatisfied with their health plans (Lillie-Blanton, p. 322).

Health care consumers are concerned that managed care companies serve health plan economic interests over patient interests by restricting their choice to physicians within the managed care network (Remler et al., 1997). In addition, access to advanced technological care may be managed by additional limits (Sennett, 1997). Managed care organizations may contract for specialty care, such as state-of-the-art cancer care, outside the geographic region of the enrollee, frequently at large academic teaching hospitals or other specialty care facilities. This may place additional emotional and financial burdens on the patient or family as the resultant travel, housing, and other costs may not be a covered benefit.

In addition, access to certain types of treatments that are the most advanced care but are not recognized as standard medical practice are generally excluded from coverage (Sennett, 1997), and thus may deny the consumer access. For example, large teaching hospitals, the source of major medical research, may offer procedures that are performed routinely, but exclusively, at that institution. These same procedures may be considered experimental by a managed care organization and access to that procedure would be restricted (Pardes et al., 1999).

Medical technological advances and managed care cost-containment strategies have a direct impact on the location of service provision and how care is accessed and utilized. The focus of diagnosis and treatment has changed from acute and unpredictable illness to disease prevention and management of chronic, multiple health problems (Berkman, 1996). Services that once required inpatient admission to an acute-care hospital are now available on an outpatient basis, frequently in out-of-hospital sites. Ambulatory care is now the primary mode of health care delivery (Robinson, 1996; Shortell et al., 1995; Stoeckle, 1995), accounting for approximately 98% of all medical encounters including 70% of surgical procedures (Shortell et al.). While managed care strategies reduce the sheer number of dollars spent on health care, they may generate societal costs that are not readily apparent. The shift to population-based care may affect all patients whether or not they are enrolled in managed care plans. Changes in location of service from inpatient to outpatient settings, decreased redundancy of costly medical technologies and equipment, reductions in the size of hospitals, and changes in the number and types of physicians practicing in markets alter the health care choices within that geographic area. Physicians practicing outside a managed care system may adapt to the accepted practice patterns of their peers. As more physicians move to a population-based pattern of care, this may affect practice patterns among physicians who treat mostly fee-for-service patients. Increased outpatient services and shorter in-patient admissions result in greater dependence on the support and assistance of informal caregivers (Kuhlthau et al., 1998; Stroul et al., 1997; Pensiero, 1995; Simmons & Goforth, 1997). Lost wages, increased caregiver strain (and possible increases in medical costs as a result of that strain) as well as individual patient financing of private homecare assistance are examples of cost-shifting, a confounding variable in cost-benefit analysis.

IMPACT ON HEALTH AND MENTAL HEALTH SERVICE DELIVERY

Changes in access and utilization of care, particularly among vulnerable populations, are mirrored in the changes that are taking place in service delivery. Health and mental health service delivery has changed significantly with the advent of managed care. As capitation funding models become more common, the shift to population-based care presents barriers to traditional long-term treatment strategies. Care is restructured. Physicians are responding to capitation by using utilization-management techniques that were previously used only by insurers. These approaches can include using gatekeeping and preauthorization for certain referrals or tests. Most also use profiling of utilization patterns (79%), clinical practice guidelines (70%), and managed care education (69%) (Kerr et al., 1995). Clinical practice guidelines, sometimes called critical pathways, are standardized intervention and treatment protocols designed to insure timely and appropriate care. These guidelines are effective quality improvement and cost-containment tools (Kane, 1998). Providers who serve privately insured, younger, and healthier populations have a wider margin of financial error as they adjust to population-based practice. High-risk populations leave little room for miscalculations of predicted costs of care. This leaves vulnerable groups (such as patients who need long-term care) at risk for gaps in service.

A model of care has been developed to address the growing need for long-term health care and lessen the financial risk to providers. The Program of All-Inclusive Care for the Elderly (PACE) is a new capitated benefit authorized by the Balanced Budget Act of 1997 (BBA). PACE is a model of care that combines Medicare and Medicaid funds to provide acute and long-term health care services for older patients who are eligible for nursing home care. Interdisciplinary teams provide integrated services beyond those provided by traditional Medicare and Medicaid coverage. The PACE model includes in-home services, day health care, primary care, acute hospital care, laboratory and ambulance services, skilled nursing facility care, medical specialty services, and restorative/supportive services (Lee et al., 1998). This program is expected to grow but the BBA limits annual growth of the PACE program to twenty new sites per year (HCFA, 1999). PACE is limited to a vulnerable patient group but the move toward integrated health care is becoming more common as providers transition into a population-based care system (Rabkin, 1998). This transition has been more easily accepted in medical care settings than in mental health care settings (Carpenter & Platt, 1997; Colenda et al., 1998), although managed care has also become the dominant method for financing and delivering mental healthcare.

Growing awareness of the social and psychological determinants of health status (Ell, 1996) results in increased emphasis on both medical and behavioral health interventions (Volland, 1996). Health and mental health comorbidity rates are estimated between 15% to 60% of patients in general medical settings and 50% in a psychiatric population (Kathol, 1997).

Common to all managed care mental health service delivery models are biopsychosocial assessments, brief interventions, and the use of standardized treatment to attain functional outcomes. Biopsychosocial assessments in a managed care environment are designed to identify functional problems within the patient or the patient's family care system. Strengths-based and systemic in nature, biopsychosocial assessments identify issues that either inhibit or promote the treatment process. This may in turn affect access and eligibility to certain types of interventions if an assessment uncovers functional deficits that would significantly interfere with a patient's ability to cooperate and participate in treatment. Mental health clinicians must be able to assess across a broad spectrum of functioning, risk factors, and major health/mental health conditions (Almgren, 1998; Durham, 1998). In addition, the ability of the individual patient as well as the patient's family to adapt to a member's medical condition must be accurately assessed in order to avoid inadequate home care services and premature readmissions because of physical or mental regression.

Goal setting, prioritizing of problems, and planned treatment strategies are expected to be established quickly. Crisis-intervention and case-management skills are at a premium. Clinicians must develop problem-focused assessment skills, expertise in short-term intervention, and effective management of acute episodes of illness. For patients with chronic and severe mental illness, care coordination and supportive interventions to maintain optimal functioning replace long-term psychotherapy (Shera, 1996). Empirical practice—i.e., practice guided by outcome measures—will become more commonplace. Skills for empirical practice include knowledge of standardized instruments for screening and assessment of psychosocial problems (Berkman, 1996) and the ability to conduct timely assessments and develop treatment plans that are defined by contractual agreement between provider and patient as well as provider/payer. For many managed care organizations, mental health providers must submit evidence of empirical practice knowledge before they are credentialed and accepted into the organization (Sennett, 1997).

Cost concerns and recognition of variability in health care delivery practices led to the development of strategies to better standardize health care delivery. Critical pathways guide the intervention and clinical decision process for individual patient conditions. When incorporated into routine medical practice along with appropriate outcome measures, they lead to improved cost-effective health care provision. Substantial problems exist, however, in the development of care-plans and integration of mental health service into the infrastructure of routine clinical practice (Pryor & Fortin, 1995, p. 105).

> Despite the fact that most mental health problems may first become evident in the context of general medical care, a separation remains between general medical services and specialty mental health care. This separation can make it difficult for primary care physicians to receive timely consultation in managing less severe problems or patients who resist referral, it limits helpful collaborative treatment arrangements, and it may make it more difficult to achieve cost offsets in medical care by appropriately treating depression and related impairments that contribute to much general disability (Mechanic, 1998, p. 89).

"Some forms of managed care have strong potential for integrating mental health care and primary health care, as some mental health professionals have advocated" (Mechanic, 1998, p. 84) but many managed care organizations use *carve-outs* to manage complex mental health needs. A carve-out refers to separate management of a particular service such as mental health, through an organization or network of providers that functions independently of the medical provider network. For example, substance abuse services are often managed separately from other medical benefits. Carve-outs can create significant discontinuities of care for persons with multiple conditions and families with multiple problems. Pharmaceutical services may also be carved out, which can cause additional coordination problems. In contrast, merging mental health into general medical care usually involves the generalist physician as a gatekeeper to specialized mental health services and encourages closer communication between primary and specialty care. Proponents of carve-outs argue that they reduce risk selection and offer a specialized network of providers to manage particular problems through the use of standardized treatment protocols. Opponents of carve-outs argue that they artificially separate the comorbidity of health and mental health care and unnecessarily divide the two domains (Slay & Glazer, 1995). Furthermore, they propose that integrated service is a more effective means of managing complex and interrelated health and mental health problems (Colenda et al., 1998).

Despite the arguments for improved integration, general physicians do not receive extensive mental health education. That, along with increased pressures to manage a population-based practice, may hinder their ability to provide appropriate assessment and intervention to persons with mental health needs (Gomez, Grimm, Yee & Skootsky, 1997). Current efforts to develop management strategies in organized primary care settings, building on team efforts of primary care physicians and mental health professionals and well-established practice guidelines, may be more effective. Comparisons of varying models for integrating versus carving out services (Mechanic, 1997) are limited, in part, because the variables of quality, provider incentive, workload, and skill level are confounded and difficult to differentiate in evaluation research. Currently, we have insufficient data to assess the pervasiveness of problems within either system (Mechanic, 1997).

IMPACT ON EDUCATION OF HEALTH PROFESSIONALS

The sheer volume of literature dedicated to the topic of managed care suggests that conflicts between the business of managed care and the practice of health care can be resolved. However, engagement among health care providers, managed care organizations, and health care policy developers is understandably focused on current, or imminent, changes in clinical practice and health care financing. Providers have been forced to adapt relatively quickly to market-driven changes, but educational programs in health care do not reflect these changes.

Managed care penetration is unevenly distributed throughout the United States. This geographic inconsistency and the fact that, until recently, managed care was primarily the domain of private insurers, have delayed changes to the current hospital-based system of medical teaching. Medicare is a major funder of academic health centers but clinical revenues subsidize teaching and research activities (Bazell & Salsberg, 1998). The shift from hospital-based care to ambulatory or community-based care depletes those revenues and creates problems for an education system that relies on an inpatient population of patients to be available to medical residents (Golditch, Anderson & Williams, 1998). In-patient admissions are shorter and the opportunity for learning is limited. Those patients who are admitted for longer periods are often suffering from acute episodes of complicated illnesses with narrowly focused teaching opportunity. The financial pressure, combined with decreasing patient populations, challenges the current system of health education and research. To develop community-based teaching programs, Medicare financing would have to be shifted from the hospital to the community, a move that has received limited support.

At the same time, managed care organizations are demanding that providers be prepared to work effectively within a managed care environment but have provided little financial support for academic teaching. Health care education is expensive and for-profit organizations have no financial incentive to engage in activities that could substantially reduce their profit. Health care education has traditionally been the purview of nonprofit and government organizations, but the market-driven changes have created a problem by moving the focus of care from an inpatient setting. Future providers must be prepared to work in the market created by managed care, but teaching cannot happen outside that market (Hanson, Stone, Penk, Flannery & Goldfinger, 1998; Nash & Veloski, 1998; Stevens, Leach, Warden & Cherniack, 1996). Managed care organizations often restrict medical resident or other health care students from providing services. This limits the opportunity to train providers to practice within a managed care system.

Medical schools, teaching hospitals, and managed care organizations have a vested interest in shaping the knowledge, skills, and attitudes of the next generation of providers, who must adapt to significant changes in the financing and delivery of health care (Nash & Veloski, 1998). Recognizing the need to incorporate managed care education into health care education programs, some schools are forming collaborative education programs that are mutually beneficial to the managed care organization and the health care education program (Hanson et al., 1998; Nash & Veloski, 1998; Stevens et al., 1996). For example, the Pew Charitable Trusts is funding academic health and managed care organization educational partnerships. The program of support aims to "accelerate the growth of joint ventures in teaching and research" (AAMC, 1998). In addition, several major academic health centers have joined with established managed care organizations to incorporate managed care strategies into the medical curriculum (Nash & Veloski, 1998). For example, Tufts Managed Care Institute is a collaboration between Tufts University School of Medicine and Tufts Health Plan, an independent-practice-association-model (IPA-model) health maintenance organization (HMO). Many of the Institute's programs have been developed as continuing education for practicing physicians and other health care professionals. For medical students, the approach has been to blend managed care principles and practices into existing courses, problem-based learning cases, and clerkships, rather than creating separate managed care courses. Public and private sources have been generous in providing venture capital to support many of these innovations but their continued operation will depend on models for health care networks that can identify and manage the revenue and costs associated with the missions of education, clinical services, and research (Nash & Veloski, 1998).

Although academic medicine is beginning to change its approach to education, other mental health professions have lagged behind. For example, social work education has made little movement beyond nominal recognition of the need to integrate managed care knowledge into social work education curriculum (Almgren, 1998; Bisno & Cox, 1997). Social workers serve those who are at the highest risk in society, groups that are especially vulnerable to managed care abuses due to their potential need for high-cost care and inadequate understanding of their choices and rights within managed care. Social workers and other mental health professionals must not only understand managed care systems but be prepared to assume an expanding, and changing, role in these evolving systems (Strom-Gottfried, 1997). Successful managed health care delivery requires multidisciplinary collaboration and many medical school curricula are beginning to include references to the significant roles of other health professionals. Mental health professionals must actively delineate how and where their skills can be utilized in the continuum of care. Following the lead of academic medicine, mental health practitioners would benefit from collaborative educational partnerships within managed care plans.

Needed curriculum changes are similar across all health care professions. Certainly there are practitioner-specific needs, but discussion of those needs is beyond the scope of this chapter. In general, all health care disciplines must integrate epidemiologic thinking, knowledge of human behavior, organizational behavior, information systems, quality measurement and improvement, health system financing and delivery, ethics, systems-based care, critical pathways, utilization management, and risk management into their curriculums (Bischof et al., 1997; Lurie, 1996). The necessary level of expertise may vary greatly across disciplines but it is clear that providers should move outside their traditional circle of knowledge to practice effectively in the new environment. Current and future changes in health care practice need to be incorporated at all levels of health care education. Students coming into health and mental health educational programs may not have realistic expectations of the training process and potential future jobs (Field et al., 1998; Raskin & Blome, 1998). Students should be clearly informed at the beginning of their education that the skills needed for successful professional practice are changing. Education that once prepared students for private practice and long-term mental health interventions must now prepare students for collaborative management of illness. Although current managed care strategies are new, the practice of health and mental health collaboration is not. For example, nurses and social workers have a history of collaborative expertise in community-based models of care (Hawkins, Veeder & Pearce, 1998) that can guide development of collaborative community-practice models. These skills are equally applicable across health and behavioral health care practice. Building on current expertise and reviving historical collaborative partnerships through systems of health care education may ultimately be the bridge to resolving the struggle of restructuring health care delivery.

CONCLUSIONS

There are no easy solutions to the conflict between the goals of increasing quality and decreasing expenditures. Managed care as it exists today is the latest attempt to restructure health care financing and service delivery. Although it is uncertain what the final health care delivery system (if any) will look like, it is unlikely that we will return to a fee-for-service-based health care market.

Biotechnology, clinical programs, and health care policy are linked together and although they have distinct domains, the boundaries among them are static and permeable. Biotechnology is emerging as an economic force similar to the computer industry two decades ago and holds the potential of changing our physical and mental health at the molecular level. At the same time, technological advances in food production, disease eradication, and health promotion are occurring in the midst of major demographic changes within our population that highlight the inadequacy of current health care financing strategies for the population that is to come.

Acute illness is no longer the focus of clinical practice or health care education. Disease management and prevention taking place outside the traditional hospital setting is likely to continue. Population-based care returns decision-making to the provider but the provider must now weigh the costs and benefits of intervention.

Policy implications revolve around issues of finance. The changing demographics alter the dependency ratio of working individuals who pay into the health care system and nonworking individuals who take from the system. Mandatory retirement ages may be inappropriate given the expected increases in health and increased years of wage-earning capability.

Program implications will also continue to evolve. We must devise accurate outcome measures to determine which programs are effective under what circumstances. The interconnectedness of health and mental health cannot be fully understood outside the context of quality outcome measures.

Research and education implications are being felt keenly in today's market. Federal dollars allotted to academic health centers are shrinking and managed care organizations have shown little interest in supporting research that is not specific to their patient populations. Collaborative partnerships show promise in bridging the gap between managed care and academic medicine.

Although this changing market is, in effect, a moving target, a common theme is identified that will affect the separate spheres of policy, programs, and research. This theme is a shift to greater accountability and stronger collaboration in health care policy, programs, and research. A balance of cost, demand, and quality across populations will continue to provide challenges into the future.

REFERENCES

Association of American Medical Colleges. (1998, August 28). *Managed Care Organizations/Academic Health Centers Partnership Initiative*. Association of American Medical Colleges. Available: http://www.aamc.org/meded/pew [1999, March 7].

Almgren, G. (1998). Mental health practice in primary care: Some perspectives concerning the future of social work in organized delivery systems. *Smith College Studies in Social Work, 68*(2), 233–253.

Ancker, A. B. (1888). *The Municipal Hospital.* Paper presented at the National Conference of Charities and Correction, Boston, MA.

Baker, J. J., Chiverton, P., & Hines, V. (1998). Identifying costs for capitation in psychiatric case management. *Journal of Health Care Finance, 24*(3), 41–44.

Baker, L. C. (1999). Association of managed care market share and health expenditures for fee-for-service Medicare patients [see comments]. *Journal of the American Medical Association, 281*(5), 432–437.

Bazell, C., & Salsberg, E. (1998). The impact of graduate medical education financing policies on pediatric residency training. *Pediatrics, 101*(4 Pt 2), 785–792; discussion 793–794.

Berkman, B. (1996). The emerging health care world: Implications for social work practice and education. *Social Work, 41*(5), 541–551.

Bischof, R. O., Smith, R. L., Nash, D. B., Murray, J. F., Louis, D. Z., Hanchak, N. A., & Schlackman, N. (1997). Bridging the gap between managed care and academic medicine: An innovative fellowship. *American Journal of Managed Care, 3*(1), 107–111.

Bisno, H., & Cox, F. (1997). Social work education: Catching up with the present and the future. *Journal of Social Work Education, 33*(2), 373–387.

Bloomgarden, Z. T. (1996). American Diabetes Association annual meeting 1996: Managed care and change in medicine. *Diabetes Care, 19*(10), 1169–1173.

Broyles, R. W., Brandt, E. N., Jr., & Biard-Holmes, D. (1998). A practical method of adjusting for risk in the prospective costs of capitated systems. *Health Care Management Review, 23*(2), 63–75.

Carpenter, M. C., & Platt, S. (1997). Professional identity for clinical social workers: Impact of changes in health care delivery systems. *Clinical Social Work Journal, 25*(3), 337–350.

Carpinello, S., Felton, C. J., Pease, E. A., DeMasi, M., & Donahue, S. (1998). Designing a system for managing the performance of mental health managed care: An example from New York State's prepaid mental health plan. *Journal of Behavioral Health Services & Research, 25*(3), 269–278.

Cerminara, K. L. (1998). The class action suit as a method of patient empowerment in the managed care setting. *American Journal of Law & Medicine, 24*(1), 7–58.

Chandler, D., Meisel, J., Hu, T., McGowen, M., & Madison, K. (1998). A capitated model for a cross-section of severely mentally ill clients: Hospitalization. *Community Mental Health Journal, 34*(1), 13–26.

Chang, C. F., Kiser, L. J., Bailey, J. E., Martins, M., Gibson, W. C., Schaberg, K. A., Mirvis, D. M., & Applegate, W. B. (1998). Tennessee's failed managed care program for mental health and substance abuse services. *Journal of the American Medical Association, 279*(11), 864–869.

Colenda, C. C., Banazak, D., & Mickus, M. (1998). Mental health services in managed care: Quality questions remain. *Geriatrics, 53*(8), 49–52, 59–60, 63–44.

Colone, M. A. (1993). Case management and managed care: Balancing quality and cost control. *Social Work Administration, 19*(3), 6–13.

Costello, K., Connors, K., & Beavan, P. (1996). Managed care: What will it mean for nurses? *Lamp, 53*(5), 26–29.

Davidson, J. R., & Davidson, T. (1996). Confidentiality and managed care—ethical and legal concerns. *Health & Social Work, 21*(3), 208–215.

Davidson, T., & Davidson, J. R. (1995). Cost-containment, computers and confidentiality. *Clinical Social Work Journal, 23*(4), 453–464.

Donelan, K., Blendon, R. J., Benson, J., Leitman, R., & Taylor, H. (1996). All payer, single payer, managed care, no payer: Patients' perspectives in three nations. *Health Affairs, 15*(2), 254–265.

Durham, M. L. (1998). Mental health and managed care. *Annual Review of Public Health, 19,* 493–505.

Ell, K. (1996). Social work and health care practice and policy: A psychosocial research agenda. *Social Work, 41*(6), 583–592.

Field, T. S., Baldor, R. A., Casey, L. M., Chuman, A., Lasser, D., Ehrlich, A., & Gurwitz, J. H. (1998). Introducing managed care to the medical school curriculum: Effect on student attitudes. *American Journal of Managed Care, 4*(7), 1015–1021.

French, M. T., Dunlap, L. J., Galinis, D. N., Rachal, J. V., & Zarkin, G. A. (1996). Health care reforms and managed care for substance abuse services: Findings from eleven case studies. *Journal of Public Health Policy, 17*(2), 181–203.

Globerman, J., & Bogo, M. (1995). Social work and the new integrative hospital. *Social Work in Health Care, 21*(3), 1–27.

Golditch, I. M., Anderson, R. J., & Williams, S. B. (1998). Managed health care and resident education. *American Journal of Obstetrics and Gynecology, 178*(6), 1157–1162.

Gomez, A. G., Grimm, C. T., Yee, E. F. T., & Skootsky, S. A. (1997). Preparing residents for managed care practice using an experience-based curriculum. *Academic Medicine, 72*(11), 959–965.

Grasso, M. E., Weller, W. E., Shaffer, T. J., Diette, G. B., & Anderson, G. F. (1998). Capitation, managed care, and chronic obstructive pulmonary disease. *American Journal of Respiratory & Critical Care Medicine, 158*(1), 133–138.

Grimaldi, P. (1998a). Medicare's new capitation method. *Journal of Health Care Finance, 24*(4), 7–21.

Grimaldi, P. L. (1998b). Risk adjustment for health status. *Nursing Management, 29*(3), 18–21.

Hanson, M. A., Stone, E. L., Penk, W. E., Flannery, R. B., Jr., & Goldfinger, S. M. (1998). Public–academic liaison research centers in an era of managed care. *Psychiatric Quarterly, 69*(1), 61–68.

Haugh, R. (1998). Who's afraid of capitation now? *Hospitals & Health Networks, 72*(11), 30–32, 34, 36–37.

Health Care Financing Administration. (1999, February 7). *Program of All-Inclusive Care for the Elderly (PACE) History*. Department of Health & Human Services. Available: www.hcfa.gov [1999, April 12].

Holahan, J., Zuckerman, S., Evans, A., & Rangarajan, S. (1998). Medicaid managed care in thirteen states. *Health Affairs, 17*(3), 43–63.

Kane, R. L. (1998). Managed care as a vehicle for delivering more effective chronic care for older persons. *Journal of the American Geriatrics Society, 46*(8), 1034–1039.

Kathol, R. G., Kick, S. D., & Morrison, M. F. (1997). Let's train psychiatric residents to use their medical skills to meet twenty-first century demands. *Psychosomatics, 38*(6), 570–575.

Kerr, E. A., Mittman, B. S., Hays, R. D., Siu, A. L., Leake, B., & Brook, R. H. (1995). Managed care and capitation in California: How do physicians at financial risk control their own utilization? [see comments]. *Annals of Internal Medicine, 123*(7), 500–504.

Krop, J. S., Powe, N. R., Weller, W. E., Shaffer, T. J., Saudek, C. D., & Anderson, G. F. (1998). Patterns of expenditures and use of services among older adults with diabetes: Implications for the transition to capitated managed care. *Diabetes Care, 21*(5), 747–752.

Kuhlthau, K., Walker, D. K., Perrin, J. M., Bauman, L., Gortmaker, S. L., Newacheck, P. W., & Stein, R. E. (1998). Assessing managed care for children with chronic conditions. *Health Affairs, 17*(4), 42–52.

Lee, W., Eng, C., Fox, N., & Etienne, M. (1998). PACE: A model for integrated care of frail older patients: Program of All-inclusive Care for the Elderly. *Geriatrics, 53*(6), 62, 65–66, 69, 73; quiz 74.

Lillie-Blanton, M., & Lyons, B. (1998). Managed care and low-income populations: Recent state experiences. *Health Affairs, 17*(3), 238–247.

Lurie, N. (1996). Preparing physicians for practice in managed care environments. *Academic Medicine, 71*(10), 1044–1049.

Manton, K., Corder, L., & Stallard, E. (1997). *Proceedings of the National Academy of Science.* Paper presented at the National Academy of Science, USA.

McDaniel, C., & Erlen, J. (1996). Ethics and mental health service delivery under managed care. *Issues in Mental Health Nursing, 17*(1), 11–20.

Mechanic, D. (1999). The changing elderly population and future health care needs. *Journal of Urban Health: Bulletin of the New York Academy of Medicine, 76*(1), 24–38.

Miller, E. A., Weissert, W. G., & Chernew, M. (1998). Managed care for elderly people: A compendium of findings. *American Journal of Medical Quality, 13*(3), 127–140.

Miller, R. H., & Luft, H. S. (1997). Does managed care lead to better or worse quality of care? *Health Affairs, 16*(5), 7–25.

Moon, M. (1996). *Medicare Now and in the Future.* (2nd ed.). Washington, DC: Urban Institute Press.

Nash, D. B., & Veloski, J. J. (1998). Emerging opportunities for educational partnerships between managed care organizations and academic health centers. *Western Journal of Medicine, 168*(5), 319–327.

Newhouse, J. P. (1998). Risk adjustment: Where are we now? *Inquiry, 35*(2), 122–131.

Pardes, H., Manton, K. G., Lander, E. S., & Tolley, H. D. (1999). Effects of medical research on health care and the economy. *Science, 283*(5398) 36–37.

Pensiero, L. (1995). Stage-IV malignant melanoma—Psychosocial issues. *Cancer, 75*(2), 742–747.

Perloff, J. D. (1996). Medicaid managed care and urban poor people: Implications for social work. *Health & Social Work, 21*(3), 189–195.

Pryor, D. B., & Fortin, D. F. (1995). Managing the delivery of health care: care-plans/managed care/practice guidelines. *International Journal of Bio-Medical Computing, 39*(1), 105–109.

Rabkin, M. T. (1998). A paradigm shift in academic medicine? *Academic Medicine, 73*(2), 127–131.

Raskin, M. S., & Blome, W. W. (1998). The impact of managed care on field instruction. *Journal of Social Work Education, 34*(3), 365–374.

Reamer, F. G. (1997). Managing ethics under managed care. *Families in Society the Journal of Contemporary Human Services, 78*(1), 96–101.

Remler, D. K., Donelan, K., Blendon, R. J., Lundberg, G. D., Leape, L. L., Calkins, D. R., Binns, K., & Newhouse, J. P. (1997). What do managed care plans do to affect care? Results from a survey of physicians. *Inquiry, 34*(3), 196–204.

Robinson, J. C. (1996). Decline in hospital utilization and cost inflation under managed care in California. *Journal of the American Medical Association, 276*(13), 1060–1064.

Roth, D., Snapp, M. B., Lauber, B. G., & Clark, J. A. (1998). Consumer turnover in service utilization patterns: Implications for capitated payment. *Administration and Policy in Mental Health, 25*(3), 241–255.

Schmalzried, T. P., & Luck, J. V., Jr. (1998). Capitated reimbursement for medical services returns control of the patient to the surgeon. *Orthopedics, 21*(6), 620, 629–631.

Scutchfield, F. D., Lee, J., & Patton, D. (1997). Managed care in the United States. *Journal of Public Health Medicine, 19*(3), 251–254.

Sennett, C. (1997). Models for measuring quality in managed care: Analysis and impact. In J. Seltzer & D. B. Nash (Eds.), *Faulkner & Gray's medical outcomes and practice guidelines library* (Vol. 1, p. 355). New York: Faulkner & Gray's Healthcare Information Center.

Shera, W. (1996). Managed care and people with severe mental illness: Challenges and opportunities for social work. *Health & Social Work, 21*(3), 196–201.

Shine, K. (1998). The health sciences, health services research, and the role of the health professions. *Health services research, 33*(3 Part 1), 439–445.

Shortell, S. M., Gillies, R. R., & Devers, K. J. (1995). Reinventing the American Hospital. *Milbank Quarterly, 73,* 131–160.

Simmons, W. J., & Goforth, L. (1997). The impact of managed care on cancer care: Review and recommendations. *Cancer Practice, 5*(2), 111–118.

Slay, J. D., Jr., & Glazer, W. M. (1995). "Carving in," and keeping in, mental health care in the managed care setting. *Psychiatric Services, 46*(11), 1119–1120, 1125.

Stevens, D. P., Leach, D. C., Warden, G. L., & Cherniack, N. S. (1996). A strategy for coping with change: An affiliation between a medical school and a managed care health system. *Academic Medicine, 71*(2), 133–137.

Stoeckle, J. D. (1995). The citadel cannot hold: Technologies go outside the hospital, patients and doctors too. *Milbank Quarterly, 73*(1), 3–17.

Strom-Gottfried, K. (1997). The implications of managed care for social work education. *Journal of Social Work Education, 33*(1), 7–18.

Stroul, B. A., Pires, S. A., Roebuck, L., Friedman, R. M., Barrett, B., Chambers, K. L., & Kershaw, M. A. (1997). State health care reforms: How they affect children and adolescents with emotional disorders and their families. *Journal of Mental Health Administration, 24*(4), 386–399.

Stuart, M. E., & Weinrich, M. (1998). Beyond managing Medicaid costs: Restructuring care. *Milbank Quarterly, 76*(2), 251–280.

Volland, P. J. (1996). Social work practice in health care: Looking to the future with a different lens. *Social Work in Health Care, 24*(1–2), 35–51.

White, M., Wimmons, W. J., & Bixby, N. (1993). Managed care and case management: An overview. *Discharge Planning Update, 13*(1), 17–19.

Wholey, D. R., Burns, L. R., & Lavizzo-Mourey, R. (1998). Managed care and the delivery of primary care to the elderly and the chronically ill. *Health Services Research, 33*(2 Pt II), 322–353.

◆ CHAPTER 3 ◆

The Intersection of Fee-for-Service, Managed Health Care, and Cultural Competence

Implications for National Health Care Policy and Services to People of Color

KING DAVIS

PUBLIC HEALTH POLICY AND PEOPLE OF COLOR

Throughout the twentieth century, a large number of studies and authors have confirmed that access, quality of care, and years of healthy living showed a significant relationship to race, ethnicity, income, and social class under the traditional fee-for-service system prevalent in the United States (Abe-Kim & Takeuchi, 1996; Ayanian, 1994; Center for Health Economics Research, 1993; Clinton, 1998; Cole & Pilisuk, 1976; Council on Ethical and Judicial Affairs, 1989; Garretson, 1993; Gaston, Barrett et al., 1998; Hadley, Steinberg et al., 1991; Hawkins & Rosenbaum, 1993; Jang, Lee et al., 1998; Jones & Gray, 1986; Livingston, 1994; Moy & Bartman, 1995; Mutchler & Burr, 1991; McWhorter & Moyer, 1987; Rice & Winn, 1990; Peterson, Wright et al., 1994; Weiss, 1997). These articles and studies show that under the American fee-for-service system the health and mental health problems of low-income people of color were misdiagnosed frequently, diagnosed more severely than the symptoms warranted, but treated less frequently with current medical procedures than were whites, even when there were no differences in ability to pay for services (Mutchler & Burr, 1991; Peterson, Wright et al., 1994). The absence of equitable access is the key variable, identified in analysis of secondary data by the Robert Wood Johnson Foundation, and used to explain why low-income people of color have higher rates of preventable acute and chronic health conditions and excess mortality (Center for Health Economics Research, 1993). However, more recent studies (Schulman, Berlin et al., 1999) suggest that the response by the health care provider to the race and gender of the patient influences the health care decisions that are made. Both these sets of findings raise important questions about the relationship between health care polices, access, and cultural competence.

Interest in the health and mental health status of populations of color, as well as the extent to which their status differs from white Americans, has been evident in the literature for decades (Babcock, 1895; Cartwright, 1851; Davis, 1998; Dreger & Miller, 1960; Evarts, 1914; Fischer, 1969; Gould, 1981; Green, 1914; Hawkins & Rosenbaum, 1993; Jang, Lee et al., 1998; Jarvis, 1852; Kleiner, Tuckman et al., 1960; Rice & Winn, 1990; Thomas & Sillen, 1972; Zane, Takeuchi et al., 1994; Weiss, 1997). However, many of these studies show that the data generated and used to form public health policy for people of color have not been accurate. For example, Thomas and Sillen (1972) and Fischer (1969) show that data on African Americans and mental illness, gathered systematically by the federal government in the 17th century, was contradictory, based on falsified census data, and was designed to be used politically to support the continuation of slavery. Public policy on African Americans with severe mental illness has wavered between two extreme positions: Blacks were portrayed prior to 1863 as being immune from mental illness (Jarvis, 1852) and were generally denied admission to state hospitals, while after 1865 blacks were considered to be at the highest risk and became disproportionately represented in state hospitals up to the 1980s (Drewry, 1916; Malzberg & Lee, 1956; Malzberg, 1959; Malzberg, 1963; Manderscheid & Sonnenschein, 1987; Pasamanick, 1959; Pasamanick, Lemkau et al., 1960; Pasamanick, 1963; Pasamanick, 1963). By 1963 community mental health programs saw the migration of rural blacks and the stresses of urban life as key risk factors that contributed to an excessive rate of severe mental illness and need for hospitalization. Data developed more recently, however, refutes these earlier findings and concludes that there is no significant statistical difference in the frequency of severe mental illness by race or color (Fischer, 1969; Jackson, Neighbors et al., 1986; Neighbors, 1984; Neighbors, Bashshur et al., 1992; Neighbors & Jackson, 1996; Regier, Farmer et al., 1993). Many of the earlier studies were based on rates of admission to psychiatric facilities, a research design that Neighbors (Neighbors, Bashshur et al., 1992) suggests results in bias. When false data on the incidence of mental illness was combined in a racially insensitive fee-for-service system, inpatient hospitalization, diagnostic error, and involuntary treatment become more frequent for people of color (Ramm, 1989).

Few of the health research studies produced over the past several decades focused on the prevalence, incidence, or utilization data trends in Asian and Pacific Islander American populations (Jang, Lee et al., 1998; Zane, Takeuchi et al., 1994). Where data has been available on this population, the quality of this data, assumptions, and conclusions have been questioned (Gardner, 1994; Gaston, Barrett et al., 1998; Zane, Takeuchi et al., 1994). The absence of accurate data on Asian Americans has contributed to an undercount of the actual prevalence and incidence of mental disorders in this population and has contributed to the absence of needed services (Jang, Lee et al., 1998; Zane, Takeuchi et al., 1994). The conclusion that Asian and Pacific Islander Americans have lower rates of mental illness than other parts of the population is similar to the "immunity" argument put forth in the 17th and 18th centuries about African Americans and used to justify the denial and absence of services (Davis, 1998; Thomas & Sillen, 1972).

The national health care approach appears to have been built around the false assumptions that there are no clinical or policy-worthy differences in people by culture, ethnicity, race, or social class that significantly influence their health or mental health status or the way services should be designed and delivered, or how they are actually sought and consumed. Donald Wing Sue characterizes this approach as monoculturalism and sees it as another key variable for interpreting and understanding the different patterns of service utilization by people of color (Sue, 1998). The impact of services based on monocultural policies is seen in psychiatric admissions data gathered by the National Institute of Mental Health in the 1980s, shown in Table 3.1 (Manderscheid & Sonnenschein, 1985; Manderscheid & Sonnenschein, 1987).

Regardless of the type of inpatient psychiatric setting, the frequency of admissions of African Americans and Native Americans significantly exceeded or approximated the national rate per 100,000 population. In some mental health settings (state hospitals) the rates for these two groups are close to double the rates for all others. For Asian and Pacific Islander American populations, the rates of psychiatric admissions are consistently lower than for all other groups. However, Jang (Jang, Lee et al., 1998; Lee & Sue, 1997) and Zane (Zane, Takeuchi et al., 1994) warn that such data may reflect serious undercounting of the extent of service need in these populations.

One reason for the longitudinal public policy interest in people of color and health care has been major concern that providing health and mental health care to these populations—in which close to one-third has low income, long-term double-digit rates of unemployment, and lower rates of personal health insurance—will increase the long-term health care costs to business and government employers. Some mortality and morbidity data suggest that chronic and acute illness, long-term disability, and early death are more common occurrences in some African, Hispanic, and Native American populations (Center for Health Economics Research, 1993; Robert Wood Johnson Foundation, 1991; U.S. Bureau of the Census, 1995; U.S. Department of Health and Human Services, 1985). Although it is not clear from these and earlier studies why there are such marked differences by race and eth-

Table 3.1
Admissions per 100,000 by Race, Ethnicity, and Type of Psychiatric Facility

Population	Total	State Hospital	Private Hospital	General Hospital	Veterans' Hospital
All Groups	593.0	163.6	62.6	295.3	70.4
African American	931.0	364.2	62.9	386.6	118.0
Asian American	268.1	75.4	25.0	161.0	6.6
Hispanic American	452.3	146.0	34.4	227.0	44.1
Native American	818.7	306.4	41.2	371.6	99.2
White American	550.0	136.8	63.4	284.9	67.9

nicity, public policies should consider the service and cost implications of these differences and how application of cultural competence could result in significant reductions in expenditures for inpatient services.

If the cost to serve people of color is perceived to be higher than for other populations there will be few incentives for managed care plans, stimulated by profit and cost savings, to voluntarily seek to cover these lives in existing health care plans without additional compensation. However, it seems important to consider that the cost of serving people of color may be artificially higher because of diagnostic and treatment errors stemming from a monocultural frame of reference that results in inappropriately higher utilization rates of expensive inpatient care. The emphasis in managed care on input and outcome data may result in a reduction of overconsumption of inpatient psychiatric care for people of color. A number of authors in mental health and health care (Collins, Sorel et al., 1990; Council on Ethical and Judicial Affairs, 1989; Jenkins-Hall & Sacco, 1991; Jones & Gray, 1986; Leigh, 1992; Mukhergee, Shukla et al., 1983; Neighbors, Jackson et al., 1989; Peterson, Wright et al., 1994; Thomas & Sillen, 1972; Williams, 1986; Willis, 1989; Yergan, Flood et al., 1987) have noted the frequency with which clinicians make serious diagnostic errors when examining people of color. These diagnostic errors may be causally related to the disproportionate frequency of admissions to mental institutions by race, gender, and ethnicity (Manderscheid & Sonnenschein, 1987).

As political and economic pressures increase to shift the service and payment mechanism in American health care from fee-for-service to managed care, a series of critical public policy questions must be raised and debated about the linkages between race, health status, and the cost of service:

1. Is there a significant difference in the cost of providing physical and behavioral health care to people of color? What factors explain these differences?
2. To what extent is there a difference in the utilization of inpatient mental health care by people of color and other populations? What factors explain these differences?
3. To what extent, if any, is there a relationship between the quality of general medical care provided to people of color and mental health status?
4. What are the policy implications for the uninsured, unemployed, and underemployed people of color in a managed care environment?
5. What is the impact of shifts towards managed care for providers of color and the health networks that currently exist in their communities?
6. What managed care programs have demonstrated success in designing services and policies consumed by people of color?
7. What factors explain these successful programs?
8. How can existing health care professionals in public and private settings be retrained to provide culturally competent services to people of color? How will these costs for training be absorbed? And by whom?

9. What does cultural competence offer to help resolve issues of service quality, differential utilization rates, help-seeking, and assumed differences in cost?
10. What are the clinical standards of care that are necessary in a behavioral health care environment to provide effective services to people of color with severe mental illness?

It is equally important to determine how to get these questions and issues of culturally based health disparities and the potential role of cultural competence on the national health care policy agenda when the nation appears to have adopted managed care.

CLINTON'S HEALTH CARE EQUITY POLICY INITIATIVE

Interest on the part of President Clinton may offer an avenue for policy efforts to address issues of racial and ethnic disparities in health care. President Clinton (Clinton, 1998) indicated that one of the more significant unresolved policy dilemmas and opportunities for the United States is to utilize a portion of its abundant budgetary surplus to structure, deliver, pay for, and guarantee access to quality health care for all its population—income, race, age, gender, language, immigrant status, and welfare status not withstanding. Clinton's intent is to insure that "all Americans, no matter what their background, have a better opportunity to live healthier lives" (Clinton, 1998). However, the president recognizes that race, ethnicity, and low income continue to act as the major impediments to equity in health status, as well as access to health care services. In an effort to rekindle interest as well as reduce racial disparities in health status, the president developed a new policy initiative in February 1998 designed to bring about equity for populations of color by the year 2010 (Shalala & Satcher, 1998; Clinton, 1998). Clinton's policy initiative is to be financed with $400 million of federal monies and with cooperation from 136 American foundations (Clinton, 1998). The relationship that is anticipated between Clinton's policy initiative and the existing fee-for-service and managed care policies is not yet clear. However, this relationship may be crucial to actual change in the dismal health care status of low income people of color, since the disparities to be addressed have survived through a number of prior policy initiatives and a number of administrations (Braithwaite & Taylor, 1998; Davis, 1997; Leigh, 1992; Rice & Winn, 1990; Rosenbaum, Serrano et al., 1997; U.S. Department of Health and Human Services, 1985; Weiss, 1997).

Previous federal and private health care policy initiatives have been contradictory, exceptionally uneven, and financially prohibitive (Robert Wood Johnson Foundation, 1991). At the same time, the annual cost of health care and the share of the GDP gobbled up by health care threatened to destabilize the economy over the past decade (White House Domestic Policy Council, 1993) by reducing the pre-tax profits and increasing the costs of goods and services produced by American corporations and increasing the cost of governmentally sponsored health care programs (Medicaid and Medicare). It was the continuous pressure of annual health care premium increases on small and large businesses that fueled the acceptance of managed health care as de facto national health care policy in 1993 (Bowles & Thorpe, 1998). Health policy analysts and health economists contend that the preeminent challenge at the core of the health care policy debate in America, over the last several decades, has been to identify a set of ubiquitous processes to decrease the rapid growth in costs in ten (see Figure 3.1) overlapping areas (White House Domestic Policy Council, 1993; Hurst, 1991; Scanlon, 1997; Robert Wood Johnson Foundation, 1991; Bowles & Thorpe, 1998). The majority of these costs characterized the fee-for-service reimbursement system in which almost all economic risks were assumed by private employers and government while providers and consumers carried minimal risk. It is assumed that there is a direct relationship between the level of risk carried and the subsequent interest in identifying policies to reduce costs.

Previous American health policies (fee-for-service, Medicaid, Medicare) have not been able to solve the problem of marked differences in access to quality care, years of health living, risk and vulnerability to illness, and disproportionately high death rates of America's poor, severely mentally ill, unemployed, and underemployed populations, as well as populations of color considered medically underserved (Gardner, 1994; Gaston, Barrett et al., 1998; Jang, Lee et al., 1998; Rice & Winn, 1990; Short, Cornelius et al., 1990; Weiss, 1997; Whittle, Conigliardo et al., 1993). Infant mortality and rates of HIV infections in the United States showed minimal abatement in the final decade of the twentieth century among lower-income populations, and the problems of adolescent pregnancy and violence are now conceptualized as major public health crises (Center for Health Economics Research, 1993; Davis, Aguilar et al., 1998; Robert Wood Johnson Foundation, 1991). Clin-

1. Health care premiums
2. Annual increases above inflation
3. Total annual increases
4. Costs per capita
5. Health costs as a proportion of the GDP
6. Health costs as a proportion of pre-tax profits of corporations
7. Health costs as a percentage of total wage compensation
8. Health care as a percentage of the current federal budget
9. Health care as a percentage of future federal budgets
10. Health care as a proportion of state and local government expenditures

Figure 3.1 Areas of Growth in Health Care

ton's newest policy approach seeks to pare the extensive health disparities of racial minorities by focusing limited federal dollars and energies on six related health problems—infant mortality, cancer screening, cardiovascular disease, diabetes, HIV/AIDS, and immunizations (Shalala & Satcher, 1998)—without altering existing managed care policies or obtaining permanent monetary participation from the business sector through tax increases. Part of the Clinton strategy may be attributed to an effort to avoid stimulating the extensive resistance, animosity, and fear of governmental intervention that contributed to the failure of his managed health care competition initiative in 1993 (Johnson & Broder, 1996).

Unparalleled growth in the United States economy and the projection of unprecedented surplus dollars at the federal and state levels may make Clinton's quest for equity in health care far more of a realistic policy goal than in any previous decade (Clinton, 1998; Congressional Budget Office, 1999). Equitable health care for people of color as a national policy goal, however, will require unprecedented visionary leadership and agreement across political ideologies about the desired direction of national health care policy and the acceptable role of government. Of equal importance in the possible transformation of American health care policy is the need to find a culturally relevant conceptual framework for services.

INTERSECTION OF MANAGED CARE AND FEE-FOR-SERVICE POLICY

Despite both growth in costs for the population generally and inequity in health care throughout the twentieth century for populations of color specifically, the nation has established a policy direction in which de facto managed health care policy intersects the traditional fee-for-service system and the two governmental health care programs (Medicaid and Medicare). The health care policy dilemma the United States faces is to determine the impact of the intersection of managed health care and fee-for-service on the president's policy initiative to equalize health status and on access for populations of color. One potential approach is to examine the intersection of these two distinctively different health care reimbursement policies and to analyze their prospective impact on the recent Clinton policy initiative to equalize health care by race, access to, and health status of populations of color.

Rather than pursue fundamental legislative change in American health care policies in 1993, the House, Senate, executive branch, and major corporations compromised on managed care as the de facto national health policy (Johnson & Broder, 1996). At the same time, no specific Congressional action was taken to dismantle the existing fee-for-service reimbursement system, nor were guidelines provided to govern how the two systems would operate within Medicaid or Medicare. Both systems of health care were permitted to remain and operate simultaneously in the health care market. The adoption of managed care was based primarily on a desire to curb health care costs for business and government, with limited attention to insuring that the health care needs of people of color were targeted specifically. As a result of the laissez faire actions by the Congress and the executive branch, managed health care policy intersected and competed with the long-standing policy of fee-for-service for customers insured through employment, Medicaid, or Medicare eligibility. States were given wide latitude in designing their Medicaid Waiver programs to interface with the emerging managed care effort. The intersection of managed care and fee-for-service policies has created a hybrid American health care system that potentially changes the stakes, relationships, and exchanges between four traditional elements in the health care system shown in Figure 3.2.

In the traditional fee-for-service system, power, authority, and decision-making were held principally by the individual, group, or hospital providers and to a lesser extent by the consumer. Providers determined the diagnosis, course of treatment, length of treatment, and the costs to be paid. Insurance companies and employers (governmental and private) held limited power and authority to intervene but bore the major financial risks for annual increases in insurance premiums and provider fees. Providers and consumers assumed only limited risk for the financial costs of health care. As a result of the imbalance in power between providers and payers, relationships and exchanges tended to be equally imbalanced and strained. Under traditional fee-for-service, access to quality health care was limited for poor people of color, resulting in a higher-than-expected frequency of illness and early death (Boutwell & Mitchell, 1993; Center for Health Economics Research, 1993; Peterson, Wright et al., 1994).

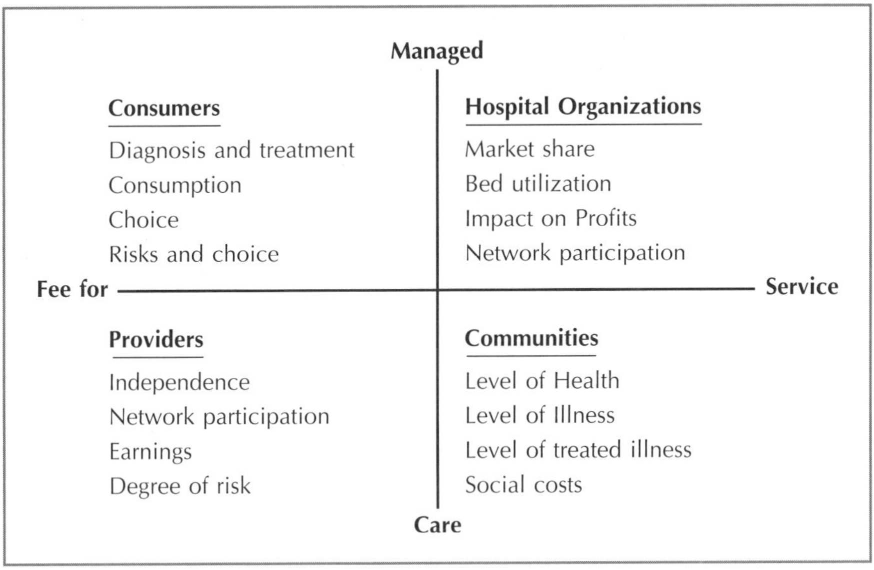

Managed

Consumers	**Hospital Organizations**
Diagnosis and treatment	Market share
Consumption	Bed utilization
Choice	Impact on Profits
Risks and choice	Network participation

Fee for —— **Service**

Providers	**Communities**
Independence	Level of Health
Network participation	Level of Illness
Earnings	Level of treated illness
Degree of risk	Social costs

Care

Figure 3.2 Traditional health care groups and how they are affected by the intersection of fee-for-service and managed health care policies

	Consumers	Providers	Employers/Insurers
Fee-for-Service:	Overuse of inpatient Misdiagnosis Unnecessary treatment	Legal liability Profit and loss	Cost of premiums After-tax profits Productivity Market position Product cost Overconsumption
Managed Care:	Underuse of inpatient Maldiagnosis Inappropriate treatment Unlimited access Choice Quality of care Confidentiality	Autonomy Unlimited income Solo practice Decision-making Network participation Control of information Control of Pricing	Cost of premiums After-tax profits

Figure 3.3 Risk by Group and Type of Health Care Reimbursement System

The intersection of fee-for-service with payer-driven managed care policy shifts the balance of power away from fee-for-service providers while increasing the economic risks borne by this system. In the managed care system, payers (insurers and employers) have displaced providers and consumers, reducing their autonomous roles in clinical decision-making and pricing while increasing their economic risks (see Figure 3.3). In addition, managed care policies have forced providers and consumers to increase the volume of clinical information—from diagnosis to treatment and outcomes—as a condition of reimbursement or payment. Managed care has also instituted a series of policies that substantially reduce access to inpatient hospitalization and long-term care. The intersection of fee-for-service with managed health care policy has resulted in considerable anger, hostility, fear, resentment, and legal challenge by providers of health care formerly associated exclusively with the fee-for-service reimbursement systems (National Association of Social Workers, 1997). Legal suits challenging the authority of managed health care systems have achieved only modest success, although a number of states and the federal government are considering legislation guaranteeing the rights of consumers in managed care plans (Clinton, 1998). The 1999 session of the Virginia legislature extensively debated the value of passing legislation to increase the rights of consumers (including the right to sue) vis-à-vis health maintenance organizations (Intress, 1999). The final vote in the Virginia legislature overwhelmingly supported an increase in consumer rights, but fell short of giving consumers the right to sue their HMOs.

Ideally, fundamental legislative change in national health care policy, based on an analysis of historical patterns of utilization, would have substantially replaced the flawed, costly, and inequitable fee-for-service system with a singular national policy direction (perhaps universal coverage). A new direction in national health care policy would have ideally addressed and resolved the question of whether access to health care is a right of all citizens, a fringe benefit of employment or welfare, or an increasingly scarce commodity available only to those who can purchase it at prevailing rates. Manderscheid (Manderscheid, 1997) proposes that managed health care converts health care to the status of commodities, not unlike any other goods or services bought and sold in the economic marketplace. Fundamental change in the direction of national health care policy too would have addressed and sought to resolve the long-term racial and ethnic disparities in health care access and status that were noted in the United States throughout the past two centuries (Braithwaite & Taylor, 1998; Center for Health Economics Research, 1993; Clinton, 1998; Davis, 1998; Duffy, 1967; Faris & Dunham, 1939; Flaskerud & Hu, 1992; Garretson, 1993; Hawkins & Rosenbaum, 1993; Hollingshead & Redlich, 1958; Jackson, 1988; Jarvis, 1852; Leigh, 1992; Livingston, 1994; Malzberg, 1959; Neighbors & Lumpkin, 1990; Office of Minority Health, 1993; Randall, 1994; Rice & Winn, 1990; U.S. Department of Health, 1979). In the short term, the adoption of managed care policy and its intersection with existing fee-for-service policy seems to confirm that access to health care continues to be viewed as an important fringe benefit of full-time employment and a reluctant short-term feature of welfare benefits for specific classes of the disabled, the aged, or dependent children and their mothers (see Figure 3.4).

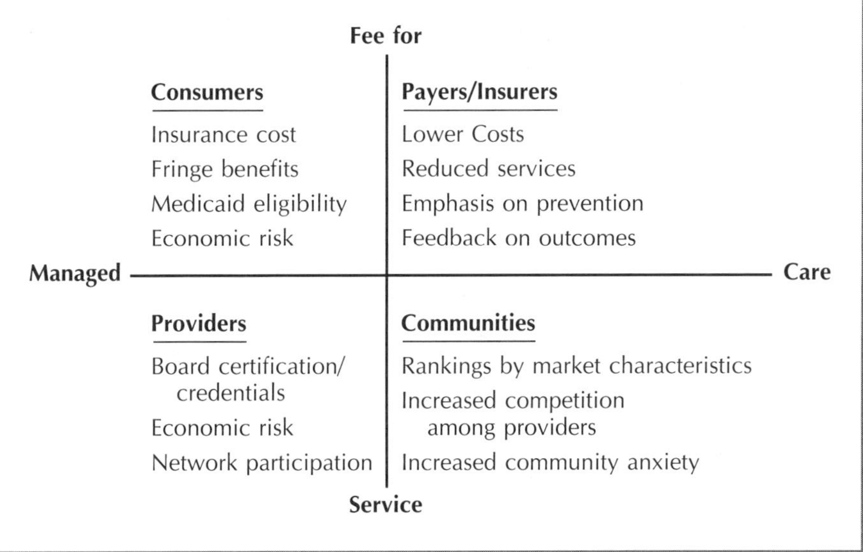

Figure 3.4 Impact on Markets when Policy Intersects

DEFINING MANAGED HEALTH CARE AND FEE-FOR-SERVICE

Managed health care is defined in this article as any plan, process, procedure, or program that attempts to impact access to health care services, as well as its costs, quality, efficiency, satisfaction, and utilization (Davis, 1996; Mauer, Jarvis et al., 1995; Rognehaugh, 1998; United Healthcare Corporation, 1994). At least theoretically, managed health care policy would appear to offer greater access to low-income people of color than what they experienced in fee-for-service health care. The two primary mechanisms for achieving the objectives of managed care are (1) modifying the service-utilization behavior of consumers and (2) changing the professional practices and decisions of providers and organizations heretofore symbiotically linked/circumscribed in the health care system. The most powerful mechanism employed in managed care policy is the ability to require that the receipt or provision of services, participation in the system, or payment is dependent on consumers and providers sharing substantially in the financial risk formerly borne exclusively by insurers and employers. This risk-sharing requirement is based on the assumption that medically unnecessary services will be less likely requested or provided when the consumer and provider must share in the cost of those services and where there is a risk that the third-party insurer will not pay for the service or may seek reimbursement from either the provider or consumer or both. It is assumed that circumscribing services by medical-necessity criteria and shared financial risk will pare consumption of the costliest and longest-term health services prescribed by physicians.

Fee-for-service is defined as a method of paying for health care services in which the provider diagnoses the ailment, prescribes the treatment, and determines the length of care and the fees (Rognehaugh, 1998; United Healthcare Corporation, 1994). Under fee-for-service, each unit of service is billed to the consumer, insurer, or employer. In this method of health care, the financial risk is carried almost exclusively by the insurer and the employer responsible for payment of premiums. In fee-for-service policy there is less dependency on prior utilization data as a prerequisite to accessing services since neither the provider nor consumer carries substantial financial risk for the service. Framers of managed care policy see an inherent conflict of interest in fee-for-service because of the ability of the provider to profit personally from decisions about the extent or length of services needed where they do not share in the financial risks of such decisions. Under fee-for-service policy, medical providers have few incentives to either curb the extent of services provided to consumers or the cost of units of service provided. As a result, health care costs and prices are likely to increase, even as the supply of providers able to bill third-party insurers increases. As the number of providers eligible to bill third-party insurers increases, the overall cost of health care in the nation increases substantially.

Managed health care now appears to be the most successful short-term public health policy developed in the twentieth century for curbing the threat to profits, economic growth, competition, and budgetary balance of the private and public sectors. Simultaneously however, managed health care is among the most politically controversial of all public health care policies, based on how it has reduced the level of autonomy of medical providers and the extent of choice by employed middle-class consumers, while purportedly lowering the quality of their health care.

The Congressional Budget Office (Congressional Budget Office, 1999) recently confirmed that managed care has had the effect of lowering costs as reflected in decreases in the percentage of the consumer price index and gross domestic product consumed by health care costs. Whether the ability of managed care to reduce the cost of health care to employers and government will counterbalance significant increases in premiums forecasted for 1999 or the disaffection with the loss of autonomy and choice by providers and consumers is unclear.

What appears to be lacking in the national decision to intersect managed health care policy with fee-for-service is a conceptual frame of reference for the design and delivery of services to populations of color that will help eliminate the numerous problems of disparity and absence of quality care these populations experienced in singular fee-for-service. One key aspect of this effort is the need to shift away from monocultural approaches to health care delivery.

When managed health care policy and service approaches intersect the traditional fee-for-service system it superimposes free market concepts and insurance processes on an already flawed and inequitable national health care approach. Free market culture is comprised of three main characteristics: market virtues, non-market values, and market (dichotomous) segmentation (see Figure 3.5).

Managed care policy includes a number of virtues that have the potential for increasing both access and quality of care for low-income consumers. These virtues include an emphasis on efficiency, cost effectiveness, medical necessity, screening, outcomes, consumer satisfaction, risk sharing, credentialing, data-based decision-making, and cost controls. Where these virtues operate, managed care is likely to exceed the level of quality care offered in the traditional fee-for-service system, where similar virtues are given less emphasis and importance.

1. Market virtues
2. Non-market values
3. Dichotomous segmentation

Figure 3.5 Elements of Market Culture

Managed care policy tends to displace and deemphasize a number of values described here as non-market values. These non-market values have more currency and acceptance in the traditional fee-for-service and government-backed health care programs such as Medicaid. These non-market values include entitlement, choice, participation, autonomy, unlimited access, rights, and information sharing. It is the elimination or major reduction of these non-market values that has stimulated resistance, hostility, legal challenge, and concern from middle-class consumers, providers, legislators, and the president of the United States.

The third factor market culture brings to the intersection with fee-for-service health care is dichotomous segmentation. Segmentation refers to the identification or categorization of individuals and groups within a market or population based on some key identifiable characteristic: age, gender, religion, social class, type of employment, place of employment, education, neighborhood, race, ethnicity, or marital status. The aim of the segmentation is to provide adequate information to an organization to enable its management to decide which segments within an overall market are to be provided goods and services (Kotler, 1975). The ultimate aim of segmentation is to reach the most profitable and least costly markets, penetrate them, and sell the goods and services designed for that market. Correspondingly, the intent is to avoid investments in markets that have less potential for profit or a higher probability of increased demands and costs (Kotler, 1976).

On close analysis, managed health care policy and processes tend to introduce and rely on what is termed here as dichotomous segmentation in the health care market. These dichotomous segments are shown in Figure 3.6. Market segments that involve greater costs and heightened needs for services, or are located in urban areas are less likely to receive needed services in a managed care environment (Center for Health Economics Research, 1993). Poor populations of color, women, children, and the aged are overrepresented in these medically underserved groups (Gaston, Barrett et al., 1998) while providers and services are often underrepresented (Center for Health Economics Research, 1993).

Managed Care	**Other Policies**
Employed	Unemployed
Insured	Uninsured
Short term	Long term
Acute	Chronic
Licensed	Unlicensed
Limits	Unlimited
Board certified	Uncertified
Managed	Unmanaged

Figure 3.6 Dichotomous Segments

When these three factors of managed health care policy intersect the existing fee-for-service system, the potential impact on low-income consumers, providers of color, organizations, and communities can include heightened short-term competition for their enrollment and a reduction in available services without a clear understanding of their needs or how to provide culturally appropriate services in the market.

Managed health care, unlike other policies and health care approaches tried in prior years, is more dependent on the accuracy, quality , and extent of data and information that is available about the market of potential and actual consumers. Information about these markets is critical for making decisions about design, location, delivery, evaluation, and pricing of services based in part on prior patterns of utilization and predictions of future usage.

To achieve its multiple goals of impacting access, cost efficiency, quality service, and utilization, managed care plans require accurate and comprehensive knowledge and information about the consumer and provider, as well as service utilization patterns, medications provided, service outcomes, consumer satisfaction, unit costs, and detailed information about the community, neighborhood, and groups in which people are born, live, work, and develop health risks. In this regard, managed care is best and appropriately viewed as a data-driven and data-dependent process. Where such data and information are unavailable, inaccessible, inaccurate, biased, prejudiced, distorted, or do not exist, managed care plans cannot achieve their goals of cost efficiency and quality of service and may show only marginal differences in outcomes from the fee-for-service plans they intersected.

USING CULTURAL COMPETENCY TO ACHIEVE EQUITY IN MANAGED CARE POLICIES AND SERVICES

Heretofore, cultural competence has been described and utilized as a tool for shaping clinical services and systems of care for people of color (Davis, 1998; Davis-Chambers, 1998; Fleming & King, 1997; Lee & Sue, 1997; Pumariega & Balderrama, 1997). However, in this discussion, the proposal is to utilize the concepts and features of cultural competence as the logical nexus for binding and redirecting such public health policies as fee-for-service, managed health care, and the Clinton initiative, as well as Medicaid and Medicare. Such a nexus and redirection seem necessary since the traditional fee-for-service policy and programs seemed unable, even with the boost from Medicaid funding, to make more than modest gains in resolving ethnic and racial disparities over the past several decades. Although the structure of managed care policy and its links to insurance and risk offer a greater probability of improved access for low-income populations of color, the emphasis on cost-containment processes may result in improved access but undertreatment or demarketing of these groups (Kotler, 1975). What the Clinton policy seems designed to do is to heighten national attention on the long-term failure of prior policy initiatives to solve the problem of disparities by race. However, the president's initiative has not yet provided the nation with clear direction or strategies for achieving equity in health status. Without such clear direction and accompanying strategies, the political and economic weight wrought from the intersection of these multiple policy initiatives may increase the complexity and confusion of these policies and their subsequent plans for low-income populations of color.

What must occur conceptually and operationally is for all of the existing health care policies and initiatives that affect low-income people of color to be redesigned through a cultural competence framework into a singular national health initiative. Such a redesign would include altering the relationships between and among each of the policies, as shown in Figure 3.7.

One of the earliest definitions of cultural competence was developed by Cross (Cross, Bazron et al., 1989). These researchers suggest that "cultural competence is a set of congruent attitudes, behaviors, and policies that come together in a system, agency, or among professionals to enable them to work effectively." However, culturally competent policy must integrate and transform attitudes, behaviors, knowledge, information, facts, patterns, history, and data about individuals, groups, and communities of color into specific problem statements, policy direction, goals, strategies, desired outcomes, organizational structures, service locations, and service standards that match the individual's culture (Davis, 1997). It is the overall public policy that determines the nature of the services that are provided to low-income populations of color regardless of whether the reimbursement mechanism in place pays for each unit of service provided, or pays by diagnosis or groups. The

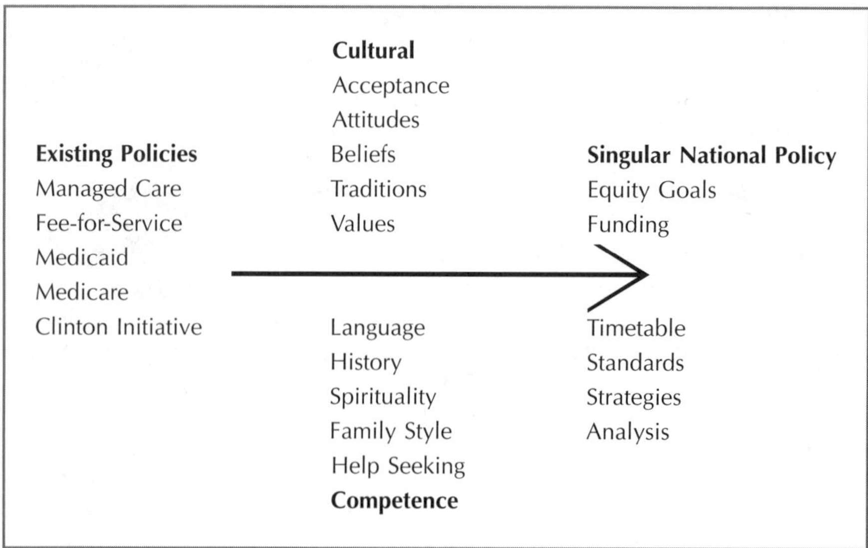

Figure 3.7 The Intersection of Health Care Policy by Cultural Competence

ultimate aim of culturally competent policy is to increase the quality and appropriateness of health care services to low-income populations of color.

It can be hypothesized that the greater the degree a health care policy is based on cultural competence, the greater the probability the goals of cost efficiency, quality services, and equity of health status will be achieved (Abe-Kim & Takeuchi, 1996; Anderson, Eaddy et al., 1990; Brach, 1996; Chess, Clark et al., 1953; Collins, Sorel et al., 1990; Cross, Bazron et al., 1989; Davis, 1997; Lecca, Quervalu et al., 1998).

POLICY, PROGRAMS, AND RESEARCH IMPLICATIONS

In the past twenty-five years, the American health care system has been faced with an overt and a covert dilemma that threatens its overall stability and the quality of health care in the United States. The overt dilemma stems from the enormous increases in the proportion of the gross domestic product consumed by the health care industry and individual consumers of services. Although the annual increases in costs (above inflation) appear to have been temporarily halted by managed health care processes, both government and the private business sector have felt this cost dilemma more intensively than health care providers, hospitals, or individuals consumers, since the latter three groups have been insulated from the economic risk and burden of increasing costs. It has been assumed by government and by key business interests that the primary reason health care costs have increased so steeply has been the inherent conflict of interest of health care providers who prescribe both the care needed (including the length of care) and the price. The absence of economic risk or participation by consumers that would be expected to accrue normally with increased personal consumption of goods and services is also viewed as an instrumental factor in maintaining the high cost of health care. The futher consumers are divorced from the cost of health care decisions, the greater the probability that they will not manage the cost of the health care decisions that are made, or participate in health maintenance.

As the nation entered the final decade of the 20th century, health care costs, purportedly fueled by the unconstrained behavior of providers and consumers, threatened to exceed 22% of the nation's overall monetary resources. Rather than absorb these increased costs, private companies passed the costs on to the goods and services they manufactured or sold. As a result, American goods and services are believed to have become less competitively priced on the world market. Additionally, when compared to other highly technological societies, the American health care system cost substantially more but produced less in terms of years of healthy living for its population. American corporations and government concluded that the threat to America's competitive position, coupled with an absence of a demonstrative linkage between the cost and outcomes of health care decisions, required a drastic change in public health policy.

In response to the growth in health care costs over the past several decades, the federal government, with support from the business sector, has passed numerous public policies to stem the escalation in health care. Up to 1992 and the implementation of managed health care, almost every previous policy had failed to substantially reduce the annual assault on the GDP from health care. In response to each new policy direction, the health care field adjusted its practices to insure that revenues remained high. In lieu of the extensive revisions in the health care system proposed by President Clinton's administration in 1993, the nation passively adopted managed care. It seems clear now that few Americans understood managed health care or the implications of allowing insurance companies and private and governmental employers to manage their health care as though it were regular insurance or similar products and services. What has become clear to the general public with the implementation of managed health care is the extent to which they have lost their right to choose who provides them with health care, and the extent to which the personal and financial risks associated with their health plans have increased.

The second dilemma in the American health care system has been and remains more covert, albeit as pernicious in effect as the escalation in overall and annual costs. The health status of many of America's poorest populations—particularly African Americans, Native Americans, and Mexican Americans—resembles that found in populations in more economically underdeveloped countries rather than that of their fellow citizens in this country. Major disparities in health status, access, and years of healthy living by race, ethnicity, income, and social class have characterized this nation throughout the century. Populations of color have had higher infant and maternal mortality rates and die more frequently from hypertension, heart disease, cancer, and job-related accidents than other Americans. Importantly, these populations have realized only modest improvements in their health risks and mortality over the century, compared to other segments of the population. As health care expenditures have increased under fee-for-service medicine, low-income communities of color have seen an exodus of health care providers and the entry of catastrophic rates of HIV deaths, adolescent pregnancies, and violence. Managed health care appears to offer these communities a greater chance of equalizing access to health care, but may substantially reduce services and overall quality, and may rupture the long-standing community-based health system on which low-income people have relied for decades. The health status of low-income people of color may be as harmful in the long term to the American economy as the steady rise in overall health care costs.

What distinguishes these two dilemmas in health care in the United States is the differential policy response by government (federal and state) and the private sector. The substantive public policy response to the crisis of cost has not been replicated in the crisis of health care disparity by race and ethnicity. One of the first indicators of federal recognition of the health status disparities experienced by people of color was the 1985 report of Margaret Heckler (U.S. Department of Health and Human Services, 1985). Heckler's report found "a continuing disparity in the burden of death and illness experienced by black and other minority Americans as compared with our nation's population as a whole" (p. x). Heckler recommended a series of action steps to Congress, including establishment of a special office in the federal government that would carry responsibility for health issues of this population. The Bureau of Primary Health Care was established in response to her recommendations, and now provides primary health care services to 20% of the medically underserved population in the United States (Gaston, Barrett et al., 1998). More recently, other federal agencies have issued reports similar in content to Heckler's. What these reports do is to reflect the incremental and slow pace of change in the national health policy, but more importantly the health status of low-income populations and their relatively modest priority in the nation.

The most substantive recognition of the unmet health care needs of people of color is the announcement by the president in February 1998 of his initiative designed to promote equity in health status by 2010 (Clinton, 1998). The Clinton proposal, however, has yet to outline a specific plan of action for achieving its goal or how it will interface with existing polices such as fee-for-service, managed care, Medicaid, or Medicare. Mr. Clinton's administration has not answered the multiplicity of research questions that surround these populations and account for the absence of equity in health status, access, or years of healthy living. Is low income the cause of lowered health status? Is discrimination at the core of the health care access dilemmas of the poor? Are there significant cultural differences in help-seeking and utilization that impede access to health care for the poor? It is also unclear how Mr. Clinton will be able to eke out the billions in additional federal dollars from Congress that will be required to make a substantive change in the dismal health status of people of color. Without a clear commitment from Congress, it may not be possible to alter the health care conditions of the poor in America, even as the amount of surplus federal and state dollars increases.

Two national policy actions seem required to transform the level of health care access and status of people of color. First, the nation must be helped to recognize that all health care is cultural. This is true as far as the environmental antecedents of illness, the course of specific diseases, and the nature of help-seeking and service utilization within different cultural groups. It is equally valid that differences in culture appear to influence whether health care providers deliver equitable levels of needed health services. "It should be remembered that culture impacts the client as well as the health care professional. For both the client and the health care professional, culture determines what is considered to be a health problem, how symptoms and concerns about the problem should be expressed, who should provide treatment for the problem, and what type of treatment should be given" (Pinderhughes, 1989). Many studies over the century illustrate the extent to which the health status of people of color and their access to quality care is compromised and endangered by discrimination and racism on the part of health care systems. The United States must recognize that the disparities in health status by race and ethnicity are as deleterious and costly to the nation's economy as the overall rise in health care costs. At the same time, the nation must exercise a willingness to use its political processes to improve the fairness in health care policies for people of color, as well as that of the private business sector.

The second action needed is to change the zeitgeist of health care policies by reconceptualizing them through cultural competency. Cultural competency is an excellent means for conceptualizing the health care disparity problem as well as the basis for formulating and evaluating responsive policies. Cultural competence offers the nation's conglomeration of public health policies a clear vision of the future and a route to attain it: equity in health status and access for all Americans. Cultural competence may also allow managed health care policy to achieve its fiscal savings objectives by retraining health care providers to improve the accuracy of their diagnoses, prescriptions, and treatment of people of color.

It is clear that all health care is cultural. The challenge in the new millennia is to use this knowledge of culture to build culturally competent policies that will connect all of our existing health care policies and redirect them toward a singular public health policy vision of equity of access and health status for all Americans.

REFERENCES

Abe-Kim, J., & Takeuchi, D. T. (1996). Cultural competence and quality of care: Issues in mental health service delivery in managed care. *Clinical Psychology. Science and Practice,* 3(4), 273–295.

Anderson, L. P., Eaddy, C. L., & Williams, E. A. (1990). Psychosocial competence: Toward a theory of understanding positive mental health among black americans. In D. S. Ruiz & J. P. Comer (Eds.), *Handbook of Mental Health and Mental Disorder among Black* Americans. (pp. 224–272). New York: Greenwood Press.

Ayanian, J. Z. (1994). Race, class and the quality of medical care. *Journal of the American Medical Association, 271,* 1207–1208.

Babcock, J. W. (1895). The colored insane. In National Conference of Charities and Corrections (Ed.), *Proceedings of the National Conference of Charities and Corrections, 1895:* Boston: National Conference of Charities and Corrections.

Bell, C. C., & Mehta, H. (1980). The misdiagnosis of black patients with manic depressive illness. *Journal of the National Medical Association, 72,* 141–145.

Boutwell, R. C., & Mitchell, J. B. (1993). Diffusion of new technologies in the treatment of the Medicare population: Implications for patient access and program expenditures. *International Journal of Technology Assessment in Health Care,* 9(Winter), 62–75.

Bowles, E., & Thorpe, A. (1998, September, 16). *Press briefing by Erskine Bowles, administrator, Small Business Administration.*

Brach, C. (1996). *Cultural competency and managed care.* Washington, DC: Mental Health Policy Resource Center.

Braithwaite, R. L., & Taylor, S. E. (1998). *Health issues in the black community.* San Francisco: Jossey-Bass.

Cartwright, S. (1851). Report on the diseases and physical peculiarities of the Negro race. *New Orleans Medical Surgical Journal, 7,* 692–705.

Center for Health Economics Research. (1993). *Access to health care: Key indicators for policy.* Robert Wood Johnson Foundation. Princeton, NJ: Robert Wood Johnson Foundation.

Chess, S., Clark, K. B., & Thomas, A. (1953). The importance of cultural evaluation in psychiatric diagnosis and treatment. *Psychiatric Quarterly, 27,* 102–114.

Clinton, W. J. (1998, February 21). *Radio address by the president to the nation.*

Clinton, W. J. (1998, September 19). *Remarks by the president to the Congressional Black Caucus.*

Cole, J., & Pilisuk, M. (1976). Differences in the provision of mental health services by race. *Orthopsychiatry, 46* 510–525.

Collins, J. L., Sorel, E., Brent, J., & Mathura, C. B. (1990). Ethnic and cultural factors in psychiatric diagnosis and treatment. In D. S. Ruiz & J. P. Comer (Eds.), *Handbook of mental health and mental disorder among black Americans.* (pp. 151–166). New York: Greenwood Press.

Congressional Budget Office. (1999, January). *Economic and budget outlook: Fiscal years 2000–2009.* Washington, DC: Author.

Council on Ethical and Judicial Affairs. (1989). Black–white disparities in health care. *Journal of the American Medical Association, 273,* 2344–2346.

Cross, T. L., Bazron, B., Dennis, K., & Isaacs, M. (1989). *Toward a culturally competent system of care.* Washington, DC: Georgetown University Child Development Center.

Davis-Chambers, E. (1998). *Cultural competence performance measures.* New York: New York State Office of Mental Health, The Research Foundation.

Davis, K. (1998, June). *Slaves don't get stress: The evolution of mental health policies and services for African Americans: Implications for current and future public policy.* Rockville, MD: Center for Mental Health Services.

Davis, K., Aguilar, M. A., & Jackson, V. H. (1998). Save low income women and their children first. *Health and Social Work,* 23(2), 83–85.

Davis, K. (1996, March). *Managed care and populations of color: A conceptual framework.* Paper presented at the Statewide Public Psychiatry Conference, Cleveland, OH.

Davis, K. (1997). Managed care, mental illness and African Americans: A prospective analysis of managed care policy in the United States. *Smith College Studies in Social Work, 67*(3), 623–641.

Davis, K. (1997). *Exploring the intersection between cultural competency and managed behavioral health care policy.* Alexandria, VA: National Technical Assistance Center for State Mental Health Planning.

Davis, K. (1998). *Consumer-driven standards and guidelines in managed mental health for populations of African descent.* Rockville, MD: Center for Mental Health Services.

Dreger, R. M., & Miller, K. S. (1960). Comparative psychological studies of Negroes and whites in the United States. *Psychological Bulletin, 57,* 361–402.

Drewry, W. F. (1916). *Central state hospital.* Baltimore, Johns Hopkins Press.

Duffy, J. (1967). Slavery and slave health in Louisiana, 1766–1825. *Medical Faculty, 26,* 1–6.

Evarts, A. B. (1914). Dementia praecox in the colored race. *Psychoanalytic Review, 1,* 388–403.

Faris, R., & Dunham, H. W. (1939). *Mental disorders in urban areas.* Chicago: University of Chicago Press.

Fischer, J. (1969). Negroes, whites and rates of mental illness: Reconsideration of a myth. *Psychiatry, 32,* 438–446.

Flaskerud, J. H., & Hu, L. T. (1992). Racial/ethnic identity and amount and type of psychiatric treatment. *American Journal of Psychiatry, 149(3),* 379–384.

Fleming, C. M., & King, J. (1997). *Cultural competence guidelines in managed care mental health services for Native American populations.* Boulder, CO: Western Interstate Commission for Health Education.

Gardner, R. (1994). Mortality. In N. W. S. Zane, D. T. Takeuchi, & K. N. J. Young (Eds.), *Confronting critical health issues of Asian and Pacific Islander Americans.* Thousand Oaks, CA: Sage Publishers.

Garretson, D. J. (1993). Psychological misdiagnosis of African Americans. *Journal of Multicultural Counseling and Development, 21,* 119–126.

Gaston, M. H., Barrett, S. E., Johnson, T. L., & Epstein, L. G. (1998). Health care needs of medically underserved women of color: The role of the Bureau of Primary Health Care. *Health and Social Work, 23(2),* 86–95.

Gould, S. J. (1981). *The Mismeasure of Man.* New York: W.W. Norton.

Green, E. M. (1914). Psychoses among Negroes—A comparative study. *Journal of Nervous and Mental Disease, 41* 697–708.

Hadley, J., Steinberg, E., & Feder, J. (1991). Comparison of underinsured and privately insured hospital patients. *Journal of the American Medical Association, 265,* 374–379.

Hawkins, D. R., & Rosenbaum, S. (1993). *Lives in the balance: The health status of America's medically underserved populations.* Washington, DC: National Association of Community Health Centers, Inc.

Hollingshead, A. B., & Redlich, F. C. (1958). *Social class and mental illness: A community study.* New York: Wiley.

Hurst, J. W. (1991). Reforming health care in seven European nations. *Health Affairs, 10,* 7–21.

Intress, R. S. (1999, February 26). Health care package passes 98–0: More control over choice and treatments is key point. *Richmond Times Dispatch,* 1.

Jackson, J. S., Neighbors, H. W., & Gurin, P. (1986). Findings from a national survey of black mental health: Implications for practice and training. In M. W. Miranda & H. H. L. Kitano (Eds.), *Mental Health Research and Practice.* Washington, DC: U.S. Department of Human Services, National Institute of Mental Health.

Jackson, J. S. (1988). *Mental health problems among black Americans: Research needs.* Washington, DC: American Psychological Association, Division 37.

Jang, M., Lee, E., & Woo, K. (1998). Income, language, and citizenship status: Factors affecting the health care access and utilization of Chinese Americans. *Health and Social Work* 23(2),136–145.

Jarvis, E. (1844). Insanity among the colored population of the free states. *American Journal of the Medical Sciences, 7,* 71–83.

Jenkins-Hall, K., & Sacco, W. P. (1991). Effect of client race and depression on evaluations by white therapists. *Journal of the Society of Psychology, 10,* 322–333.

Johnson, H., & Broder, D. S. (1996). *The system: The American way of politics at the breaking point.* Boston: Little, Brown & Co.

Jones, B. E., & Gray, B. A. (1986). Problems in diagnosing schizophrenia and affective disorders among blacks. *Hospital and Community Psychiatry, 37,* 61–65.

Kleiner, R.J., Tuckman, J., & Lavell, M. (1960). Mental disorder and status based on race. *Psychiatry, 23,* 271–274.

Kotler, P. (1975). *Marketing for nonprofit organizations.* Englewood Cliffs, NJ: Prentice-Hall, Inc.

Kotler, P. (1976). *Marketing management.* Englewood Cliffs, NJ: Prentice-Hall, Inc.

Lecca, P. J., Quervalu, I., Nunes, J. V., & Gonzales, H. F. (1998). *Cultural competency in health, social, and human services: Directions for the twenty-first century.* New York: Garland Publishing, Inc.

Lee, E., & Sue, S. (1997, June). *Managed care mental health services for Asian and Pacific Islander American Populations.* Boulder, CO: Western Interstate Commission for Health Education.

Leigh, W.A. (1992). *A health assessment of black Americans: A fact book.* Washington, DC: Joint Center for Political and Economic Studies.

Livingston, I. L. (1994). *Handbook of black American health: The mosaic of conditions, issues, policies and prospects.* Westport, CT: Greenwood Press.

Malzberg, B., & Lee, E. S. (1956). *Migration and mental disease: A study of first admissions to hospitals for mental disease, New York 1939–41.* New York: Social Science Research Council.

Malzberg, B. (1959). Mental disease among Negroes: An analysis of first admissions in New York State, 1949–1951. *Mental Hygiene, 43,* 422–459.

Manderscheid, R. W. (1997). *Changes in managed care and the implications for cultural competence.* Alexandria, VA: National Technical Assistance Center for State Mental Health Planning.

Manderscheid, R. W., & Sonnenschein, M. A. (1985). *Mental health United States, 1985.* Rockville, MD: National Institute of Mental Health.

Mauer, B., Jarvis, D., Mockler, R., & Trabin, T. (1995). *How to respond to managed behavioral health care.* Tiburon, CA: Centralink.

McWhorter, W. P., & Moyer, W. J. (1987). Black–white differences in type of initial break cancer treatment and implications for survival. *American Journal of Public Health, 77,* 1515–1517.

Moy, E., & Bartman, B. A. (1995). Physicians' race and care of minority and medically indigent patients. *Journal of the American Medical Association, 273,* 1515–1520.

Mukhergee, S., Shukla, S. S., Woodle, J., Rosen, A. M., & Olarte, S. (1983). Misdiagnosis of schizophrenia in bipolar patients: A multiethnic comparison. *American Journal of Psychiatry, 140,* 1571–1574.

Mutchler, J. E., & Burr, J. A. (1991). Racial differences in health and health care service utilization in later life: The effects of socioeconomic status. *Journal of Health and Social Behavior, 32(4),* 342–356.

National Association of Social Workers. (1997, July). Suit targets managed care. *NASW News, 42,* 1.

Neighbors, H.W. (1984). The distribution of psychiatric morbidity: A review and suggestions for research. *Community Mental Health Journal 20,* 5–18.

Neighbors, H. W., Jackson, J., Campbell, L., & Williams, D. (1989). The influence of racial factors on psychiatric diagnosis: A review and suggestions for research, *Community Mental Health Journal, 250*(4), 301–311.

Neighbors, H. W., & Lumpkin, S. (1990). The epidemiology of mental disorder in the black population. In D. S. Ruiz & J. P. Comer (Eds.), *Handbook of mental health and mental disorder among black Americans.* (pp. 55–70). New York: Greenwood Press.

Neighbors, H. W., Bashshur, R., Price, R., Donavedian, A., Selig, S., & Shannon, G. (1992). Ethnic minority mental health services delivery: A review of the literature. *Research in Community and Mental Health, 7,* 55–71.

Neighbors, H. W., & Jackson, J. S. (1996). *Mental health in black America.* Thousand Oaks, CA, Sage Publications.

Office of Minority Health. (1993). *Toward equality of well-being: Strategies for Improving minority health.* Washington, DC: U. S. Department of Health and Human Services, Office of the Assistant Secretary for Health, Office of Minority Health, 93-50217.

Pasamanick, B. A. (1959). *The epidemiology of mental disorder.* Washington, DC: American Association for the Advancement of Science.

Pasamanick, B. A., Lemkau, P. V., Robers, D., & Kruger, D. E. (1960). *A survey of mental disease in an urban population III: Prevalence and demographic distribution of some "psychosomatic" disorders* (1st ed.). Washington, DC: American Psychiatric Association.

Pasamanick, B.A. (1963). Some misconceptions concerning differences in the racial prevalence of mental disease. *Orthopsychiatry. 33,* 72–86.

Pasamanick, B.A. (1963). Mental disease among negroes. In M. M. Grossack (Ed.), *Mental health and segregation.* (pp. 150–157). New York: Springer.

Peterson, E. D., Wright, S. M., Doley, J., & Thibault, G. E. (1994). Racial variations in cardiac procedure use and survival following acute myocardial infarction in the Department of Veterans' Affairs. *Journal of the American Medical Association, 271,* 1175–1180.

Pinderhughes, E. (1989). *Understanding race, ethnicity, and power: The key to efficacy clinical practice.* New York: Free Press.

Pumariega, A. J., & Balderrama, H. H. (1997). *Cultural competence guidelines in managed care mental health services for Latino populations.* Boulder, CO.: Western Interstate Commission for Higher Education Mental Health Program.

Ramm, D. (1989). Overcommitted. *Southern Exposure, Fall,* 14–17.

Randall, V. R. (1994). Impact of managed care organizations on ethnic Americans and underserved populations. *Journal of Health Care for the Poor and Underserved, 5*(3), 225–236.

Regier, D. A., Farmer, M. E., Rae, D. S., Meyers, J. K., Kramer, M., Robins, L. N., George, L. K., Karno, M., & Locke, B. Z. (1993). One-month prevalence of mental disorders in the United States and sociodemographic characteristics: The epidemiologic catchment area study. *Acta Psychiatrica Scandinavica, 88,* 35–47.

Rice, M. F., & Winn, M. (1990). Black health care in America: A political perspective. *Journal of the National Medical Association, 82*(6), 429–437.

Robert Wood Johnson Foundation. (1991). *Challenges in health care: A chartbook perspective.* Princeton, NJ: Author.

Rognehaugh, R. (1998). *The managed health care dictionary.* (2nd ed.). Gaithersburg, MD: Aspen.

Rosenbaum, S., Serrano, R., Magar, M., & Stern, G. (1997). Civil rights in a changing health care system. *Health Affairs, 16*(1), 90–105.

Scanlon, W. J. (1997, May). *Health insurance: Management strategies used by large employers to control costs.* Washington, DC: General Accounting Office. GAO/HEHS-97-71.

Schulman, K. A., Berlin, J. A., Harless, W., Kerner, J. F., Sistrunk, S., Gersh, B. J., Dube, R., Taleghani, C. K., Burke, J. E., Williams, S., Eisenberg, J. J., Escarce, J. J., & Ayers, W. (1999). The effect of race and sex on physician's recommendations for cardiac catheterization. *New England Journal of Medicine, 340*(8), 618–626.

Shalala, D., & Satcher, D. (1998, February, 21). *Press briefing, secretary of Health and Human Services and the Surgeon General.*

Short, P. F., Cornelius, L. J., & Goldstone, D. E. (1990). Health insurance of minorities in the United States. *Journal of Health Care for the Poor and Underserved, Summer*(l), 9–24.

Sue, D. W. (1998, May). *Cultural competence and mental health care.* Paper presented at the North Carolina Medical Association Conference, Greensboro, NC.

Thomas, A., & Sillen, S. (1972). *Racism and psychiatry*. New York: Brunneer Mazel, Inc.

U. S. Bureau of the Census. (1995). *Census of the United States update*. Washington, DC: United States Department of Commerce.

U. S. Department of Health and Human Services. (1985). *Report of the secretary's task force on black and minority health: Vol. 1. Executive summary*. Washington, DC: U.S. Government Printing Office.

United Healthcare Corporation. (1994). *A glossary of terms: The language of managed care and organized health care systems*. Minnetonka, MN: Author.

Weiss, L. D. (1997). *Private medicine and public health: Profit, politics, and prejudice in the American health care enterprise*. Boulder, CO: Westview Press.

White House Domestic Policy Council. (1993). *Health security: The president's report to the American people*. Washington, DC: Author.

Whittle, J., Conigliardo, J., Good, C. B., & Lofgren, R. P. (1993). Racial differences in the use of invasive cardiovascular procedures in the Department of Veterans' Affairs medical system. *New England Journal of Medicine, 329*, 621–627.

Williams, D.H. (1986). The epidemiology of mental illness in Afro-Americans. *Hospital and Community Psychiatry, 37*, 42–49.

Willis, D. P. (1989). *Health policies and black Americans*. Brunswick, NJ: Transaction Publications.

Yergan, J., Flood, A. B., Lo Gerfo, J. P., & Diehr, P. (1987). Relationship between patient race and the intensity of hospital services. *Medical Care, 25*, 592–603.

Zane, N. W. S., Takeuchi, D. T., & Young, K. N. J. (1994). *Confronting critical health issues of Asian and Pacific Islander Americans*. Thousand Oaks, CA: Sage Publishers.

◆ CHAPTER 4 ◆

Ethics and Managed Care Policy

FREDERIC G. REAMER

In recent years, discussions of managed care have changed tone. In the early 1980s, much of the literature focused on whether managed care strategies should or should not be implemented. In contrast, today we are much more inclined to accept—perhaps with misgivings—that managed care is here to stay. Even managed care's harshest critics typically acknowledge that the movement's momentum is inexorable. Exactly how managed care policies and procedures should be formulated and implemented is a debatable topic; whether managed care policies and procedures will be formulated and implemented is an issue that now seems moot.

For social workers, managed care broaches a wide range of implications. Much of the profession's literature on the subject has focused, understandably, on clinical implications (see, for example, Grossberg, 1996; Kanter & Silva, 1996; Myers, 1998; Schamess & Lightburn, 1998; Weimer, 1996). A number of social work authors have written commentaries on the implications of managed care for administrators and program directors (see, for example, Brach & Scallet, 1998; Matorin, 1998; Siskind, 1997). Much less has been written about the ethical implications of managed care for social workers, especially related to education and training (Reamer, 1997a, 1998a; Strom-Gottfried & Corcoran, 1998).

There is no question that managed care raises many complex ethical issues. Focused narrowly, many of these issues are clinically germane, related to issues of, for example, client informed consent, confidentiality, client abandonment, and fraudulent billing (Reamer, 1987a; 1998a; Srom-Gottfried, 1998). In addition to these compelling issues, however, is a complex series of broader ethical issues pertaining to policy formation and implementation, program administration, and professional education. My primary purpose in this chapter is to provide an overview of these issues and speculate about their implications for social workers. My aim is twofold. First, I plan to outline a range of ethical issues in managed care that social workers must address. Many of these entail ethical dilemmas that require difficult choices.

In this respect I want to introduce a number of concepts that may assist social workers who face challenging ethical decisions. Second, I want to comment on practical risks social workers can face—in the form of lawsuits and ethics complaints, most prominently—in conjunction with their handling of difficult ethical choices. To achieve these ends I will need to devote a portion of this discussion to the broad topics of (1) ethical dilemmas and decision-making and (2) risk management in a managed care environment.

In general, ethical issues take many forms, all of which need to be considered in our discussion of managed care. What all ethical issues have in common is that they concern matters of moral right and wrong, and issues of duty and obligation. Some ethical issues are fairly straightforward in that they involve relatively uncomplicated guidelines, policies, or procedures. For example, social workers employed in managed care environments need to understand their ethical obligations to inform clients of limits to services because of the requirements of third-party payers. Social workers also must avoid falsifying insurance documents and need to document accurately the services they provide.

Social workers encounter problems, however, when two or more of these prima facie duties (Ross, 1930)—duties we ordinarily carry out—conflict, thereby producing an ethical dilemma. In short, ethical dilemmas arise when professionals face conflicting values or moral duties, obligations, or responsibilities. Without such conflicts we have no ethical dilemmas. For example, if social work administrators believe they have a moral obligation to provide services to people in need, they encounter an ethical dilemma if, as a result of managed care restrictions, their agencies will not be reimbursed for services provided to clients in need. At least in the short run, such administrators may need to choose between their duty to meet clients' needs and their duty to sustain fiscal solvency (and, ultimately, the agency's survival). Similarly, social work program directors may face difficult ethical dilemmas when scarce resources—such as staff time, agency funds, or caseload openings—need to be allocated. These circumstances often produce what moral philosophers call dilemmas of distributive justice, where a just and fair allocation mechanism needs to be established and implemented (Reamer, 1982, 1990, 1993).

Ethical dilemmas related to managed care require thoughtful decisions. Fortunately, in recent years the maturation of the applied and professional ethics field has produced an array of practical decision-making guidelines. Briefly, before the late 1970s few professions had paid serious attention to ethical dilemmas and ethical decision-making. Due to a variety of factors, nearly all professions—as diverse as engineering, medicine, law, social work, psychology, nursing, and journalism—began to explore earnestly the nature of relevant ethical issues, key ethical dilemmas, and ethical decision-making. Especially since the early 1980s, literature, education, and training on the subject have proliferated (Reamer, 1995a, 1997b, 1998b, 1999). This growth of knowledge, conceptual frameworks, and decision-making protocols can be applied fruitfully to ethical dilemmas pertaining to managed care.

The principal aim for many professionals facing ethical dilemmas is to make a morally "right" or principled decision. However, in addition to this noble agenda are a number of practical concerns. To put it bluntly, some decisions about ethical dilemmas make affected parties angry, particularly if they feel that their rights have been violated in some important way. Examples include clients who are denied additional services because their benefits have been exhausted, clients who believe their confidentiality rights were violated when service providers shared sensitive information with managed care company representatives, and employees who lose their jobs because of managed care–related cutbacks. People who believe their rights have been violated sometimes decide to take action, in the form of lawsuits or formal ethics complaints. Thus, it behooves social workers to understand the nature of ethics-related risk management—that is, strategies designed to prevent lawsuits and ethics complaints.

Like ethics, the subject of risk management is relatively new to the human services. Not until the mid 1990s does one find a critical mass of publications on the subject. By now, however, there is widespread agreement in the profession that practitioners need to understand and implement practical risk-prevention and risk-management strategies, especially as they pertain to ethical matters. I will explore these issues more fully below.

OVERARCHING ETHICAL ISSUES

Ethical issues and dilemmas related to managed care are diverse. One way to organize them is to distinguish among ethical issues that arise in relation to individuals' access to services, the delivery of services, and the termination of services.

Access to Services

One of the distressing by-products of managed care is that sometimes people are not able to access the services and assistance they need or to which they have a right. This may occur for several reasons. Employers may limit the services covered under managed care because of their cost. Social service agencies whose revenue has dropped because of reduced reimbursements under managed care may limit or cut programs and services. Also, once services have been initiated, clients in need may be denied further assistance when they have exhausted their benefits.

Such cutbacks and limitations can be particularly problematic for social workers' most vulnerable clients. Low-income clients, for example, rarely are in a position to pay for services out of pocket once third-party payments cease. Managed care restrictions thus may pose a special challenge to social workers' ethical obligation to, as stated in the introduction to the *NASW Code of Ethics* (1996), "enhance human well-being and help meet the basic human needs of all people, *with particular attention to the needs and empowerment of people who are vulnerable, oppressed, and living in poverty*" (emphasis added).

Because of funding pressures under managed care, some social workers and social service agencies have cut back on their commitment to low-income clients. It is not unusual to hear clinical social workers, for example, proclaim in frustration that no longer are they willing to deal with insurance companies because of inadequate reimbursement rates, cumbersome approval procedures, and bureaucratic annoyances. The practical result is that a growing number of practitioners are limiting their clientele to individuals who can afford to pay for services out of pocket—a form of "skimming" or "creaming." This shift in clientele served poses a fundamental threat to social work's historic moral mission of service to the most vulnerable and least advantaged, a disproportionate number of whom are people of color and members of ethnic minority groups (Brach & Scallet, 1998; Perloff, 1996). According to Rosenberg (1998, p. 5), "managed care companies avoid such enrollees unless the companies can make a profit and only if the coverage plan calls for high reimbursements." As an illustration of this phenomenon, Davis (1998) comments on the impact of managed care on African Americans in need of mental health services:

> The inveterate dilemmas and paradoxes concerning race, mental illness, and health care have not been resolved adequately. As new managed health care policies and services are being implemented, there is a great need to focus attention on the multiple issues cited here to reach, penetrate, and adequately serve African Americans with severe mental and physical illness. Although a prime concern in managed care policy is cost reduction, the role of race and service utilization remains poorly understood. As in earlier eras of change in public policy, the paradoxes associated with race are likely to have a disproportionate impact on low-income populations of color. (p. 63)

Another consequence of managed care that affects clients' access to services concerns reductions in (1) the number of providers eligible for reimbursement under managed care plans—presumably to reduce administrative costs involved in processing client claims—and (2) the reimbursement rate for the remaining approved providers. In one case that received national publicity, a statewide Blue Cross / Blue Shield company signed a letter of agreement with a managed care company to oversee mental health and substance abuse services for nearly 300,000 Blue Cross subscribers. According to a chapter of the National Association of Social Workers that monitored this situation, one of Blue Cross's goals was to "narrow the network" of providers "to save Blue Cross money" (National Association of Social Workers, Rhode Island Chapter, 1998). A serious consequence of this sort of strategy, however, is that clients' freedom to choose from whom they will receive services is greatly limited (Gorden & Kline, 1997). Clients whose current service providers cannot meet the newly established eligibility criteria would have their care disrupted if they were forced to find a new service provider approved by the managed care company. This phenomenon is directly contrary to social workers' long-standing commitment to client autonomy and clients' right to self-determination (see the *NASW Code of Ethics,* standard 1.02). As Corcoran (1997) argues:

> No longer does the client in need of services select a physician for scambosis or a social worker for treatment of depression. The selection of who will provide the services is no longer an autonomous decision between the client and providers; instead, it is likely to be determined by a utilization reviewer or a case manager performing triage. In many instances this fourth party is outside the social worker–client relationship. Consequently, there can be little doubt that some managed care procedures undermine the bioethic principle of autonomy, which in social work is called self-determination . . . . (p. 196)

Service Delivery

Among the most complex ethical issues involving managed care are those that pertain to the delivery of services. The most prominent issues concern what ethicists refer to as *divided loyalties* and *distributive justice.* In short, managed care has placed social service professionals between Scylla and Charybdis or between a rock and a hard place. More than ever, social workers find themselves caught between their clients' interests and the interests (mainly financial) of their employers or other funding bodies—a classic manifestation of divided loyalties (Sabin, 1994; Schreter, Sharfstein & Schreter, 1994). According to Schamess and Lightburn (1998: xvi), "conflicts of interest are inherent as the philosophy of service and care clashes with the philosophy of profit." On one side, social workers feel a deep-seated obligation to provide individual clients with the services they need—services that may be long-lasting and expensive; on the other side, social workers feel pressure to expedite the delivery of services conserving as much expense as possible, avoiding costly interventions to the greatest extent possible. For social workers, this is an untenable conflict. Simultaneously they must satisfy the clashing interests of their individual clients and those of a third party, such as their agency, a managed care company, or taxpayers who subsidize many social services (Havas, 1998). They may also feel pressured to choose between meeting clients' needs and their own need to earn a reasonable living. As Corcoran (1997) notes:

> Another ethical conflict faced by social workers in managed care settings concerns conflicts of interest. This is probably the most apparent, and most general, conflict between managed care and social work. A conflict of interest occurs between two legitimate and competing duties. In managed care this occurs between the duty to provide quality care (that is, the bioethical principle of beneficence) and the duty to contain costs with a managed care organization (a contractual duty) and not to waste limited societal resources (the bioethical principle of social justice). The social worker is an agent of the client but concomitantly is an agent of the managed care company and the provider of scarce and valuable societal resources; in some respects the social worker is a double agent. . . . (p. 198)

The nature of conflicts of interest for social workers in managed care took center stage in the widely publicized effort cited above involving Blue Cross's efforts to introduce a new statewide managed care plan for mental health and substance abuse services. As part of this plan, Blue Cross sought to introduce a "case rate" method of reimbursement, according to which approved providers would be paid a flat fee for each person that requests mental health or substance abuse services, regardless of the amount of care needed. Under this arrangement, clearly, providers have an incentive to limit services to avoid cost overruns, which ultimately may undermine clients' interests. For example, a child might need more counseling sessions to deal with the ramifications of childhood trauma, but the flat fee the service provider receives would not cover the cost of additional treatment.

A common alternative to case-rate reimbursement—capitation—also poses ethical challenges. Under capitation arrangements, providers and insurers share financial risk; capitation assumes that an estimated percentage of an insured subscriber pool will seek mental health and/or substance abuse services. If the estimate is high, the insurer and providers share in the "profit." If the estimate is too low, the insurer and providers share the financial burden. Even here, social workers may have an incentive to limit the number of people accepted for service and the volume of services provided to them. With this arrangement, however, unlike case-rate plans, the risk is shared between insurer and providers.

This predicament is analogous to that faced daily by many doctors who feel caught between their instincts in some cases to authorize expensive care and to conserve limited health care dollars for the greater public good (Caughey & Sabin, 1995). Traditionally doctors have always believed that their primary and fundamental duty is to provide each patient with the care and services that he or she needs. However, with the advent of various cost-containment policies in health care—including utilization review committees, diagnosis-related groups, capitation arrangements, and other managed care mechanisms—doctors increasingly find themselves forced to satisfy various, often conflicting, audiences: patients, doctors' employers, insurers, other patients who also have a claim on limited health care resources, and taxpayers who shoulder the burden of many health care expenditures (Medicaid and Medicare dollars, for example).

Another troubling example of managed care policy with dire ethical implications stems from some managed care companies' insistence that subscribers receive services from providers (such as inpatient hospitals and other residential treatment programs) with which the managed care companies have negotiated financially favorable contracts when, in fact, clients would be better served by other providers that may be more costly, have more appropriately specialized expertise, or be more conveniently located. In one instance, for example, the social worker and psychiatrist of a client with symptoms of a serious eating disorder attempted to obtain approval to admit the client to a well-known nearby hospital with a highly regarded eating disorders clinic. However, the managed care representative informed the social worker and psychiatrist that the company would authorize hospitalization only at a psychiatric unit of a community hospital that is a 45-minute drive away, with which the managed care company had negotiated a lower daily rate. The result of such practices is that clients may receive limited or "Band-Aid" responses to complex problems, responses that ultimately drive up costs and are counterproductive therapeutically (Dumont, 1998; Geller, 1998). Matorin (1998), for example, describes how the state of New Hampshire attempted to restrict outpatient access to psychiatric medication in an effort to contain costs. A formal evaluation of this effort by Harvard public health researchers demonstrated that New Hampshire's strategy led to a significant rise in emergency room visits and partial hospitalization services at a higher net cost in the long term.

As with doctors, social workers need to formulate sound, ethically defensible policies and procedures to manage these difficult conflicts and tensions. One common argument in social work is that scarce or limited health care resources are more imagined than real—i.e., our current struggles to allocate limited and scarce resources would disappear if only the electorate and those in positions of authority had political gumption and would reorder their priorities sensibly to shift resources away from excessive and inappropriate expenditures (for example, some military expenditures and public subsidies and tax breaks for some Fortune 500 corporations) and toward human services. This is a legitimate and compelling debate; whatever the arguments and their ultimate consequences, however, practicing social workers still must address managed care as it currently exists.

One way to approach this daunting task is for social workers to enhance their understanding of issues of distributive justice and to develop practical, ethically sound procedures and policies based on these concepts. Distributive justice concerns the criteria people and organizations use to allocate limited or scarce resources, such as health care, housing, welfare benefits, and emergency services. The concept of distributive justice dates back at least to Aristotle, who offered one of the earliest formulations of justice when he distinguished between *corrective* justice, pertaining to punishment and retribution, and *distributive* justice, relating primarily to the allocation of resources.

There are several ways to think about distributive justice. The eighteenth-century philosopher David Hume, for example, viewed justice rather conservatively as an extension of property rights (Spicker, 1988). That is, justice is determined in part by defensible principles related to the acquisition of property, transfer of property, occupation of property, and so on. As long as people acquire their wealth through "legitimate" means—which would enable them to purchase whatever health care they wish, for example—justice has been served. That some people are not able, for a variety of reasons, to acquire the wealth necessary to purchase adequate health care is a separate issue. For Hume, extreme concentrations of wealth and property may not be a problem as long as established property rights are respected (see Hayek [1976] and Nozick [1974] for more contemporary defenses of the concept of property rights and related ethical issues).

In contrast, Herbert Spencer, the nineteenth century English philosopher, defined justice in terms of moral *desert* or merit; what people have a right to is a function of what they contribute to the broader society. This harkens back to the distinction during the poor-law and charity-organization-society eras between the so-called "worthy" and "unworthy" poor (Leiby, 1978; Lubove, 1965; Trattner, 1979). From yet another perspective, Kropotkin, the Russian anarchist, argued that a just allocation of resources should be based on need; in order to meet people's needs, a redistribution of resources may be necessary.

This is more than academic or intellectual rhetoric. At the root of debate about managed care is controversy about what kind of health care people have a right to, in an ethical sense, and the nature and extent of "society's" obligation to meet this need. Those who believe that individuals who acquire property and wealth through legitimate means have a right to retain these assets and use them for their own purposes (for example, to pay for their own health care but no one else's) are likely to favor managed care policies and principles that maximize individual control over personal resources and minimize public subsidy and mandated insurance benefits and coverage. Such individuals are likely to be critical of any type of redistributive strategy designed to promote equality among individuals' access to health care that entails increased taxation and mandated subsidies for lower-income people. Ideologically and philosophically, proponents of this perspective want to minimize manipulation of and interference in the free market. As Spicker (1988, p. 138) summarizes the argument, "In the simplest terms, redistribution would be theft." Further, as Schoek (cited in Spicker, 1988, p. 138) argues, such redistribution is nothing more than envy—the envy of people who want the possessions of others.

At the philosophical heart of much debate about the ethics of managed care is the concept of equality, particularly in relation to social workers' concern about individuals' right to health care. As R. H. Tawney (1964) noted in his classic book *Equality* in relation to class differences in wealth:

> What is repulsive is not that one man should earn more than others, for where community of environment, and a common education and habit of life, have bred a common tradition of respect and consideration, these details of the counting house are forgotten or ignored. It is that some classes should be excluded from the heritage of civilization which others enjoy, and that the fact of human fellowship, which is ultimate and profound, should be obscured by economic contrasts, which are trivial and superficial. (p. 113)

The concept of equality has been defined in various ways (Dworkin, 1981). First there is *absolute equality*, which assumes that resources should be divided among people into equal portions. The implication here is that all persons, regardless of economic standing, should have the right to the same amount of social services; all people would be entitled to the same number of physical examinations or counseling sessions, for example, over a period of time. This is also known as the *equality of result* (Spicker, 1988). In contrast there is *equality of opportunity,* which is concerned primarily with individuals' opportunity to gain access to desired resources, such as health care, more than the actual distribution of the resource. At one level this means that individuals should have the education and job training they need in order to have jobs with health care benefits that provide the opportunity to access the services they need. At another, more practical level, this means that individuals should have equal opportunity to obtain services from providers and agencies when the need arises, by ensuring that adequate numbers of providers are located throughout various geographical areas, sufficient transportation services exist, and so on. The concept of equality of opportunity can also entail the use of a lottery (for example, to determine which of two equally "qualified" individuals will receive the one organ available for transplantation or which of two equally qualified individuals will receive the one available shelter bed) or the principle of "first come, first served" to distribute social service resources.

In a thought-provoking analysis, Rae (1981) suggests that four practical mechanisms can be used to maximize equal access to resources and minimize inequality (Spicker, 1988). The first is the *maximin* policy (maximizing the minimum), where, for example, minimum standards for access to resources under managed care are raised. A second approach is to address the *ratio* of inequality, or inceasing the resources of those who are the worst off in relation to those who are best off. A third policy aims for the *least difference,* where the goal is to reduce the range of inequality. And the fourth approach is the *minimax* principle, whose goal is to reduce the advantage of those who are most privileged—that is, to minimize the maximum. (Also see Rawls's compelling discussion in his *A Theory of Justice* [1971] for in-depth analysis of similar ideas.)

The pressing challenge for social workers is to reflect thoughtfully on distributive justice concepts and debates and formulate ethically sound guidelines to govern practice in a managed care environment. This is especially important in those circumstances where social workers feel caught between their clients' interests and those of third parties (employers, funding agencies, insurers, taxpayers). On the one hand, social workers do not want to abandon their long-standing and primary commitment to their clients' best interests. On the other hand, social workers recognize their ethical obligation to balance clients' interests with those of the broader society. As the *NASW Code of Ethics* (1996, p. 6) states, "social workers are cognizant of their dual responsibility to clients and to the broader society. They seek to resolve conflicts between clients' interests and the broader society's interests in a socially responsible manner consistent with the values, ethical principles, and ethical standards of the profession."

In addition to the broad ethical issues involving divided loyalties and distributive justice, social workers also need to be concerned about several other issues that arise in the delivery of services: confidentiality, the use of less experienced and qualified providers, and fraud or misrepresentation. Confidentiality has always been a cornerstone in the delivery of human services. It is an essential element of the trust developed between professional and client.

Human service organizations and agencies understand their obligation to take assertive steps to protect client confidentiality (Dickson, 1998; Wilson, 1978). With relatively few exceptions (for example, when confidential information must be disclosed in extraordinary circumstances to prevent serious, foreseeable, and imminent harm to a client or identifiable third party or when laws or regulations require disclosure without a client's consent), clients' confidential information should be sacrosanct. Managed care, however, poses some unique ethical challenges to this practice. To obtain authorization for services, clients and social workers must be willing to disclose some confidential information to third-party payers. As a result, various professional and administrative staff affiliated with insurers and managed care companies may have access to very sensitive, confidential information (Davidson & Davidson, 1996). As Strom-Gottfried (1998) notes:

> Not only is more information required to obtain approval to serve clients, but the use of electronic methods for conveying and storing data results in less control over who has access to this information and how it is used. This quest for data is particularly distressing in the behavioral health field, where personal disclosures are often at the core of treatment. An additional concern is that sensitive information may be accessed by employers and future insurers, and that such information may affect job security or the ability to obtain future health coverage. (p. 299)

It is essential for managed care officials to establish and enforce stringent safeguards to protect clients' privacy and confidentiality. Specifically, these safeguards should address ways to protect the confidentiality of clients' computerized records in managed care company databases. Davidson and Davidson (1996) suggest that managed care companies should be required to have periodic reviews of their record-handling and client data storage by an independent, external examiner with the authority to establish penalties if confidentiality has not been safeguarded. In addition, clients should be informed of disclosures that are or will be made to insurers and of the risks associated with such disclosure (for example, social workers' inability to strictly control access to the confidential information once it is shared with insurers). Several *NASW Code of Ethics* standards are relevant:

> Social workers should inform clients, to the extent possible, about the disclosure of confidential information and the potential consequences, when feasible before the disclosure is made. This applies whether social workers disclose confidential information on the basis of a legal requirement or client consent. (standard 1.07[d])

> Social workers should discuss with clients and other interested parties the nature of confidentiality and limitations of clients' right to confidentiality. Social workers should review with clients circumstances where confidential information may be requested and where disclosure of confidential in-

> formation may be legally required. This discussion should occur as soon as possible in the social worker–client relationship and as needed throughout the course of the relationship. (standard 1.07[e])
>
> Social workers should not disclose confidential information to third-party payers unless clients have authorized such disclosure. (standard 1.07[h])

Another by-product of managed care in some settings is that financial pressures have led agencies to use less experienced and qualified providers in an effort to reduce labor and personnel costs. Staff with less education and training (such as paraprofessionals) may be assigned duties that otherwise would have been carried out by more experienced and qualified personnel (Anders, 1996; Karon, 1995; Strom-Gottfried, 1998; Sunley, 1997). Although this tendency does not necessarily result in inferior care or services, it does increase the possibility.

In addition, agencies should be careful not to overstate or exaggerate claims concerning services they are able to provide under managed care arrangements. Social service agencies and providers have a responsibility to "market" themselves honestly and forthrightly (Geraty, Hendren & Flaa, 1992; Munson, 1996). If managed care places limits on what agencies are able to provide clients, agencies should be candid about that fact, acknowledge any limitations to services because of managed care, and consult with clients about the potential implications. Service delivery or treatment goals should be realistic in light of available resources. According to the *NASW Code of Ethics,* social workers should ensure that their representations to clients, agencies, and the public of results to be achieved are accurate (standard 4.06[c]).

Also, agencies must avoid misrepresenting who on their staff has provided the services for which the agencies bill insurers (Vandivort-Warren, 1998; Geraty, Hendren & Flaa, 1992). In some instances, for example, agencies have arranged for psychiatrists to "sign off" on services that were actually provided by other staff who, absent the psychiatrists' signature, would have triggered a lower reimbursement or no reimbursement. As the *NASW Code of Ethics* asserts, "social workers should not participate in, condone, or be associated with dishonesty, fraud, or deception" (standard 4.04).

Termination of Services

One of the persistent ethical challenges in a managed care environment concerns the termination of services provided to clients whose benefits have been exhausted. Agencies need to establish policies designed to protect clients and to minimize malpractice and liability risks to the agencies and their employees (Houston-Vega, Nuehring & Daguio, 1997; Reamer, 1994, 1997b). Agencies cannot simply "abandon" clients whose benefits have run out; rather, they are obligated to engage in a series of steps in an effort to ensure that clients' needs are met. This may entail providing services pro bono or for a reduced fee—an intimidating challenge for underfunded public or charitable programs (Haas & Cummings, 1991; Strom-Gottfried, 1998)—or referring clients to other agencies or practitioners that may be in a position to provide services that clients can afford. As the *NASW Code of Ethics* states, "Social workers should take reasonable steps to avoid abandoning clients who are still in need of services" (standard 1.16[b]). Further, "social workers who anticipate the termination or interruption of services to clients should notify clients promptly and seek the transfer, referral, or continuation of services in relation to the clients' needs and preferences" (standard 1.16[e]).

Agency policies concerning termination of services should address a variety of issues. Staff should be clear about steps they should take to consult with colleagues and supervisors about termination decisions; consider all reasonable options to continue services; provide clients with as much advance warning as possible if services must be terminated; provide clients with the names, addresses, and telephone number of appropriate referrals; and follow up with clients who have been terminated with respect to the clients' attempts to arrange alternative services (Austin, Moline & Williams, 1990; Reamer, 1994; Schutz, 1982). As I will discuss in more detail, social workers and their agencies must be sure to inform clients about any options they have to appeal unfavorable managed care representatives' decisions and offer to assist clients with any such appeal.

GUIDELINES FOR ETHICAL MANAGED CARE

Guidelines designed to govern the delivery of services under managed care should have multiple (albeit sometimes conflicting) goals: meeting clients' needs; enhancing client freedom of choice for providers and services; enhancing professionals' autonomy and ability to meet clients' needs consistent with their best judgment; and allocating limited resources in a fair, just, and cost-effective manner consistent with social workers' obligation to be "diligent stewards" of resources (see standards 3.07[b] and 3.09[g] of the *NASW Code of Ethics* [1996]).

The most ambitious, prominent, and widely publicized attempt to develop ethical guidelines for professionals working in a managed care environment was conducted recently by the American Medical Association. The AMA's Council on Ethical and Judicial Affairs recognized the need to develop principles and policies to govern the allocation of resources in a managed care environment, with an eye toward helping professionals address the nagging problem of divided loyalties. After much analysis, discussion, and debate, the council issued a comprehensive set of guidelines. Underlying these guidelines was the council members' belief that it is patently unfair for individual practitioners to engage in "bedside rationing" of health care resources—that it is unreasonable to expect the individual practitioner, case by case, to balance individual patients' needs and interests with those of other patients and the broader society: "Allocation decisions should be determined not by individual physicians at the bedside but according to guidelines established at a higher policymaking level. Physicians should contribute their expertiese in the development of the guidelines and should advocate for the consideration of differences among patients" (American Medical Association, 1995, p. 332).

Further, and with particular relevance to social workers' enduring commitment to client empowerment, the AMA council also concluded that patients should be actively involved in allocation decisions:

> In addition to the physician's role in making rationing decisions, there is an equally critical role for patients. The decision making process should include some mechanism for taking into account the preferences and values of the people whom the rationing decisions will most directly affect. Accurate and full disclosure is most important. In addition, a managed care organization could use "town meetings" and other mechanisms whereby subscribers could voice their preferences and "vote" on what treatments should be included in their benefits package.
>
> Once guidelines and criteria are developed at the policy level, physicians are free to make clinical decisions based on those guidelines and criteria. (p. 332)

In my view, the AMA guidelines and principles constitute the wisest available approach to a very difficult problem and can be applied usefully to the predicament faced by the social work profession. Drawing on and adapting this framework, I offer comparable guidelines for social workers:

1. The duty of client advocacy is an essential, fundamental element of the social worker–client relationship; it should not be altered by the managed care system in which social workers practice. Social workers should continue to place the interests of their clients first and advocate on their behalf.

2. When managed care plans place restrictions on the care that social workers may provide to their clients, the following principles should be followed:

   a. Any broad program-wide or agency-wide allocation guidelines that restrict care and choices—which go beyond the cost-benefit judgments made by social workers as a part of their normal professional responsibilities—should be established at a policy-making level so that individual social workers are not asked to engage in ad hoc rationing case by case.

   b. Regardless of any allocation guidelines developed at a policy or administrative level, social workers must advocate for any care they believe is in their clients' best interest. Social workers should take assertive steps on their clients' behalf in instances when their clients' needs conflict with allocation guidelines social workers are expected to follow. This may entail advocacy with managed care or social service agency administrators. Another option is for social workers to bring the matter to their agency ethics committee. Ethics committees exist in many agencies, particularly in health care settings, to help staff and clients address complex and controversial ethical issues. Ethics committees can help the parties involved to identify key ethical concerns, mediate disputes, explore options, and navigate organizational paths (Cohen, 1988; Conrad, 1989; Cranford & Doudera, 1984; Reamer, 1987b).

c. Social workers should seek and be given an active role in contributing their expertise to any allocation process and should advocate for guidelines that are sensitive to differences among clients, including differences of race, ethnicity, national origin, color, sex, sexual orientation, age, marital status, political belief, religion, or mental or physical disability (see *NASW Code of Ethics,* standard 4.02). As the *NASW Code of Ethics* asserts, social workers should be especially mindful of the needs of "all people, with particular attention to the needs and empowerment of people who are vulnerable, oppressed, and living in poverty" (p. 1), and "social workers should have a knowledge base of their clients' cultures and be able to demonstrate competence in the provision of services that are sensitive to clients' cultures and to differences among people and cultural groups" (standard 1.05[b]). Managed care plans should create structures that allow social workers to have meaningful input into the plan's development of allocation guidelines. Guidelines for allocating resources should be reviewed on a regular basis and updated to reflect advances in knowledge and changes in relative costs and benefits. According to the *NASW Code of Ethics,* "social workers should advocate for resource allocation procedures that are open and fair. When not all clients' needs can be met, an allocation procedure should be developed that is nondiscriminatory and based on appropriate and consistently applied principles" (standard 3.07[b]).

d. Adequate appellate procedures and mechanisms for both clients and social workers should be in place to address disputes regarding access to and delivery of services. Clients should be informed about appellate options and procedures, and social workers should offer to assist clients with them. Cases may arise in which a managed care plan has an allocation guideline that is generally fair when considering clients as a broad group but which, in particular or individual circumstances, results in unfair denials of care that in the social worker's judgment would benefit the client significantly. In such cases, the social worker's obligation as client advocate requires that the social worker challenge the denial and argue for the provision of services in the specific case.

Cases may also arise in which a managed care plan has an allocation guideline that is generally unfair in its design or implementation. In such cases social workers should challenge any denials of care based on the guideline and advocate at the managed care company's or relevant agency's policy-making level to eliminate or modify the guideline. Social workers should assist clients who wish to seek additional appropriate care outside the plan when the social worker believes the care is in the client's best interest.

e. Managed care plans must adhere to the requirement of informed consent that clients be given full disclosure of relevant information (Reamer, 1987a). Full disclosure requires that managed care plans inform potential subscribers of limitations or restrictions in the benefits package when they are considering participating in the plan. This requirement is consistent with the *NASW Code of Ethics,* which states that "social workers should provide services to clients only in the context of a professional relationship based, when appropriate, on valid informed consent. Social workers should use clear and understandable language to inform clients of the . . . limits to services because of the requirements of a third-party payer . . ." (standard 1.03[a]).

f. Social workers should disclose treatment alternatives to clients. Full disclosure includes informing clients of all their treatment options, even those that may not be covered under the terms of the managed care plan. Clients may then determine whether an appeal is appropriate or whether they wish to seek care outside the plan for treatment alternatives that are not covered.

g. Clients should not participate in any plan that encourages or requires care at or below minimum professional standards. Social workers should seek to ensure that managed care policies do not lead to serious compromises in the quality of care provided to clients.

3. When social workers are employed or reimbursed by managed care plans that offer financial incentives to limit care, serious potential conflicts are created between the social workers' personal financial interests and the needs of their clients. Efforts to contain costs should not place client welfare at risk. Thus, financial incentives are permissible only if they promote the cost-effective delivery of quality care and not the withholding of necessary care.

a. Any financial incentives to limit care must be disclosed fully to clients by plan administrators at the time of enrollment and at reasonable intervals thereafter (for example, annually).

b. Limits should be placed on the magnitude of fee withholds, bonuses, and other financial incentives to limit care. Calculating incentive payments according to the performance of a sizable group of comparable professionals rather than on an individual basis should be encouraged.

c. Managed care plans and other organizations should develop financial incentives based on quality of care. Such incentives should complement financial incentives based on the quantity of services used. As the AMA Council on Ethical and Judicial Affairs concluded:

> The most effective way to eliminate inappropriate conflicts is to create the use of financial incentives based on quality rather than quantity of services.

Reimbursement that serves to promote a standard of "appropriate" behavior helps to maintain the goals of professionalism. Unlike incentives based on quantity of services, which punish the provision of both appropriate and inappropriate services, incentives based on quality of care punish only inappropriate services. (p. 333)

Part of the challenge, of course, is establishing criteria to assess quality of care. In principle, there are four important components (see American Medical Association, 1995, for additional discussion of this point):

i. *Outcome Data*. Managed care officials should favor services with demonstrated effectiveness. Although many social work interventions have not been formally evaluated, many have been (Myers & Thyer, 1997). When data on effectiveness exist, managed care officials should take them into account. Curtis (1996) described four categories of empirical validation, with increasing levels of substantiation: (a) tentative or suggestive evidence, including anecdotal observations, single-case reports, or uncontrolled or open trials; (b) promising or interesting evidence, based on completion of several uncontrolled trials with fairly positive and consistent results; (c) probable effectiveness, when one rigorous controlled study or several less rigorous investigations have positive results; and (d) established effectiveness, when several well-designed, controlled studies show the treatment to be superior to other accepted treatments.

ii. *Adherence to Practice Guidelines*. Preferred interventions should be consistent with the social work profession's practice standards. In legal circles, these are known as standards of care. Standards of care are defined as how an ordinary, reasonable, and prudent professional with similar education and training would act under the same or similar circumstances (Austin, Moline & Williams, 1990; Cohen & Mariano, 1982; Hogan, 1979; Meyer, Landis & Hays, 1988; Reamer, 1994, 1998a; Schutz, 1982).

For many years, courts defined the standard of care by comparing a practitioner's actions with those of similarly trained professionals in the same community (the locality rule). The underlying assumption was that levels of training, education, and skill varied from community to community because of differences in available educational programs and opportunities, teaching technology, and intervention approaches.

Today, however, the locality rule has been replaced in many jurisdictions either by judicial decision or legislation (Schutz, 1982; Austin, Moline & Williams, 1990). These more recent guidelines are based on the availability of modern technology (for example, video- and teleconferencing, computer-based publications, national journals) that enables professionals nationwide to have access to similar education, training, and information. Consequently, the standard of care now typically refers to national rather than local norms.

iii. *Client Satisfaction*. It is now widely accepted that social workers should take client satisfaction into account when assessing service effectiveness. Although it may not be the primary determinant of practitioners' effectiveness, client satisfaction is certainly an important element.

In recent years the growth of the empirically-based-practice movement has led to the creation of a number of widely used client satisfaction measures. Examples include the Client Satisfaction Questionnaire, Reid-Gundlach Social Service Satisfaction Scale, Session Evaluation Questionnaire, and Working Alliance Inventory (Fischer & Corcoran, 1994a, 1994b; Reamer, 1998c).

iv. *Judgment of Professional Peers*. This criterion is an extension of the concept of standard of care. One of the key elements of standards of care is the extent to which intervention approaches are endorsed by one's professional colleagues.

4. Clients should exercise their autonomy by public participation in the formulation of benefits packages and by prudent selection of benefit packages and coverage that best suit their needs. Clients must realize that under the best of circumstances it may not be possible to fund all desired services; some limitations may be essential. As the AMA Council on Ethical and Judicial Affairs asserted in their discussion of health care, "patient autonomy does not guarantee the right to have all treatment choices funded. Some limits on personal freedom are inevitable in a society that tries to provide all of its members with adequate health care" (p. 334).

CONCLUSION

Managed care poses a wide range of complex ethical issues for social workers, especially related to clients' access to services, the delivery of services, and the termination of services. To address these issues adequately, social workers need to consider a number of compelling policy, programmatic, and research implications.

Policy Implications

It is essential for social workers in positions of authority to explore and address ethical issues related to a number of specific policy issues. Social workers must be mindful of their obligation to advocate in the public policy arena for adequate resources and against draconian managed care policies. Social workers are uniquely educated and qualified to advocate with legislators and administrators for sufficient funding to meet clients' needs, particularly for those who are poor, vulnerable, and oppressed. Social workers are also in a position to challenge managed care policies that undermine the profession's efforts to meet clients' needs (Gil, 1995, 1998). According to the *NASW Code of Ethics:*

> Social workers should engage in social and political action that seems to ensure that all people have equal access to the resources, employment, services, and opportunities they require to meet their basic human needs and

> to develop fully. Social workers should be aware of the impact of the political arena on practice and should advocate for changes in policy and legislation to improve social conditions in order to meet basic human needs and promote social justice. (standard 6.04[a])

As social workers struggle with these challenging issues, they must recognize differences of opinion and divergent interests within the profession. Many social workers are critical of many managed care policies that, they allege, limit clients' access to services, threaten the quality of services provided, and undermine social workers' commitment and careers. At the same time, however, significant numbers of social workers support and benefit from managed care. Some social workers have thriving careers under managed care contracts; others are well-compensated officials in managed care companies. Social workers must recognize that sustained, vigorous, and principled discussion and debate *within* the profession is needed as much as discussion and debate between social workers and the managed care industry.

It is particularly important for professional education to address the ethical aspects of managed care policy. Today's students will be entering a professional world dominated by managed care models and it is incumbent on educators to ensure that fledgling practitioners have the knowledge they need to function competently, effectively, and ethically in this environment. In addition, human service agencies and professional associations and societies should sponsor continuing education for more experienced professionals. With specific respect to ethics, educators and trainers should address several key topics (Correse & Wright, 1998; Reamer, 1997a, 1998a; Strom-Gottfried & Corcoran, 1998). First, students and practitioners should be thoroughly acquainted with the origins, purposes, and methods of managed care in order to enhance their understanding of the context in which pertinent ethical issues arise. How is managed care defined and operationalized? How and why did it begin? What cost-containment efforts preceded managed care? Second, how has managed care shaped the ways that professionals function in their roles as clinicians, caseworkers, supervisors, and administrators? How has managed care influenced clients' access to services, professionals' gatekeeping role, the ways in which services are delivered, the continuity of services, and the termination of services? What impact has managed care had on phenomena such as client confidentiality, trust, autonomy, informed consent procedures, conflicts of interest, and fraud and misrepresentation? Third, how should professionals handle issues of distributive justice, rationing, and the allocation of resources available under managed care? What ethical criteria and frameworks can be used to inform such decisions? Finally, what steps can professionals take to address ethical problems that arise under managed care? Professionals need to be informed about and comfortable with their role as advocates for just and humane services. They need to know what kinds of advocacy strategies they can engage in to confront unethical, oppressive, and exploitative managed care policies, procedures, and practices (Dumont, 1998). Vandivort-Warren (1998) reinforces this critical point: "Advocacy forms the root of this profession and is needed now more than ever to infuse social work values into insurance-dominated interests. The office insulation of clinical practice can no longer preclude advocacy efforts. As always with social work, this advocacy entails promoting both social good for vulnerable consumers and social work services and skills" (p. 263).

Programmatic Implications

In addition to this wide range of policy and educational issues, social workers need to focus on the ethical implications of program design in managed care environments. Especially important are issues related to the size and characteristics of provider panels authorized for reimbursement, reimbursement rates, agency intake criteria, conflicts of interest, the allocation of resources, confidentiality and privacy, fraud and misrepresentation, and the termination of services. Social workers need to shed light on the ethical trade-offs involved in reducing the size of provider panels, which may limit clients' choice and their right to self-determination. In addition, social workers must address the ethical implications of managed care policies and procedures that discourage especially proficient, experienced, and seasoned practitioners from participating in managed care plans (because of inadequate reimbursement rates and overly stringent approval and authorization procedures and criteria) and encourage inappropriate termination of services.

Research Implications

Social workers are just beginning to understand the complex ethical implications of managed care. In order to address these issues adequately, social workers need to cultivate a database and research evidence—both qualitative and quantitative—in five areas. First, social workers need to conduct surveys concerning the extent to which services to clients under managed care have been refused or denied, scaled back or limited, and terminated prematurely. Second, social workers must gather data concerning the numbers and characteristics of practitioners who have "opted out" of managed care because of their frustration with this system. Such research should explore especially the extent to which practitioners with considerable experience and skill have discontinued their association with managed care and limited their practice to clients who are able to pay for services out of pocket. These data would help us understand the extent to which managed care policies have reduced the availability of services and service providers to low-income clients.

Third, social workers need to gather data on practitioners' and clients' experience with confidentiality breaches that may occur as a result of managed care. Thus far we have only anecdotal evidence of confidentiality problems. If in fact the problem is a serious one—and this remains an empirical question—we need empirical evidence of the extent to which confidential information has been mishandled by managed care personnel.

Fourth, social workers must gather data on the prevalence of fraudulent billing practices under managed care. To what extent are practitioners exaggerating client diagnoses in order to obtain authorization for service? To what extent are practitioners overbilling insurance providers to compensate for low reimbursement rates?

Finally, social workers need to develop empirical tools—again, both qualitative and quantitative—to document the extent to which managed care has had a significant impact on client outcome. To what extent have limits on clients' access to services and service providers affected their efforts to address problems in their lives? Is there evidence that managed care's authorization and reimbursement procedures are causally related to client progress?

Managed care is not, by definition, anathema to the human services. In fact, managed care's broadest goal—the delivery of services in the most cost-effective way possible—is, *in principle,* consistent with social work's values and ethical norms. What is at issue, of course, is the extent to which prevailing managed care policies and procedures are ethical. In this respect, social workers have a great deal to offer. Social workers' core values and ethical traditions can and should be used to guide the formulation and implementation of managed care policies and procedures. It is this set of values and moral tradition that offers the greatest hope that managed care will be ethical both in design and operation.

REFERENCES

American Medical Association, Council on Ethical and Judicial Affairs. (1995). Ethical issues in managed care. *Journal of the American Medical Association, 273,* 330–335.

Anders, G. (1996). Dismantling the old system. In G. Anders (Ed.), *Health against wealth: HMOs and the breakdown of medical trust* (pp. 16–34). New York: Houghton Mifflin.

Austin, K. M., Moline, M. E., & Williams, G. T. (1990). *Confronting malpractice: Legal and ethical dilemmas in psychotherapy.* Newbury Park, CA: Sage Publishers.

Brach, C., & Scallet, L. (1998). Managed care challenges for children and family services. In G. Schamess & A. Lightburn (Eds.), *Humane managed care?* (pp. 99–108). Washington, DC: NASW Press.

Carrese, J. A., & Wright, S. M. (1998). Commentary: Time to teach about ethical issues encountered in managed care. *Academic Medicine, 73,* 1128.

Caughey, A., & Sabin, J. (1995). Managed care. In D. Calkins, R. J. Fernandopulle, & B. S. Marino (Eds.), *Health care policy* (pp. 88–101). Cambridge, MA: Blackwell Science.

Cohen, C. B. (1988). Ethics committees. *Hastings Center Report, 18,* 11.

Cohen, R. J., & Mariano, W. E. (1982). *Legal guidebook in mental health.* New York: Free Press.

Conrad, A. P. (1989). Developing an ethics review process in a social service agency. *Social Thought, 15,* 102–115.

Corcoran, K. (1997). Managed care: Implications for social work practice. In R. L. Edwards (Ed.-in-Chief), *Encyclopedia of social work* (19th ed., 1997 Suppl., pp. 191–200). Washington, DC: NASW Press.

Cranford, R. E., & Doudera, E. (Eds.). (1984). *Institutional ethics committees and health care decision making*. Ann Arbor, MI: Health Administration Press.

Curtis, G. C. (1996). The scientific evaluation of new claims. *Research on Social Work Practice, 6,* 117–121.

Davidson, J. R., & Davidson, T. (1996). Confidentiality and managed care: Ethical and legal concerns. *Health & Social Work, 21,* 208–215.

Davis, K. (1998). Managed care, mental illness, and African Americans: A prospective analysis of managed care policy in the United States. In G. Schamess & A. Lightburn (Eds.), *Humane managed care*? (pp. 51–64). Washington, DC: NASW Press.

Dickson, D. T. (1998). *Confidentiality and privacy in social work*. New York: Free Press.

Dumont, M. P. (1998). Privatization and mental health in Massachusetts. In G. Schamess & A. Lightburn (Eds.), *Humane managed care*? (pp. 123–130). Washington, DC: NASW Press.

Dworkin, R. (1981). What is equality? Part 2: Equality of resources. *Philosophy and Public Affairs, 10,* 283–345.

Fischer, J., & Corcoran, K. (1994a). *Measures for clinical practice: A sourcebook: Vol. 1. Couples, Families, Children* (2nd ed.). New York: Free Press.

Fischer, J., & Corcoran, K. (1994b). *Measures for clinical practice: A sourcebook: Vol. 2. Adults* (2nd ed.). New York: Free Press.

Geller, J. L. (1998). Mental health services for the future: Managed care, unmanaged care, mismanaged care. In G. Schamess & A. Lightburn (Eds.), *Humane managed care*? (pp. 36–50). Washington, DC: NASW Press.

Geraty, R. D., Hendren, R. L., & Flaa, C. J. (1992). Ethical perspectives on managed care as it relates to child and adolescent psychiatry. *Journal of the American Academy of Child and Adolescent Psychiatry, 31,* 398–402.

Gil, D. (1994). Confronting social injustice and oppression. In F. G. Reamer (Ed.), *The foundations of social work knowledge* (pp. 231–263). New York: Columbia University Press.

Gil, D. (1998). *Confronting injustice and oppression*. New York: Columbia University Press.

Gorden, R., & Kline, P. M. (1997). Should social workers enroll as preferred providers for for-profit managed care groups. In E. Gambrill & R. Pruger (Eds.), *Controversial issues in social work ethics, values, and obligations* (pp. 52–62). Boston: Allyn & Bacon.

Grossberg, S. H. (1996). A successful short-term treatment case in managed care. *Smith College Studies in Social Work, 66,* 335–341.

Haas, L. J., & Cummings, N. A. (1991). Managed outpatient mental health plans: Clinical, ethical, and practical guidelines for participation. *Professional Psychology: Research and Practice, 22,* 45–51.

Havas, E. (1998). Managed care: Business as usual. In G. Schamess & A. Lightburn (Eds.), *Humane managed care*? (pp. 75–84). Washington, DC: NASW Press.

Hayek F. A. (1976). *Law, legislation, and liberty: Vol. 2. The mirage of social justice*. London: Routledge.

Hogan, D. B. (1979). *The regulation of psychotherapists: Vol. I. A study in the philosophy and practice of professional regulation.* Cambridge, MA: Ballinger.

Houston-Vega, M. K., Nuehring, E. M., & Daguio, E. R. (1997). *Prudent practice: A guide for managing malpractice risk.* Washington, DC: NASW Press.

Kanter, J., & Silva, M. (1996). Depression, diabetes, and despair: Clinical case management in a managed care context. *Smith College Studies in Social Work, 66,* 358–369.

Karon, B. P. (1995). Provision of psychotherapy under managed health care: A growing crisis and national nightmare. *Professional Psychology: Research and Practice, 26,* 5–9.

Leiby, J. (1978). *A history of social work and social welfare in the United States.* New York: Columbia University Press.

Lubove, R. (1965). *The professional altruist: The emergence of social work as a career.* Cambridge, MA: Harvard University Press.

Matorin, S. (1998). The corporatization of mental health services: The impact on service, training, and values. In G. Schamess & A. Lightburn (Eds.), *Humane managed care?* (pp. 159–170). Washington, DC: NASW Press.

Meyer, R. G., Landis, E. R., & Hays, J. R. (1988). *Law for the psychotherapist.* New York: Norton.

Munson, C. E. (1996). Autonomy and managed care in clinical social work practice. *Smith College Studies in Social Work, 66,* 241–260.

Myers, L., & Thyer, B. A. (1997). Should social work clients have the right to effective treatment? *Social Work, 42,* 288–298.

Myers, R. (1998). Managed care as a transference object: A clinical study. *Journal of Analytic Social Work, 5,* 5–23.

National Association of Social Workers. (1996). *NASW Code of Ethics.* Washington, DC: Author.

National Association of Social Workers, Rhode Island Chapter. (1998). *Fact Sheet: Frightening changes in Blue Cross to affect social workers, consumers.* Providence, RI: Author.

Nozick, R. (1974). *Anarchy, state, and utopia.* New York: Basic Books.

Perloff, J. D. (1996). Medicaid managed care and urban poor people: Implications for social work. *Health & Social Work, 21,* 189–195.

Rae, D. (1981). *Equalities.* Cambridge, MA: Harvard University Press.

Rawls, J. (1971). *A theory of justice.* Cambridge, MA: Harvard University Press.

Reamer, F. G. (1982). Conflicts of professional duty in social work. *Social Casework, 63,* 579–585.

Reamer, F. G. (1987a). Informed consent in social work. *Social Work, 32,* 425–429.

Reamer, F. G. (1987b). Ethics committees in social work. *Social Work, 32,* 188–192.

Reamer, F. G. (1990). *Ethical dilemmas in social service* (2nd ed.). New York: Columbia University Press.

Reamer, F. G. (1993). *The philosophical foundations of social work.* New York: Columbia University Press.

Reamer, F. G. (1994). *Social work malpractice and liability: Strategies for prevention.* New York: Columbia University Press.

Reamer, F. G. (1995). Ethics and values. In R. L. Edwards (Ed.-in-Chief), *Encyclopedia of social work* (19th ed., Vol. 1, pp. 893–902). Washington, DC: NASW Press.

Reamer, F. G. (1997a). Managing ethics under managed care. *Families in Society, 78,* 96–101.

Reamer, F. G. (1997b). Ethical standards in social work: The *NASW Code of Ethics*. In R. L. Edwards (Ed.-in-Chief), *Encyclopedia of social work* (19th ed., Suppl., pp. 113–123). Washington, DC: NASW Press.

Reamer, F. G. (1998a). Managed care: Ethical considerations. In G. Schamess & A. Lightburn (Eds.), *Humane managed care?* (pp. 293–298). Washington, DC: NASW Press.

Reamer, F. G. (1998b). *Ethical standards in social work: A critical review of the NASW Code of Ethics*. Washington, DC: NASW Press.

Reamer, F. G. (1998c). *Social work research and evaluation skills*. New York: Columbia University Press.

Reamer, F. G. (1999). *Social work values and ethics* (2nd ed.). New York: Columbia University Press.

Rosenberg, G. (1998). Social work in a health and mental health managed care environment. In G. Schamess & A. Lightburn (Eds.), *Humane managed care?* (pp. 3–22). Washington, DC: NASW Press.

Ross, W. D. (1930). *The right and the good*. Oxford: Clarendon.

Sabin, J. E. (1994). Caring about patients and caring about money. *Behavioral Sciences and the Law, 12,* 317–330.

Schamess, G., & Lightburn, A. (Eds.). (1998). *Humane managed care?* Washington, DC: NASW Press.

Schreter, R. K., Sharfstein, S. S., & Schreter, C. A. (Eds.). (1994). *Allies and adversaries: The impact of managed care on mental health services*. Washington, DC: American Psychiatric Press.

Schutz, B. M. (1982). *Legal liability in psychotherapy*. San Francisco: Jossey-Bass.

Siskind, A. B. (1997). Agency mission, social work practice, and professional training in a managed care environment. *Smith College Studies in Social Work, 67,* 16–19.

Spicker, P. (1988). *Principles of social welfare*. London: Routledge.

Strom-Gottfried, K. (1998). Is "ethical managed care" an oxymoron? *Families in Society, 79,* 297–307.

Strom-Gottfried, K., & Corcoran, K. (1998). Confronting ethical dilemmas in managed care: Guidelines for students and faculty. *Journal of Social Work Education, 34,* 109–119.

Sunley, R. (1997). Advocacy in the new world of managed care. *Families in Society, 78,* 84–94.

Tawney, R. H. (1964). *Equality*. New York: Barnes and Noble.

Trattner, W. I. (1979). *From poor law to welfare state* (2nd ed.). New York: Free Press.

Vandivort-Warren, R. (1998). How social workers can manage managed care. In G. Schamess & A. Lightburn (Eds.), *Humane managed care?* (pp. 255–267). Washington, D.C.: NASW Press.

Weimer, S. E. (1996). The development of self-love and managed care—or, reflections on being a tutor. *Smith College Studies in Social Work, 66,* 342–348.

Wilson, S. J. (1978). *Confidentiality in social work*. New York: Free Press.

◆ CHAPTER 5 ◆

System Care Management

Purpose, Structure, and Function

SUSAN SAUNDERS

Health care delivery in the United States is undergoing a profound transformation in response to changes in health care financing and market dynamics. The future viability of health care systems depends, in part, on their ability to manage service, delivery, quality, consumer appeal, and cost. Effective service management, in turn, depends on the existence of a sophisticated care management infrastructure that is capable of affecting service access, utilization, and outcome across the care continuum.

Though *system care management* capability is essential for effective health network performance, few comprehensive models currently exist. This chapter offers one perspective on the nature and operational requirements of system care management. The chapter highlights health care trends that necessitate system care management, delineates the broad objectives of a system care management program, describes care management functions and staffing patterns for designated sectors of the health delivery system, provides an overview of the information management requirements associated with system care management, and frames questions to be addressed in measuring the outcome of care management interventions.

HEALTH CARE TRANSFORMATION

Predictions abound about the nature of health care delivery in the early twenty-first century (Aschenbrener, 1996; Churchill, 1997; Davis, 1996; Ginzberg, E., 1998; Ginsburg, P., and Grossman, 1995; Iglehart, 1997; Marmor, 1998; Taylor & Lessin, 1996; VanderLaan, de la Houssaye, Janousek & Derus, 1998; Weil & Jorgensen, 1995). For some, health care delivery will be dominated by capitated reimbursement, "covered lives," and rationed health care. For others, managed care will be doomed by its own access, quality, and financial inadequacies and washed away by waves of consumer and provider protest. Whichever overarching paradigm emerges, certain trends observable today in the health care arena likely will continue.

Issel and Anderson (1996) predict that six transformations will shift the focus in health care delivery from (1) person as customer to population as customer; (2) illness care to wellness care; (3) revenue management to cost management; (4) professional autonomy to professional interdependence; (5) continuity of provider to continuity of information; and (6) patient as non-consumer to consumer of cost and quality information.

Other trends projected to influence the nature of emerging health care systems include growth in the uninsured population (Churchill, 1997); increased managed care enrollment of individuals with Medicaid and Medicare insurance (P. Ginsburg & Grossman, 1995); continued pressure from purchasers of service for reduction in service volume, intensity, and cost (P. Ginsburg & Grossman, 1995); continued insurer risk shifting to providers (VanderLaan et al., 1998); continued downsizing of inpatient bed capacity, and an accompanying shift of care to the home, physician office, and multi-specialty ambulatory care center (E. Ginzberg, 1998); increased provision of health care through physician-directed (interdisciplinary) management teams (E. Ginzberg, 1998); cost and market driven aggregation of health care providers into mega-sized health delivery systems (Davis, 1996); increased emphasis on care management, including effective strategies for medical, utilization, case, and disease management (VanderLaan et al., 1998); and public demand for convenient, high quality, and affordable service (Weil & Jorgensen, 1995).

Materialization of these trends in the early years of the twenty-first century will present significant challenges to health systems. Each system will be required to achieve optimum efficiency, sustained cost management, and superior quality of care.

Systems will achieve cost-efficiency through a variety of means, including (1) continued channeling of care to lower-cost ambulatory environments, (2) further reduction in staff-to-patient ratios, (3) group purchasing and tightly controlled supply consumption, (4) care standardization to cap clinical resource utilization, (5) elimination of cost-leader programs, and (6) continued system consolidation to achieve greater cost control across the continuum of care.

As each health system reduces its work force, exerts stronger controls over practice, and regulates use of diminishing resources it will have to meet two additional objectives: positive clinical outcomes and high levels of consumer satisfaction. Achievement of these objectives is essential if the health system is to maintain preferred-vendor status in a marketplace increasingly dominated by quality-shopping businesses and demanding consumers.[1]

In other words, each system will have to provide excellent care at the lowest possible price with fewer providers, while achieving outcomes that compare with or exceed those of regional health care competitors. It is this paradoxical requirement for "better, cheaper" health care that elevates the importance of system care management in twenty-first century health care delivery.

THE NATURE AND TARGETED IMPACT OF SYSTEM CARE MANAGEMENT

As health networks engage in the process of creating viable care management models for the twenty-first century, they must (1) define care management and delineate the objectives it is intended to achieve within the health care system, and (2) create structures through which care management can be implemented effectively. Figure 5.1 provides a schematic representation of the structure objectives and of a model system care management program.

In the author's view, system care management is a collection of integrated policies, operations, protocols, and incentives that (1) span the health care continuum; (2) are implemented and coordinated by teams of interdisciplinary professionals; (3) support medical providers in the delivery of care; and (4) ensure the identification and management of system, provider, and patient barriers to optimum health care access, utilization, and outcomes.

Care management systems exist to accomplish objectives critical to health system viability and effectiveness. Core objectives include:

1. *Consumer Empowerment.* Accomplished through education that enables consumers to (a) effectively access care, (b) appropriately utilize the health system, (c) understand their condition, (d) enhance their self care capabilities, and (e) participate fully in all phases of their treatment and recovery.

2. *Improved Health.* Achieved through health promotion interventions that (a) expand consumer knowledge of the physical, environmental, psychosocial, and spiritual bases of health; and (b) enhance population capacity to sustain optimum health status.

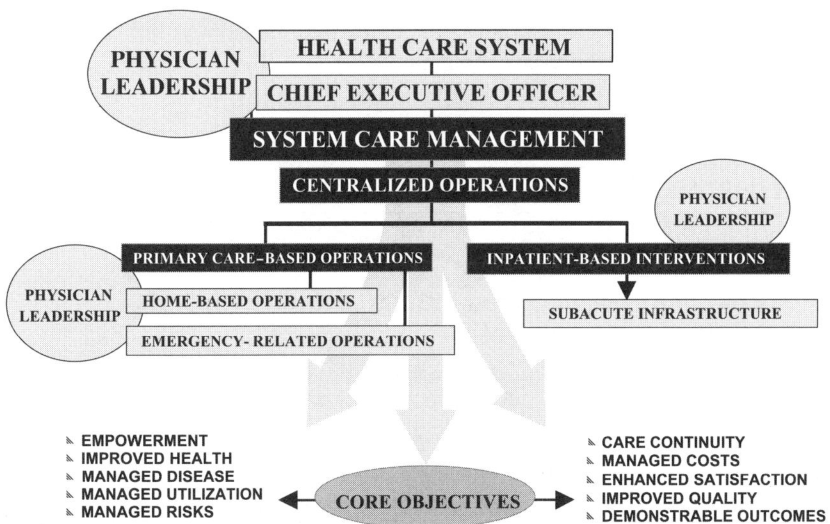

Figure 5.1 Structural Framework for System Care Management

3. *Managed Disease.* Enhanced by (a) early identification of illness, (b) effective medical management, (c) enhanced patient self-care, and (d) continuous application of new knowledge in the management of chronic illness.

4. *Managed Utilization.* Accomplished through (a) consumer education, (b) service accessibility, (c) level of care management, and (d) targeted case management that, together, enable clients to receive appropriate and timely care from the provider most suited to meet their care requirements.

5. *Managed Risks.* Optimized by comprehensive screening that permits identification and management of patient risks that jeopardize access, appropriate utilization, medical management, or patient safety.

6. *Care Continuity.* Brought about through implementation of system-wide protocols that ensure timely transfer of medical, psychosocial, and risk information between levels of care so that receiving providers are prepared optimally to meet the patient's care requirements.

7. *Managed Cost.* Addressed through comprehensive referral, utilization, and resource management operations that permit care to be rendered in a cost-efficient and nonredundant manner throughout the system.

8. *Enhanced Satisfaction.* Augmented by care management operations that are (a) well understood by patients and providers, (b) carried out with consistent attention to customer requirements,[2] and (c) associated with improved efficiency and health outcomes.

9. *Improved Quality.* Optimized by operations that (a) reduce barriers to care, (b) enhance provider risk management, (c) manage utilization and cost, and (d) improve patient compliance and outcomes.

10. *Demonstrable Outcomes.* Derived from the implementation of a comprehensive system plan that measures care management impact on the access, utilization, cost, and clinical status of targeted populations.

In order to meet these objectives, care management functions must be designed and implemented at the system level, within primary care, and in the acute hospital setting.

CENTRALIZED CARE MANAGEMENT

Fully functional care management models of the future will be guided by a central care management component devoted to (1) strategic planning, (2) development and integration of care management functions across the continuum, (3) execution of *centralized* care management functions, and (4) coordination of care management outcome measurement across the system.

Program Locus, Authority, and Leadership

In optimally designed models, the centralized component of care management reports directly to the system's chief executive officer. This structural arrangement positions the program appropriately for information access, rapid decision-making, integration with other system components, and significant "ascribed power" within the system. Such influential placement is essential for program credibility, operational influence, and service effectiveness across the network.

Physician Sanction

Physician sanction and sponsorship are prerequisites for effective care management. Physicians with credibility and system stature, selected from a variety of practice settings (primary care, specialty care, emergency medicine, radiology, and laboratory medicine), must participate as full partners with central care management leaders, information technologists, and financial experts in the development of any system care management model.

Critical physician contributions include (1) leadership in the design and marketing of system care management; (2) provision of professional, technical, and political consultation in development of care management operations for diverse practice settings; (3) creation of physician utilization profiling methods;[3] (4) collaboration in development of the system's physician care management incentive structure;[4] and (5) development of disease management models for use throughout the network.

Centralized Direction and Functions

The director of the system care management program[5] is invested with full authority to (1) ensure development and integration of care management operations across the care continuum, (2) articulate and ensure system-wide compliance with care management requirements, and (3) mobilize from other system divisions the operational support necessary to achieve care management objectives. The director also ensures effective execution of centralized care management functions. Figure 5.2 provides an overview of these centralized functions.

Functions include:

1. *Contract Review and Consultation.* Ensuring that managed care agreements provide for delegation of appropriate care management functions to the health system.[6,7]

2. *Incentive Development.* Collaborating with physicians and senior system administrators in creation of incentives that enhance provider compliance with care management requirements.

3. *Data Management.* Distilling information from payer and system databases into standardized membership, cost, and utilization reports available to care management stakeholders throughout the network.

4. *Physician Profiling.* Creating effective and professionally acceptable mechanisms for communicating utilization, referral, and cost information to physician groups throughout the network.

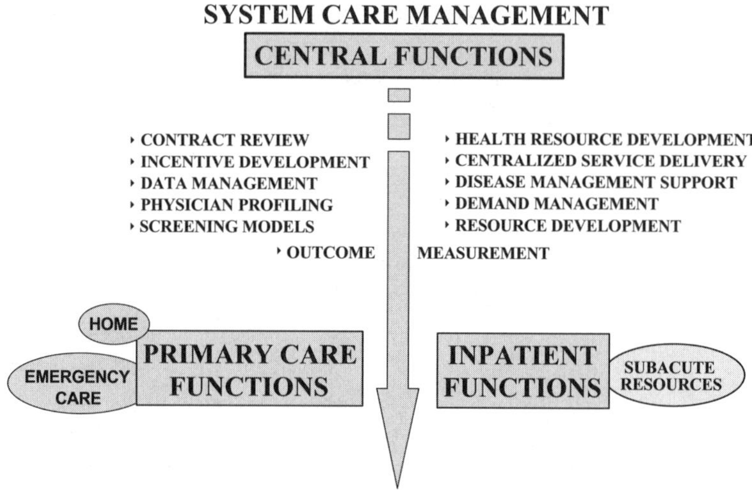

Figure 5.2 Centralized Care Management Functions

5. *Health and Risk Appraisal Development.* Selecting and disseminating standardized tools and analytic software for use by care management professionals across the system.

6. *Health Resource Development.* Targeting high-cost and high-volume diseases. Providing related prevention and health promotion resources to populations, providers, and care management professionals.

7. *Central Service Management.* Ensuring availability of centralized wellness and disease management resources (for example, diabetes education) for use by system providers and consumers.

8. *Disease Management Support.* Coordinating physician development and system dissemination of medical management approaches to high-cost and high-volume diseases such as congestive heart failure.

9. *Demand Management.* Managing the system's 24-hour call center that offers (1) health information, (2) self-care and decision counseling, (3) medical triage, (4) physician referral and scheduling, and (5) compliance reminders.

10. *Resource Development.* Coordinating efforts to fill service gaps in the spectrum of care, such as lack of subacute bed availability, to optimize service accessibility and efficient patient movement through the system.

11. *Outcome Measurement.* Overseeing processes that (1) target system-wide care management outcomes, (2) measure system performance against targets, and (3) report outcomes to stakeholder groups throughout the network.

In addition to carrying out its assigned tasks, the centralized care management component supports care management operations in primary and acute care settings.

CARE MANAGEMENT IN THE PRIMARY CARE ARENA

Primary care, with its large provider and consumer base, provides diverse opportunities for care management. Principal care management objectives in this setting include (1) health education and promotion, (2) early disease detection and management, (3) utilization and risk management, (4) system access management, (5) enhanced patient satisfaction and outcomes, and (6) optimum provider efficiency.

The patient's primary care physician, often in partnership with an office-based nurse practitioner, directs the care management process within each primary care setting.[8] Figure 5.3 summarizes care management functions implemented in this arena.

Medical providers within the physician office perform care management functions such as health education and disease management. Other functions, such as case management, are performed by nursing and social work care managers assigned to the physician practice. Care management interventions occur in office, home, and community settings.

Core care management functions carried out in primary care settings include:

Universal Health and Risk Screening

Centralized care management makes available to each physician office or clinic standardized instruments for use in patient health and risk assessment. The health status and health vulnerability profile of each patient is obtained at the point of office enrollment and at specified intervals.[9] Risk screening is conducted at the point of enrollment and, thereafter, at scheduled intervals determined by the initial level of identified risk.[10] Screening identifies

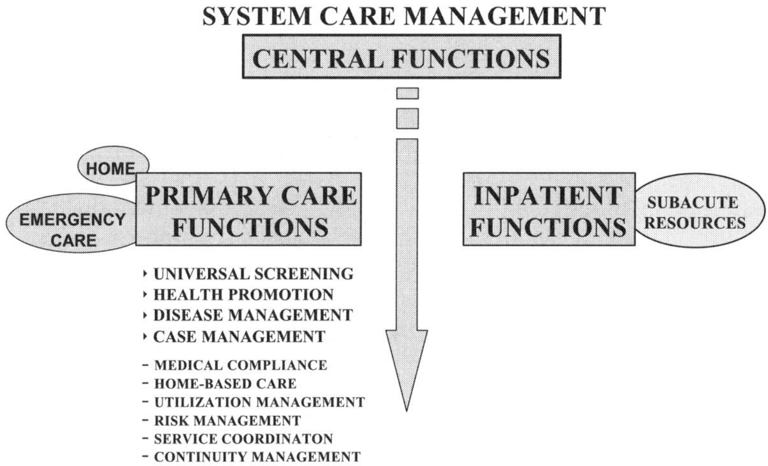

Figure 5.3 Care Management Functions in Primary Care

medical, cognitive, psychosocial, functional, utilization, and environmental risk factors. Health and risk screening data are utilized in determining the office approach to health promotion, medical management, and case management for each patient.

Health Promotion

All patients served through a primary care practice receive generic health and wellness information developed and disseminated through central care management. Generic educational materials focus on prevention of common illnesses, infection control, and principles of health maintenance, such as exercise and nutrition. In addition, each office is provided with materials (such as brochures, videotapes, and interactive software applications) that can be utilized on a targeted basis with patients at risk for developing disease—for example, patients with higher than normal blood pressure. Each primary care physician also may refer patients requiring more structured health promotion services to central wellness resources where patients receive individual and group assistance with such things as stress management and smoking cessation.

Disease Management

Office-based health screening identifies patients with an illness acuity level that requires intensive disease management—for example, patients with cardiovascular or pulmonary conditions. Providers offer these patients comprehensive medical management plans, often utilizing standardized disease management protocols developed by physician consensus groups at the central care management level. In addition, patients receive education and skill-development assistance to enhance their capacity for self-care and disease management in the home setting. Patients managed with the support of pathways and protocols receive a structured office visit schedule designed to optimize disease monitoring and care compliance.

Case Management[11]

Case management services in the primary care setting are provided by social workers and nurses working in partnership with the referring physician and office-based nurse practitioners. Ideally, case management teams occupy offices within the practice setting. Given the space constraints in the typical physician office, the team may be stationed in an offsite setting and receive referrals via telephone or fax transmission.

Core case management services include:

1. *Medical Compliance*. Provided to patients who demonstrate lack of adherence to medical-management plans. Interventions include (i) education, (ii) in-home observation and teaching, (iii) behavioral contracting, (iv) trans-

portation, and (v) mobilization of financial resources required for equipment or supplies not covered by medical insurance.

2. *Home-Based Patient Management.* Provided by an interdisciplinary team consisting of a physician, nurse practitioner, and social worker. Services are targeted to patients with chronic or terminal illness and age-related frailty whose *functional status limits their capacity to access primary care services in the physician office setting.* Interventions include (i) patient assessment and monitoring, (ii) medical and disease management, (iii) patient and family education, (iv) pain management, (v) medication management, (vi) functional optimization, (vii) caretaker support, (viii) medical triage to other levels of care, and (ix) mobilization of resources required for in-home care such as home health and hospice care.

3. *Utilization Management.* Provided to patients who inappropriately use health care services. Interventions include (i) patient orientation to appropriate use of health resources; (ii) outreach support; (iii) transportation and escort to primary care; (iv) behavioral contracting; (v) collaboration with emergency service professionals for inappropriate visit management; (vi) joint planning with pharmacists to monitor and appropriately limit drug dispensing; (vii) specialist referral monitoring and physician consultation to minimize medically unnecessary referrals and optimize utilization of in-plan specialists; (viii) appropriate emergency service diversion through 24-hour-a-day outreach, assessment, crisis intervention, and medical triage; and (ix) admission diversion, securing appropriate placement of patients in home or subacute levels of care as an alternative to acute-care admission.[12]

4. *Risk Management.* Provided to patients evidencing risk factors with potential to impair their personal safety, utilization, or compliance. Interventions include (i) 24-hour crisis intervention; (ii) liaison to family, neighbors, and police to create environmental watch and safety nets for the patient; (iii) in-home assessment and modification for enhanced safety; (iv) referral to protective resources; (v) institution of in-home meal, chore, or aide services; (vi) referral to mental health services; (vii) intensive home visiting and monitoring; and (viii) application for guardianship, when necessitated by the patient's lack of capacity.

5. *Service Coordination.* Provided to patients who receive care from multiple providers within or external to the health system. Interventions include (i) physician education on resource availability; (ii) service information, eligibility determination, and referral; (iii) patient transportation and escort to required services; (iv) intersite case management; and (v) patient advocacy when access and justice concerns must be addressed.

6. *Continuity Management.* Case managers ensure that primary care risk patients triaged to other levels of care, such as specialist consults or inpatient care, experience a managed transition between care settings. Interventions include (i) patient and family transition preparation; (ii) notification to receiving providers of the patient's special needs, known risk factors, and case

management plan; and (iii) in the case of transition to inpatient care, joint patient rounding and discharge planning with facility-based case managers.

Systematic use of these case management interventions in the primary care setting enhances health outcomes, utilization and cost management, and provider and patient satisfaction.

CARE MANAGEMENT APPLICATIONS IN THE ACUTE CARE SETTING

Despite the best efforts of physicians and care management professionals to optimize wellness, manage disease, and channel utilization appropriately, a percentage of patients will continue to require treatment in acute care settings. Inpatient care management activities occur in two distinct phases: the preadmission period and the inpatient stay. Figure 5.4 summarizes care management functions executed in the inpatient setting.

Preadmission Care Management Functions

Preadmission care management functions are performed by admission schedulers, utilization review nurses, preadmission clinical nurses and social workers, and interdisciplinary staff associated with the emergency admission process. Target objectives of preadmission care management include (1) level of care management, (2) appropriate service reimbursement, (3) preadmission care planning for patients with elevated risk profiles, and (4) length-of-stay management through early discharge planning.

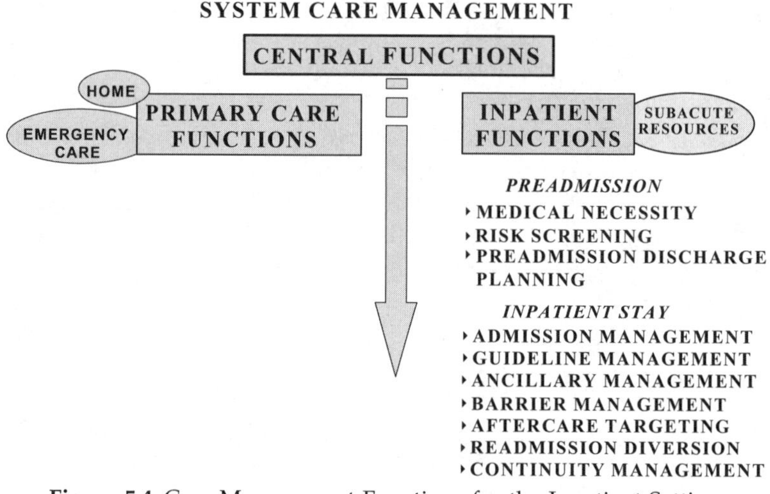

Figure 5.4 Care Management Functions for the Inpatient Setting

Preadmission professionals execute a variety of functions in achieving these objectives:

1. *Medical Necessity Review.* A collaborative process between referring physicians and hospital preadmission personnel that ensures that patients referred for admission are qualified by condition and severity for the acute level of care.

2. *Precertification.* A process through which clinical staff obtain required authorization from insurance companies for patient admission to a designated level of care.

3. *Broad-Band Risk Screening.*[13] (Provided for elective admissions.) A process through which a patient risk profile is obtained from the referring physician and patient. Screen findings may trigger preadmission discharge planning or outreach assessment to determine how best to manage the risk patient's acute care episode.

4. *Preadmission Discharge Planning.* (Available for elective patients.) A process through which professional staff assist patients with a variety of preadmission tasks, including (a) transportation, (b) insurance verification, (c) Medicaid application, (d) assessment of postcare environment and requirements, and (e) aftercare planning and facility selection.

Preadmission risk and discharge information is documented through automated mechanisms and available to inpatient staff on the day of patient admission to a specific acute care unit.

Inpatient Care Management Functions

care management functions within the acute care setting are carried out by physicians, nurse practitioners, nurses, social workers, and utilization review nurses.[14] Core objectives of inpatient care management are (1) continuity and risk management as the patient enters and departs from the acute care setting, (2) enhanced patient outcomes, and (3) managed utilization and costs.

Effective care management in the acute care environment must be supported by sophisticated informational and operational infrastructures that provide for:

1. *Automated Patient Data.* On-line availability of demographic, financial, clinical, and case management information obtained in other system sites that permits inpatient staff to provide continuous and nonredundant care management service to patients.

2. *Automated Length-of-Stay Assignment.* Application of a targeted length of stay based on the patient's working diagnosis at admission and adjusted as needed to accommodate identified co-morbidities or complications.

3. *Automated Clinical Pathways.* On-line availability of medical guidelines, companion interdisciplinary care maps, and associated standing order

sets for use in the care of patients in targeted diagnostic or procedure groups (such as pneumonia or craniotomy).

4. *Automated Variance Tracking.* An on-line function that flags and specifies patient departure from guidelines.

5. *Daily Patient Tracking.* An automated capability that enables the patient's physician and health team to effectively monitor length-of-stay against target and identify barriers impeding target achievement.

6. *Interdisciplinary Rounds.* A daily clinical conference attended by physicians and health team members in which patient care planning, length-of-stay, discharge barriers, and aftercare requirements are addressed.

7. *Discharge Resources.* Sufficient home health, terminal care, subacute, and long-term care services to ensure timely patient discharge.

8. *Provider Incentives.* Designed to reward effective length-of-stay and cost management in the acute care setting.

Interdisciplinary teams execute a variety of care management functions directed toward management of the patient's inpatient episode of care. Core functions include:

1. *Admission Management.* Ensuring that patient advance directives, risk factors, initial orders, and preliminary aftercare requirements are addressed within a targeted time frame.

2. *Patient and Family Orientation.* Communicating the course of care, targeted discharge date, probable aftercare requirements, and tasks that must be addressed by the family in order to optimize patient discharge within the targeted time frame.

3. *Guideline Management.* Ensuring that medical management guidelines are assigned and followed to optimize care standardization, clinical resource utilization, patient outcome, and cost management.

4. *Ancillary Services Management.* Ensuring that radiographic, laboratory, pharmacy, and clinical consult services are provided within time standards to avoid unnecessary delays in patient care and discharge.

5. *Barrier Management.* Ensuring identification and management of provider, patient, and system barriers that may negatively affect length-of-stay management, patient discharge, and safe patient return to the community.

6. *Aftercare Targeting.* Developing individualized discharge plans that direct patients to aftercare resources that are clinically appropriate, in concert with patient preference whenever possible, and cost-effective from a health system perspective.

7. *Continuity Management.* Ensuring that each patient leaving the inpatient care unit is scheduled for appropriate medical and case management service after discharge.

8. *Readmission Diversion.* Ensuring that patients with potential for unplanned readmission to the hospital benefit from development of risk-management plans that optimize patient stability in the post-discharge period.

The staffing pattern required to effectively carry out core inpatient care management functions varies by patient population and care unit type. Five professional positions, however, are essential across inpatient populations and settings. These positions are (1) a physician director responsible for delivery of appropriate clinical care, efficient medical management, and length-of-stay mangement;[15] (2) a nurse practitioner responsible for overseeing patient guideline compliance and variance management; (3) a nurse care coordinator responsible for ancillary service management, daily care coordination and task management, and discharge barrier management in collaboration with the unit social worker; (4) a social worker responsible for ensuring patient and family readiness for discharge, collaborative barrier management, psychosocial risk management, identification of appropriate aftercare placement resources, and expedited access to required aftercare facilities; and (5) a utilization review nurse responsible for daily continued stay reviews, collaborative benefit management with insurers, and preparation of automated length-of-stay and variance reports.

INFORMATION MANAGEMENT

System care management is driven by information. Sophisticated care management models of the future must be supported by system-wide computer applications that permit population, utilization, and cost analysis.[16] Care management professionals utilize information technology to:

1. *Access Lifetime Clinical Records.* Ensuring provision of continuous medical and care management services to patients within facilities and across system sites.

2. *Access Longitudinal Health Status Information.* Permitting identification of populations with health vulnerabilities that require care management service to avert health decline.

3. *Analyze Member Utilization and Cost.* Identifying patients who exceed targeted service and cost thresholds and require case management intervention.

4. *Analyze Utilization by Diagnosis and Provider.* Facilitating development of targeted disease management initiatives and provider profiling interventions.

5. *Identify High-Cost Diseases and Sites of Care.* Permitting focused utilization and cost-management interventions by level of care.

Accumulation of the information required for effective care management must be accompanied by stringent data control. Access protocols, tracking mechanisms, and misuse penalties must be enforced universally to protect the privacy of patients, providers, and the health system.

OUTCOME MEASUREMENT

The fundamental question addressed through outcome measurement is, *How does system care management affect health behavior, utilization, cost, and outcome?* Measurement activities focus on:

1. *Longitudinal Health Status.* Highlighting the impact of care management on the overall health status of targeted populations.
2. *System Utilization.* Documenting the impact of care management interventions on key system use indicators such as (a) admissions per thousand, (b) days per thousand, (c) readmission rate, (d) emergency visit rate, and (e) specialist referral volume.
3. *Sub-Population Utilization.* Analyzing the impact of care management initiatives on the use patterns of targeted disease-management groups, such as patients with congestive heart failure.
4. *Targeted Clinical Outcomes.* Correlating specific care management interventions with shifts in individual patient outcomes, such as changes in blood pressure levels.
5. *Cost Per Case.* Demonstrating the impact of care management interventions on the average cost per case by target population, focal diagnosis, or site of care.
6. *System Cost Distribution.* Tracking the impact of care management on expenditure shifts across outpatient, emergency, inpatient, and subacute care levels.
7. *Satisfaction.* Measuring changes in provider and patient perception of system service and process after receipt of care management service.

care management utilization outcomes (for example, increased immunization rates for at-risk children following an outreach care management initiative) are measured at designated intervals (1) against the prior experience of the target population in the system, and (2) against regional and national utilization benchmarks for similar populations. In addition, each targeted care management outcome is examined in relationship to other key outcomes for the target population. Use of this *relational analysis framework* is necessary for care management professionals to accurately assess the true value of achieved outcomes.

An example of relational analysis illustrates its importance. Through systematic application of practice guidelines in emergency and acute care settings, a case management program targets and achieves a reduction of 1.5

days in the average length of inpatient stay for patients with community-acquired pneumonia. From the unilateral perspective of inpatient utilization, this outcome has significant value for a system attempting to reduce inpatient utilization and cost. From a relational perspective, however, the assessed value may be quite different. The ultimate value of reduced length of stay for patients with pneumonia is dramatically reduced if patients affected by the enabling care management intervention are readmitted within seven days. Such readmissions result in poor quality of care and clinical outcome for the patient and a cost increase for the system.

Care management professionals must systematically document the relative impact of targeted care management interventions on health and clinical status, satisfaction, utilization patterns, and cost distribution. Such documentation is a vital asset in garnering the universal support required for care management success from the sponsoring system, its medical providers, and system consumers.

CONCLUSION

System care management is an important ingredient in the capacity of health networks to manage continuity, utilization, cost, and outcomes. To ensure incorporation of care management in future health-delivery models, care management professionals, collectively, must ensure completion of three developmental tasks: definition, measurement, and marketing.

Definition

Care management must be defined so that the nature of this *complex health care process* is widely understood. The functional components of the care management process (health management, disease management, utilization management, case management, and demand management) must be agreed upon and defined. Interventions associated with each of the functional components (such as health education, risk management, medical adherence, and continuity management) must be delineated and described in standardized operational terms. In addition, the skills and qualifications required for execution of each intervention must be specified and serve as the universal basis for care management education, employment, and performance assessment.

Measurement

Care management professionals must engage in research efforts at provider sites across the country, rigorously testing the ubiquitous but unproven assumption that care management interventions are correlated with desired changes in health care utilization, cost, and outcomes. Only through amassment of reliable and valid data will it be possible to *prove* the precise ways in which implementation of discrete care management interventions result in targeted changes in health behavior and outcomes.

Marketing

The ultimate prominence of care management in health systems of the future depends on the ability of care management professionals to successfully market their product to health insurers and providers who must pay for it. Care management experts must be able to clearly articulate the nature of the care management process, describe care management components and cost, and predict care management outcomes with reasonable certainty. In short, they must explain persuasively what health systems can expect as return on the considerable investment that is required to support the care management process.

Vigorous intellectual debate, sophisticated inquiry, and instrumental influence are prerequisites for ensuring the inclusion of care management in future models of health delivery. Without this concerted effort the care management process will remain poorly understood, inadequately funded, and operationally fragmented, deprived through professional lassitude of its proper standing in emerging health paradigms.

NOTES

1. Golodner (1999) provides an interesting perspective on the changing status of consumers in the health care system.
2. Taylor & Lessin (1996), Issel & Anderson (1996), and Weil & Jorgensen (1995) highlight the importance of consumer satisfaction in future health care models.
3. Evans, Hwang & Nagarajan (1995) offer detailed commentary on the impact of physician profiling on one aspect of care management: length-of-stay reduction.
4. For discussion of the professional, ethical, legal, and technical aspects of physician incentives programs, consult Hillman (1995), Grimaldi (1996), Hellinger (1996), Lederberg (1997), and Pearson, Sabin & Emanuel (1998).
5. Directors of care management may be selected from any of a number of disciplines typically involved in the process, including nursing, social work, and utilization review.
6. Central to the future design of system care management is the outcome of the current debate on the authority for care management. Health insurance companies retain control of a significant range of care management functions and retain premium dollars for their support and expansion. Many health systems, on the other hand, maintain that care management activities are best done by professionals who work in close daily collaboration with providers and patients. From the system perspective, premium dollars for care management are best concentrated in the health system.
7. Gates (1996) provides a summary of common financial contracts available under managed care.

8. For commentary on care management in the primary setting, refer to Anker-Unnever & Netting (1995), Gaillour (1996), and Wynn (1996).
9. Ware (1984) and Greenfield & Nelson (1992) offer important perspectives on health status measurement and its application in contemporary health settings.
10. A number of standardized risk-screening instruments are available. Critical in the effective use of any screening tool is the systematic and immediate transmittal of risk information to designated medical or care management professionals. These providers assume responsibilities for entry of risk information into a database, risk management, and longitudinal risk tracking.
11. The conceptual framework for case management in the primary care office outlined in this section of the chapter was developed by the author in collaboration with interdisciplinary colleagues from the University of Rochester Medical Center and the Rochester Physicians' Organization. Design team members included Elizabeth Slavinskas, RN, MS; Kelly Luther, MSW; Chrissie Copolus, RN, MS; and Drs. Peggy Bergin, Wally Johnson, Robert Kerper, George Plain, and Patrick Wilmot.
12. Subacute care is defined in this instance as a level of service intensity that falls between acute and long-term care.
13. The concept of broad-band risk screening and the functional framework for preadmission discharge planning were developed by the author in collaboration with the Preadmission Continuity of Care Team of the University of Rochester's Medical Center Continuity of Care and Case Management Program. Original design team participants included ElizabethSlavinskas, RN, MS; Lisa Schwark, MSW; Mandy VanderHorst, RN; and Joanne Lembach, RN, MS.
14. The framework for inpatient care management described in this section of the chapter was developed by the author in collaboration with interdisciplinary colleagues participating in the design and implementation of the URMC Continuity of Care and Case Management Program's Inpatient Care Management Model for Strong Memorial Hospital. Lisa Norsen, RN, MS, collaborates with the author in development of all inpatient care management components. Carol Sammann, RN, MS, serves as the project manager for inpatient model development. Key participants in the original design process included: Andrew Rudman, MD; Lisa Clas-Nobel, RN, MPA; Nancy Resseguie, RN; Mary Ellen Kunz, RN, MS; Kelly Luther, MSW; Susan Luxemburg, MSW; and Chris Kokkoris, MSW. We are aided in the ongoing refinement of the model by physicians, nurses, social workers, utilization review nurses, physical therapists, pharmacists, radiologists, and laboratory administrators involved in the delivery and coordination of care on the hospital's medical/surgical inpatient services.
15. Wachter & Goldman (1996) discuss the potential contribution of a physician "hospitalist" in the enhancement of efficiency and quality management in the acute care setting.
16. Simpson (1999) outlines criteria for use in selecting an information management system. Weydt, Hertz, Frahm & Frederick (1999) discuss computer applications across components of the health care system.

REFERENCES

American Health Consultants. (1998). *Critical pathways across the continuum of care.* Atlanta, GA: Author.

Anker-Unnever, L., & Netting, F. E. (1995). Coordinated care partnership: Case management with physician practices. *Journal of Case Management, 4*(1), 3–8.

Anonymous, (1998). Do-it-yourself disease management programs. *Medical Management Network, 6*(2), 1–6.

Anonymous, (1998). Get ready for population-based disease management. *Demand & Disease Management, 4*(7), 97–98.

Armstrong, E. P. (1996). Monitoring and evaluating disease management: Information requirements. *Clinical Therapeutics, 18*(6), 1327–1333.

Aschenbrener, C. A. (1996). News from the future: Health care summit caps decade of transformation, 1996–2005. *Academic Medicine, 71*(8), 823–827.

Bartolozzi, P. R., & Levin, L. (1997). Strategies in a managed care system: One agency's experience. *Journal of Case Management, 6*(3), 114–118.

Berenson, R. A. (1997). Beyond competition. *Health Affairs, March/April,* 171–180.

Bernard, S., & Frist, W. H. (1998). The healthcare quality debate: The case for disease management. *Disease Management, 1*(2), 91–98.

Boland, P. (1991). Market overview and delivery system dynamics. In P. Boland (Ed.), *Making managed health care work: A practical guide to strategies and solutions* (pp. 20–23). New York: McGraw-Hill, Health Professionals Division.

Bower, K. A. (1991). *Case management by nurses.* Kansas City, MO: American Nurses Publishing.

Bronstein, J. M. (1996). The politics of U.S. health care reform. *Medical Anthropology Quarterly, 10*(1), 20–28.

Chamberlain, R., & Rapp, C. A. (1991). A decade of case management: A methodological review of outcome research. *Community Mental Health Journal, 37,* 171–188.

Churchill, L. R. (1997). Market mediotopia: A glimpse at American health care in 2005. *Hastings Center Report, 1,* 5–6.

Cline, B. G. (1990). Case management organizational models & administrative methods. *CARING Magazine, July,* 14–18.

Coons, S. J. (1996). Disease management: Definitions and exploration of issues. *Clinical Therapeutics, 18*(6), 1321–1326.

Davis, J. (1996). Predicting future health system change. *Health Affairs, Winter,* 107–108.

Epstein, R. S., & Sherwood, L. M. (1996). From outcomes research to disease management: A guide for the perplexed. *Annals of Internal Medicine, 124*(9), 205–206.

Evans, J. H., III, Hwang, Y., & Nagarajan, N. (1995). Physicians' response to length of stay profiling. *Medical Care, 33*(11), 1106–1119.

Favor, G., & Ricks, R. (1996). Preparing to automate the case management process. *Nursing Case Management, July/August, 1*(3), 100–106.

Gadomski, A. M., Perkis, V., Horton, L., Cross, S., & Stanton, B. (1995). Diverting managed care Medicaid patients from pediatric emergency rooms. *Pediatrics, 95,* 170–179.

Gaillour, F. R. (1996). Good-bye gatekeeper. *Group Practice Journal, November/December,* 20–24.

Gates, D. M. (1996). Changes in health care financing: Effects on the delivery of health care services in the 1990s. *The Journal of Cardiovascular Nursing, 11*(1), 1–13.

Geary, C. R., & Smeltzer, C. H. (1997). Case management: Past, present, future—the drivers for change. *Journal of Nursing Care Quality, October,* 9–19.

Ginsburg, P. B., & Grossman, J. M. (1995). Health system change: The view from Wall Street. *Health Affairs, 14*(4), 159–163.

Ginzberg, E. (1998). The changing US health care agenda. *Journal of the American Medical Association, 279*(7), 501–504.

Golodner, L. F. (1999). Consumer voice: From whisper to roar. In E.L. Cohen & V. DeBack (Eds.), *The Outcomes Mandate: Care Management in Health Care Today* (pp. 20–26). St. Louis, MO: Mosby.

Greene, R. R. (1992). Case management: An arena for social work practice. In B. Vourlekis & R. Greene (Eds.), *Social Work Case Management* (pp. 11–25). New York: Aldine de Gruyter.

Greenfield, S., & Nelson, E. C. (1992). Recent developments and future issues in the use of health status assessment measures in clinical settings. *Medical Care, 30*(5) Supplement, MS23–MS41.

Grimaldi, P. L. (1996). Federal rules expanded for physician incentive plans. *Nursing Management, 27*(8), 12–14.

Hawkins, C. W., Veeder, N. W., & Pearce, J. W. (1998). *Nurse Social Worker Collaboration in Managed Care.* (pp. 123–149). New York: Springer Publishing Company, Inc.

Hellinger, F. J. (1996). The impact of financial incentives on physician behavior in managed care plans: A review of the evidence. *Medical Care Research and Review, 53*(3), 294–314.

Hillman, A. L. (1995). The impact of physician financial incentives on high-risk populations in managed care. *Journal of Acquired Immune Deficiency Syndromes and Human Retrovirology, 8* (Suppl. 1), S23–S30.

Holdford, D. A. (1996). Barriers to disease management. *American Journal of Health-System Pharmacies, 53,* 2093–2096.

Iglehart, J. (1997). Forum on the future of academic medicine: Session 1—setting the stage. *Academic medicine, 72*(7), 595–599.

Issel, L. M., & Anderson, R. A. (1996). Take charge: Managing six transformations in health care delivery. *Nursing Economics, 14*(2), 78–85.

Korr, W. S., & Cloninger, L. (1991). Assessing models of case management: An empirical approach. *Journal of Social Service Research, 14,* (1/2), 129–146.

Kretz, S. E., & Pantos, B. S. (1996). Cost savings and clinical improvement through disease management. *Journal of Case Management, 5*(4), 173–181.

Langley, P. C. (1996). Assessing the input costs of disease management programs. *Clinical Therapeutics, 18*(6), 1334–1340.

Lederberg, M. B. (1997). New HCFA physician incentive plan regulations: A physician's guide. *Medicine and Health/Rhode Island, 80*(5), 173–174.

Lieberman, P. B., Wiitala, S. A., Elliott, B., McCormick, S., & Goyette, S. B. (1998). Decreasing length of stay: Are there effects on outcomes of psychiatric hospitalizations? *American Journal of Psychiatry, 155*(7), 905–909.

Loomis, J. F. (1988). Case management in health care. *Health and Social Work, 13,* 219–225.

Macko, P., Dunn, S., Blech, M, Ashby, F., & Schwab, T. (1995). The social HMOs meeting the challenge of integrated team care coordination. *Journal of Case Management, 4*(3), 102–106.

Marmor, T. R. (1998). Forecasting American health care: How we got here and where we might be going. *Journal of Health Politics, Policy and Law, 23*(3), 551–571.

Milstein, A., Bergthold, L., & Selbovitz, L. (1993). In P. Boland (Ed.), *Making Managed Healthcare Work: A Practical Guide to Strategies and Solutions,* (pp. 371–388). Gaithersburg, MD: Aspen Publishers.

Mitchell, E. (1997). Medicaid, Medicare, and managed care Case management for dually eligible clients. *Journal of Case Management, 6*(1), 8–12.

Niemi, K. (1997). Integrating clinical and support process design for effective health services. *Managed Care Quarterly, Summer,* 1–10.

O'Grady, K. F. (1993). Physician utilization profiling: The key to managing ambulatory utilization. In P. Boland (Ed.), *Making Managed Health Care Work: A Practical Guide to Strategies and Solutions,* (pp. 394–399). New York City: McGraw-Hill, Health Professions Division.

Pearce, C. W., & Trabka, E. (1998). The community view: New models, new links. In J. Hawkins, N.W. Veeder, & C.W. Pearce (Eds.), *Nurse–Social Worker Collaboration in Managed Care: A Model of Community Care Management,* (pp. 123–149). New York: Springer Publishing Company.

Pearson, S. D., Sabin, J. E., & Emanuel, E. J. (1998). Ethical guidelines for physician compensation based on capitation. *The New England Journal of Medicine, 339*(10), 689–693.

Rothman, J. (1991). A model of case management: Toward empirically based practice. *Social Work, 36*(6), 520–528.

Schraeder, C., Shelton, P., Britt, T., & Buttitta, K. (1996). Case management in a capitated system: The community nursing organization. *Journal of Case Management, 5*(2), 58–64.

Simpson, R. L. (1999). Automated outcomes management: Criteria for selection of information systems. In E.L. Cohen & V. Deback (Eds.), *The Outcomes Mandate: Case Management in Health Care Today,* (pp. 226–243). St. Louis, MO: Mosby.

Taylor, R., & Lessin, L. (1996). Restructuring the health care delivery system in the United States. *Journal of Health Care Finance, Summer,* 33–60.

VanderLaan, B. F., de la Houssaye, M., Janousek, K., & Derus, C. (1998). Performance under capitation: The true cost of infrastructure. *Journal of Health Care Finance, Summer,* 27–38.

Van Horn, R. L., Burns, L. R., & Wholey, D. R. (1997). The impact of physician involvement in managed care on efficient use of hospital resources. *Medical Care, 35*(9), 873–889.

Vourlekis, B. S., & Greene, R. R. (Eds.). (1992). *Social Work Case Management.* New York: Aldine de Gruyter.

Wachter, R. M., & Goldman, L. (1996). The emerging role of "hospitalists" in the American health care system. *The New England Journal of Medicine, 335*(7), 514–517.

Ware, J. E., Jr. (1984). Conceptualizing disease impact and treatment outcomes. *Cancer, 53* (Supplement), 2316–2323.

Weil, T. P., & Jorgensen, N. E. (1995). Why market-driven forces in our health industry might eventually stumble: What could happen then? *Journal of Health Care Finance, Winter,* 1–12.

Weydt, A. P., Hertz, L., Frahm, L., & Frederick, J. (1999). Computers across the continuum. In E.L. Cohen & V. DeBack (Eds.), *The Outcomes mandate: Case Management in Health Care Today,* (pp. 244–251). St. Louis, MO: Mosby.

Wynn, P. (1996). The role of physicians in disease management. *Managed Care, October,* 19–22.

Zablocki, E. (1995). Using disease state management to coordinate care across the continuum. *The Quality Letter, November,* 2–10.

◆ PART TWO ◆

MANAGED CARE: SERVICE DELIVERY DOMAINS FOR SPECIAL NEEDS AND AT-RISK POPULATIONS

In this section, a variety of managed care services delivery domains and target populations are discussed, as are training needs for child welfare practitioners.

In "Managed Care and Child Welfare Practitioner Training Needs," Vivian Jackson, Charlotte McCullough, and Jan McCarthy discuss the knowledge and skill requirements for child welfare practice in a child welfare environment. These knowledge and skill requirements pertain to both practitioners at the direct practice and management or executive levels.

The authors point out that child welfare is a new domain for managed care. General knowledge, skill, and attitude training needs for all groups practicing at all levels in child welfare include change management, cross-system training to support integrated systems of care, multi-level training within an agency, leadership in addressing attitudinal changes, knowledge about managed behavioral health care, applying managed care to child welfare, and implications for public purchases and private providers.

For those child welfare practitioners and managed care organizations (MCOs) not familiar with the child welfare practice area, the authors suggest specific training in child welfare managed care, health and behavioral health care, and child welfare, to include goals, statutory requirements, core values, family dynamics, role of the courts, state-of-the-art treatment approaches, and funding sources.

Scott Miyake Geron's "Managed Care and Care Management for Older Adults" reviews recent developments in Medicare managed care for older adults. He asks, and answers, the following questions: Is the system of managed care working for older adults? If so, how? If not, what are the barriers to the use of managed care by older adults?

Geron discusses the unique health and related service needs of older adults, summarizes the Medicare program, and discusses specific federal efforts to promote acute and post-acute managed care plans. He also presents federal and state initiatives to manage long-term care, or acute care and long-term care combined. Finally, Geron focuses on case management (or *care management,* as it is currently called) and describes how it is now being adapted in services delivery to older adults.

Roberta R. Greene and W. Patrick Sullivan's "Managed Care and the Ecological Perspective: Meeting the Needs of Older Adults in the Twenty-First Century" focuses on the ecological, person-environment perspective model of geriatric health based on ecological principles, individualized multidisciplinary treatment plans, and designs that promote optimal functioning among older adults.

The chapter argues for continued use of ecological principles in health and behavioral health care for older adults. Greene and Sullivan outline major features of managed care in which the large majority of older adults receive health and behavioral health services. Finally, the chapter explores the important public policy question of whether managed care is a service delivery system that can meet the needs of the elderly in the 21st century.

The next four chapters in this section focus on issues associated with managed health and behavioral health services delivery to at-risk populations (children, the elderly, the under- and unemployed, the poor, handicapped, mentally ill, substance abusers, and minorities of color). In two of the chapters, policy and programmatic actions are described. In the other two chapters, research needs are outlined in relation to outcomes research for children and adolescents and in the managed care of substance-abusing adults.

Susan B. Stern's "Outcomes Research for Children and Adolescents: Implications for Children's Mental Health and Managed Care" gives an overview and discussion of recent outcomes research pertinent to the mental health needs of children and adolescents, as well as research bearing upon managed care's impact on the provision of services to this population. Consideration is given to the relevance of this research to managed care, the mental health professions, policy-makers, and consumer groups.

Stern enumerates several important research questions to be empirically assessed (or assessed in more depth, with more controlled studies) in the future: What treatments work best and why? How can the service delivery system be adapted to maximize positive treatment outcomes for children and adolescents? What does research suggest about ethical practice? How can this be adapted to better serve clients and contribute to a more effective service system? Where do preventive services fit within managed care? What research outcomes will best inform managed care and the mental health services delivery community for future collaboration, advocacy, and prevention efforts?

Susan M. Chandler's "Facilitating the Enrollment of Elderly and Disabled Persons into Medicaid Managed Care" describes the challenges faced and the lessons learned when a large state human services agency began planning for the enrollment of elderly and disabled people into a managed health care environment. This particular case study critically examines the pros and cons of attempting to plan for the smooth transition of elderly and disabled people from a traditional fee-for-service medical system into a highly complex, sometimes hostile managed care Medicaid contractual system. Political factors in this state system further complicated already complex managed health and behavioral health systemic roadblocks.

In "Managed Care and the Severely Mentally Ill: Current Issues and Future Challenges," Wes Shera asserts that if social work is to survive and thrive in managed mental health care, it must undertake action on a number of fronts simultaneously. These action fronts include understanding current knowledge and practice in managed care, both domestically and internationally; using efficacy and best-practices information to design systems of care; promoting cultural competence in the delivery of services; and supporting consumer involvement in the design and monitoring of managed mental health care.

Wilma Peebles-Wilkins and Nancy W. Veeder's "Research Needs in the Managed Care of Substance-Abusing Patients" provides an overview of managed care systems and addresses current general issues relating to treatment of substance-abusing patients. The authors go on to review existing research in this field, both in terms of methodological issues and findings, as well as examine research needed in the future.

Future research needs include controlled studies comparing traditional treatments of substance-abusing patients and new prevention and treatment innovations to more effectively deal with the growing social problem of substance abuse.

More specifically, Peebles-Wilkins and Veeder suggest several areas where future research is needed: cost effectiveness (is managed care cost effective? with whom? with which treatments? and for what duration?); services provided by which professional or non-professional?; the effect of various payment approaches on the provision and outcomes of care; the comparative cost-effectiveness of for-profit and not-for-profit service delivery systems; immediate versus long-term cost benefits of managed care systems; needs assessments to assess both services needed by specific target groups and professional competencies needed for behavioral health care practice; assessment, diagnostic, and outcome instrument development (intervention and treatment protocols, patient-assessment tools, case recording for quality assurance); access and rationing (which groups have and do not have access to behavioral health services and why?); rationing of services (for whom and why?); and market research to identify and target underserved groups and increase access and utilization.

Additional research needs in the managed care of substance-abusing patients include comparative studies of different innovations; how various lower cost treatments are affecting the addictive disorders and other quality-of-life factors, comparisons of different professions delivering the same and different services, effectiveness of interdisciplinary teams versus solo interventions; effects of managed care policies, short- versus longer-term interventions with the chronic relapsing conditions, intensive treatment versus periodic interventions, provider decision-making, and follow-up studies across the board.

A final area of needed research is in professional social work education and practice: the nature and effectiveness of social work leadership in policy and program design and implementation, outcomes of advanced case management versus less skilled interventions, the viability of community-building, the viability of preventive interventions, and more short-term and strengths and competency approaches to assessment and interventions versus psychodynamic approaches.

Again, the theme of this section is that more attention needs to be paid to the "effectiveness" of managed care and the only way to assess services delivery accountability to all stakeholders is through empirical research.

◆ CHAPTER 6 ◆

Managed Care and Child Welfare Practitioner Training Needs

VIVIAN JACKSON, CHARLOTTE MCCULLOUGH,
JAN MCCARTHY

AN OVERVIEW OF MANAGED CARE AND CHILD WELFARE

The term "managed care" describes a wide variety of financing and service-delivery operations. What all managed care operations have in common is the effort to balance cost, quality, and access. Because multiple human service systems have turned to managed care, child welfare practitioners may find themselves confronted with several different managed care operations for the children within their responsibility. For example, primary health care may be offered through a network of Health Maintenance Organizations (HMOs) that offer limited mental health benefits for acute care. A separate behavioral health carve-out plan may provide both acute care and some extended services for children and families. And finally, the child welfare system itself may use managed care technology to provide some of its services.

This chapter will focus on the knowledge and skill requirements for child welfare in a managed care environment. This includes managed care under an auspice apart from child welfare, such as medical and behavioral health services. It also includes changes within child welfare that use managed care technology. This discussion will address both the knowledge and skill requirements of those practitioners at the direct practice level and at the management/executive level. We will consider both pre-service and in-service training needs.

Managed Care Methodology

In general, managed care is a collection of tools to manage the costs of service delivery to achieve certain defined outcomes for a defined population. It is the unique blend of these strategies that separates one managed care endeavor from another. The theory is that if the right set of incentives and disincentives is constructed, consumers and providers will interact with each other to achieve maximal outcomes in a cost- and time-efficient manner. In many ways we are still at experimental stages in defining what sets of conditions create that type of environment.

The functions of the strategies most frequently attributed to managed care technology are listed below. These strategies:

- Control the pricing of services, using methods such as capitation, case rates, discounted fees, etc.
- Codify the circumstances under which a type of service can be offered, such as medical necessity criteria, social necessity criteria, and clinical criteria
- Define and limit who can provide the services by developing provider networks and establishing provider credentialing criteria
- Establish a system to route the recipient of care to the service deemed most appropriate by using preauthorization and gate-keeping methods
- Monitor and track utilization of services deemed to be appropriate for the recipient by using case/utilization management and best-practices guidelines
- Monitor and track the outcomes of services and provider performance by establishing outcomes-management processes, provider profiling, continuous quality improvement strategies, consumer satisfaction analyses.
- Monitor and track the expenses related to service delivery through careful claims processing and contract management

The capacity to perform these functions is dependent on information technology capable of capturing the needed information through management information systems. The data collection requires relevant analysis and decision-making as reflected in quality-improvement processes.

The management information system must be able to:

- Track clients and families through the system in real time
- Provide information for utilization management
- Track individual and aggregate outcomes
- Support structures for financial management
- Track contract requirements and performance requirement.

In the best of worlds, managed care technology could assure that the recipient of services receives the correct care for his/her need provided by the best person/system to provide that service in the briefest period of time necessary and at the lowest cost possible. In the ideal, funds would be redirected to services that provide the best outcomes for the least cost. Dollars would be shifted from more expensive services to less expensive services and gaps in the service system would be filled. The expectation is that the provider will discover methods to obtain desired outcome in the shortest time and in the most efficient manner possible. Also, it is anticipated that customer choice and customer satisfactions will stimulate system improvements.

However, we are far from that ideal. There is still a great deal of experimentation on how to achieve that perfect balance, and great debate within the field regarding the merits and demerits of managed care. Indeed, there are many examples of reconfiguration of services that yield better results for more people in a cost-efficient manner. But there are those who question the motivations for change. Is the goal purely cost reduction by the public entity and profit-taking by large managed care organizations? Others raise concerns regarding the lack of appreciation of the level of skill and resources required to achieve the desired outcomes. Should RNs or nursing assistants be used to provide a service? If Medicaid is already underfunded, how will reducing the funds even more in managed Medicaid achieve required change? Still others point to the difficulties inherent in trying to match need with the right intervention in communities where there is not a sufficient array of service diversity. And finally, they note that the pressure to restrict spending has led to more intense debate over the questions of who should pay for what services. Should costs be paid by the mental health system, school systems, or child welfare system? Is the service medically necessary or socially necessary?

From the perspective of child welfare stakeholders in a ten-state impact analysis, there was some degree of consensus with respect to the benefits and concerns about the impact of health care reform, especially behavioral health care reform on children in the child welfare system. The reforms they were referencing were generally managed care endeavors.

Benefits

- Access to behavioral health services has increased so that more children in the child welfare system are getting at least a basic level of behavioral health care services.
- Managed care reforms have drawn attention to the need for discrete planning related to behavioral health services for children and adolescents in the child welfare system.
- Short-term treatment models and level of care/decision-making criteria have led to more purposeful, focused treatment and clinical accountability. Clinical decision-making has become more standardized.
- Managed care reforms have resulted in a trend toward providing services in less restrictive environments, creating less opportunity for children to remain inappropriately in long-term treatment settings.
- Awareness has been raised to the need for qualitative data, benchmarks, and measurement of outcomes for children and families in the child welfare system.
- In some states, there has been increased joint planning among agencies, better communication, and newfound willingness for the behavioral health system to be involved in the provision of treatment services for the child welfare population, increasing the feeling of shared responsibility for services to children and families in the child welfare system.

CONCERNS

- Managed care tends to exacerbate the difficulties at transition points in a child's life and makes continuity of care at those times more difficult, particularly for children who experience many placements.
- There is quicker access, but to insufficient amounts of service. Some of the children require sufficient intervention to address the complex problems associated with profound trauma.
- This environment stimulates cost-shifting and "dumping" of children from one system to another.
- Managed care organizations (MCOs) frequently are unfamiliar with the child welfare population.
- The sometimes overzealous focus on reduction in length of stay in hospitals overshadows the need for attention to child safety and step-down services.
- Workload is not adjusted for child welfare workers who now have the tasks of negotiating with multiple MCOs to obtain services for children and families.
- Families of children in the child welfare system are frequently left out of the planning process for both individual service planning and system-level planning for managed care activities.
- Managed care systems tend to focus on services for individual children, making it difficult to obtain services for families that would prevent placement or enhance reunification efforts.
- Essential child welfare services such as post-adoption services or services for youthful sexual offenders are not covered adequately by the behavioral health managed care initiatives.
- Some MCOs have not recognized, understood, or respected the role of the courts in the child welfare system, leading to disagreements about service plans and court orders for services.

Managed Care and Child Welfare

The benefits and concerns noted above suggest some of the knowledge needs required of stakeholders in a managed care environment serving children and families in child welfare systems. It is within this environment of multiple types of managed care, operating within the multiple systems that touch the lives of the children and families, that the child welfare system must make decisions. We will discuss briefly three major venues of managed care of relevance in child welfare.

Health Care The first is Managed Medicaid. In 1982, 2% of Medicaid recipients were enrolled in managed care plans. By 1995, over 40% were enrolled in such plans. And in 1998 over 65% were enrolled in Managed Medicaid plans. Since most of the children who enter foster care are Medicaid eligible, the decisions on a policy level regarding whether they should be in managed Medicaid plans is a significant consideration. If the child is included in managed Medicaid, it is most likely that the services will be provided through a Health Maintenance Organization. On a case level, the caseworker and foster family will need to address the administrative logistics unique to that particular HMO. On a program level, the HMO will need to address the special needs of the youth in foster care. They need rapid eligibility determination, immediate and thorough assessment, continuity of health care information, stability of health care providers. Many of these children are at higher health risk that the general Medicaid youth population. The HMO will need to be prepared to address issues of special concern to this population, such as substance-exposed children, poor immunization history, untreated or undertreated chronic health issues, and trauma histories. One of the critical questions is whether the capitation rate for the HMOs serving the children are established at a level appropriate to address these complicated needs.

Behavioral Health Care The behavioral health services are also often managed. The arrangements for financial responsibility for the mental health needs of children under child welfare auspice is variable. In some cases, the HMO will address the acute mental health needs. Those services may be provided by the HMO itself or the mental health services may be carved out to a specialty managed mental health entity. Oftentimes, longer-term behavioral health services are financed by the public mental health system and/or the child welfare system. In either case, these services may be offered through a managed care operation. The MCO operation could be conducted by a public authority or contracted to independent not-for-profit or for-profit entities. Again, there is a policy decision that must be made as to whether to include these children in the population to be served through managed care. If so, the child welfare staff and caretakers must learn how to access and use those services. In addition, the behavioral health providers need to be cognizant and skilled regarding some of the issues confronting this population. Issues regarding separation, attachment, and trauma must be well understood in addition to depression, attention deficit disorder, substance abuse, conduct disorders, and other issues that bring youngsters to the attention of mental health professionals.

Managed Child Welfare The most recent evolution is the use of managed care within child welfare systems themselves. Having observed the use of managed care technology in health and mental health services, legislators, state and county executives, and child welfare executives began to consider the possibilities within child welfare. In these scenarios, the child welfare system uses managed care techniques to perform one or more of the following activities:

- Transform its own operations
- Take the lead to organize specific services for which it is responsible (like mental health) in a managed care framework

- Engage in a privatization process, using managed care technology for implementation
- Participate in multi-systemic reforms that use managed care technology

This process is very new. Based on studies in 1998 there are under fifty child welfare managed care initiatives in the country that are in the early stages of implementation or in earnest planning. As of winter 1998 only four initiatives had been underway for more than a year.

Public Trust

The role given to child welfare systems by society require a set of constraints and parameters that are different from those in health and behavioral health. Society has declared that children who are at risk be assured safety, well-being, and permanency. Successful managed care operations require accurate anticipation of the level of demand for services and the intensity of services that will be required for a given population. Child welfare systems cannot predict the number of children and families that will be referred for service. Child welfare systems do not have the option of refusing service or placing a child or family on a waiting list. Child welfare systems have an obligation of public trust to assure the safety of a child. Once a child is in the custody of the state, the child welfare system has a responsibility to the total well-being of that child, not just the provision of a specific services.

The Courts

Child welfare systems operate with an ever-present stakeholder that does not exist in other managed care operations. There is little the child welfare system can do successfully if the judges and court staff do not understand, support, and help guide these initiatives. At minimum, there must be agreement and understanding of the approach being used and who will present cases and make recommendations on the case. If contracted, and once the case has been referred, the managed care entity will be deciding when to seek court intervention, placement for children still in their homes, reunification, and closure.

Custody

The question of custodial authority must be clearly answered. Thus far, the public entities have maintained custody of the child. The question must also be answered for voluntary custody arrangements and temporary custodial arrangements. This arrangement requires careful communication between the public authority and the private entity that may have day-to-day responsibilities for the child.

Public Scrutiny

The child welfare system remains under intense scrutiny by the public to examine the ability of the system to care for those in its care. Any time that harm comes to a child who is in the care of the public system, there is often an expression of public outrage. The public entity holds ultimate responsibility. The fact that services may be contracted to a private entity does not relieve the public authority from responsibility. Plans for crisis management must be established. Those plans must include considerations for media management.

With those concerns and responsibilities as a backdrop, child welfare systems have approached the introduction of managed care somewhat cautiously. In contrast to managed health care, the public child welfare system has maintained significant control and involvement in the managed care operation. They may use the managed care technology themselves or, when they contract out responsibilities, they may maintain some responsibility and involvement with the children and families. Some contracts even delineate the conditions under which total responsibility reverts back to the public entity. The public expectation of safety for the children stimulates interest in the positive potential for managed care strategies as well as providing a basis for caution.

Characteristics of Managed Child Welfare

The Child Welfare League of America (CWLA), with university research support, has been tracking and evaluating the use of managed care in child welfare in recent years. A review of their findings provides an excellent snapshot of the status of child welfare managed care.

What Do We Know? The Child Welfare League of America has conducted surveys of state child welfare administrators since 1996 to learn how managed care was used in their states. That first survey revealed curiosity about managed care's potential, especially to make child welfare services more effective while containing costs for the most expensive "deep end" services. The states and some counties were surveyed in 1997 and again in 1998. As of December 1998, twenty-nine states had reported a total of forty-seven initiatives. The study focused on management changes, services delivery changes, and/or financing changes that would meet a broad definition of managed care. For their purposes, privatization was also included in the survey.

The Heath Care Reform Tracking Project took on the task of exploring the impact of state mental health care reforms on children and families served by the child welfare system who need mental health and substance abuse services. It also looked at the impact efforts to reform public child welfare systems have had on child with mental heath and substance abuse service needs and their families. This targeted effort, part of a larger program, was funded by the David and Lucille Packard Foundation. The analysis of child welfare managed care was taken from 1997 survey and covers twenty-five child welfare managed care initiatives.

Just as there is great variability in the specifics of managed care in health and behavioral health, it became clear that there is no single model of managed care in child welfare. Each community differs in the manner in which the state and localities divide financial responsibility, administrative authority, and implementation tasks for the administration of the child welfare program. Each community has its own political dynamic. Each community has its own demographic issues, all of which influence the nature of any given managed care operation. A state like Ohio, which has a strong county-centered system, has a variety of managed care structures. A state like Kansas, which has a strong state-administered system, has chosen to privatize across the entire state.

In general, child welfare managed care is limited to serving portions of populations or to addressing specific services. Many are in the early implementation stage. Few are statewide initiatives. The focus seems to be on children in out of home care or those at risk of placement. There is an increase in the use of wraparound approaches to reduce the need for initial placement and to shorten length of stay when placement is required.. The specific services are for placement, family preservation and support, and also adoption. In most cases, the state or county retains most of the responsibilities and tasks for child protective services, particularly investigation and substantiation, although the assessment and service delivery may be a function included in a contracted/privatized managed care operation. Most often, public systems maintain the role of managed care entity rather than contracting it out to an external managed care entity, although some use lead agencies as a quasi-leader or use traditional MCOs in an ASO arrangement. But the financing strategies that are changing to include shared financial risk also lead to shared authority for critical decision-making with contractors that bear that risk. It should be noted that private for-profit MCOs see themselves as tooling to compete more fully in this market.

This is an example of the way in which the public authority could separate the roles and responsibilities. The state agency could maintain the functions of determining Medicaid and Title IV-E eligibility, contracting with the managed care organizations, overseeing and approving the development of a certain level of care criteria, monitoring performance, and ensuring payment. It could maintain custody of the children, speak before the court, and function as the spokesperson in public relations circumstances. The managed care organization may have responsibility for provider network development, provider contract management, utilization management, billing, and reimbursement to providers in the network.

Goals

In general, legislators and public agency administrators view managed care as a way to achieve greater cost efficiencies. They also identified other key goals and expectations for managed care, such as:

- Creating more individualized services for children
- Reducing length of stay in care

- Averting unnecessary out-of-home placements
- Promoting adoptions
- Improving permanency planning
- Providing the locality with greater authority, responsibility, and flexibility
- Supporting a seamless system of care, establishing unified care managed processes
- Improving their accountability

Legislation and Regulatory Mandates

The capacity of the jurisdictions to proceed frequently involves legislative or regulatory changes. Some of the initiatives receive sanction through the Title IV-E waivers prompted by the Adoption and Safe Families Act. Some states have invoked a legislative mandate for competitive contracting and statewide privatization of foster care. Other changes have included the shift in rate-setting authority from the state to the county. Some states expanded the possibilities for options in care delivery by establishing the expectation of development of alternatives to group home care through the development of expanded family-based programs and individualized or wraparound services.

Planning of the Process

Generally there were extensive and inclusive planning processes. Some jurisdictions were very careful to listen to the input from providers. To a lesser degree, consumers, juvenile and family courts, and mental health systems were involved in the initial stages. The exceptions occurred when the managed care effort was part of a multi-systemic reform effort.

Population Served

In general, children in custody (and their families), children at risk of being in custody (and their families), children in high-end residential services, and children with serious emotional disturbances are those most likely to be involved in a child-welfare-initiated managed care effort.

Performance Expectations

General categories regarding performance are developed in dimensions such as access, appropriateness of services, quality of providers, cultural competency, client satisfaction, fiscal performance, safety, and permanency.

Specific measures may be linked to the particular goals of the initiative, such as:

- Reduction of length of stay or level of care for children already in the foster care system
- Prevention of initial entry
- Improved initial assessments to make better a match of appropriateness and level of care

- Increase in percentage of enrolled children who obtain high school diploma or GED
- Reduction in percentage of enrolled children who drop out or are suspended or expelled from school
- Increase in employment of enrolled children over age sixteen that are not attending school
- Increase in percentage of enrolled children who participate in community activities
- Reduction in percentage of enrolled children who are involved in noncriminal aggression, are on runaway status, or who are adjudicated

Service Array

The nature of services are not necessarily any different from those historically being used to assist the children and their families. There is the use of case management, family-support and family-preservation services, therapeutic foster care, group care, mental health services, and others. There is a programmatic and financial incentive to provide more community-based, family-focused, and diversionary services. The management of care has the goal of using the traditional array of services differently and more strategically to the benefit of the child and family.

Funding

The primary funding streams have come through partnering with Medicaid agencies, public mental health, and child welfare. In some situations the funds were blended and pooled into a central authority. In other situations they were tracked separately, but used to support the goals of the program.

TANF (Temporary Assistance for Needy Families) funds were also used for child care for children in kinship and foster care.

Pricing

Two types of risk-sharing are being tried: One shares risk between the state and the county; the second shares risk between the public authority and the provider. In general, the method used for sharing risk has been through the establishment of case rates. Capitation is the method that is generally used for a defined population. This is harder to do for child welfare, where the defined population could be an entire community. An exception could be the youth currently in residential treatment with the goal of bringing them back into the community. The localities and the providers have felt it a better option to use a case rate with a defined range of services provided over a discreet period of time. The protections for the provider include a risk corridor in which the public authority establishes a stop/loss framework, including triggers to go to a fee-for-service payment strategy. The protection to the public authority is a warranty on the status of the child and family at the time of case closure, in which there is financial obligation to serve the child and family if there is reentry to the system within a certain designated time period.

Networks

The child welfare agencies could chose to act as their own managed care organization and establish their own provider network to deliver services. Alternatively, they could designate a lead agency that would have administrative functions over service delivery and might also provide some direct services as well. The tendency of child welfare agencies has been to provide the managed care function itself or to use private nonprofit agencies. The use of for-profit managed care entities is the exception rather than the rule.

Practice

Managed care in child welfare has created new practices. For example, the eligibility determination and gatekeeping function in some communities requires preauthorization by a team. In one community the individual child and family team makes the service plan and a community team that includes the contractor, the funding partners, public agency administrators, community members, and family members handles oversight and referral screening. Case management includes tracking of data related to outcomes and expenditures. System-of-care values and wraparound philosophy are encouraged. The agency may be the gatekeeper for mental health services but the managed care vendor determines the level of care and selects the provider.

WHAT PUBLIC AND PRIVATE ADMINISTRATORS NEED TO KNOW

Placing the Change in Context

Each community has made decisions regarding funding, administrative authority, and service delivery. Funds are received by some combination of federal, state, and local sources, each with its own sets of rules and procedures. In some states, the state has primary administrative responsibility. In other states, the counties or cities have primary authority. Finally, communities have made decisions regarding which of the services will be provided by public employees and which will be provided through private entities. The combination of public child welfare services and private community-based nonprofit organizations has been the bedrock of the child welfare service delivery system. The services provided by the community-based organizations have historically been paid on a contractual fee-for-service basis.

This system of joint public and private responsibility has generally served children and families, communities, and society well. However, in recent years, values in the political arena have changed and there is less support for public safety nets for small community-based agencies and more demands for increased cost efficiency. Public pressure is increasing to demonstrate observable results for the dollars spent. Court decisions and settlement agreements in over twenty states have highlighted difficulties in the current child welfare system. As noted in earlier sections, these factors, combined with the perceived success of managed care in the health and behavioral health arena, have led decision-makers to begin to transfer the managed care philosophy of care and technology to the child welfare arena. Managed care is being implemented in the name of greater efficiency, cost-effectiveness, and local control.

Under new managed care contracts, private child welfare agencies are being asked by public purchasers not only to deliver quality services but also to share potential rewards and financial risks in managing the money. Nonprofit child welfare executives are signing managed care contracts and assuming risks they barely understand. In this clamor for a new and better way of serving those in need, for-profit entities also see opportunities. Public purchasers, attracted by the capital, technology, and management skills that for-profit organizations bring to the table, have kept the market open to both for-profit and nonprofit agencies. Even traditional nonprofit agencies are finding new ways to collaborate with proprietary agencies, creating joint ventures or subcontracting with one another.

The presumed benefit of allowing competition and managed care approaches in the public sector social service marketplace is that it will lower costs and increase quality. Some of the new child welfare alliances created by managed care may, in fact, introduce needed innovation into an underfunded system. But, as public and private child welfare agency administrators embrace managed care, inherent conflicts and tensions should be recognized and time and resources should be committed to prepare for the transition. Managed care requires that public and private child welfare executives change how think about what they do and how they conduct business. At a minimum, private executives and public purchasers must be equipped with the knowledge, skills, and attitudes to handle their new responsibilities and guide their agencies into the future.

KNOWLEDGE, SKILLS, AND ATTITUDES

Few public or private child welfare administrators came to their current jobs equipped with formal education or a background in managed care. Until several years ago, this was not a serious barrier to managing a child welfare agency. But today, if public administrators and private providers are going to successfully shape and adapt managed care to fit the child welfare system and/or continue to advocate for managed health care systems that work for vulnerable populations, they must find opportunities to grasp the principles and tools of managed care and stay abreast of the changes in the behavioral health and child welfare marketplace nationwide.

Change Management

The move to managed care requires that public and private administrators acquire new knowledge and reassess values and attitudes. It requires them to manage the organizational culture-change process, reassess human resource needs, and shift the service delivery philosophy. It requires them to manage during times of rapid growth and organizational upheaval and reach out to new and unfamiliar partners. And, it requires them to create a process for developing new skills and new technologies throughout the agency.

In some instances, the public purchaser will specify in a Request for Proposal (RFP) or contract which new technologies and tools must be developed and used by the contract agency. In other cases, the potential bidder will be asked to describe current or proposed methodologies for meeting the requirements of the RFP. In either case, much of what s being asked for in new child welfare managed care contracts has not previously existed in the child welfare field. Both public purchasers and potential contractors need time and resources to create or adapt managed care tools to fit child welfare, and then they have to develop and implement a training program to prepare staff to use the tools to improve quality and enhance efficiency. Visionary child welfare leaders are not waiting for an RFP or contract to begin reengineering, product development, and skill building within the agency.

Cross-System Training to Support Integrated Systems of Care

In more recent years, there has been a growing recognition that both child welfare and behavioral health managed care systems can best achieve programmatic and fiscal goals if their plans are purposefully integrated or linked together. In many states and local communities, public purchasers across multiple systems are pooling resources and releasing interdepartmental RFPs to contract for integrated systems of managed care for children. To succeed in this effort, cross-system training is essential.

Planners and administrators in behavioral health managed care systems need to understand the unique needs of the child welfare population, the legal mandates of the system, the federal, state, and local funds supporting child welfare, the role of the courts in approving case plans and services, the complexity of the child welfare service system, and the role of traditional service providers.

Child welfare planners and administrators need cross-system training to develop and adapt the skills and technologies that have proven effective in managing high quality behavioral health services. For example, they need to adapt medical-necessity criteria to fit the social needs of the child welfare population, revise the credentialing requirements of providers to meet the casework needs of public and private staff, adapt the financing options to adjust to a system with inadequate or inaccurate data to price the system, and build the MIS capability to support the information-driven needs of managed care systems.

The Need for Multi-Level Training within an Agency

Since this is still a new and emerging trend, much of the training that has taken place has been targeted to the top administrators in an agency. Both public and private administrators must assure training for all levels of the agency's staff and board. Too often, managed care plans have failed to be smoothly implemented because staff were ill prepared and not invested in the system change.

Public agency administrators must begin to develop training to prepare staff for their new roles and responsibilities under new contract arrangements. Public agency administrators face challenging transition tasks—from having to address possible staff reduction, to low morale, to shifting from direct services to oversight responsibilities. They must also anticipate the challenges in moving to risk-based contracting—from cash flow problems to reporting difficulties.

The new risk-based contracts with providers, new service delivery options, and new management technologies will require a different skill mix of public sector staff. Efficiency in the use of staff can result in the merging of redundant positions, the elimination of some positions, and the creation of new positions requiring new skills. Public agencies with union agreements may have special challenges in making necessary changes in their staffing structure. At a minimum, public agency workers must be given the training and retraining opportunities to develop the skills needed to shift from direct services to new responsibilities related to contract oversight and quality assurance.

Private agency executives must create training opportunities to prepare their staff to assume new case management roles, use MIS technology and meet new reporting requirements, develop new clinical skills and management tools, learn how to create and manage or participate in networks, and prepare for the chaos inherent during times of rapid growth and upheaval. For providers operating under risk-share contracts, new risk-management skills and tools are essential. Governing boards must be prepared to make significant investments and weigh different options for strategically positioning the agency to survive.

Leadership in Addressing Attitudinal Challenges

As the child welfare field moves to managed care, staff culture and morale will be affected in both public and private agencies and administrators and supervisors must be equipped to address the human side of change. The transition to managed care may not suit every public or private administrator or staff member. After becoming familiar with managed care practices and technologies, child welfare administrators need to assess whether their personal values and beliefs and leadership styles are consistent with managed care philosophies and systems of care. They also have to create a forum for their staff members and other agency stakeholders to share concerns.

In order to succeed in the transition, the organization's leaders must work through the perceived and real cultural changes brought about by managed care and support the staff in adjusting to new roles and expectations. The following are among the most common concerns expressed by both administrators and staff members:

- The financial cost-containment emphasis is inconsistent with the agency's mission.
- Managed care will emphasize short-term indicators of progress at the expense of long-term outcomes.
- Criteria used to make clinical decisions regarding treatment will undermine individual clinical judgement.
- The agency will have financial incentives to restrict care in ways that jeopardize client well-being.
- The agency will lose its credibility and standing in the community.
- By participating in new collaborations, the agency will lose control over key decisions and cease to have its separate organizational culture.

Gaining Knowledge about Managed Behavioral Health Care

Most child welfare administrators first became interested in managed care in order to advocate for health and behavioral health managed care plans that better met the needs of the child welfare population. In the early 1990s, public and private administrators began receiving their basic training in managed care through training events planned for health or behavioral health care practitioners. At that time, managed health and behavioral health plans were already in place in most states. Child welfare leaders had not had a significant role in designing such systems and they were struggling to access the care needed by the children and families they served. They attended training conferences to learn about the principles, practices, and technologies of managed care.

These training events exposed child welfare administrators to core managed care concepts, such as gatekeeping and preauthorization for care, risk-based contracting options, provider panels and credentialing, the use of medical-necessity criteria and clinical protocols to guide decisions, utilization-management tools, new treatment methodologies, and the use of information systems to monitor costs and outcomes. After learning some of the basics, administrators were better prepared to navigate the maze of health and behavioral health care managed care plans erupting across the country.

Basic managed care training should ensure that participants have knowledge of:

- Centralized intake and eligibility requirements
- Gatekeeping and prospective authorization
- Medical-necessity criteria and the use of clinical protocols
- Coordinated case-management procedures
- Network development and credentialing
- Different financial risk-sharing options
- Claims adjudication and payment
- MIS requirements, including a central database of utilization, cost, claims, and performance information
- Outcomes-based treatment planning
- Prospective, concurrent, and retrospective utilization review
- Quality management and monitoring
- Grievance and appeals procedures

But few administrators left a behavioral health conference with an understanding of how these tools could be applied to child welfare services.

Applying Managed Care to Child Welfare

As it became clear that managed care systems were not going to be confined to the health care field, there was a critical need for additional training. In 1995, the Child Welfare League of America (CWLA) offered the first child welfare managed care training series designed specifically for public and private child welfare agency administrators. The goal was to take managed care constructs and have participants apply them to the finance and delivery of child welfare services through a simulated Request for Proposal (RFP) exercise.

Since managed care or privatization approaches change how child welfare services are managed, how they are reimbursed, and how they are organized and delivered, the proposal development exercise required public and private administrators to address key questions that would have to be answered in planning for managed care in real life. Proposals had to define:

- The broad goals of the plan
- The population to be covered

- The services and supports to be included in the plan and the services to be provided outside the plan
- How quality would be ensured and outcomes defined and measured under the plan
- How public and private roles would change
- How the plan would be funded and how risks would be shared

Implications for Public Purchasers and Private Providers

Managed care or privatization efforts continue to increase in number in the child welfare field. Forty-nine states and the District of Columbia responded to the 1998 CWLA Managed Care Institute survey (making a total of forty-seven initiatives). Of those responding, twenty-seven states reported one or more initiatives that include management or finance changes consistent with managed care or privatization models.

There is great variability in the scope of initiatives and timetables for implementing managed care or privatization efforts. A few states have already implemented statewide or large countywide initiatives, affecting entire child welfare populations and broad service areas. Most states are moving more slowly, using pilots to test innovative models before going statewide.

The process of developing these programs should include careful attention to the following issues that emerged in the CWLA survey: covered populations, services and supports, structural designs, quality and outcomes accountability, management changes, and different financial risk-sharing arrangements.

Covered Populations The survey attempted to find out which of the children and families in a community or state would be covered by the proposed initiative. Would plans cover all children who are at risk of abuse or neglect? Or only those who come to the attention of child welfare after an allegation of abuse or neglect? Or only those children with substantiated abuse or neglect histories? Or only those children in need of out-of-home care placement? Or only those children in the most restrictive, intensive out-of-home care settings? Or only those children in out-of-home care with diagnoses of serious emotional disturbance? Would initiatives cover the families of these children? If so, what services and supports would be provided to them?

As in previous years, findings indicate that the specific populations vary from one initiative to another, with most initiatives targeting children in custody and, specifically, those in out-of-home care settings. But in 1998, there was an increase in the number of initiatives that also include children at risk of placement, and also more plans focusing efforts on the families of children in custody and at risk of placement.

This finding has implications for both public purchasers and private executives. The child welfare field has had historically inaccurate or inadequate data about the children and families it serves. Under managed care contracts it becomes critical for the public purchaser to have information on the population's service needs and utilization history in order to accurately price the initiative. For the potential bidder, systems must be created or adapted to capture information on population characteristics and service utilization on an ongoing basis.

Services and Supports A central tenet of an effective managed care system is that a full array of services are in place for the covered population to ensure that individuals can access the services they need, when they need them, in the amount and intensity they need, in order to achieve desired outcomes in the most cost-effective manner. The survey attempted to find out which services and supports are included in each of the initiatives. Service areas covered by the various current or proposed initiatives vary, but most of the initiatives include out-of-home care options above the level of traditional family foster care. Case management is the most likely service to be included. Child Protective Service (CPS) intake and investigations and post-adoption supports and services are the least likely to be included.

Continuing a trend identified in 1997, it appears that some initiatives are focusing attention on the front-end of the child welfare system and are including a variety of services for at-risk families before or after the investigation phase of CPS to prevent placement.

Structural Designs There are many different structural designs for managed child welfare initiatives. In over half of the initiatives, the public agency

At a minimum, public and private administrators must develop the skills and technology to understand the service need characteristics of the target population, including:

- Conducting a demographic analysis by age, sex, and geographic area
- Creating client profiles of service need characteristics
- Understanding the most common presenting problems in the child and the family
- Developing knowledge of which populations are most and least likely to succeed
- Understanding the relationship between presenting problems and actual services used
- Understanding current performance related to key outcomes for the target population
- Tracking claims or encounter data for the target population

Both public and private administrators have to assess the current service array, identify gaps, and take steps to match services to the needs of the target population. In most communities this will require

- Significant restructuring
- Improved collaboration between the public and private sectors
- Creation of new preventive and community-based services to supplement or replace more restrictive service delivery options
- Reassessment of human resource skills needed to deliver and manage a full array of coordinated services.

is contracting for services in ways that stimulate the development of service-delivery networks, often managed by a lead, nonprofit agency, functioning as a managed care entity. The lead agency assumes varying levels of responsibility for coordinating and providing all the necessary care to the covered population, managing subcontracts with other providers in the network, and delivering some services. In a very few initiatives, the MCE is not a provider but rather a managed care organization (MCO) that is responsible for creating networks and managing the care of all children referred.

In other states, the public agency has incorporated managed care practices—such as more rigorous gatekeeping and utilization management procedures or the creation of cross-system public collaboratives—and the

After a careful strategic planning or positioning process, agency executives must:

- Re-examine the current service array, treatment philosophy and planning approach, and clinical capacity
- Fill in the service array to match the needs of the target population
- Find partners and create strategic alliances and collaborations
- Learn how to create or function in an integrated network
- Create a centralized intake and case-management process
- Develop and implement utilization management systems
- Develop and implement a cross-system, cross-agency training agenda for all levels of staff within the network to learn to use common protocols and treatment/case-planning methodologies.

Both public purchasers and private contractors have to develop skills and technologies to:

- Define and manage outcomes/indicators and measures
- Define and implement the MIS capability needed
- Manage critical information and monitor performance
- Continuously evaluate progress, and redesign systems to enhance performance
- Agree on what reports will be generated to provide timely, accurate information on the characteristics of children and families served, the services provided, the results of services, and the costs of care

public agency functions as the managed care entity. In some instances, public agencies across systems have created an interagency collaborative to manage the care of children across systems. The collaborative might also have a designated lead public agency that bears risk for managing care and resources within a set budget.

Again, the implications are obvious for public or private agencies that want to function as a lead agency and for those that want to be a part of a service-delivery network.

Quality and Outcomes Accountability The twin promises of managed care—cost containment and access to quality care—have to be closely monitored. Public agencies report a range of quality-assurance mechanisms and reporting requirements to ensure that clients have access to needed care and that contractors are accountable for achieving outcomes consistent with the legal mandates of the system.

In the majority of initiatives the public purchaser has set performance standards related to access, availability, and appropriateness of care, and established outcomes related to child and family functioning and permanency. Contractors are being monitored for progress in meeting specified goals. In some instances, financial bonuses and penalties are being linked to performance in key outcome areas.

States and counties are using multiple means to collect and manage quality and outcomes data. Since managed care systems are information-driven, many of the plans will rely heavily on reports generated from the automated MIS and provided to the state by the lead agency, managed care entity, or individual service providers.

Public purchasers have to define reporting requirements they will use to ensure quality in the initiatives they design, and they must ensure that staff responsible for quality and performance monitoring and oversight are trained to interpret the reports they receive and respond appropriately to any issues that arise.

Private contractors must demonstrate their ability to enter and report outcomes and quality data required in the contract. This will be the first time many agencies have had to have an externally monitored outcomes and quality-management approach to service delivery. It requires specially trained quality-assurance staff and an automated information system to manage real-time information and respond to external and internal quality-improvement requests.

Management Changes There are many ways the responsibility for managing child welfare services can be divided between public and private agencies. However, even when services are managed and delivered by private agencies that are bearing financial risks, the survey reveals that public agencies tend to remain involved to varying degrees in decision-making at key strategic points. If a managed care or privatized initiative is in place, the referral to the plan is done or approved by the public agency. In that regard the public agency remains the child welfare system's gatekeeper.

However, many private, nonprofit agencies under contract with public

---

Private agencies or other entities responsible for key management functions will have to develop tools and skilled staff to handle:

- Pre-authorization for care
- Gatekeeping
- Utilization management, including prospective, concurrent, and retrospective review
- Creation of provider networks and contract management with providers
- Tracking of data related to outcomes, expenditures, and quality
- Case management related to permanency planning
- Case management related to treatment decisions
- Billing, reimbursement, and claims adjudication
- Grievances and appeals

Because many tasks are shared between public and private agency staff, public/private agency cross training is essential to:

- Build trust
- Clarify roles and responsibilities
- Resolve day-to-day conflicts

---

purchasers are assuming many responsibilities and administrative tasks formerly held by public agencies. For example, some nonprofit providers have had to learn about federal and state claiming and reimbursement systems. All contractors bearing financial risks have had to develop new risk-management skills. Since all contracts require some quality and outcomes reporting, nonprofit agencies have had to develop mechanisms for documenting utilization and the results of services in new ways. In the case of lead agencies, they have had to develop contract-management and monitoring skills and learn how to manage and coordinate the care of individual children outside their agency walls.

A majority of public agencies retain certain duties, such as determining Medicaid and Title IV-E eligibility, contracting with managed care entities or lead agencies, overseeing and approving the development of certain level-of-care or service-necessity criteria, monitoring performance in key outcome and quality areas, and ensuring payment for services. It is most common for public agencies to contract for provider network development, provider contract management, utilization management, billing and reimbursement to providers in the network, quality monitoring, tracking of outcomes, and other critical data-reporting functions.

Different Financial Risk-Sharing Arrangements Seventy-four percent of the initiatives currently include or plan to include financial incentives or financial risk. Public purchasers vary in their approaches to risk—both in terms of the nature of the risk and how risk will be introduced into initiatives. When risk-sharing has been introduced, it has typically been between the public agency and a nonprofit entity. The level of risk ranges from capitation or case rates to lower-risk performance-based, incentivized contracts. Some initiatives will introduce financial risk-sharing from the initial implementation; others will phase in risk after some period of time.

The reimbursement rate gets set in various ways. In some initiatives, the public agency provides a spending ceiling in the Request for Proposal and allows the competitive bidding process to set the price parameters that are then negotiated in final contracts. The challenge with this method is that providers who are eager to win the business but inexperienced in managing risk-based contracts may seriously underprice their services. The public agency can also put a price on the services when the RFP is released. Bidders may then have to determine if they can survive the rate being proposed. If the public agency sets the rate, it is likely that the agency began by examining historical costs of purchasing similar services. It is also likely that the rate will not include the full costs of delivering and managing services. Under most initiatives it appears that the public agency expects the contractor to supplement the contract rate with funds from other sources—either other state or local dollars, grants or charitable dollars, or federal programs such as Medicaid. This expectation is explicit in most RFPs and contracts. The introduction of financial risk-sharing poses perhaps the greatest challenge to both public and private agency administrators. This is a new experience for both the purchaser and the contractor and the areas of uncertainty are great—from accurately pricing the system to being able to implement sound risk-management strategies to allow contractors to survive the risk over time. At a minimum, private agencies need to use state-of-the-art risk-management technologies and have trained staff responsible for tracking day-to-day utilization and cost data. The public agency contract-monitoring staff need to carefully review performance reports to ensure that quality and access are not being jeopardized as a means of containing costs.

TRAINING NEEDS FOR THE CHILD WELFARE PRACTITIONER

The earlier discussion focused on the general content issues related to child welfare and the skill and knowledge needs of child welfare administrators in both public and private agencies. This section will focus on the knowledge needs of the direct practitioner.

Why Train Child Welfare Practitioners?

When any system reform occurs, front-line service providers play a most important role in its success; however, they are often the last to be informed and trained in the changes that result from the reform. Managed care imposes changes in the roles and responsibilities for both public agency practitioners and for private providers as traditionally public functions are shifted to private providers or to managed care organizations. However, in any managed care or privatization initiative the child welfare system remains legally responsible (and under public scrutiny) for both the care of children in its custody and for appropriate decision-making and service for children and their families' needed child protective services.

Child Welfare Managed Care In child welfare managed care, *public agency social workers,* who had traditionally been the persons with the most direct contact with children and families, now have responsibility for overall case management and become contract managers, monitors, and quality assurance workers. On the other hand, direct service staff from *private provider agencies,* who formerly offered specific services to individual children, become responsible for managing all services, networking with other providers, complying with federal and state procedural requirements, and measuring and demonstrating outcomes. This is often done within a specified reimbursement rate for all services that allows the provider flexibility but no longer provides open-ended reimbursement for each service provided.

Health Care Child welfare practitioners must learn a new set of skills in addressing managed health care systems. Prior to managed care they had the authority to control referrals paid for through Medicaid on a fee-for-service basis. They had more influence on the type, level, and duration of services. In managed health care, they are reliant on other independent organization such as the MCO for authorization and delivery of health and behavioral health services. These MCOs typically retain both the decision-making authority and the financial risk related to the health care services that are provided.

Child welfare workers need to be knowledgeable about the details of the health plans, benefits, requirements, and procedures for access. Their role is shifting from provider of service or even purchaser of service to that of advocate for appropriate and timely services and of facilitator, assisting families to navigate the managed care system.

Private practitioners also must change the way that they work. In a ten-state analysis of the impact of health care reform on children with significant behavioral health care needs, respondents described a range of changes in front-line practice attributed to managed care reforms. The use of briefer, more problem-focused approaches to treatment was reported in all ten states, as was increased paperwork requirements. According to stakeholders, managed care reforms have resulted in the need to train child- and adolescent-service providers, specifically in brief interventions and also in various home- and community-based service approaches, which are in increased demand as reduction in length of stay in hospitals and residential care requires providers to work with children and adolescents in more vulnerable or fragile conditions.

What the Training Should Look Like As noted above, the impact and knowledge needs of practitioners vary according to their specific role in the service-delivery system. There are distinct audiences that will be discussed in this section:

- Public and private child welfare practitioners new to managed care
- Front-line staff in MCOs and private providers new to child welfare

Child Welfare

As a baseline, all front-line practitioners, whether in public or private agencies, need to have the basic content on managed care, as noted in the section for administrators. Whether the managed program is the child welfare services or external services such as health or behavioral health, the practitioners will need to understand the operations of the system sufficient to interact in a manner sufficient to promote the needs of the child and family.

The most significant change for many front-line *public practitioners* is the shift from the role of service provider and case manager to the roles of monitoring and oversight functions. It becomes the public practitioner's responsibility to assure that someone else (the MCO or private provider) provides comprehensive services for children and families. To function in this new role the practitioner will need to master skills such as

- Managing critical information
- Utilization review
- Measuring and tracking outcomes
- Determining consumer (youth and family) satisfaction

Public practitioners will feed the information they gather back to agency administrators so that the managed care initiative is continually assessed and adapted to meet family and child service needs. Practitioners will be responsible for assuring the providers are working with other child-serving systems, community resources, and families in a collaborative, team-driven model.

MCOs not Familiar with Child Welfare

Just as child welfare practitioners must learn skills required to function in a managed care environment, MCOs and other private entities entering this process now must understand both how the child welfare system works and the strengths and needs of the children and families it services. The ten-state analysis conducted in 1997 found that in all of the states using for-profit MCOs in health care reform initiatives, respondents complained that the MCOs were unfamiliar with the Medicaid population in general and in particular with children with emotional disorders, adolescents with substance-abuse problems, and children involved in the child welfare system. A 1997–98 survey of all states showed that just less than half of these states were offering training to MCOs and providers related to children and families involved in the child welfare system.

For MCOs and private providers unfamiliar with the child welfare system, at a minimum training in the following areas should be provided so that they may adequately service children and families: goals and statutory requirements, core values, family dynamics, role of the court, state-of-the-art treatment approaches, and funding sources.

Goals and Statutory Requirements Child welfare and behavioral health systems operate under different statutory requirements that create differing missions for each system. Child welfare systems are mandated to service all children in need of protection and are guided by goals of safety, permanence, and child well-being. Meeting these goals may involve providing long-term care, treatment, and supports. Behavioral health systems are charged with reducing symptoms and improving functioning in the child's environment. As mentioned previously, managed care systems typically implement this mission through short-term treatment models. "Mission collision" may occur when the child welfare system goal of safety and permanence leads to a different assessment of treatment and support needs for a child than the assessment made by the behavioral health system, which sees its role as limited to providing active treatment interventions for diagnosable disorders. For example, an MCO may order that a child be discharged from a psychiatric hospital because adequate interventions have been provided for his most immediate needs. However, due to lack of appropriate step-down services in the community or a safe placement setting, the child welfare system believes that this child's safety would be in danger if he were to leave the hospital. Appropriately trained practitioners in both systems are more likely to find a solution to such a mission collision than those who do not understand the system goals and statutory requirements

Because statutory requirements that guide the child welfare system change, it is important that professional education programs and agency administrators stay abreast of current driving legislation. Current and past key legislation that all MCOs and private providers should understand includes, but is not limited to, the 1980 Adoption Assistance and Child Welfare Act (PL 96-272), the National Child Abuse Prevention and Treatment Act, the Family Preservation and Support Services Program (name changed to the Promoting Safe and Stable Families Program in 1997), the 1997 Adoption and Safe Families Act, and the 1996 Personal Responsibility and Work Opportunity Reconciliation Act (welfare reform).

Core Values It is also imperative that MCOs and private provider practitioners understand the core values that frame the approach to services. In 1994 two national organizations, the American Public Welfare Association and the National Association of State Mental Health Program Directors, worked to identify values, principles, and practices common to both child welfare and mental health that should be used to develop partnerships among the two systems and to guide the creation of systems of care for children, youth, and their families. They specified the following core values:

- *Be Family-Centered.* The needs of the child and family dictate the theory of services provided. Families are the single best place for a child. When a child's safety cannot be guaranteed within the family, provide an alternative home-like setting in the least restrictive environment possible, and maintain relationships between the family of origin and the child while planning for reunification.
- *Be Community-Based.* Children's needs can best be met within the context of their community. Therefore, the locus of service as well as the management and decision-making should rest at the community level.
- *Respect and Value Cultural Diversity.* All components of a system of care must ensure respect for cultural and racial diversity and cultural competency in policy development, program administration, service delivery, and program evaluation.
- *Seek Permanency.* All must recognize the need for and value of permanent, stable relationships for all children and youth and must develop practices to ensure that children are placed in stable, permanent settings.

Family Dynamics Out-of-home placements create new dynamics for both children and parents. In spite of efforts to provide stable placements, many children in the child welfare system continue to experience multiple placements and have ties to several families. Treatment providers and persons who authorize services must understand attachment issues and the dynamics created by multiple placements in order to provide appropriate services and to include all of the persons involved with the child. Foster families and adoptive families too often find themselves working with service providers who do not understand the special complexities of their families.

Role of the Courts Juvenile and family court judges are the gatekeepers of the nation's foster care system. They ultimately decide wither families in crisis will be broken apart and children placed in foster care or whether placement can be safely avoided. Judges make critical legal decisions and oversee social service efforts to rehabilitate and maintain families or provide permanent alternative care for child victims. Their involvement in all child service system reforms is absolutely essential. To successfully work with children and families served by the child welfare systems, MCOs and private practitioners must understand and accept the role of the courts.

State-of-the-Art Treatment Approaches MCOs and private practitioners must provide access to state-of-the-art treatment approaches such as systems of care, the wraparound service process, family group conferencing, and family-centered alcohol and drug treatment programs.

Funding Sources Multiple federal state and local funding sources are available for children served by the child welfare system, (e.g., Title IV-E, Title IV-B, Temporary Assistance for Needy Families, Social Services Block Grant, Title XIX–Medicaid). In addition, other child-serving systems—such as mental health, education, juvenile justice, and health, as well as special foundation projects—fund services for these same children and families. As complicated as funding streams may be, it is critical for practitioner to know what sources of funds can be used to pay for various services. This knowledge serves as a tool to enhance the opportunity to provide comprehensive services to avoid funding wars among agencies, to fill service gaps, and to provide a seamless system for families and children.

NOTES TO EDUCATORS AND TRAINERS

This chapter has provided an overview of the multiple issues of concern regarding child welfare and managed care. As noted, managed care interfaces with child welfare due to the fact that child welfare systems must use services that are now managed, such as health or mental health. In addition, the child welfare itself may use managed care tools in its own system reform or as part of a multisystem reform effort. In addition to the complexities of the structures of the reforms, the managed care tasks include a variety of participants: federal, state, and local (city/county), public and private child welfare agencies, and not-for-profit and for-profit managed care entities. There are a host of educational needs that are unique to each stakeholder of the system.

The most central need of trainers at the in-service education level is to assure that all levels of all of the systems involved have the baseline information on the policies, procedures, values, and principles guiding the various systems involved in the managed care endeavor. In general, the content will need to address the changes in roles and functions brought about by the reform or restructuring. As with most managed care initiatives, skills involving data-driven decision-making in a time-sensitive, least restrictive level of care will be essential. Within the child welfare arena, the issues of safety and legally mandated public accountability are core issues that guide and drive decision-making. The structure and pricing of services will need to account for this significant issue.

Pre-service education needs to account for the changing environment. Most notably, those in preparation for administration and management functions will need to be prepared to function in a role in which the emphasis is shifting from managing large bureaucracies to managing multiple contracts, financial risk arrangements, and extensive data analysis. Similarly, the preparation for practice requires the skills to work with data-driven, cost- and time-aware systems. Practitioners will need to develop capacity for flexibility in intervention strategies in the direction of community-based interventions. Students will need to adopt a value for constant learning to stay abreast of cutting-edge interventions as they evolve. In addition, they will need to learn to work alongside families and consumers in intervention planning rather than play the "expert." Collaboration at the system and case level is a key skill.

In summary, the challenge to educators is to prepare students to be innovators. Managed care represents a strategy of innovation that deliberately includes costs and measurable outcomes as part of the equation for decision-making regarding human services. It represents a factor that had not been examined sufficiently in the past. Managed care is not a magical potion. Communities are still struggling with how to be healthy, nurturing, and self-renewing entities. The practitioners and decision makers of today need to be able to master the technology of today's environment, but our future is dependent on the innovations made toward the goal of healthy communities.

REFERENCES

American Public Welfare Association, the Federation of Families for Children's Mental Health, the National Association of State Mental Health Program Directors. (1994). *Child welfare, children's mental health, and families: a partnership for action.* Washington, DC: National Technical Assistance Center for Children's Mental Health, Georgetown University.

Board of Children, Youth and Families, Commission on Behavioral and Social Sciences and Education. (1996). *Paying attention to children in a changing health care system.* Washington, DC: National Academy Press.

Connecticut Department of Children and Families. (1999, February). *IV-E waiver demonstration project: Singe contract/continuum of care: A state initiative to restructure the delivery and funding of residential services.* Paper presented at the Child Welfare League of America Conference, Washington, DC.

Ferriman, D. (no date given). *Issues to be considered in developing managed care in child welfare.* [Newsletter]. Franklin County, OH: Franklin County Children Services.

Foley, R. (1997). Issues for consideration in the privatization of child welfare services. *Family Matters, Dec/Jan.*, 6–7.

Jackson, V. (1994). *A brief look at managed mental health care.* Washington, DC: NASW Press.

Jackson, V. (Ed). (1995). *Managed care resource guide for social workers in agency settings.* Washington, DC: NASW Press.

McCullough, C. (1996). *Managed care and child welfare: Is your agency prepared?* Washington, DC: Child Welfare League of America.

McCullough, C., & Schmitt, B. (1998). *Managed care and privatization child welfare tracking project: 1998 state and county survey results.* Washington, DC: Child Welfare League of America.

Osher, T., McCarthy, J., Koyanagi, C., Pires, S., & Webman, D. (1997). Achieving success at managing integrated systems for children and families: Critical consideration. *Behavioral Healthcare Tomorrow, 6*(5), 40–47.

Oss, M. (1999, February). *Emerging trends in child mental health care.* Paper presented at the Child Welfare League of America Conference, Washington, DC.

Pires, S.A., Armstrong, M. I., & Stroul, B.A. (1999). *Health care reform tracking project: Tracking state managed care reforms as they affect child and adolescents with behavioral health disorders and their families—1997–1998 state survey.* Tampa, FL: Research and Training Center for Children's Mental Health, University of South Florida.

Publication Development Committee, Victims of Abuse Project. (1995). *Resource guidelines: Improving court practice in child abuse and neglect cases.* Reno, NV: National Council of Juvenile and Family Court Judges.

Schulzinger, R., McCarthy, J., Meyers, J., Irvine, M., & Vincent, P. (1999). *Health care reform tracking project: Tracking state managed care reforms as they affect children and adolescents with behavioral health disorders and their families: A special analysis—child welfare managed care reform initiatives: The 1997/98 state survey.* Washington, DC: National Technical Assistance Center for Children's Mental Health, Georgetown University.

Simms, M., & Halfon, N. (1994). The health care needs of children in foster care: A research agenda. *Child Welfare, 73*(5), 505–523.

Stroul, B. A., Pires, S.A., & Armstrong, M.E. (1998). *Health care reform tracking project: Tracking state health care reforms as they affect children and adolescents with behavioral health disorders and their families—1997 impact analysis.* Tampa, FL: Research and Training Center for Children's Mental Health, University of South Florida.

◆ CHAPTER 7 ◆

Managed Care and Care Management for Older Adults

SCOTT MIYAKE GERON

Contending with a medical emergency, health problem, or chronic illness is never easy. For older adults, who are more likely to have health limitations, cognitive impairment, or problems with memory, and less education than younger adults, facing health problems can be particularly difficult. The vulnerability of the elderly population has long been recognized in American society—the elderly are almost the only constituency in the United States with an entitlement of health insurance. Virtually all elderly Americans receive their health insurance from Medicare, the landmark health care program for people over sixty-five. Today, more than six million older adults participate in managed care through the Medicare program, 16% of all Medicare beneficiaries (Gage, 1997).

As other authors in this book have described, the U.S. health care system has undergone profound changes in the past two decades. The development of managed care and other new forms of delivering care, the change from fee-for-service and retrospective payment to capitated and prospective financing systems, the growth of investor-owed hospital and nursing home chains and other organizations providing care, and the emergence of a new array of settings outside of the hospital where services are delivered have combined to fundamentally alter the health care landscape. The Medicare program—and hence health care for older adults—played a bellwether role in initiating these changes. In 1983, the Medicare program instituted a prospective payment system called Diagnostic Related Groups (DRGs) to reimburse hospitals for treatment for Medicare beneficiaries (Rogers, Draper, Kahn, Keeler, Rubenstein, Kosecoff & Brook, 1990). In other ways, however, the Medicare program has been one of the last major segments of the health care industry to change, with a smaller percentage of elderly Americans receiving managed care than younger adults. Still, an increasing numbers of older people are enrolled in managed care plans, and current estimates are that more than 25 percent of the Medicare population will be enrolled in managed care plans by the year 2002 (Dallek, 1998).

Older people potentially have much to gain from managed care, given their particular health and financial needs and the focus in managed care on prevention and follow-up. Managed care theoretically could be more coordinated, more efficient, more cost-effective. But will managed care actually provide better care for less cost, as its proponents claim, or will the incentives in the system lead to "management" of care simply by providing less care or substandard care for this most vulnerable population?

This chapter will review recent developments in Medicare managed care for older adults, and will address the questions of whether the system of managed care is working for older adults. If so, how? If not, what are the barriers to its use? The first section describes the health and related service needs of older adults, highlighting some of the unique service issues that make the application of managed care to this population promising but also problematic. The second section summarizes the Medicare program and discusses specific federal efforts to promote acute and post-acute managed care plans. Existing research on these programs is reviewed, with special attention paid to low-income elderly and persons with chronic and service illnesses. A third section describes private initiatives to manage long-term care or acute care and long-term care combined, such as Social Health Maintenance Organizations (S/HMOs) and the Program for All-Inclusive Care for the Elderly (PACE) demonstrations. We conclude by briefly examining how a single example of an intervention that has long been used in providing care to older people—case management, or care management as it is now more commonly called—is currently being adapted for use in managed care.

HEALTH CARE AND RELATED SERVICE NEEDS OF OLDER ADULTS

Older adults share some health and service needs with other patient populations, but also are more likely to have chronic and long-term care service needs that pose special burdens. As adults age, they are more likely than younger adults to require expensive medical treatment (including the use of prescription drugs) and to develop chronic health problems (Kane & Kane, 1997). Older adults who need long-term care and personal-assistant services typically also need acute care from time to time, requiring an integration between these two service sectors. Sometimes their need for long-term care is precipitated by an episode of acute care and sometimes long-term care customers experience acute exacerbations of a chronic condition.

Efforts to address the social, health, and long-term-care needs of elderly Americans are hampered by existing fragmentation in funding and service provision. Paying for health or long-term care privately is an enormous financial burden that few can meet. Among government programs, Medicare is largely responsible for financing acute care, while another set of programs (Medicaid, Older Americans Act, and various state-funded programs) finances long-term care. Unlike Medicare, which is primarily an age-based entitlement program assuring almost universal coverage to acute care for adults aged sixty-five and above, Medicaid is a means-tested welfare-type state program administered by the states that requires older adults to spend down their resources in order to quality for support for long-term care. In the present system, each level of government has incentives to shift costs to another, and has little incentive to save money for other levels of government. Care provision is similarly fragmented, with one set of organizations and delivery systems responsible for acute care (including hospitals, ambulatory clinics, and physicians' practices for acute care) and another for nursing homes, home care agencies, and long-term care services.

ACUTE AND POST-ACUTE MANAGED CARE

Since almost all elderly people get health insurance through Medicare, understanding Medicare is essential to understanding the growth of Medicare managed care for this population. The original Medicare program was modeled after the system of "third-party" employment-based insurance developed in the decades after World War II for younger, working adults. Like these private plans, Medicare beneficiaries paid only a fraction of the true cost of care and providers (doctors, hospitals, nursing homes, pharmacists, and so on) were reimbursed on a fee-for-service basis or retrospectively. As third parties, both private insurers and government programs effectively insulated patients from the true cost of treatment decisions. Under this system, the consumers, doctors, hospitals, and other health providers bore little to none of the financial risk for the cost of care; moreover, because providers received more reimbursement if they provided more services, they had an incentive to maximize the volume of services.

The original fee-for-service Medicare has two parts. Part A covers hospital care, post-acute care (rehabilitation, skilled nursing facility care, and skilled home health), and 80% of the cost of durable medical equipment and is universally available to all beneficiaries. Part B, which covers physician/special services, is an optional program for which beneficiaries must pay monthly premiums. Importantly, Medicare does *not* provide coverage for long-term care in nursing homes or other residential settings, and Medicare also does not provide coverage for outpatient prescription drugs. Several types of Medicare supplemental insurance policies (called "Medigap") have been available to supplement the benefits provided by Medicare, with some options paying for prescription drugs, deductibles, and premiums.

Beginning in 1980, the Health Care Financing Administration (HCFA), the federal agency that administers the Medicare program, funded a set of demonstrations to test the feasibility of enrolling Medicare beneficiaries by health maintenance organizations (HMOs). In 1982, Congress passed the Tax Equity and Fiscal Responsibility Act (TEFRA), establishing a program of risk-based, capitated Medicare HMOs, which became known as TEFRA HMOs. Medicaid beneficiaries were paid a fixed amount per beneficiary enrolled per month. Participating managed care plans were, therefore, at financial risk if their costs exceeded the payment amount and, for the same reason, they profited if costs fell below the payment. These managed care organizations were responsible for providing the beneficiary with the same benefits he or she would receive under the regular Medicare program. In most cases, additional benefits were offered without additional premiums and with low costs to the enrollee in order to attract beneficiaries. Popular additional benefits include preventive services, outpatient drugs, eye exams and eyeglasses, hearing exams and hearing aides, and dental services.

In 1985, HCFA established new Medicare payment rules based on TEFRA of 1982. The new payment structure reimbursed plans 95% of what it cost to care for regular Medicare program beneficiaries who lived in the same county. Plans were permitted to keep the difference between the program payment and their allowable costs. The risk-adjusted payment amount, called AAPCC for "adjusted average per capita cost," is adjusted for geographic cost differences and differences in age, gender, Medicaid eligibility (yes or no), institutional (nursing home) status, employment status, and basis of Medicare eligibility (disability or age). Initially, enrollment grew rapidly under this new payment formula, from 32 plans in 1985 to 152 in 1987; however, enrollment began to decline in 1988, and between 1988 and 1990 57% of the plans had dropped out of the program, citing financial losses (Gage, 1997).

Participation began to increase again in 1990 for a number of reasons. Managed care organizations, who had already begun to dominate the health insurance market for younger adults, began to view Medicare as a viable new area of expansion. Because the AAPCC payment structure is essentially a variation of fee-for-service, the payment rates were relatively high in some areas, and thus attractive to managed care organizations. The attraction of these plans to older adults also reflected the difficulty in finding an affordable way to pay for the gaps in basic Medicare coverage. Many elders were being forced out of the traditional Medicare plan because of the rising costs of Medigap insurance, which can now cost anywhere from $400 to $7,000 a year (Dallek, 1998; Pham, 1999). In contrast, most Medicare managed care plans offer prescription drugs and other benefits not covered by regular Medicare at no cost or less cost to members. Additionally, the Medicare program began an initiative designed to promote greater participation and consumer choice. In October 1995, Medicare provided guidelines to Medicare risk plans regarding a point-of-service (POS) benefit for members of these plans. The POS benefit allows plan members to go outside of the plan's network of health care providers to receive health care services, although covered services are limited and members are typically responsible for a larger share of the cost for those out-of-plan services. For all of these reasons, enrollment has increased steadily so that, by May 1998, about 6.3 million (or 16%) of Medicare's beneficiaries were enrolled in managed care plans.

Is managed care working for these elders? The first point to realize is that, given the restrictions of the Medicare program to acute or post-acute care, the large majority of Medicare managed care options are limited to these areas. Thus, one of the major health care needs of older adults when they experience chronic illnesses—the need to integrate acute and long-term care—is not met by most of the existing Medicare managed care plans. In the next section, we will review recent efforts by states and local agencies and demonstration programs supported by the Medicare program to address this issue.

Research on managed care programs for the delivery of acute care to the elderly is comparatively recent, and the results of the relatively few evaluations are mixed. As previously noted, most Medicare managed care plans provide prescription drugs and other benefits that are not provided in the regular Medicare program—an attractive feature for all elders, but especially for those with low incomes. In general, studies show that the quality of Medicare managed care is generally as good as care provided in traditional fee-for-services plans, but has not achieved the kinds of outcomes in cost, patient health status, and functioning that most proponents of managed care had expected. Alarmingly, there is a growing body of evidence to suggest that older adults most in need of health care—e.g., those with the most severe chronic illnesses—fare worse in managed care plans than in traditional Medicare.

For example, in a follow-up to their comprehensive 1994 analysis of managed care and fee-for-service delivery systems, Miller and Luft (1997) reviewed fifteen recent evaluations and found that an equal number demonstrated better and worse HMO results compared with non-HMO plans. Three of the five studies with significant negative HMO results included samples of patients with chronic conditions or diseases most in need of care.A study by John Ware and his colleagues (1996) confirmed these findings. Their study examined differences in four-year outcomes for the elderly and for poor, chronically ill patients treated in HMOs compared to fee-for-service systems. Patients were selected who were between eighteen and ninety-seven years of age living in Boston, Chicago, or Los Angeles who had any of five chronic problems: hypertension, non-insulin-dependent diabetes mellitus, recent acute myocardial infarction, congestive heart failure, and depressive disorder. For elderly Medicare patients, declines in physical health were significantly more common in HMOs than in fee-for-service plans. Mental health outcomes were significantly better for elderly patients in HMOs in one site, but not in the other two study sites.

Several studies suggest that older persons with chronic problems receive fewer services in managed care plans than in the regular Medicare program. Findings from a series of studies by Mathematica, Inc. of the Medicare TEFRA HMO programs indicated that HMO enrollees were not as likely to receive as many chronic and long-term care services (home health care, rehabilitative services) as those in the fee-for-service sector, they had fewer visits with their physicians, and they reported somewhat lower satisfaction with the quality of care received (Brown, Bergeron, Clement, Hill & Retchin, 1993). Shaughnessy, Schlenker, and Hittle (1994) compared home health care use and patient outcomes in Medicare HMO patients and regular Medicare patients and found that the Medicare HMO patients received fewer home visits and had longer intervals between visits than fee-for-service Medicare patients. They also found that the fee-for-service patients had significantly better health status and service utilization outcomes than the HMO patients and that the costs of home services in the HMOs averaged two-thirds those of the fee-for-service Medicare costs for similar services. In a more recent study, Stone and Nutfeld (1998) found little empirical evidence suggesting significant differences between managed care and fee-for-service for the typical Medicare beneficiary, but did find that persons with multiple health conditions had more limited access to certain specialized services and may be receiving poorer quality of care.

The broader context of these findings is that our limited experience with Medicare managed care programs to date reveals problems of "risk selection"—that is, of the tendency of plans to select patients who are at lower risk of incurring high health costs. As other writers in this book have described, segmentation of the healthy from the sick is one of the major problems with managed care for younger adults. Risk selection poses a potentially serious barrier to care for the elderly, who are more likely to use health services than younger adults, but particularly serious access problems for older adults with severe health problems. Several analysts have noted the AAPCC payment mechanism for Medicare managed care does not sufficiently adjust for risk. Without adequate risk adjustment, plans have incentives to enroll relatively health patients and incentives to discourage patients who have or who are likely to have severe health problems. Even those plans that do not discriminate may find themselves at a competitive disadvantage in the market if other plans attract relatively health patients away from these plans. Examination of enrollment and disenrollment patterns in Medicare HMOs confirms that Medicare beneficiaries choosing to enroll in Medicare HMOs tend to be younger and healthier, while disenrollment rates were higher for those who were older than eighty-five years of age, were disabled, black, and had Medicaid coverage (Riley, Ingber & Tudor, 1997; Morgan, Virnig, DeVito & Persily, 1997).

In the coming years, the managed care environment for Medicare beneficiaries will be profoundly affected by the Balanced Budget Act of 1997 (BBA). The legislation contained a host of controversial proposals to address rising costs in the Medicare program, several of which are designed to encourage Medicare beneficiaries to choose a risk-based, capitated health plan rather than traditional Medicare. The BBA created Part C of Medicare, authorizing the program to contract with a host of new of new types of plans, referred to as Medicare + Choice. Medicare beneficiaries will have the choice of unrestricted fee-for-service plans, managed care plans with or without a POS option, preferred provider organizations (PPOs), provider sponsored organizations (PSOs), and a limited medical savings acount (MSA), a type of voucher program. The BBA also eliminated the provision that plans have more than half of their members as Medicare beneficiaries. Continuous enrollment and disenrollment, provisions which allow beneficiaries to sample a managed care plan but also to return if they choose to regular Medicare, were also changed. Through 2001, Medicare enrollees will be able to disenroll from any of these choices and return to traditional fee-for-service Medicare or join another plan at any time during the year. In future years, enrollees will face restrictions on the time in which they may enroll or disenroll in a plan.

These changes present further challenges to Medicare's traditional role of providing universal coverage for all older adults. Theoretically, Medicare's new choices will encourage the growth of health plan options that are responsive to the needs of patients, and that hopefully provide more coordinated and affordable care with no decline in quality. However, moving Medicare to emulate the private insurance market poses significant risks of increasing the "risk selection" problem described earlier. Medicare beneficiaries will self-select plans with lower premiums, and those premiums will remain low if the plan they choose has relatively more healthy than sick people. Similarly, health plans have incentives to favorably select relatively healthy enrollees, as these members will use less resources on average and generate greater profits as a result. Unfortunately, Medicare's experience with the BBA suggests that this type of "risk selection" is already taking place. Last year, more than ninety managed care plans that had offered some type of risk-based Medicare managed care plans withdrew or curtailed their Medicare options, leaving more than 400,000 beneficiaries with few Medicare options (Hatch, 1998).

INTEGRATING ACUTE AND LONG-TERM CARE IN MANAGED CARE

Although most managed care for older adults to date has been directed at acute care, some promising developments include long-term care as well. Two of the most highly visible federal demonstration programs have involved an integration of acute care and long-term care on a capitated basis. The Social Health Maintenance Organization (S/HMO) demonstrations, begun in 1985 with four sites and eventually expanded to ten in 1995, provide all acute and ambulatory services available in the regular Medicare program, plus preventive medical care. S/HMOs also provide chronic and long-term care services to members who are assessed as eligible for nursing home care. Because S/HMOs receive a higher institutional rate for these patients even if the member remains in the community and receives no extra long-term care services, there is an incentive to maintain members in the community (Manton, Newcomer, Lowrimore, Vertrees & Harrington, 1993; Macko, Dunn, Blech, Ashby & Schwab, 1995). If the S/HMO member is on Medicaid, the plans entered into a capitation with the state for the Medicaid component of the expenditures. S/HMOs receive 100% of the Medicare AAPCC for the geographic area they serve (unlike 95% of the AAPCC received by Medicare HMOs). In order to keep premiums competitive with other Medicare HMOs, the level of long-term benefits in the S/HMOs is relatively modest, and the S/HMOs were able to limit the number of enrollees with deficits in activities of daily living.

The other major federal demonstration designed to integrate acute and long-term care services is the Program for All-Inclusive Care for the Elderly (PACE) demonstration (Kane, Illston & Miller, 1992; Branch, Coulam & Zimmerman, 1995). The PACE program is a replication of On Lok Senior Services in San Francisco, which was established in 1971. Like that model, PACE is targeted to frail, low-income older persons who are eligible for nursing home care but are living in their home or community. The programs are funded by pooling the enrollees's Medicare and Medicaid premiums. Members eligible only for Medicaid or for both Medicaid and Medicaid pay nothing, but those eligible only for Medicare pay a monthly premium. Funds are paid to a provider who is then responsible for providing (directly or under contract) the full range of Medicare and Medicaid benefits. The PACE programs operate as staff model HMOs in which the physicians are employees of the program, with most services coordinated and provided by a multidisciplinary team with training in geriatrics. PACE programs are built around regular attendance at adult day health centers, where enrollees receive preventive and primary care services and participate in social activities. The results of initial asssessments of the PACE projects have suggested positive patient outcomes, lower nursing home utilization, and cost savings over traditional Medicare HMOs (Eng, Padulla, Eleazer, McCann & Fox, 1997).

Some Medicare HMO demonstrations have been targeted at special long-term care populations. One of these is EverCare, a Minnesota-based program operated by United Health Care which is designed to improve nursing home care for Medicare beneficiaries and decrease hospitalizations from nursing homes (Kane, Kane, Kaye, Mollica, Riley, Saucier, Snow & Starr, 1996). EverCare enrolls nursing home residents under a conventional risk-based Medicare HMO. Medicare-related costs under Part A (hospitals) and Part B (physician services) are covered, while costs for providing nursing home care beyond the post-acute care covered by Medicare are not included in the plan. Evercare is operating at six locations (Minneapolis/St. Paul, Boston, Baltimore, Atlanta, Phoenix, and Tampa).

In the past several years, numerous states have begun or have planned initiatives to integrate Medicare and Medicaid resources to provide health and/or long-term services to low-income elderly and persons with disabilities who are eligible for both programs—the "dually eligible." Ten states—Arizona, California, Illinois, Kentucky, Nebraska, Oregon, Pennsylvania, Tennessee, Utah, and Washington—require some of all of the Medicare beneficiaries also covered by Medicaid to participate in managed care for the

Medicaid acute care services (Mollica & Riley, 1997). Capitation for acute and long-term-care services is very limited, although planning in several states has begun. Minnesota is the first state to operate a program that combines Medicaid and Medicare funding and an acute and long-term care service delivery system. The Minnesota Senior Health Options (MSHO), which operates in the Minneapolis/St. Paul area, is a voluntary program in which enrollees have a choice of three plans. Arizona has operated a capitated Medicaid long-term-care system for the frail elderly and persons with developmental disabilities for the past eight years, but Medicare benefits continue to be provided on a fee-for-service basis. The Arizona Long-Term Care System (ALTCS) covers all traditional Medicaid program services, including mental health services, nursing home care, intermediate care for persons with developmental disabilities, and home and community-based long-term care services. Colorado, a consortium of New England states, and several other states have begun plans for similar programs.

These programs, while promising, remain limited in scope. The S/HMO and PACE demonstrations provide the best experience with capitated long-term and acute care. The S/HMOs provide only limited long-term care benefits as part of an HMO plan, and provide only limited coverage to low-income persons or persons with severe disabilities. The PACE demonstrations, which are directly targeted to serve this population, have such high program expenditures that they are unlikely to serve as an affordable option for most people. Both programs have had difficulty attracting enrollees, and neither program has successfully demonstrated that their approaches for combining long-term care and acute care into a single program can serve as a feasible model for care for most older Americans.

CARE MANAGEMENT AND MANAGED CARE

In this final section, we examine in detail how one service that has evolved to play a critical role in coordinating care for older adults has been adapted to managed care. Over the past twenty years, care management has occupied a central place in efforts to help coordinate care for the frail elderly and others with chronic care needs in the United States and abroad (Applebaum & Austin, 1990; Austin, 1987; Kodner, 1993; Geron & Chasler, 1994; Challis, Darton, Hughes, Huxley & Stewart, 1998). Originally funded in large part by federal and state initiatives and developed by private service agencies as a way to coordinate home-based services to frail elders residing in the community, care management has evolved with new applications, models of practice, and target populations. Recent managed care applications include health insurance policies that use care management services to coordinate services for beneficiaries with chronic or long-term care needs; private practice care management that has grown in response to demands for services from individuals ineligible for or not wishing to participate in publicly funded programs (Mahoney, Parker & Geron, 1997); and care management in capitated funding environments such as the S/HMOs and PACE demonstrations, in which a broad range of acute and long-term care services may be within the authorization purview of care managers (Kane et al., 1996).

Care management has a number of features that make it an attractive service model for managed care, particularly for integrating acute and long-term care. Care managers are experienced at conducting the kind of multidimensional psychosocial assessments needed in managed care to identify the social, health, and service needs of patients who still reside in the community but have episodic acute care needs. The boundaries of care management have long extended beyond a single-service setting, making care management useful as a way to integrate fragmented services. Care managers frequently work with physicians and other health care professionals; indeed, one of their essential roles is to help integrate acute and long-term care services for consumers who move in and out of the need for acute care. Care managers often seek to involve physicians and other health professionals to maximize the effectiveness of medical diagnosis and treatment. Moreover, care management's responsibility to coordinate and link long-term care with other services (such as housing, mental health, and social programs) is growing as a result of increased programmatic responsibilities to multiple payers, changing client problems, and the proliferation of managed care.

As managed care organizations continue to expand their services for older adults, care management is continuing to adapt as well. For example, state departments on aging, Area Agencies on Aging funded by the Older Americans Act, and private care management organizations—all of which have developed a capability for management of home- and community-based services—have begun to market care management as a service that could be vended by managed care organizations, which may or may not also contract for direct services (Coleman & Graves-Tucker, 1997; Mollica & Riley, 1997; Polivka & Robinson-Anderson, 1999). For example, Elder Services of Merrimack Valley, Inc., an Area Agency on Aging located in Lawrence, Massachusetts, has contracted with a managed care organization to provide assessments to identify enrollees who are at risk of developing costly chronic illnesses. The managed care organization pays Elder Services a negotiated fee for each assessment. The Atlantic Regional Commission / Area Agency on Agency maintains an electronic database of elder service providers which it sells to managed care organizations. The publicly supported home care corporations of Massachusetts have organized an independent for-profit consortium to negotiate contracts with managed care organizations for community-based care management services. Finally, several managed care organizations in Michigan are developing an alliance to become a qualified managed care organization in order to assume capitated contracts for acute and long-term care services. Although limited in scope, these initiatives illustrate the emerging opportunity for organizations that provide care management to contract to managed care organizations or to receive a capitation rate directly to do care management and also purchase long-term care services.

CONCLUSION

Theoretically, managed care has the potential to improve the delivery of services to older adults by developing better financial and service integration between acute and long-term care; allowing more creative care and integrated services for the consumer; improving the coordination and communication at the clinical level, in part by adopting successful service interventions such as care management; and stressing better opportunities for cost-saving and efficiency. Managed care employs financial incentives to encourage the use of less expensive alternative services to hospital care, such as home care and residential care. Managed care also encourages investment in areas such as primary care, prevention, and care management for high-risk enrollees. For example, older adults need ongoing primary care and preventative health services, which are two of the basic strengths of managed care (achieved by providing these services as a basic benefit). Whenever such activities can be expected to lower the risk of subsequent expensive events like hospitalization without reducing patient care, the interests of consumers and cost-conscious health managers will coincide.

Managed care has clearly been an attractive option to elderly Americans, as the strong recent growth represents. The surge in enrollment was largely unexpected. Many analysts questioned whether the elderly would voluntarily restrict their service choices, since by choosing to join a managed care organization, these enrollees, like any other enrollee in a managed care organization, would give up their guaranteed rights to select their personal physician and to have access to specialists of their choosing. These findings suggest that, on the whole, older adults choosing an HMO have received similar care to that provided under the regular Medicare program, but have had increased benefits, such as prescription drug coverage. Have elders been joining Medicare HMOs because of better quality care? Unfortunately, the evidence does not support this view.

Most observers agree that the early experience with managed care for older adults has emphasized the cost reduction much more than the increased coordination and efficiency, and that plans have incentives to selected younger and healthier beneficiaries over those who are older, have lower incomes, and who are disabled. The large majority of Medicare managed care organizations serving older adults only cover acute or post-acute care, and thus fail to address the need to integrate acute and long-term care for this population. Those initiatives that do integrate across the continuum of care are relatively small and have not grown beyond small demonstrations. The passage of the Balanced Budget Act of 1997 has led many plans to drop out of the program because they are concerned that the services they are required to provide to beneficiaries pose too great a financial risk. Dr.

Paul Ellwood, who coined the term "health maintenance organization," recently criticized the quality of health care provided in HMOs and called for greater government regulation (1999).

For older adults, who we know are more likely than others to have serious or chronic health problems and to require both acute and long-term care, the success or failure of managed care is obviously a critical personal issue that will contribute in no small way to the quality of their lives. It is also a societal issue of extreme importance. It is a truism that measuring how a society cares for some of its most vulnerable citizens provides a good lens through which to view the society as a whole. This is a review in which we do not want to be found wanting. We have learned that providing health care and long-term care to older adults while maintaining high quality and controls on cost surely presents a host of clinical, policy, and financing issues. We have also learned, at least based on experiences to date, that relying on managed care to provide a marketplace solution is not a panacea.

REFERENCES

Applebaum. R., & Austin, C. (1990). *Long-term case management: Design and evaluation*. New York: Springer Publishing Company.

Austin, C. (1988). History and politics of case management. *Generations, 7*(5), 7–10.

Beeuwkes, B., & Newhouse, J. P. (Summer 1998). Paying Medicare managed care plans. *Generations, 12*(2), 37–42.

Branch, L. G., Coulam, R. F., & Zimmerman, Y. A. (1995). The PACE evaluation: Initial findings. *The Gerontologist, 35*(3), 349–359.

Brown, R., Bergeron, J., Clement, D., Hill, J., & Retchin, S. (1993). *The Medicare risk program for HMOs: Final summary report on findings from the evaluation*. Princeton, NJ: Mathematica Policy Research, Inc.

Challis, D., Darton, R., Hughes, J., Huxley, P., & Stewart, K. (1998). Emerging models of care management for older people and those with mental health problems in the United Kingdom. *Journal of Case Management, 7*(4), 153–160.

Coleman, B., & Graves-Tucker, N. (1997, October). *Managed long-term care: What role do area agencies on aging play?* Washington, DC: AARP Public Policy Institute.

Dallek, G. (1998, Summer). Shopping for managed care: The Medicare market. *Generations, 12*(2), 19–24.

Eng, C., Padulla, J., Eleazer, G. P., McCann, R., & Fox, N. (1997). Program of All-inclusive Care for the Elderly (PACE): An innovative model of integrated geriatric care and financing. *Journal of the American Geriatrics Society, 45*, 223–232.

Ellwood, P. M. (1999, May 2). HMOs creater urges reform in quality of care. *Boston Globe*, pp. A1, A34.

Gage, B. (1998, Summer). The history and growth of Medicare managed care. *Generations, 12*(2), 11–18.

Geron, S. M., & Chassler, D. (1994). *Guidelines for case management across the long-term care continuum: A report of the National Advisory Committee on Long-Term Care Case Management*. Bristol, CT: Connecticut Community Care, Inc.

Hatch, A. (October 12, 1998). Medicare risk HMOs gamble future: HCFA ponders enforcing re-entrance ban. *News and strategies for Medicare and Medicaid, 4*(37), 1.

Kane, R. A., Illston, L. H., & Miller, N. A. (1992). Qualitative analysis of the Program of All-inclusive Care for the Elderly (PACE). *The Gerontologist, 32,* 771–780.

Kane, R. A., & Kane, R. L. (1997). *Long-term care: Principles, programs and policies.* New York: Springer Publishing Co.

Kane, R. L., Kane, R. A., Kaye, N., Mollica, R., Riley, T., Saucier, P., Snow, K. I., & Starr, L. (1996). *Managed care: Handbook for the aging network.* University of Minnesota: National LTC Resource Center.

Kodner, D. (1993). *Case management: Principles, practice and performance.* (GeronTopics #1) Brooklyn, NY: Institute for Applied Gerontology.

Macko, P., Dunn, S., Blech, M., Ashby, F., & Schwab, T. (1995). The social HMOs: Meeting the challenge of integrated team care coordination. *Journal of Case Management, 4*(3), 102–107.

Mahoney, K., Quinn, J., Geron, S. M., & Parker, M. (1997). Case management for private payers. In R. Newcomer & A. Wilkinson (Eds.), *Annual review of gerontology and geriatrics* (Vol. 15). New York: Springer.

Manton, K. G., Newcomer, R., Lowrimore, G. R., Vertrees, J. C., & Harrington, C. (1993). Social/health maintenance organizations and fee-for-service health outcomes over time. *Health Care Financing Review, 15*(2), 173–202.

Miller, R., & Luft, H. S. (1997, September/October). Managed care performance: Is quality of care better or worse? *Health Affairs, 16*(5), 7–25.

Mollica, R., & Riley, T. (1997). *Managed care for low income elders dually eligible for Medicaid and Medicare: A snapshot of state and federal activity.* Portland, ME: National Academy for State Health Policy.

Morgan, R. D., Virnig, B. A., DeVito, C. A., & Persily, N. A. (1997). The Medicare–HMO revolving door—the healthy go in and the sick go out. *The New England Journal of Medicine, 337*(3), 169–175.

Riley, G. F., Ingber, M. J., & Tudor, C. G. (1997, September/October). Disenrollment of Medicare beneficiaries from HMOs. *Health Affairs, 16*(5), 117–124.

Retchin, S. M., Brown, R. S., Yeh, S. J., Chu, D., & Moreno, L. (1997). Outcomes of stroke patients in Medicare fee-for-service and managed care. *Journal of the American Medical Association, 278*(2), 119–124.

Rogers, W. H., Draper, D., Kahn, K. L, Keeler, E.B., Rubenstein, L, V., Kosecoff, J., & Brook, P. H. (1990). Quality of care before and after implementation of the DRG-based prospective payment system. *Journal of the American Medical Association, 264*(15), 1989–1994.

Pham, A. (1999, March 3). Push grows for drug coverage: Many back Medicare change. *Boston Globe,* pp. A1, A4.

Polivka, L., & Robinson-Anderson, R. (1999). Managed care and the role of the aging network. *Long-Term Care Policy Series* (Vol. IV, rev. ed.). Tampa, FL: The Florida Policy Exchange Center on Aging.

Stone, R. J., & Nutfeld, M. R. (1998). Medicare managed care: Sinking or swimming with the tide. *The Journal of Long-Term Home Health Care, 17*(1), 7–16.

Shaughnessy, P., Schlenker, R., & Hittle, D. (1994). Home health care outcomes under capitated and fee-for-service payment. *Health Care Financing Review, 16*(1), 187–221.

Ware, J. E., Bayliss, M. S., Rogers, W. H., Kosinski, M., & Tarlov, A. R. (1996). Differences in 4–year health outcomes for elderly and poor, chronically ill patients, treated in HMO and fee-for-service systems: Results from the Medical Outcomes Study. *Journal of the American Medical Association, 276*(13), 1039–1047.

◆ CHAPTER 8 ◆

Managed Care and the Ecological Perspective

Meeting the Needs of Older Adults in the Twenty-First Century

ROBERTA R. GREENE AND W. PATRICK SULLIVAN

Gerontologists are increasingly exploring models of geriatric health care that are based on ecological principles, individualized multidisciplinary treatment plans, and designs that promote optimal functioning among older adults. At the core of this care process is a person-environment perspective—or, the patient in his or her milieu. Gerontologists use comprehensive assessments to examine a patient's ability to function successfully in his or her environment and mobilize resources to improve interpersonal functioning (Coulton, 1981; Fandetti & Goldmeir, 1988; Fillit, Hill, Picariello & Warburton, 1998; Greene, in press).

Historically, the motivation behind a comprehensive team assessment was linked to a central ecological construct: everyday competence. Everyday competence—akin to functional capacity—is concerned with older people's ability to care for themselves, manage their affairs, and live independent, quality lives in their communities (Tinetti & Powell, 1993; Willis, 1991, Willis, 1996a, b). With the graying of U.S. society and the sharp rise in acute and disabling illnesses, health professionals are giving increased attention to the concept of competence among older adults (Diehl, 1998; Silverstone, 1996). Older adults continue to account for a disproportionate use of health care services—that population recently represented one-eighth of the U.S. population and accounted for more than one-third of health care expenditures (U.S. Senate Special Committee on Aging, 1992). Given this sharp rise in chronic illness and the use of health care services, policymakers fear that by 2030, growing numbers of frail older adults with health problems will require health and other services that will surpass the capacity of delivery systems. Researchers (Zedlewski, Barnes, Burt, McBride & Meyer, 1990) have found that the elderly population's need for supportive services will far exceed the general increase in the elderly population.

In this context, the ability of older adults to handle everyday concerns has become a critical societal issue. As increased numbers of older adults enroll in managed care plans, which are characterized by measures to contain costs and discourage the use of unnecessary medical services, what will happen to geriatric practice (Edinburg & Cottler, 1995)? Managed care includes a range of services intended to increase access to care and perhaps has the potential to improve care (Friedland & Feder, 1998). Managed care, at its best, may also reduce an older adult's overuse of physicians, drugs, and medical equipment (Dallek, 1998). In addition, managed care may direct consumers to the best care for the best cost and transfer insurance risk from the payer to the provider (Edinburg & Cottler, 1995; White, Simmons & Bixby, 1993).

According to *Consumer's Research Magazine* in 1997, Medicare is the nation's largest purchaser of managed care services. However, to date, there is little evidence documenting how elderly people with functional impairments and chronic conditions are experiencing managed care (Friedland & Feder, 1998). What is known is that differences exist between older adults who enroll in managed care and those who are in fee-for-service arrangements (Riley et al., 1996; Wiener, 1996). Medicare beneficiaries enrolled in managed care tend to be younger and healthier, and have fewer chronic conditions. Within managed care plans, 7.3% of elderly consumers have problems with activities of daily living, compared with 14.1% in fee-for-service plans who have reported such difficulties (Friedland & Feder, 1998). In 1995, 5.8 million older adults (17% of the elderly population) had some functional limitation that would require assistance (Komisar, Lambrew & Feder, 1996). How do older adults with functional difficulties who are enrolled in managed care plans experience their care? Will managed care meet long-term care needs (Wiener, 1996)? Does managed care make a difference to the quality of care and meet older adult's needs and expectations (Sofaer, 1998)?

This chapter argues for the continued use of ecological principles in health care for older adults. It outlines the major features of managed care through which the large majority of older adults receive health services. The chapter also explores the public policy issue of whether managed care is a service delivery system that can meet the needs of the elderly population in the twenty-first century.

ECOLOGICAL PRINCIPLES FOR UNDERSTANDING EVERYDAY COMPETENCE AMONG OLDER ADULTS

Assessment

What are the benefits of using an ecological focus in health care? Social workers who use the ecological perspective as a conceptual framework examine older clients' behavior as a "complex outcome of person-environment transactions at multiple systems levels" (Greene & McGuire, 1998, p. 9). Social workers in health care can extend the concept of *goodness-of-fit*—the extent to which there is a match between the individual's adaptive needs and the qualities of the environment—to the health care system. Practitioners must understand if health care services are compatible with an older adult's needs, resources, and demands; if so, then there is a goodness-of-fit.

Practitioners who use the ecological perspective in health care emphasize everyday competence among older adults and take the perspective that such ability is a multidimensional phenomenon best understood as the outgrowth of transactions between person and environment over time (Bronfenbrenner, 1979). Everyday competence among older adults involves a person's total life situation, his or her personal, psychosocial, cultural, political, and economic contexts. An understanding of everyday competence requires an ecological assessment that "addresses the totality of the client's life experience and contexts as a harmonious whole" (Greene & Watkins, 1998, p. 64). An ecological view of the older adult's functional capacity considers the concept of the *life course*—how a person has functioned over time, the timing of life events, and the historical changes associated with those events. The attention to changing social conditions helps practitioners assess the older adult's present functioning in the context of life events.

"Ecological approaches also focus attention on the connections among individuals at various systems levels" (Greene, 1999). A multilevel assessment ranges from personal expressions of competence to environmental-systems factors. Bronfenbrenner (1979) proposed a useful assessment schema for visualizing a client's connections to his or her family and other systems in the environment. He conceptualized systems at four levels: (1) the *microlevel* is the older adult's immediate environment, which consists of face-to-face relationships, such as family and friends; (2) the *mesolevel* includes the relationship or linkages among small-sized systems, such as the family and a house of worship; (3) the *exosystems level* includes linkages among systems in which the older adult is not (physically) involved, such as between the insurance company and the nursing home; and (4) the *macrolevel* system encompasses large-scale social, political, legal, and economic beliefs of a particular society, such as the social security system.

When a social worker assesses a client at the microlevel, the practitioner must remember that a person's everyday competence is a biopsychosocial phenomenon, encompassing the whole person from the strengths perspective (Greene, 1999). Biological factors may encompass energy levels, physical flexibility, propensity to exercise, disease or medical condition, and wellness. Psychological factors include everyday memory, affective state, and level of stress. The more psychologically adaptive an older adult, the more likely he or she is to attain a sense of well-being and to successfully master his or her environment (Germain & Gitterman, 1987). Social variables involve cultural rituals, recreation, peer support, or lifelong social economic advantages or disadvantages.

Self-efficacy, the perceived power to be effective in one's environment, is a central psychological variable in everyday competence (Bandura, 1986). For an older adult, self-efficacy may involve the sense of security that he or she may not slip and fall or that the person has the capacity to drive a car (Tinetti & Powell, 1993). The literature (Mcvay, Seeman & Rodin, 1996) has suggested that the stronger the older adult's sense of self-efficacy, the more positive the health-promoting behaviors and health outcomes. Lifelong patterns of self-efficacy, which are different for each individual, are also related to the importance of health or wellness activities such as exercise, not just to illness avoidance (Pender, 1982). Because everyday competence is related to a person's ability to perform tasks associated with daily living (Lawton, 1982), practitioners need to understand how a person copes within his or her milieu by exploring how well the older adult functions in his or her home. For example, can the older adult traverse the stairs, get in and out of the bath, or prepare his or her own meals?

Social workers in health care also must understand that everyday competence is related to availability of family and other social support systems at the mesolevel. To achieve such understanding requires an assessment of how successfully people interact and connect with others in their environments. Social workers are particularly concerned about the strength of a person's support networks, which may serve as a source of mutual aid. As families continue to be the primary caregivers for older adults, it is critical that practitioners view families not only as a resource, but when appropriate as the client system. A key social work activity is obtaining resources to enhance family functioning on behalf of the older adult.

Furthermore, social workers in health care must appreciate mesolevel aspects of human functioning, particularly those expressions of diversity within everyday competence. During assessment, practitioners must recognize that an older adult is a member of a particular cohort—for example, the older adult may be a member of a group born in a particular year or era; he or she may have grown up during the Great Depression, experienced school segregation, or been a survivor of the Holocaust. Availability of friends and opportunities for recreation and spiritual life also play a role in everyday competence (Canda & Furman, 1999). A comprehensive assessment addresses predisposing factors that influence competence and service use, including age, gender, marital status, race, and family composition (Kosloski & Montgomery, 1994). In addition, assessment examines macrolevel conditions such as economic trends, personal income, living arrangements and adequacy of housing, and educational level (Rowland, Feder & Keenan, 1998).

Interventions

Just as with assessment, ecological principles may guide social workers to make appropriate interventions—interventions that treat the entire patient. From an ecological perspective, which involves an understanding of an older adult's level of functioning in a particular environment, social workers direct their interventions to promote personal competence. Furthermore, interventions based on an ecological perspective may allow for a more effective use of health and human services, given that functional decline has been associated with poor quality of life for elderly people, and such functional limitation has been associated with expensive health-related care (Boult, Kane, Louis, L. Boult & McCaffrey, 1994). For example, to treat older adults' fear of falling, Tinetti and Powell (1993) suggested enhancing self-efficacy.

> The medical component of intervention should target those physical factors that constitute the relevant skills for safe transfers and ambulating. Because these skills simultaneously constitute the essential mobility skill, the important risk factor for falls, and . . . the relevant skills contributing to self-perception of physical ability, it is possible their remediation will have a multiplying effect on function. . . . In addition, because individuals function within an environment, attention to environmental factors such as good lighting, nonslippery surfaces, appropriate footwear, and safe furniture is essential. (p. 37)

Managed care, according to Dallek (1998), "can ensure that medical interventions are appropriate to the problem and that the entire patient, not just the particular disease, is treated" (p. 19).

Social workers also may make interventions based on an ecological perspective to address older adults' adaptiveness. Numerous studies have suggested that the more functional older adults experience greater psychological and physical well-being. The less functional the older adult, the less likely he or she is to experience life satisfaction, and the greater the likelihood he or she will use home health care, and the greater the risk of hospitalization, institutionalization, and mortality (Diehl, 1998). Furthermore, despite the improvement in income among elderly people, there still are low-income elderly persons, primarily women, minorities, and the very old. Rowland et al. (1998) have suggested that if Medicare and Medicaid promoted the use of managed care that would facilitate access to quality care, such an initiative would assist low-income elderly people. Minority elderly people also continue to be at high levels of risk for incompetent health care, particularly care that is not culturally competent (Davidhizar & Giger-Newman, 1996). Despite health promotion efforts among African-American older adults, that population continues to be at a health disadvantage (Yee & Weaver, 1994). Another major concern is whether to integrate mental health into general health managed care (Olsen, Rickles & Travik, 1995; Robinson, Crow & Scallet, 1998). What might be the advantage of managed care?

MANAGED CARE

Managed care is a term that evokes strong negative emotions for many professionals. For some, managed care is a euphemism for those efforts that place cost considerations above the needs of people. Others, however, may view managed care—particularly through the behavior of managed care organizations (MCOs)—as an infringement on professional autonomy and decision making.

Actually, managed care comprises so many forms that, like *case management,* it is difficult to define. As Hoge, Jacobs, Thakur, and Griffith (1999) put it, "if you've seen one managed care program, you've seen one managed care program" (p. 51). The inability or unwillingness of health care professionals to define managed care has added to the emotionality of the debate and has resulted in the substitution of personal experience for objective analysis in evaluating the merits of this health care delivery model (Bachrach, 1995). What most forms of managed care have made explicit is that the provision of care is inseparable from the costs of doing business; thus, in an arena of scare resources, practitioners and clients alike must confront difficult choices (Hoge, Davidson, Griffith, Sledge & Howenstine, 1994). Certainly, from a macro perspective, professionals have understood that inequalities are inherent in health care and that access, scope, and intensity of service vary among individuals. Yet, on the experiential level, it is easier to accept the abstract notion that variation exists among individuals in terms of their eligibility for services rather than to accept that a health care provider will not authorize specific services for reimbursement. Managed care has pierced the omnipresent denial systems that many professionals maintain in the face of dauntingly tragic choices. Recognizing the present tension, Hoge and associates (1994) commented that:

> This aspect of managed care has been the most difficult for patients and their primary caregivers to accept, because, to them, the rationale for denying the most optimal services is seldom evident and the needs of other patients are of less concern. . . . A managed care approach involves making these difficult decisions in a deliberate and rational manner rather than allowing such decisions to evolve from diffuse, unorganized, and often conflicting administrative, political, and economic forces. (p. 1087)

Whether professionals recognize it or not, fiscal policies shape the structure of service delivery systems and professional practice. The present challenge is to develop and implement fiscal polices that support best practices and help create organized systems of care. A vision of quality services for older adults must inform this effort, which also must affirm values consistent with professional social work. The gold standard for success is the ability of the service delivery system to support older adults in the quest to maximize their overall quality of life. Good social work practice requires the development of individually tailored care plans that account for older adults' strengths and needs, and involve the procurement and organization of the necessary services and supports older adults need to attain their goals and desires. The necessary services and supports may be formal, such as health care and transportation, or informal, such as leisure activities, support groups, or the ability to stay active with family.

Although some professionals may long for those days that preceded the managed care movement, it is wise to recall that models of care based on indemnity insurance arrangements and fee-for-service systems also created a set of vexing problems for older adults, families, and professional helpers. For example, Rose (1997) pointed out that:

> Indemnity based, fee for service reimbursement embodies medicalized interventions in discrete service units, delivered through contracts with isolated providers or fragmented provider "networks" to discrete individual patients whose categorical malady as well as insurance card confer eligibility and service delivery. The mechanism is inherently episodic, reactive, and premised upon high volume for solvency or profit. (pp. 61–62)

In the classic fee-for-service model, doing more means more income for providers. Indeed, there is often an inherent incentive for providers to use the most intensive and expensive medically oriented services available. In the fee-for-service model, providers may consider nursing homes and inpatient hospitalization as the first option rather than the least preferred alternative (Dorwart & Epstein, 1992). By comparison, in the new paradigm of health care, providers must control or "manage" all services which are now cost centers. In addition, reimbursement mechanisms that are based on the provision of discrete service units and episodes help create a fragmented system of care (Wiener, 1996). These funding silos result in a host of specific rules, policies, and procedures and, in the final analysis, work against organized systems of care. This is a critical problem for older adults, who often need a wide range of services that cut across social agencies or are outside of the formal service sector. Older adults must negotiate a confusing world of regulations and deal with a host of service providers; furthermore, they must piece together a web of supports critical to their well-being. Oftentimes, providers may not view the supportive services and activities that may be central to older adults' continued success as medically necessary; thus, the funding streams to support those services may be lacking.

Consequently, as counterintuitive as it may seem, managed care presents a golden opportunity to fashion a delivery system that is person-centered; yet, managed care plans may jeopardize older adults' health, quality of life, and longevity. The remainder of this chapter discusses the challenges presented by managed care, and suggests ways to structure managed care systems to support the goals of quality care. A word of caution: Any model falls short in the real world of practice and requires modification based on the uniqueness of each service setting and the population served. Robinson (1999) astutely noted that:

> Public policymakers and industry analysts often assume that there exists somewhere a truly efficient form of physician and hospital organization, an optimal benefit package, an evidence-based set of clinical protocols, and one best method of marketing and enrollment. But even a cursory examination of the medical marketplace quickly reveals that no one size fits all and that consumers do not agree on what they want, purchasers on what they are willing to pay for, and providers on what they are willing to deliver. (p. 9)

THE STRUCTURE OF MANAGED CARE SYSTEMS

The diversity of models under the managed care umbrella leaves program designers and policymakers with a host of important decisions to make when structuring a service-delivery system. One basic decision concerns the range and type of services a program will offer to an enrolled population. For example, the distinction between carve-in and carve-out models of managed care has frequently been a key topic of discussion in behavioral health care. For example, health care providers have hotly debated the advisability of including mental health and addictions service as a part of the overall benefits package to individuals enrolled in a health care plan versus separating (or "carving out") those services. Advocates of clients with serious mental illness have expressed concern that providers will exclude from coverage or provide fewer than required services to those clients most in need, who by definition will require more costly treatment. In addition, mental health problems vary widely in course and outcome, and the entire process of care—from diagnosis to treatment—is less precise and known than occurs with other medical conditions. By carving out behavioral health care, it is argued that providers will solely devote attention to mental health conditions, and, over time, actuarial sophistication and improvements in treatment protocols may bring more predictability to the field.

In many respects, particularly given the use of medical services in the last years of life, older adults and their advocates face similar concerns. Are there unnecessary restrictions on services or the scope of services offered? Are there efforts to exclude coverage or drop coverage as people age? With older adults, a carve-in health care package is conceptually attractive. Like all people, older adults face emotional challenges, which may become more pronounced as their health declines and concerns about the future emerge. A benefits package that features one-stop shopping has obvious appeal. Integrated or organized systems of care may feature primary care physicians or medical practice groups as the linchpin, or may operate through an MCO. At times, the MCO serves as an intermediary agent and is not involved in the direct provision of services. These administrative-service-only organizations may subcontract with medical or specialty groups or with a host of "preferred providers." At other times, medical and specialty health care groups are full-service, linking administrative services with the provision of care. In theory, MCOs offer the full range of services specified for an enrolled population for a defined reimbursement rate, which is commonly set on a per-member, per-month basis.

Managed care also may serve as a vehicle to control health care costs. Over the past two decades, health care costs have risen dramatically for business and industry as well as for the public sector. Although the rate of growth for health care spending will ebb and flow, the graying of America will ensure that this issue will not abate. Weiner and Stevenson (1998) reported that, in 1995, nursing home and home health care accounted for 12% of all personal health care expenditures and 14% of state and local health care spending. Long-term health care expenditures will likely double in inflation-adjusted dollars in the first two decades of the twenty-first century. Equally compelling and alarming is Fuch's (1999) finding that health care expenditures on the elderly population "outpaced the Gross Domestic Product by 3.5 to 4.0 percent in recent decades" (p. 11). Given these statistics, it is not surprising that industry leaders, public officials, insurers, and citizens have been searching for methods to retard the rapid growth of health care spending. Managed care models control health care spending through a variety of key mechanisms. These methods appear to have little to do with advancing the health and well-being of older adults. However, these same techniques, coupled with a supportive fiscal policy, can advance person-centered social work practice.

One control mechanism is case-management. Here, the classic "medical" case-management model is described. In this model, case managers provide clinical and fiscal oversight and are involved in the titration of care (Weiner & de Lissovoy, 1993). Case managers may or may not be clinicians—oftentimes a source of consternation for professionals who deal with MCOs. A key component of the model is the search for alternatives to expensive and restrictive care (Landress & Bernstine, 1994). Over time, a medical case manager may be knowledgeable about accepted treatment protocols, standard length of treatment, and costs associated with care. In the management-information age, much of this information may be readily available online.

Closely related to the functions of case management are various oversight procedures such as precertification or medical necessity reviews. Each of these procedures curbs the autonomous behavior of professionals; subsequently, most professionals find such reviews onerous. Precertification and medical necessity reviews are self-explanatory and essentially ask the question, Is this intervention justified at this time? As a gatekeeping mechanism, this procedure in particular controls access to expensive treatments. In addition, these reviews often set limits on the number of sessions, visits, or days of treatment.

Concurrent review, another quality-assurance method, features ongoing monitoring of the course and the outcomes of treatment to date. Synchronous with this review process is the collection of fiscal and clinical data to assist the case manager to develop clinical pathways and thus develop standard treatment protocols. Ultimately, the manager will link this information to ascertain the costs associated with care and the costs of obtaining various levels of acceptable outcomes.

Through managed care, it is relatively easy to control health care spending and succeed financially as well. For example, given the exponential growth in health care spending, managed care providers have been able to secure a contract in the public or private sector by simply guaranteeing that expenditures would not exceed current levels. Prudent managers who observed the escalating costs of providing coverage for employees considered managed care an important strategy to protect their organization. However, as the managed care industry has matured and competition in terms of price alone has become fierce, these risk-bearing organizations have been forced to consider new strategies to gain a competitive advantage. One trend is the consolidation and merger mania that allows large health maintenance organizations (HMOs), insurance agencies, and other organizations involved in the managed care world to cover more lives. The goal is to improve the profit margin through increased volume or the ability to spread the risk (Robinson, 1999). An alternative theme is to gain market share by emphasizing quality of care and consumer responsiveness (Schaeffer & Volpe, 1999). Furthermore, purchasers of managed care services, having grown wiser through experience, are becoming more sophisticated in contracting. They, too, have learned how to craft a contract that benefits their host organization and the constituents they represent. Certainly, many of the fiscal and human disasters that have garnered public attention are due, in part, to inattentiveness in the initial contracting between a host organization and the managed care industry (Camp, Pizer & McCarty, 1997).

TOWARD AN INTEGRATED MODEL OF SERVICE DELIVERY FOR OLDER ADULTS

It would be foolish to deny that serious problems exist in some managed care programs and delivery systems. However, it would be equally foolish to deny that health care professionals must make difficult choices regarding health care provision as we head toward the twenty-first century. One may reasonably assert that there is no such thing as national health care policy. Rather, public policy that lacks a unified theme guides U.S. health care, which is provided in an uncoordinated fashion.

The following is a discussion of a model of practice that can help create the context that may positively affect the older adults' quality of life through the use clinical and fiscal tools. Within this framework is a myriad of opportunities for social workers to practice in a manner consistent with the longstanding strengths of the field that will allow professionals to use those skills in new roles and settings. To this end, Rose (1997) has suggested that the new world of health care should emphasize wellness, prevention, and health promotion as well as create incentives to treat people in a cost-effective manner. Accordingly, "these sociocultural parameters offer exceptional opportunities for social work to operationalize our values of human dignity, diversity, and social justice" (Rose, 1997, p. 60).

Several years ago, Moore (1992) argued that positing direct-service case management as a solution to system fragmentation was unrealistic. He suggested that, "when delivery systems lack an administrative structure and adequate resources, case management is, at best, an attempt to cope with a chaotic service environment" (p. 418). This chaos has a deleterious impact on professionals and the consumers for whom they care. For this reason, social workers must attend to the organizational and policy context that can support best-practice models. Organized systems of care provide one such context. According to Shortell, Gillies, and Anderson (1994), *organized systems of care* comprise "a network of organizations that provides or arranges to provide a coordinated system of services to a defined population and is willing to be held clinically and fiscally accountable for the outcomes and health status of the population served" (p. 47).

Given the aim to provide good care to many vulnerable or potentially vulnerable populations, health care must not be narrowly defined as pertaining solely to the disease of the body and mind. Good social work practice, particularly when guided by ecological principles, must consider the range of individual and environmental factors that affect the quality of the social niche occupied by people. Unfortunately, social policy and the social programs that result rarely reflect this holistic orientation. In the face of compelling evidence and the experience of most people, programs and policies that aim to solve social and personal problems or help us reach individual or social aspirations continue to operate in a piecemeal fashion. As a result, the United States continues to pay, in the words of Lisbeth Schorr (1988), "the high cost of rotten outcomes" (p. 8).

Managed care plans, particularly when narrowly focused, may reflect the tyranny of reductionist thinking. To manage care and not simply costs, organized systems of care must focus on the whole person and the quality of person-environment interactions—because health and wellness is more than a personal experience; it is, in part, a cultural phenomenon. To that end, the concept of the social health maintenance organization (S/HMO) offers a method to "provide a coordinated and comprehensive system of health and social service" (Moore, 1992, p. 420). This chapter argues that, given the range of needs—broadly defined—of older adults, the S/HMO framework provides a useful template to tease out key features of a progressive managed care system. Two sources guide the ensuing discussion: (1) the schemata of key dimensions for a public sector managed care model offered by Hoge and associates (1994) and (2) the guidance offered by Camp et al. (1997), surmised from their review of state-level initiatives in the area of managed behavioral health care. Throughout this discussion, the words of Ogles, Trout, Gillespie, and Penkert (1998) ring true: "not only is a system of care a collection of coordinated services, the system of care also includes a philosophy about the way services should be delivered" (p. 253).

Gatekeeping

Hoge (1994) has advanced that "the initial step in managing care involves defining a target population and instituting procedures to ensure that services are provided to those—and only those—in the targeted group" (p. 1086). Beyond this initial step, the gatekeeping system will limit access to services health care providers deem unnecessary and costly in favor of equally effective and less costly alternatives. Although some critics have decried this aspect of managed care as unethical, there are no ethical violations present if a less costly treatment or intervention can produce similar outcomes. Furthermore, when the level of responsibility is population-based, resources must be managed for the good of all. Therefore, it is essential to reserve scarce and expensive resources for those for whom no alternative is feasible. For services to be effective, they must be person-centered and not program centered. Thus, institutional arrangements, although often convenient, may not match the consumer's true goals and desires.

Gatekeeping in some managed care arrangements may be synonymous with traditional direct-care case management. This process must begin with comprehensive assessments that devote equal attention to the consumer's strengths and ability and gain insights into their goals and aspirations. An assessment of strengths is a cornerstone of person-centered treatment plans. Such an assessment begins with the basic assumption that providers will take action clues from the customer. Undoubtedley, there are areas of involvement in which professionals' specialized knowledge and skills will hold sway. Nonetheless, attention to the process of collaboration can appreciably reduce common points of friction in the consumer-professional relationship.

Case management practice differs from gatekeeping in a managed care environment in that case managers may make purchasing decisions and remain sensitive to the fiscal parameters of care. Not surprisingly, in classic carve-in models of managed care, the primary care physician occupies the case-manager role. Within the context of an S/HMO, it may be inappropriate for a physician to serve in such a capacity for many reasons. For one, classical medical assessment may overlook or fail to recognize important issues impacting older adults, such as alcohol and drug abuse, and emotional problems such as depression (Olfson, Sing & Schlesinger, 1999). Furthermore, effective care plans may require an awareness of a host of formal and informal resources that are likely beyond the purview of physicians.

It is not surprising then, that social workers have become prominent actors at all levels of MCOs. In part, the social worker's ability to complete multidimensional assessments and his or her awareness of both formal and informal community resources have proved to be invaluable in systems in which providers are in a risk-based or shared-risk environment. An alternative strategy is to use multidisciplinary teams in the assessment and treatment-planning phase. In all cases, the effort is guided by the desire to help consumers surmount those barriers to optimum functioning and to do so in the environments of their choice. Consider a consumer who has experienced a serious health condition but strongly desires to remain in the home. A traditional approach would proceed by assessing the level of impairment and then search for the right program or available specialty service that could compensate for the impairment. From a person-centered model, the focus is on what level of supports are essential for this consumer to meet his or her goal—in this case, to remain in the home.

PROVISION OF COMPREHENSIVE SERVICES

In situations in which individuals enjoy good mental and physical health and some degree of economic security, it is less difficult to secure the range of services and supports needed to enhance the quality of their life. Basic medical insurance can cover costs for the acute problems that people face throughout their lives, whereas work and social affiliations provide support and the needed stimulus to thrive on a daily basis. Without second thought, many people use formal and informal systems with regularity. However, chronic illness, loss of social roles and support systems, and economic setbacks can overwhelm the routine social structures that sustain people.

For a system of care to be effective and efficient for older adults, comprehensive services must be available. Since the 1990s, there has been a horizontal integration of some health care systems. Thus, hospitals have attempted to increase their reach and market share by expanding into programs as varied as skilled nursing care, home health, assisted living programs, and hospice. Motivators for this expansion have included demand for such services and pressure from third-party payers who have become keenly aware of and have invested in the use of less costly alternatives to inpatient care. The attempt to maintain a competitive advantage has resulted in a dizzying number of mergers and acquisition and consolidation of health care industries.

With respect to the effort to integrate services and functions vertically, health care organizations are becoming active in the insurance arena, and pharmaceutical companies are acquiring health care systems, all of which contribute to an already turbulent health care world. Having witnessed these trends, Robinson (1999) observed that everyone seems to "be dabbling with great enthusiasm and little success in the others' business" (p. 9).

The kinds of comprehensive systems previously described involve the formal health care sector. In contrast, the intent of the S/HMO model is to coordinate health and social services to better match consumers' needs. Thus, in the ideal world, few barriers would exist when professionals, older adults, and their families worked together to devise and implement an individually tailored care plan for an older adult. The needs of many older adults, in particular those in the greatest need, rarely fall into one category or service system. The conceptualization of resources and services goes way beyond formal systems, and even beyond those informal services and settings practitioners customarily use in daily practice. A comprehensive assessment should explicate the strengths and needs in all spheres of life: health and social, material and spiritual. These components and others encompass who the client is as a person. Such an assessment also should include the relative fit among an ideal quality of life, what is preferred, and what is experienced at the moment. For a service system to function optimally, it must match the needs and experience of those served. Therefore, flexibility and versatility characterize an effective service system.

CONTINUITY AND FLEXIBILITY OF CARE

Continuity of care, as described by Hoge and associates (1994), is reflected in the effectiveness of services to follow and match consumers' needs over time and also allow for consistency in the professional-consumer relationship. Particularly when people are most in need and most fearful about their future, consistency and predictability become important. Far too often, consumers must adjust to a new range of faces, procedures, and settings as they move through the formal and informal service system. Some change is inevitable. However, an ideal goal is to develop a seamless system of care.

Furthermore, professionals should not provide care in a lockstep manner, or care should not manifest unnecessary rigidity. When considering the array of services for older adults, it is likely that the home is at one end of the continuum, with nursing home care on the other. Furthermore, a pessimistic view of aging sees movement along the continuum in a predictable fashion consistent with declining health and social facility. Grouping older adults on the basis of the presumed severity of their impairment is abetted by categorical funding—and movement between programs and level of care becomes difficult. Greater flexibility should characterize a person-centered model, which should reflect the basic principle that people require different levels of support and intensity of services at various times.

In such a model, it is essential that there is a consistent case or care manager who ensures that the person gets the right service, at the right time, for the appropriate duration. In many respects, this assessment is part and parcel of use and concurrent review procedures common to managed care. The important modifier here is the addition of the human link that focuses on care of the person, not simply the cost of such care. The requirements for an effective person-centered model of care for older adults are hardly new. However, several key issues remain to be addressed. One question is, How can such care be paid for? Another is, How could such a system be structured to provide flexible, comprehensive, and continuous care?

PUBLIC SECTOR MANAGED CARE

With slight modifications, the definition of *public sector managed care* offered by Hoge and associates (1994) has great utility for this analysis:

> Public sector managed care involves the organization of an accessible and accountable service delivery system that is designed to consolidate and flexibly deploy resources so as to provide comprehensive, continuous, cost-efficient, and effective . . . services to targeted individuals in their home communities. (p. 1087)

The designation of this model as a public model of managed care does not preclude the possibility of applying these principles in the proprietary world.

However, it is not only the business world that is interested in containing health care costs. State authorities in particular have also made an effort to curb rising Medicaid costs. The range of state and local services designated for older adults is broader than health care alone; hence, it is suggested that an integrative service-delivery system can be effective and cost effective.

To address the issue of cost-effectiveness, public officials must answer to multiple constituencies, including the taxpayers. Conceptually, whether providing services directly or contractually, public agents purchase services for older adults on behalf of the taxpaying public. In addition, like many of the human services, programs for older adults involve a greater demand for services with fewer available resources. Therefore, public agents must make an effort to define and delimit the service population and efficiently deploy scarce resources. These decisions cannot be decoupled from clinical decision-making.

The human services landscape varies state by state. Some states directly operate a wide range of public services; in others, there are more contractual arrangements between the state and nonprofit and profit-seeking vendors. At the state level, responsibility for services to older adults may all fall under a distinct and autonomous department, be included in a large umbrella agency, or be represented in a range of agencies with differing primary foci. The variations alone conspire to render a limited discussion of ideal models. The task in this chapter is to glean those key principles that are portable to diverse locales.

One potential approach is to reconfigure the role of a lead state agency. For example, an agency can reshape itself to function like an insurance company and offer a standard benefits package for eligible citizens either directly or through vendors tied to the agency contractually. In this model, the lead state authority has the power to identify the target population through explicit criteria, define the parameters of the benefits package, and perform the customary functions of managed care. In practice, such agencies deal with limited budgets and are unlikely to be capable of assuming risk for a defined population. State agencies may address limitation contractually by devising a full or shared-risk relationship with vendors. In some states, county boards or designated agencies assume primary responsibility for a defined region, and usually they, too, operate with a fixed budget.

Unlike insurance contracts with business and industry, the number of covered lives often is unknown and therefore an assessment of likely risk—determined through actuarial analysis—is difficult. In an environment marked by uncertainty, agencies may use different techniques to manage care and costs. Consider the wide range of efforts undertaken by states to curb the rising cost of Medicaid. Given that Medicaid is an entitlement program, states primarily control costs through configuration of reimbursement rates, eligibility criteria (which are defined in a plan unique to each state), or contracts with managed care firms that engage in the range of cost-control methods described in this chapter. Regardless of the direction undertaken, professionals must consider several key functions in the development of a managed care or managed care hybrid plan (Camp et al., 1997).

One key issue is the degree of integration between agencies with partial or primary responsibility for services to older adults (Camp et al., 1997). Moore's (1992) extension of the S/HMO model suggested the importance of integrating and consolidating the service system at each level, from the provider to the financing method chosen. It is difficult to argue with service integration on a conceptual plane, but how might this be accomplished?

One strategy to increase cooperation and coordination between agencies is through contractual language, memoranda of understanding, and other forms of joint agreements. An alternative strategy is to physically locate offices in proximity. Unfortunately, in the absence of fiscal rewards or penalties, these written agreements simply become areas of contested turf, and co-location simply reduces logistics problems. Fiscal policy must support public policy goals and directions. Therefore, a successful managed care model must blend funds from diverse sources (thus, memoranda of agreement will also involve a level of financial contribution) and flexibly use such funds at the individual consumer level. In the proprietary world of managed care, purchasing authorities establish the parameters of practice by defining critical elements such as the target population, the package of benefits, performance standards, consumer rights, and consumer protections. In practice, however, the ability and desire to tailor services to match the consumers' distinct needs and goals is an important consideration in both the private and public sector.

In the public model of managed care, a lead agency or agencies must be designated, and this entity becomes the point of contact for the consumer. In all cases, the model specified here is predicated on the ability to provide the range of services (or "wraparound services" in the popular vernacular) that the older adult needs. This ability underscores the connection between mind and body and person and environment, and creates opportunities to ameliorate problems and actuate potentialities by way of a wide spectrum of interventions and social resources. There are few limits on how such a program could be structured or what kind of organizations can serve as the front door to care. The only requirement would be that such organizations provide the necessary array of services either directly or contractually. Ogles and associates (1998) have argued that, in the children's service arena—an area that also suffers from extreme fragmentation—managed care can serve as a platform to integrate services. They see utility in contracting with a private MCO, and their observations are applicable in the area of services for older adults.

Typically, local government entities resist integration of funding for fear of losing money through cost shifting. Contracting with an independent, private MCO, though, would allow each public entity to contract separately, thus maintaining its unique accountability for funds while allowing management to occur within an organization that can address cross-system needs. The unique vantage point created by an MCO may provide the only real breakthrough for creating a genuine child-serving system that removes barriers between typically opposing and artificially separated child welfare, juvenile justice, and behavioral systems (Ogles et al., 1998, p. 256–257).

The person or team that greets the older adult and his or her family at the point of contact is key to the success of any intervention. In addition to the basic clinical procedures that are germane to the early stage of contact, that person or team must communicate specific consumer rights, such as grievance protocols. Practitioners must present consumers with a range of options, including benefit plans and providers, and must institute a peer counselor system. Indeed, consumer involvement should be ubiquitous, from formal and informal feedback mechanisms to participation on oversight boards.

Managed care is a data-driven model of service. Most of the information a clinician needs will be at his or her fingertips. Such information will include accepted treatment protocols, standardized assessments that link clinical and fiscal data, comprehensive service records, and reports specific to individual consumers. Obviously, as the field moves in such a direction, there are both opportunities and hazards. At some point, collection and interpretation of such data will be common at point of intake. If this system improves clinical and fiscal outcomes and expedites care for the consumer, it is indeed a sign of progress.

Blended funding and capitation provide the needed fiscal context to support holistic consumer-focused treatment plans. That capitation can benefit consumers may be a surprising concept. Unfortunately, many social work practitioners fail to consider what costs are associated with serving consumers. Yet, in the context of socially defined scarce resources, all human services organizations operate within fiscal parameters. In the days of indemnity insurance, there was no disincentive to overserving consumers. That all citizens would eventually pay for these kinds of decisions was a reality that rarely broke through the consciousness of practitioners. This has changed in the managed care environment. In this new world, providers are routinely given an enrollment fee for each consumer covered or, as began in the days of diagnostic related groups, a flat fee for a consumer on enrollment. For many social workers, this aspect of managed care is anathema, for it is seen as restricting or withholding care. Intriguingly, the possibility that providing a consumer more than she or he needed was rarely viewed as an ethical issue, when in the presence of scarcity it is equally troubling.

If necessity is the mother of invention, then capitation forces provider and provider systems to scrutinize what they do, what works and what doesn't, and what service might be equally efficacious at less cost. If the old incentives to use intensive restrictive services have vanished, in their stead are incentives to use home- and community-based interventions. Such interventions can rely on formal and informal systems, and, in a supportive structural context, be unfettered by unnecessary medical necessity requirements and other rigid guidelines that restrict the ability to practice creatively. In such a system, social workers should thrive, and the profession may actually have a chance to operationalize key components of some of the primary conceptual frameworks and models that guide the profession, such as the ecological model and the strengths perspective. Thus, "although a focus on cost may initially appear to clash with system-of-care values, the managed care emphasis on appropriate care in fact matches nicely with the system-of-care values of community-based care in the least restrictive setting" (Ogles et al., 1988, p. 255).

Other positive possibilities are encouraged in a managed care environment in which shared or at-risk contracting is featured. If an MCO can either profit or expand services through wise stewardship of dollars, several kinds of initiatives should rise in prominence. First, a central feature of managed care is a focus on a population—or, in the parlance of business, "covered lives." There are incentives to promote health and wellness as opposed to treating illness. It stands to reason that the better the overall health of the covered population, the less risk for the provider. Health promotion can include standard medical interventions, such as regular physicals and dental maintenance, or efforts in the area of nutrition and exercise. Additionally, home-based case-management services allow a person to keep constant contact with a consumer, thus ensuring that existing problems are treated and monitored, or that the person maintains a level of activity that reduces the likelihood of physical or emotional decline. Rose (1997) has extended the potential of a population focus even more broadly, to include efforts to ascertain and ameliorate environmental, community, and even political impediments to health and well-being. When a provider is at risk, the provider has an invested financial interest in promoting and maintaining the health of those for whom they are held accountable.

Fragmented services are not only detrimental to older adults; they also increase costs to individuals, business, specialty providers, and society. An example is the underrecognition of substance abuse and emotional problems common in primary care. Through accurate assessment and intervention when substance abuse and emotional problems are detected, practitioners may recoup the costs associated with future medical care, absenteeism, and lost productivity for those in the workforce, and the indirect costs associated with reduced individual functioning. The cost of providing care in the area of behavioral health care pales in comparison to the medical costs associated directly or indirectly when such conditions go untreated (England, 1999).

Olfson et al. (1999) strongly stated that the integration of health and mental health care can reduce unnecessary expenditures for physical health care. They suggested three ways to accomplish such savings while improving care, strategies that have been highlighted throughout this chapter:

> The delivery and financing of health care can be structured in three ways to reduce patients' use of excess medical care services because of mental health factors. First, health care systems can be organized so that financing and management of medical and mental health services is integrated. Sec-

> ond, utilization managers and primary care physicians can be trained to identify patients whose excessive use of medical care is driven by mental health factors and to facilitate their access to mental health care. Third, in a managed care environment, pricing policies can be combined with utilization management techniques to increase access to mental health treatment where offset savings are possible. (p. 85)

Organizational context and financing strategies have been key themes in this chapter. Yet, although context is critical, quality care is still an interpersonal event; it is reflected in the dynamic of the professional-consumer relationship and the skill and proficiency of those entrusted to help. England (1999) for example, strongly advocated for clinically and fiscally integrated services, but also recognized the upper limits of structural changes to promote humanistic goals. She argued that "assessment and care management tools at the point of entry into the health system should be used to promote more patient-centered care" (England, 1999, p. 93).

This chapter has suggested that social workers are suited to play a vital role in consumer-centered managed care systems. By virtue of training in the area of comprehensive assessment, social workers are well positioned to greet people at the point of entry either individually or as members of a multidisciplinary team. The long experience of working within systems, both in the formal and informal sector, particularly through case management and historically as caseworkers, also prepares practitioners to serve in an augmented care coordinator role.

In the hypothetical managed care model posited from the previously described guidelines and functions, a central organization would be entrusted for the care for a specifically defined target population. On enrollment into such a program, a defined capitated rate would be credited to the program. This could be a simple flat rate for the number of covered lives or could be risk-adjusted based on the actuarial analysis. From this point, the MCO would be responsible for the care of the identified population. Given that the contract would be for the entire population, the enrollment fees would be pooled, therefore allowing flexibility on a consumer-by-consumer basis. In this model, the MCO must provide needed services for each consumer based on the length of the contract period. Thus, the MCO would not deny or cap services for each individual, yet, like indemnity insurance, the provider would profit in those instances in which individuals needed little care over the contract period.

In this model, it behooves the MCO to develop its own utilization review and quality-improvement capabilities. The external payer or contractor will focus less on the internal process of service position and more on the actual outcomes of service. The emphasis will be on a range of outcome indicators such as consumer satisfaction, consumer health and well-being, and the coverage or penetration rates within the defined population. It will also be important for the primary funder to profile consumers to ensure that "creaming" (or selectively selecting and serving those at least risk) or "dumping" (removing high-risk consumers from care) does not occur. This leaves the risk and the responsibility with the provider. In return, the MCO enjoys relative freedom to provide the services it deems to be clinically efficacious and cost-effective.

This is a real opportunity to put social work values in action. Without being encumbered by discrete reimbursement streams, the ways in which a consumer can be helped is limitless and can proceed from the goals established in the assessment and contracting helping phase. Such interventions must be justifiable on empirical and commonsense grounds and, as always, one must be cognizant of true cost limitations. In this model, a lead person serves as the care coordinator but will work within a multidisciplinary team. In practice, it is expected that classic medical and emotional services will still predominate. Yet, in this model, rent assistance, gym memberships, and the purchase of a pet companion are potential interventions chosen to address a consumer's goal and stated area of concern. If the overriding principle is accountability for actual outcomes of services, the process to get there can be widely diverse.

There are obvious challenges to such a model. First, this is an intensive model of service, as most person-centered models are; thus, caseload size becomes critical. In the absence of reasonable caseloads, case managers become crisis managers, and there is a great push to develop lockstep, organization-centered services. Second, there may be political problems to surmount both internally and externally. Any person-centered helping system that strays from medical predomination also alters the base of power. Establishing a nonphysician care coordinator, and imbuing the role with some power, is likely to create a stir in the professional ranks. Externally, it is always easy to stir public unrest when programs that are funded in part by taxpayers appear to engage in frivolous activity. Paying rent or for exercise classes, for example, do not seem like standard "medical" interventions and thus may be susceptible to condemnation. This is but one more reason to assess the outcomes of such programs both clinically and fiscally.

CONCLUSIONS: POLICY, PROGRAMS, AND RESEARCH ISSUES

Clearly, attempting to integrate ecological principles into managed care designs raises many issues. These include, among others:

- How is health care defined?
- What range of health and social services will be provided?
- Will only interventions that are medically indicated be provided?
- Will prevention, health promotion, and wellness programs be included?
- Will older adults be able to engage in "one-stop shopping?"

- Who will monitor the course of treatment?
- What are the ethical dilemmas involved in the use of scarce resources and access to care?
- What is the process of authorization and denial of care?
- What services support quality of life?
- What outcome studies need to be done to document best practices?
- How can best practices receive fiscal support?

In any respect, some forms of managed care are here to stay. Social workers must do more than bemoan this trend in health care financing. Aspects of managed care can create opportunities for social work professionals and afford us the opportunity to practice in a manner that encourages creativity and person-centered care. For some time, geriatric social workers have played an active role in conducting multifaceted assessments of older adults and in using case management to ensure that individuals are appropriately matched and receive health and social services (White, Simmons & Bixby, 1993). Such results suggest the "superiority of a functional approach as compared with the 'classical' disease-oriented approach in making decisions concerning treatment and the need for supportive care in older persons" (Ferrucci et al., 1991, p. 52). These findings have serious implications for competing health plans, which must examine the package of services they offer (Frank, McGuire, Bae & Rupp, 1997).

REFERENCES

Bachrach, L. (1995). Managed care: Delimiting the concept. *Psychiatric Services, 46*(12), 1229–1232.

Bandura, A. (1986). *Social foundations of thought and action: A social cognitive theory.* Englewood Cliffs, NJ: Prentice Hall.

Boult, C., Kane, R. L., Louis, T. A., Boult, L., & McCaffrey, D. (1994). Chronic conditions that lead to functional limitations in the elderly. *Journal of Gerontology: Medical Sciences, 49*(1), 28–41.

Bronfenbrenner, U. (1979). The *ecology of human development.* Cambridge, MA: Harvard University Press.

Camp, J., Pizer, C., & McCarty, D. *Designing and implementing managed behavioral health care in the public sector: Lessons learned and future directions.* Waltham, MA: Institute for Health Policy, The Heller School, Brandies University.

Canda, E. R., & Furman, L. D. (1999). *Spiritual diversity in social work practice.* New York: Free Press.

Coulton, C. J. (1981). Person–environment fit as the focus in health care. *Social Work, 26*(1), 26–35.

Dallek, G. (1998). Shopping for managed care: The Medicare market. *Generations, 22*(2), 19–25.

Davidhizar, R., & Giger-Newman, J. (1996). Reflections on the minority elderly in healthcare. *Hospital Topics, 74*(3), 20–29.

Diehl, M. (1998). Everyday competence in later life: Current status and future directions. *The Gerontologist, 38*(4),422–433.

Dowart, R., & Epstein, S. (1992). Economics and managed mental health care: The HMO as the crucible for cost-effective care. In J. Feldman & R. Fitzpatrcik (Eds.), *Managed Mental Health Care: Administrative and Clinical Issues*. Washington, D.C: American Psychiatric Press.

Edinburg, G. M., & Cottler, J. M. (1995). Managed care. In R. L. Edwards (Ed-in-Chief), *Encyclopedia of social work* (19th ed., Vol. 2, pp. 1635–1642). Washington, DC: NASW Press.

England, M. J. (1999). Capturing mental health cost offsets. *Health Affairs, 18*(2), 91–93.

Fandetti, D. V., & Goldmeir, J. (1988). Social workers as culture mediators in health care settings. *Health & Social Work, 13*(3), 171–179.

Ferrucci, L., Guralnik, J. M., Baroni, A., Tesi, G., Antonini, E., & Marchionni, N. (1991). Value of combined assessment of physical health and functional status in community-dwelling aged: A prospective study in Florence, Italy. *Journal of Gerontology: Medical Sciences, 46*(2), 52–56.

Fillit, H. M., Hill, J., Picariello, G., & Warburton, S. (1998). How the principles of geriatric assessment are shaping managed care. *Geriatrics, 53*(4), 76–84.

Frank, R. G., McGuire, T. G., Bae, J. P., & Rupp, A. (1997). Solutions for adverse selection in behavioral health care. *Health Care Financing Review, 18*(3), 109–121.

Friedland, R. B., & Feder, J. (1998). Managed care for elderly people with disabilities and chronic conditions. *Generations, 22*(2), 51–57.

Fuchs, V. (1999). Health care for the elderly: How much? Who will pay for it? *Health Affairs, 18*(1), 11–21.

Germain, C. B., & Gitterman, A. (1987). Ecological perspective. In A. Minahan (Ed-in-Chief). *Encyclopedia of social work* (18th ed., Vol. 1, pp. 488–499). Silver Spring, MD: NASW Press.

Greene, R. R. (1999). *Human behavior and social work practice.* (Rev. ed.). New York: Aldine de Gruyter.

Greene, R. R. (2000). *Social work with the aged and their families.* (Rev. ed.). New York: Aldine de Gruyter.

Greene, R. R., & McGuire, L. (1998). Ecological perspective: Meeting the challenge of practice with diverse populations. In R. R. Greene & M. Watkins (Eds.), *Serving diverse constituencies: Applying the ecological perspective* (pp. 1–28). New York: Aldine de Gruyter.

Greene, R. R., & Watkins, M. (1998). *Serving diverse constituencies: Applying the ecological perspective.* New York: Aldine de Gruyter.

Hoge, M., Davidson, L., Griffith, E., Sledge, W., & Howenstein, R. (1994). Defining managed care in public-sector psychiatry. *Hospital and Community Psychiatry, 45*(11), 1085–1089.

Hoge, M., Jacobs, S., Thakur, N., & Griffith, E. (1999). Ten dimensions of public-sector managed care. *Psychiatric Services, 50*(1), 51–55.

Komisar, H., Lambrew, J., & Feder, J. (1996). *Long term care for the elderly: A chart book?* [Mimeograph]. Washington, DC: Institute for Health Care Research and Policy, Georgetown University.

Kosloski, K., & Montgomery, R. J. V. (1994). Investigating patterns of service use by families providing care for dependent elders. *Journal of Aging and Health, 6*(1), 17–30.

Landress, H., & Bernstein, M. (1994). Managed care 101: An overview and implications for psychosocial rehabilitation services. *Psychosocial Rehabilitation Journal, 17*(2), 5–14.

Lawton, M. P. (1982). Competence, environmental press, and the adaptation of older people. In M. P. Lawton, P. G. Windley, & T. O. Byerts (Eds.), *Aging and the environment: Theoretical approaches* (pp. 33–59). New York: Springer.

McAvay, G. J., Seeman, T. E., & Rodin, J. (1996). A longitudinal study of change in domain-specific self-efficacy among older adults. *Journal of Gerontology: Psychological Sciences, 51B*(5), 243–253.

Moore, S. (1992). Case management and the integration of services: How service delivery systems shape case management. *Social Work, 37*(5), 418–423.

Ogles, B., Trout, S., Gillespie, K., & Penkert, K. (1998). Managed care as a platform for cross-system integration. *The Journal of Behavioral Health Services & Research, 25*(3), 252–268.

Olfson, M., Sing, M., & Schlesinger, H. (1999). Mental health/medical care cost offsets: Opportunities for managed care. *Health Affairs, 18*(2), 79–90.

Olsen, D. P., Rickles, J., & Travlik, K. (1995). A treatment-team model of managed mental health care. *Psychiatric Services, 46*(3), 252–256.

Pender, N. J. (1982). *Health promotion in nursing practice.* Norwalk, CT: Appleton Century-Crofts.

Riley, G. et al., (1996). Health status of Medicare enrollees in HMOs and fee-for-service in 1994. *Health Care Financing Review, 17*(4), 65–86.

Robinson, J. (1999). The future of managed care organization. *Health Affairs, 18*(2), 7–24.

Robinson, G. K., Crow, S. E., & Scallet, L. (1998). Managed care policy: Meeting the mental health needs of the aged? *Generations, 22*(2), 58–63.

Rose, S. (1997). Considering managed care. *Journal of Progressive Human Services, 8*(1), 57–65.

Rowland, D., Feder, J., & Keenan, S. (1998). Managed care for low-income elderly people. *Generations, 22*(2), 43–51.

Schaeffer, L., & Volpe, L. C. (1999). Focusing on the health care consumer. *Health Affairs, 18*(2), 25–27.

Schorr, L. (1988). *Within our reach.* New York: Anchor Books.

Shortell, S., Gillies, R., & Anderson, D. (1994). New world of managed care: Creating organized delivery systems. *Health Affairs, 13*(5), 46–64.

Silverstone, B. (1996). Older people of tomorrow: A psychosocial profile. *Gerontologist, 36*(1), 27–32.

Sofaer, S. (1998). More HMO information needed for seniors. *Generations, 22* (2), 25–31.

Tinetti, M. E., & Powell, L. (1993). Fear of falling and low self-efficacy: A cause of dependence in elderly persons [Special issue]. *Journal of Gerontology, 48,* 35–38.

U.S. Senate Special Committee on Aging. (1992). *Aging American: Trends and projections, 1991 edition.* Washington, DC: U.S. Department of Health and Human Services.

Weiner, J. (1996). Managed care and long term care: The integration of financing and services. *Generations, 20*(2), 47–53.

Weiner, J., & de Lissovoy, G. (1993). Razing a tower of Babel: A taxonomy for managed care and health insurance plans. *Journal of Health Politics, Policy and Law, 18*(1), 75–103.

Weiner, J., & Stevenson, D. (1998). State policy on long-term care for the elderly. *Health Affairs, 17*(3), 81–100.

White, M., Simmons, W. J., & Bixby, N. (1993). Managed care and case management: An overview. *Discharge Planning Update, 13*(1), 1, 18–19.

Wiener, J. M. (1996). Managed care and long-term care: The integration of financing and services. *Generations, 20*(2), 47–53.

Willis, S. L. (1991). Cognition and everyday competence. In K. W. Schaie (Ed.), *Annual Review of Gerontology and Geriatrics* (Vol. 11, pp. 80–109). New York: Springer.

Willis, S. L. (1996a). Assessing everyday competence in the cognitively challenged elderly. In M. Smyer, K. Schaie, W. Kapp, & B. Marshall (Eds.), *Older adults' decision making and the law.* New York: Springer.

Willis, S. L. (1996b). Everyday cognitive competence in elderly persons: Conceptual issues and empirical findings. *Gerontologist, 36*(5), 595–601.

Yee, B. W. K., & Weaver, G. D. (1994). Ethnic minorities and health promotion: Developing a "culturally competent" agenda. *Generations, 18*(1), 39–45.

Zedlewski, S. R., Barnes, R. O., Burt, M. R., McBride, T. D., & Meyer, J. A. (1990). *The needs of the elderly in the 21st century.* Washington, DC: Urban Institute.

◆ CHAPTER 9 ◆

Outcomes Research for Children and Adolescents

Implications for Children's Mental Health and Managed Care

Susan B. Stern

The challenge to better meet the mental health needs of children and adolescents has long occupied a position of top priority among researchers, clinicians, and policy-makers alike. Children and adolescents experience a high incidence of emotional and behavioral problems that render them less able to function at home, in school, or in their community (Cohen, Provet & Jones, 1996). Recent estimates place the prevalence of mental health disorder among this population between 14% and 26% (Brandenberg, Friedman & Silver, 1987; Tuma, 1989). The National Institute of Mental Health (NIMH, 1990) has estimated that between 11 and 14 million children under the age of eighteen are in need of mental health services. Sadly, there is a significant gap between the number of children in need of mental health services and those served. It has been estimated that over half of children in need of mental health services do not receive them and, for those who do, services are often inappropriate or ineffective (Henggeler, 1994; Saxe, Cross & Silverman, 1988; Tuma, 1989).

Such large numbers by themselves argue for the need for extensive mental health services; the form services must take, however, is far from straightforward. Not only are their numbers large, but children and adolescents present a unique set of features rendering the adequate development and provision of services to them complex. These complexities have been discussed by several authors (Kazdin & Weisz, 1998; Saxe et al., 1988) and include:

- Discriminating dsyfunctional symptomatic behaviors from individual variations in normal development, in part dependent upon the age and maturity of the child
- The tendency of children and adolescents to be referred for services by another person (typically a parent or teacher) as opposed to identifying a problem on their own

- The inherent risk because of this referral by a third party that disruptive behavioral problems will be overrepresented among children and adolescents while less obtrusive, internalizing difficulties will be slighted
- The inescapable and extensive involvement of multiple psychosocial influences in their life, partly as a function of children and adolescents' developmental dependence upon adults

Also, unique difficulties surround clinical work with individuals who are not self-referred and who may or may not share the concerns of the referring party (Kazdin & Weisz, 1998).

Although such complications are not insurmountable, they do challenge the policy-maker and mental health provider to be creative, thorough, and comprehensive in their attempts to plan for adequate service provision for this vulnerable population. One cannot proceed without a full appreciation for and understanding of the influences of basic human developmental processes upon work with children and adolescents (Cicchetti, 1984). It is likely that effective service provision will require the inclusion of parents or other primary caregivers, extended family members, peer networks, teachers, and, at times, other relevant community figures such as medical staff, court representatives, and recreational personnel. Additionally, children in need of mental health care are seen in a wide range of settings and across diverse service systems, often with multiple agency and system involvement, creating unique challenges for coordination and financing of care.

Complicating any response to this situation is the overwhelming transformation of the mental health service delivery system ushered in by managed care (Veeder & Peebles-Wilkins, 1998). Now, in addition to meeting the service needs of children and adolescents, mental health professionals are further challenged to do so in an atmosphere of restricted service options, reduced financial resources, and heightened accountability (Strosahl, 1994). Although its initial responses to managed care were less than friendly and despite continuing concerns, the professional community now largely recognizes that the mental health delivery system has been ineradicably transformed and that some form of managed care will continue into the foreseeable future (Strosahl, 1994; Veeder & Peebles-Wilkins, 1998). Managed care's emphasis upon accountability, in particular, demands that the mental health professional turn to the child and adolescent research community for information and guidance. This is not merely to stay current with the recent literature, but also actively to participate in the debates and concerns shaping the research agenda and priorities. Without such commitment and the knowledge that comes with it, the mental health community will prove unequal to the dual tasks of advocating effectively for those they hope to serve while also partnering with managed care organizations to shape the future of the mental health service delivery system.

This chapter will provide an overview and discussion of recent outcomes research pertinent to the mental health needs of children and adolescents as well as research bearing upon managed care's impact upon the provision of services to this population. Consideration will be given to the relevance of this research to managed care, the mental health professions, policy-makers, and consumer groups as well. Some of the questions that will be considered include: Which treatments have the most empirical support? How can the service-delivery system be adapted to maximize positive treatment outcomes for children and adolescents? What does research suggest about ethical practice? How can this be adopted to better serve clients and contribute to a more effective service system? What research outcomes will better inform managed care and the mental health community to guide efforts at collaboration, advocacy, and prevention? It is hoped that this discussion will help shape policy debates in such a fashion as to better render mental health services to children and adolescents within a managed care environment.

THE EFFECTIVENESS OF PSYCHOTHERAPY WITH CHILDREN AND ADOLESCENTS

The determination that psychotherapy is effective with children and adolescents is now well established within the professional literature. Over several hundred outcome studies have been identified that document psychotherapy's effectiveness (Kazdin & Weisz, 1998). Meta-analyses of earlier psychotherapy studies (Casey & Berman, 1985; Kazdin, Bass, Ayers & Rodgers, 1990; Weisz, Donenberg, Han & Weiss, 1995; Weisz, Weiss, Alicke & Klotz, 1987), literature reviews of effective practices (Kazdin & Weisz, 1998; Taylor & Biglan, 1998; Thyer, 1995), and studies of subgroups within the larger population of children and adolescents (Henggeler, Schoenwald, Borduin, Rowland & Cunningham, 1998; Kazdin, 1990, 1993) all lend further support consistent with this finding. Although this research is certain to bolster the clinician's confidence in and commitment to psychotherapy, we need to consider the findings in closer detail to better understand their specific parameters and mediating conditions. Such understanding will help insure the development of more effective, sensitive, and ethical policy practices. While certain policies will appear clear in light of specific outcomes research, other policies will undoubtedly emerge only through the process of professional debate.

With respect to the studies reviewed in this chapter, it is important to note that the preponderance of the evidence for effectiveness comes from interventions offered in the context of university-affiliated research projects. Few studies have evaluated child therapy in the context of traditional agencies and, among those that have, few have been methodologically rigorous, and little support for treatment effectiveness has been found (Weiss, Catron, Harris & Phung, 1999). There is an urgent need to expand beyond treatment efficacy studies in research settings to the study of treatment effectiveness in real-world practice settings, a point that will be returned to later in the chapter.

Outcomes research has not been restricted to the evaluation of any single model of psychotherapy. However, the vast majority of this research has focused upon behavioral and cognitive behavioral approaches to treatment, with over 70% of the research tilted in this direction (Kazdin et al., 1990). Furthermore, the consistent and overwhelming finding of all this research is that cognitive behavioral approaches to the mental health treatment of children and adolescents, as with adults, are highly effective (Kazdin & Weisz, 1998). It is quite apparent that cognitive behavioral approaches to psychotherapy have been more extensively studied, more thoroughly documented, and most successful in generating an impressive body of outcomes research that supports their efficacy and applicability with a variety of different mental health problems among children and adolescents (Thyer, 1995; Weiss & Weisz, 1995).

Cognitive Behavioral Outcomes Research Focused on Youth

Kazdin & Weisz (1998) and Thyer (1995) offer useful reviews that summarize some of the more promising examples of empirically supported treatments for children and adolescents with a variety of mental health problems. A primary focus of researchers and practitioners in this area involves the distinction between internalizing and externalizing problems, which together encompass the more prominent and typical problems within this field of practice. Internalizing problems reflects difficulties with inner-directed experience, such as might be common with depression and anxiety. These are also referred to as problems of overcontrol. Externalizing problems, on the other hand, are characterized by their impact upon the external environment. Also referred to as problems of undercontrol, externalizing problems include such examples as oppositional and aggressive behavior, delinquency, and hyperactivity. While the research evidence for these broad-based diagnostic categories and specific disorders is reviewed separately, it should be noted that in actuality disorders often coexist (e.g., co-morbidity) both within and across diagnostic bands.

Among internalizing problems, Cognitive Behavioral Therapy (CBT) has proven effective in producing therapeutic change with anxiety disorders as well as simple phobias and nighttime fears (Kazdin & Weisz, 1998; Ollendick & King, 1998). Although CBT takes many different forms, common characteristics of this approach can be identified. Typical interventions seek to help the child or adolescent to identify the biological, cognitive, emotional, and behavioral patterns associated with the experience of anxiety, to challenge negative cognitions once identified, to expand coping skills through the use of problem-solving training and relaxation or meditation, and to confront the anxiety-arousing situations through graduated exposure using such techniques as role play, imaginative exercises, and *in vivo* exposure. Use of homework is common and psychotherapy sessions are usually active, collaborative, and oriented towards rewards for effort and success. CBT outcome research for childhood anxiety is not extensive, but it has been impressive with regard to overall effectiveness with serious cases, durability of treatment results over time, specification of treatment mechanisms leading to the outcomes (change in anxious self-talk mediates change in anxiety symptoms), and replicability both across randomized controlled clinical trials and across research groups. Importantly, these studies have documented positive outcomes on multiple measures including clinical diagnosis; child, parent, and teacher report of symptom reduction; and anxiety observational measures, as well as on measures of co-morbid diagnoses such as depression (Kazdin & Weisz, 1998). Treatment of child anxiety may also include parents in some aspects; the evaluation of the systematic addition of family management training to CBT has shown strong enhancement effects (Barrett, Dadds & Rapee, 1996). CBT plus family management training appears to maintain its effects when delivered in a group format that potentially offers clinical benefits (e.g., parental support, multiple models) as well as cost benefits (Barrett, 1998).

Coping Skills Training (CST) is another empirically supported treatment that has demonstrated success with childhood depression (Kazdin & Weisz, 1998). Because of its cognitive behavioral roots, CST shares a number of characteristics with CBT. These include a focus on teaching the child or adolescent to identify cognitive schemas or attributional biases associated with the experience of depression and to learn skills to help facilitate more rewarding social interaction, maintain self esteem, and resolve conflict. Use of relaxation and exposure techniques to increase engagement in reinforcing activities are also commonly drawn upon. Although the outcomes research is similar to that of CBT for anxiety, there has been less of it and further research is needed to examine several issues raised by the research to date. For instance, stronger effects have been found for reducing adolescent depression than for depression in younger age groups; mechanisms hypothesized to mediate change have not been supported when tested; CST's differential effectiveness has not been clearly established; and, surprisingly, neither the addition of parent training or booster sessions appear to enhance the effectiveness of CST (Kazdin & Weisz, 1998). Further, participants in research on childhood and adolescent depression have been almost exclusively middle- and upper-income white youth. Given the research on the relationship between depression and stressors associated with poverty and minority status, treatment outcome research with diverse youth is badly needed (Cicchetti & Roth, 1998). Moreover, in light of what we now know about the persistence and negative consequences of childhood and adolescent depression as well as the risks for children of depressed parents (Cicchetti & Roth, 1998; Downey & Coyne, 1990), the mental health professions need to pay greater attention to the development of effective prevention as well as intervention programs (for example, see Beardslee et al., 1997; Clarke et al., 1995).

Among externalizing problems, Problem-Solving Skills Training (PSST) is a promising treatment for children and adolescents with oppositional and aggressive difficulties. PSST is based on research showing that youth with externalizing difficulties exhibit information-processing deficits and an attributional bias supporting aggression as a legitimate way to deal with conflict (Dodge & Frame, 1982; Slaby & Guerra, 1988). These youth also exhibit deficits in means-ends thinking, perspective-taking, and other problem-solving skills (Rubin, Bream & Rose-Krasner, 1991; Spivack & Shure, 1982), and have poorer communication skills than their nonaggressive peers (Dumas, Blechman & Prinz, 1994). Central to PSST is skill acquisition for the troubled child in the areas of how to approach social situations, solve interpersonal problems in a step-by-step fashion, and develop prosocial behaviors through modeling and reinforcement. Also utilized are methods such as role-playing, imagery rehearsal, and observation of peers who display valued self-control skills (Thyer, 1995). PSST, like CBT and CST, is highly structured, interactive, and predicated upon principles of reinforcement. PSST has been shown to be effective at significantly reducing aggressive and antisocial behavior among both nonclinic samples and in several well-controlled clinic studies with positive gains evident for up to one year later. Although the research clearly supports a role for focusing on cognitive processes and change in the treatment of externalizing disorders, it is not similarly clear that change in cognitive processes is what actually mediates treatment outcomes (Kazdin & Weisz, 1998).

Despite the promise of PSST, a number of caveats should be kept in mind in considering it as an intervention for children with externalizing problems, especially those exhibiting aggressive and antisocial behavior (Smith & Stern, 1997). In actual practice, PSST is often provided in a small-group setting, particularly with referred youths in schools and institutional settings. Some research suggests that placing aggressive youths together in group intervention can have iatrogenic effects (Dishion & Andrews, 1995). These effects may be mitigated by including in treatment competent children who can serve as role models (Prinz, Blechman & Dumas, 1994). PSST's effectiveness is limited among those youths with co-morbid diagnoses, learning delays, and who come from dysfunctional families (Kazdin & Weisz, 1998). Combining PSST with family interventions may produce more durable and generalizable change; for example, Kazdin, Siegal, and Bass (1992) found that PSST plus behavioral parent management training had a more marked effect on child antisocial behavior and delinquency, as well as on parental stress and depression, than either intervention alone.

Behavioral Family Interventions and Prevention

Behavioral family interventions such as Parent Management Training (PMT) have been enormously successful at garnering empirical support for their effectiveness (Kazdin & Weisz, 1998; Kendziora & O'Leary, 1992; Taylor & Biglan, 1998). Central to these approaches is a focus upon altering the dysfunctional child-parent interactions that are presumed to reinforce inadvertently the child's symptomatic behavior. Parents are trained in more effective child management strategies to increase the amount of positive parent-child interactions and minimize those that are negatively coercive. Of special note, changes in these parenting practices have been shown to alter child behavior, reinforcing the empirical base for behavioral family intervention (Patterson, 1982: Kazdin & Weisz, 1998).

Taylor and Biglan (1998) have written a comprehensive review of the research literature in this area specifically for clinicians and policy makers. They report consistently impressive outcomes for behavioral parent training focused upon improving child management skills with diverse child problems, although the most extensive evidence is for externalizing difficulties. These studies tend to be randomized, well-controlled studies; use multiple measures of child and family functioning, often including observation; and focus on the process as well as outcomes of therapy. Most of the studies are with pre-adolescent children; the research evidence for adolescents is both more limited and more mixed (Dishion & Andrews, 1995; Dishion & Patterson, 1992). This is similar to meta-analysis findings that therapy is more effective for children than for adolescents (Weisz et al., 1987). Because other variables such as poverty, quality of the marital relationship, parental mental health status, stress, and social isolation all contribute to and influence the adult's parenting capacities (Stern & Smith, 1995; Stern, Smith & Jang, 1999) and affect treatment engagement and outcome (Dumas & Wahler, 1983; Kazdin, 1990; Webster-Stratton & Hammond, 1990), parent training has also been broadened to enhance skills in other areas such as coping with extrafamilial stressors, conflict management, and couples' communication (Smith & Stern, 1997; Taylor & Biglan, 1998). Not only have parents benefited from these interventions, but their children have also been found to improve as well. Successful treatment in this area helps the parents separate parenting from non-parenting issues so as to improve their problem-solving in each domain (e.g., see Dadds, Schwartz & Sanders, 1987; Miller & Prinz, 1990; Wahler, Cartor, Fleischman & Lambert, 1993).

When teaching parents skills in behavioral parent training or family therapy, helping professionals need to take care in establishing a therapeutic relationship whereby parents do not feel blamed for their children's problems (Stern & Smith, 1999). Research on the process of behavioral parent training underscores the importance of maintaining an atmosphere of mutual collaboration when working with parents (Webster-Stratton & Herbert, 1993, 1994). Without helping families to feel that they are contributing to the solution and actively soliciting their input, behavioral family training may well be ineffective at breaking through the resistance that is so often encountered in this work. Parent stress and resistance has been shown to increase during various phases of parent training (Chamberlain, Patterson, Reid, Forgatch & Kavanagh, 1984; Spitzer, Webster-Stratton & Hollinsworth, 1991) with further teaching and confrontation increasing resistance whereas therapist reframing and support decreases it (Chamberlain et al., 1984; Patterson & Forgatch, 1985).

Behavioral family interventions offer the further advantage of maintaining their effectiveness even when offered in a group training format (which many families prefer) and, for some families, even in self-administered formats such as videotapes (Taylor & Biglan, 1998). In the former case, groups may increase access and engagement for parents least likely to seek or remain in clinic-based services (Cunningham, 1996). While both these formats are potentially cost-efficient ways to deliver effective services, this only may be the case when level of service is appropriately matched to parent and child needs. For example, Webster-Stratton (1990) found that only when parents who watched tapes also participated in a therapist-led discussion group were child changes maintained, and disadvantaged families were those least likely to maintain change. Although groups and media approaches are not for everyone, they may well prove beneficial when seeking to work with larger populations, especially as part of a prevention program. Unlike many other popular parenting approaches that attract both professionals and consumers, behavioral parenting groups and media materials (books and videotapes) are based on strong research evidence (Kazdin & Weisz, 1998; Taylor & Biglan, 1998). To the extent that managed care holds the promise to move beyond the treatment of illness towards the promotion of wellness, behavioral family interventions may well offer managed care an effective means to deliver on its promise of better care for all.

Family Therapy Approaches

Family therapy approaches that integrate structured systematic interventions and attend to multiple levels of the youth's ecology have shown the most promise in treating externalizing mental health problems in adolescents. In contrast, family therapy treatment outcome studies for youth internalizing problems are scarcer. Three interrelated areas of family-based intervention are suggested by the research on family processes and adolescent externalizing or disruptive behavior disorders (Smith & Stern, 1997). As with younger children and consistent with the behavioral family literature, the first area focuses on improving parenting skills and family management. Secondly, research on the critical role of the parent-child bond increasingly points to the need to strengthen the parent-adolescent affective relationship and youths' perceptions of supportive parenting (Liddle & Diamond, 1991; Stern, Smith & Jang, 1999). Third, family conflict has been associated with delinquency, substance abuse, and a host of other youth mental health problems (Henggeler, Schoenwald, Borduin, Rowland & Cunningham, 1998), and interventions that include adolescents in improving family members' communication and problem-solving skills to resolve conflict have been shown both to decrease negative youth outcomes and modify associated interaction patterns hypothesized to maintain them, with encouraging results at follow-up. For example, treatment outcome studies on functional family therapy (FFT), a social-learning-based approach that targets communication and negotiation skills, show that FFT reduces delinquency recidivism and out-of-home placement for status-offending and seriously delinquent youth.

Notably, changes in the family interaction patterns hypothesized to maintain adolescent problem behavior also are observed and outcomes are maintained at long-term follow-up, interrupting negative youth trajectories and resulting in significant cost savings (Alexander & Parsons, 1973; Gordon, Arbuthnot, Gustafsond & McGreen, 1988; Klein, Alexander & Parsons, 1977).

Similarly, multisystemic family therapy (MST) targets changes both in youth behavior and the family system but goes beyond most other family approaches in also systematically targeting the multiple domains in which youth behavior is embedded. Using a family-preservation model, services are provided in the youth's home and community guided by nine treatment principles that emphasize empowering parents and other caregivers with the skills and support to develop and carry out change strategies across the key systems linked with problematic child behavior (intrapersonal, family, peer, school, and neighborhood). Treatment is individualized and highly flexible, drawing on empirically based and pragmatic problem-focused interventions from a number of approaches—behavioral, cognitive-behavioral, structural, and strategic family therapies. MST has shown strong, consistent results in controlled clinical trials across settings in modifying family processes and attenuating adolescent serious antisocial behavior, including long-term reductions in delinquency recidivism, incarceration, and costs (Borduin et al., 1995; Henggeler, Melton & Smith, 1992). The effectiveness of MST in reducing youth drug and alcohol abuse and serious emotional disorders also has or is currently being investigated in randomized clinical trials with promising results on measures of symptomatology, youth and family functioning, out-of-home placements (e.g., psychiatric hospitilization), and cost dimensions (Henggeler et al., 1998). A study of MST dissemination shows that individual family outcomes are associated with adherence to the nine underlying principles (Henggeler, Melton, Brondino, Scherer & Hanley, 1997)—thus, the integrity or fidelity of treatment has important implications for program and policy decisions in provider settings under managed care.

IMPLICATIONS FOR PROGRAMS, POLICIES, AND RESEARCH

The mental health community has a professional obligation to offer treatments that are empirically supported, efficacious, and effective when implemented in a real-world setting. Managed care adds the further obligation to offer only those treatments that are maximally efficient and cost-effective without compromising quality of care. Thus, it is not enough merely to establish that a treatment works; one must also consider its cost, efficiency, and ability to sustain outcomes into the future. What does this imply for future mental health services and outcomes research under managed care? The discussion that follows is predicated upon the research findings that were reviewed earlier in this article. Several key issues will be explored and their implications for children's mental health programs, future research, and policy development will be considered.

It is common to end papers such as this with a call for further research, and this chapter will be no different. However, it is important to consider the recommendations that follow within the context of an altered mental health service-delivery system. Managed care has dramatically transformed the organizational, financial, and administrative structures of the mental health industry. It is essential that clinicians, policy-makers, and researchers all confront the implications of these pervasive changes to insure that future change is in the best interests of those children and adolescents (and their families) whom we seek to serve. Obviously, research is needed, but it must address mental health treatment mindful of the changes that have been wrought and are likely to ensue in future years. To do otherwise is to ignore the challenge of rendering treatment in a new era of accountability and frugality.

Continued Provision of and Research into Cognitive Behavioral Treatments

In light of the predominance of cognitive behavioral studies within the outcomes literature, several questions confront the policy-maker and clinician. Clearly, cognitive behavioral methodologies are strongly supported within the literature. Not only are such models effective, but they seem to meet managed care's requirement of efficiency and cost-effectiveness. A number of areas of research warrant further analysis and empirical study. These include further exploration into the contextual differences between research and natural settings in order to better understand those factors leading to differential outcomes (Kazdin & Weisz, 1998), further study of the mechanisms that lead to positive outcomes, further evaluation of the impact of the addition or deletion of collateral services (parent training and booster sessions) along with CBT for specific diagnostic problems, and a comparison between cognitive behavioral practice in a managed care environment and other practice settings.

The Need for Expanded Research into Other Treatment Modalities

Cognitive behavioral studies can prove instructive for research into other treatment modalities. The issue here is not one of the superiority of cognitive behavioral treatment over other treatments (although that argument can be made) so much as its compatibility with the research enterprise. In effect, cognitive behavioral methodologies are eminently researchable and lend themselves naturally to evaluation by objective researchers. Were other models to subject themselves to the same degree of rigor in the articulation of delineated goals, specification of clear and replicable treatment guidelines, and utilization of reliable outcome measures, greater accountability would inexorably follow. Research would then be better positioned to more adequately inform these treatments as to what works (or not) and why. This is particularly important in light of managed care's call for greater accountability and the need to develop treatment models that are empirically verifiable.

Indeed, most treatment methods in common use have not been evaluated (Saxe et al., 1988) and clinicians tend to select interventions based on treatment familiarity and philosophical preferences (Schoenwald & Henggeler, in press). This does not imply that the approaches clinicians currently use are not effective; rather, we simply have little or no evidence that many of them do work. Several approaches to child and adolescent treatment may warrant further exploration because of their popularity with either clinicians or managed care. Psychodynamic treatment continues to be a favored approach among clinicians (Kazdin, Siegal & Bass, 1990) despite little empirical support (Russ, 1998). Similarly, play therapy, a technique developed specifically for work with children, has enjoyed renewed professional attention in recent years despite the relative lack of outcome research to support its effectiveness. In part, what each of these treatments offers its practitioners is a fertile means of thinking about their clients' problems within the context of their developmental history, family relations, and current treatment circumstances. Practitioners of these approaches believe this potentially richer understanding of the internal dynamics informing their clients' problems can aid in establishing a helping relationship, developing a meaningful treatment plan, and collaborating upon and following through with this treatment plan.

Traditionally, psychodynamic methods have been considered less amenable to empirical study due to the global nature of the underlying approach, broad goals, and highly individualized treatment plans (Russ, 1998). In line with this, psychodynamically oriented child therapy is relatively untested and the outcome studies that exist tend to be methodologically flawed, with many being case studies. Concerned with this state of affairs, psychodynamic researchers recently have turned their attention to the systematic, focused study of such interventions with youth (Fonagy & Target, 1994; Target & Fonagy, 1997) with increasing recognition of the pressing need for methodologically sound research on psychodynamic and play therapy (Russ, 1998; Shirk & Russell, 1992). Given these approaches' popularity with providers, rigorous evaluation of their efficacy for specific childhood disorders is critical to support their continued use, particularly in cases where alternative evidence-based interventions exist. Clarification of who might benefit from these approaches (and under what conditions) and exploration of those elements of treatment that lead to improved outcomes would be an essential part of strengthening these treatments within a managed care environment.

Brief solutions-oriented treatment offers another even more compelling example of a specific research domain that demands further attention.

Solutions-oriented treatments have burgeoned over the past decade partly in concert with the enormous growth of managed care. These approaches towards clinical work with children and adolescents share with cognitive behavioral treatments an emphasis upon clearly articulated goals, uniform guidelines to inform treatment, and well-specified outcome measures. Such characteristics should make these models quite amenable to outcomes evaluation. Unfortunately, this research attention has not been forthcoming until just recently (Stern, 1998). And even now, only a few studies have examined outcomes of solution-focused treatment and most are limited to client follow-up evaluations, the majority from the Milwaukee Brief Family Therapy Center (De Shazer & Berg, 1997). At this time, there are no rigorously controlled studies of solution-focused treatment for child behavior problems. The lack of further research is especially surprising given the enormous popularity solution-focused treatments enjoy in managed care circles.

Yet another approach to treatment that clearly warrants providers' and policy-makers' attention is Multisystemic Treatment—in this instance, because of its wealth rather than lack of research. Given its striking success with court-involved youth, among the most difficult populations confronting society, plus encouraging findings in treating substance abuse and serious emotional disorders, MST is proving to be one of the most promising empirically supported child and adolescent treatment modalities. Studies reported to be in the planning process (Henggeler et al., 1998) that generalize MST to new youth populations and problems (e.g., internalizing ones) should be carefully watched.

Multisystemic Treatment's relevance for managed care is heightened by the MST studies of cost-effectiveness and dissemination. Of special note, a randomized clinical trial of an MST continuum of care for children's mental health under a managed care model is being conducted in a large northeastern city (S. K. Schoenwald, personal communication, November 18, 1999). Additional studies of MST are currently underway to better understand its future potential (Henggeler et al., 1998). We need to know: What are the specific treatment mechanisms leading to clinical success? What other variables help account for this treatment's success or failure? What are the limiting conditions for its effectiveness? What personal (provider) and organizational factors affect successful dissemination and adoption of MST?

Maintenance of Change

Adequate follow-up in treatment outcome studies is critical for assessing an intervention's ability to sustain outcomes (Ivanoff & Stern, 1992; Kazdin & Weisz, 1998). For example, early enthusiasm for behavioral parent training was later tempered by findings of lack of maintenance of change for some families. Identification of groups for whom treatment was less likely to succeed and factors related to treatment failure led to treatment modifications and enhancing treatment effectiveness in future work.

Maintenance of change has important implications for child outcomes and for cost effectiveness under managed care. Some treatments initially may be more expensive, yet decrease the likelihood of children reentering the mental health system. Given the stability and persistence of many child disorders, intervention needs to be of sufficient magnitude to interrupt negative trajectories. Besides the need for adequate follow-up in research studies, this requires understanding and targeting factors related to generalization and durability of change in clinical practice. Treatment course and decisions should be matched to client need based on the best available knowledge and ongoing case monitoring. This does not necessarily imply that brief treatment is not sufficient for some children and disorders. Rather, it suggests that effective treatment may require a variety of treatment lengths, intensity, and constellations, running counter to the way many managed care organizations traditionally operate, with preauthorized limited number of sessions and costs computed over an episode of treatment rather than over the long term (including future cost savings that may or may not accrue to the initial treatment authorizer).

Central Role of the Family in Child Treatment

Research on behavioral and multisystemic family therapy underscores the importance of understanding children's behavior in context and involving parents or other caregivers in treating child and adolescent disorders. With rare exceptions that need to be further investigated (e.g., CST + parent training for depressed adolescents), involving parents in treatment either enhances child treatment outcomes or is actually the key to achieving change. As an example, for child externalizing problems such as conduct and oppositional disorder, behavioral parent training is not only by far the most supported treatment but also the only one considered well established using one current classification system (Brestan & Eyeberg, 1998).

Moreover (and consistent with the empirical evidence), among those concerned with improving the delivery of child and adolescent mental health services, there is a clear consensus that any intervention efforts need to include parents and other caregivers and empower family members in a collaborative partnership in service planning and delivery (Henggeler, 1994; Stroul & Friedman, 1986, 1994). There is a concern that managed care has been associated with loss of choice and threatens family members' voice in their child's treatment, with managed care organizations making treatment decisions instead of consumers in partnership with their providers (Scallet, Brach & Steel, 1997). To increase the likelihood of meaningful participation, the Federation of Families for Children's Mental Health (1995) has developed principles for family involvement in planning and implementing children's mental health services in managed health organizations. However, the National Mental Health Association findings suggest that families continue to be underrepresented in managed care planning at every level and they do not feel they are taken seriously when they are involved (Faenza & Steel, 1999).

Systems Level Changes in Children's Mental Health Services

The research reviewed thus far speaks to clinical-level outcomes whereas children's mental health services research addresses system-level changes needed to support effective treatment. Precipitated by Knitzer's (1982) landmark study of the condition of children's mental health services in the United States and supported by the NIMH 1984 creation of the Child and Adolescent Service System Program (CASSP), the focus of systems-level reform has been on creating culturally competent, child-centered and family-focused, community-based comprehensive systems of care (for a review, see Ruffolo, 1998). Systems-level program planning and research recognizes that the complexity of children's mental health needs requires an array of services, across multiple systems (mental health, child welfare, medical, educational, juvenile justice) with implications for integration and coordination of care and financing arrangements.

The broad-based call for systems-level changes in mental health services for children and adolescents includes the reduction of restrictive services such as hospitals, improved access to home- and community-based services, heightened service integration and accountability, reformed funding mechanisms to foster other systems changes, and more training for providers in the delivery of cost-effective treatments (Henggeler, 1994; Stroul & Friedman, 1986, 1994). These changes warrant further discussion in light of managed care's dominance within the service system at present.

Whereas children and youth services have been dramatically reshaped over recent decades by the advocacy of consumers, families, and other stakeholders to insure the adequate provision of a full range of services that are informed by the values of nonrestrictiveness, open access, community-based orientation, and partnership with families, most managed care organizations operate under capitated reimbursement and typically use business strategies such as limiting the plan benefits available to consumers, negotiating lower fees from providers, and diverting consumers from more expensive to less expensive services in order to manage financial risk. The consumer advocacy perspective and business perspective intersect in some beneficial and problematic fashions. While managed care organizations are likely to support an expansion of community-based services as a means of reducing institutional care, it is unclear how far they will go in this direction. Will it be a priority to establish a full range of community services to better enable families to take advantage of them or will managed care organizations simply restrict access to the institutional services and expect families to fend for themselves in the community? Will transportation services and child care be offered to low-income families to support their participation in treatment or will such supports be viewed as outside the obligation of the managed care company's insurance plan? These are questions that go to the heart of the issue of whether managed care companies will fully seek to better the health of their members or simply limit cost to please the financial interests of stockholders and others. An ethical position stemming from a public health perspective demands that managed care organizations collaborate with the community in an effort to construct a mental health delivery system that is built on firm outcomes evaluation, accessibility of appropriate services, and partnership with those families whom we seek to help.

The philosophy and underlying principles of managed care and systems of care for child mental health are entirely compatible: most appropriate, least restrictive level of care that is simultaneously effective and fiscally responsible (Lourie, Howe & Roebuck, 1997). Unfortunately, the reality does not live up to the potential. In a national study of children's mental health private sector systems of care under managed care contracts, Lourie et al. (1997) only found five programs that met their study criteria. These sites had, encouragingly, developed integrated continuums of care, yet none could be considered systems of care with mechanisms for access, cross-system coordination, child and family case management and coordination, and strategies for funding as defined by CASSP (Stroul & Friedman, 1986).

Low-Income Families

Medicaid offers a compelling case example of the opportunity for partnership between managed care and the community. It is now well documented that a dramatically increasing proportion of Medicaid recipients are under some form of managed care (Faenza & Steel, 1999; Perloff, 1996; Scallet, Brach & Steel, 1997). This trend continues in spite of the fact that little research exists on the impact of managed Medicaid on treatment outcomes for this population (Perloff, 1996). Of concern is the fact that managed care companies have pioneered their innovations with a largely employed, lesser-risk population without the need or expectation for such supports as case management, transportation, and outreach. Managed care organizations may be inexperienced in meeting the needs of multistressed families, needs that affect treatment engagement and outcomes in child mental health. Will managed care companies limit utilization without equally attending to the full range of supports and services typically needed by poor people in order to maintain their health status? For children, innovative financing strategies will be needed to support comprehensive, preventive, family-centered and community-based services as Medicaid programs come increasingly under the influence of and are altered by managed mental health care (Meyers, 1994).

One aspect of managed care's impact upon the service system available to the urban poor is of particular cause for alarm. Because of their lack of access to private health care, many low-income families are dependent upon a potpourri of local services, both formal and informal, sometimes referred to as the urban safety net (Faenza & Steel, 1999; Perloff, 1996). These services—offered through public hospitals, local clinics, and academic institutions—tend to be marginally funded and hence more vulnerable to the impact of budget changes, and are often more responsive to the needs of the local community through the participation of local residents on their boards and planning committees. As managed care's presence has expanded within the urban setting it has redirected many medicaid recipients away from the urban safety net providers, thereby threatening the financial integrity of this informal, but local, service system. Unless managed care organizations develop service partnerships through the urban safety net, the threat exists that the local service system will be financially undermined.

Furthermore, as managed care expands within the public sector and to low-income populations, MCOs will need to serve more culturally diverse children and families. Concern has been expressed about managed care organizations' understanding of and preparedness for developing culturally competent programs and policies (Scallet et al., 1997).

Reconsideration of Outcome Evaluation

Effective outcomes research requires clarity of definition surrounding exactly what is to count as an effective outcome. Outcomes need to address the presenting problems that bring children and families into treatment in a way that is clinically meaningful. Often this has meant a narrowing of clinical focus to gauge the effect of treatment upon the relief of symptoms or reduction of the chief complaint. In effect, the treatment's effectiveness is demonstrated through a measurable reduction in the problems that led to the involvement in treatment in the first place. While such a bottom-line emphasis is understandable within a service system pressured by managed care with increasing demands for accountability and documentation of effective outcomes, it is important not to lose sight of what may be lost by such a narrowing of focus.

Clearly specified goals need not be narrowly focused. Kazdin and Kendall (1998) and Hoagwood (Hoagwood, Jensen, Petti & Burns, 1996) have argued for the importance of examining the impact of treatment on more than simply symptomatic improvement at the individual level. In addition to reducing symptoms, special attention should be given to impairment—whether a child or adolescent can meet the demands of home, school, and community life. Another important domain—consumer perspective—is frequently considered a core outcome within managed care but rarely reported in research studies. Researchers either do not tend to include the consumer perspective in outcomes evaluation or, if included, accord it as much weight as psychometrically based assessments. Consumers' subjective experience can shed light on the relationship between seeking care, retention in treatment, and outcomes (Hoagwood et al., 1996), and deserves increased attention by researchers as well as managed care service providers and policy-makers.

Given the call for broad-based systemic changes within child and adolescent services, it is essential that outcomes evaluators also gauge the effect of treatment on the larger ecosystem of the child and the service system in which treatment takes place. We have seen the importance of interventions directed at the parents' well-being that subsequently lead to improvements in the child. Were outcomes studies only to assess effectiveness at the level of individual change, important variables might be lost. The implications of this apply not just to future research but also to day-to-day treatment authorization. Treatment effectiveness can be severely hampered by a case manager or clinician who cannot see past the individual child's symptoms to consider the broader ecological field. Heightening one's awareness of these factors can lead to more effective outcomes and promising treatment for the future.

Measures of social impact including service use, consequences on systems, and monetary costs and gain are important criteria in evaluating treatment outcome (Kazdin & Kendall, 1998) and are an increasing priority under managed care. While many of the studies reviewed in the first half of the chapter report outcomes in multiple domains (e.g., symptom reduction, impairment, family functioning, recidivism), few include social impact measures beyond reporting recidivism and incarceration rates and costs in the studies of juvenile delinquency. Multisystemic Treatment research serves as an exemplar in this area, reporting service-level use, cost-effectiveness, and projected system savings through reduced out-of-home placements (e.g., foster care, incarceration, and institutionalization). Developing measurement systems in managed care that maximize the researcher's rigor in capturing treatment outcomes, have social validity from consumers' and society's perspective, and address impact measures for systems that serve children and families and for our national behavioral health care, is a challenge necessitating new types of collaborations. A number of efforts are under way that will themselves require study and evaluation (National Mental Health Services Knowledge Exchange Network Bulletin, 1998). With good measurement, research partnerships with managed care may offer a unique opportunity to improve child mental health services by capitalizing on the large amount of available data (Miller & Farber, 1995).

Evaluation of Managed Care Outcomes in Children's Mental Health

Clearly, the managed care system itself needs to be evaluated and monitored as a part of this ongoing process. While few would disagree that managed care has failed to influence, and even dominate, the provision of mental health services within this country, it is far less obvious what the full impact of this influence has been. Although many businesses and states have touted managed care's success in improved utilization rates, reduced costs, and improved service access as contrasted with traditional fee-for-service arrangements, the research evidence in this area is far from settled (Perloff, 1996). Questions related to differential impact of service structure upon varying populations and provider groups, the influence of fee structures and financial incentives upon service provision, and the range of services available under different service arrangements all need further and ongoing exploration as managed care both changes the health and behavioral health care fields and itself evolves and changes form. Research is especially critical in formulating policy for children's services as managed care enters the public sector and rapidly expands from behavioral health care systems to the array of other service systems that affect youth and their families, (Scallet et al., 1997). Beginning with managed care's "explosion" into child welfare, we can expect movement, perhaps slower, into other child-serving systems (such as juvenile justice) and impact on the educational system, with implications for systems-of-care initiatives as more child-serving systems come under or are influenced by managed care (Scallet et al., 1997, p. 6).

Unfortunately, at a time of rising emphasis on systems of care, evidence for both treatment and cost effectiveness lags behind (Hoagwood, 1997; Saxe et al., 1988). Counter to expectations, several studies have not supported the increased effectiveness of coordinated comprehensive systems of care (Bickman, 1996; Glisson & Hemmelgarn, 1998). Most notably, the first evaluation of a managed behavioral health integrated continuum of care for child and adolescent mental health—the five-year Fort Bragg study—significantly increased costs without differences in clinical outcomes compared with traditional services at two matched site (Bickman, 1996). The continuum of care did increase service access and continuity of care, use of less restrictive environments, and consumer satisfaction—service outcomes of interest to managed care organizations—but the disappointing findings in this and other system-of-care evaluations raise questions about exactly what is being evaluated and the gap between systems-level outcomes and child- and family-level treatment outcomes (Bickman, 1996, 1997; Hoagwood, 1997; Saxe & Cross, 1997; Sechrest & Walsh, 1997). Some consider the findings unsurprising given the lack of support for most child and adolescent treatment as commonly practiced in community-based settings and the lack of attention to the conceptual and empirical basis of interventions used within continuum-of-care initiatives. This is the old "black box" conundrum—i.e., more services are being delivered in a more integrated, coordinated manner, but more of what? (Henggeler, Schoenwald & Munger, 1996; Weisz, Han & Valeri, 1997). More closely linking the clinical research on treatment efficacy for child and adolescent disorders to evaluations of service delivery systems is a priority for future research on systems of care under managed behavioral health.

The Gap Between Research and Clinic Studies: Lessons from Meta-analyses

There were repeated calls for the adoption of empirically supported interventions by those in the helping professions even before the advent of managed care, and certainly these have been heightened by the demands for accountability of the current managed care environment. However, despite a substantial body of empirical evidence on treatment efficacy for selected child and adolescent behavioral and emotional problems, further evidence suggests that these are not the interventions practitioners typically use

(Kazdin, Siegal & Bass, 1992; Weisz, Weiss & Donenberg, 1992). Furthermore, when the effects of child and adolescent treatment in primarily university-based research studies are compared with outcomes of the limited number of available studies of community-based clinic practice, the latter fare poorly with small effect sizes in meta-analyses (Hoagwood, Hibbs, Brent & Jensen, 1995; Weisz et al., 1992). In addressing the gap between research and community-based studies, concerns have been raised about the differences between these settings, whether the clients served in clinic settings somehow differ, for example, in problem severity and co-morbidity, and the training, resources, and constraints for therapists across these different conditions (Kazdin & Weisz, 1998; Schoenwald & Henggeler, in press; Weisz, Donenberg, Han & Kauneckis, 1995). Weisz et al. (1995) identified and empirically investigated ten possible explanations for the differences found between research and clinic-based treatment outcomes. Only three differences between the research and clinic-based studies were associated with the better outcomes in experimental studies: the latter's use of behavioral and cognitive-behavioral methods, specific focused treatments, and the provision of preplanned, highly structured interventions (e.g., through treatment manuals) with monitoring of therapist adherence. Given the small number of clinic studies, it would be premature to conclude that there still may not be other important differences between clinical practice in research studies and in the "real world." It has been suggested that empirically supported treatments in the research literature may require considerable adaption to diverse community-based (and managed care) practice settings (Kazdin, 1995; Kazdin & Weisz, 1998). However, since the available findings on empirically supported treatments for children and adolescents (as well as those on treatment specificity and structure) constitute our best knowledge on "best practices," they should be incorporated into current programs and policies with ongoing evaluation and modification as additional data emerge. Research needed to bridge the gap between research and practice settings should focus on issues in the transportability of empirically based interventions and on studies of effectiveness in real-world settings that can inform continued treatment development.

Dissemination of Best Practices

Bridging the gap between research on empirically based practice and real-world implementation requires partnerships between researchers, providers, policy-makers, and funders. The incredible growth of the managed care industry has occurred without significant input from researchers—or, for that matter, from key stakeholders such as consumers and practitioners (Plant, 1999). There are a number of tasks to be undertaken. The case already has been made that tests of empirically based and promising treatments need to be conducted under real-world conditions. Diffusing empirically validated knowledge is another priority to inform current treatment and policy decisions, and we need to pay greater attention to the literature and studies on utilization and dissemination of innovations (Gambrill, 1994; Taylor & Biglan, 1998). Researchers need to educate the public and mental health consumers as well as providers, policy-makers, and managed care organizations on current research findings about child mental health disorders and effective treatments (NIMH, 1990)—the campaign to inform the public about adult depression and the availability of effective treatments stands as a good example. Managed care organizations are calling for the use of "best practices" and accountability in demonstrating provision of effective services. Researchers and providers need to help policy-makers understand what constitutes good evidence (Biglan & Taylor, 1998) as well as the limits of our research knowledge and the need for flexibility in applying guidelines. As treatment protocols are developed for specific domains, the helping professions need to collaborate to bring their data to the table to influence these protocols and place them in the wider psychosocial and environmental context of our clients' lives as well as join together around the value base and respective codes of ethics that undergird our professions and provision of services (Cornelius, 1994; Thyer, 1995).

A call for an emphasis on accountability is not new to social work or to the other helping professions. Managed care is, perhaps, pushing this agenda forward, but the professions need to act not *because* of managed care but because of our professional and ethical obligation to provide effective services to children and families in need. Most importantly, we should be leading and partnering managed care, not just responding to it. The recent emphasis on evaluating treatments under "real world" conditions needs to be extended to the study of empirically based treatments under managed care so that research results will, in time, inform mental health care policy and standards of care. Recent efforts in this direction are promising, and although much is left to be done, developing empirically validated, efficacious, and effective child mental health interventions is a national priority (NIMH, 1990) and, for the behavioral health care community, a professional trust, even if managed care were to disappear tomorrow.

The author would like to acknowledge the contribution of Gary Eager in the development of this chapter and also thanks Marianne Berry and Sara Bachman for their thoughtful comments on the manuscript.

REFERENCES

Alexander, J. F., & Parsons, B. V. (1973). Short-term behavioral intervention with delinquent families: Impact on family processes and recidivism. *Journal of Abnormal Psychology, 81,* 219–225.

Barrett, P. M (1998). Evaluation of cognitive-behavioral group treatments for childhood anxiety disorders. *Journal of Clinical Child Psychology, 27,* 459–468.

Barrett, P. M., Dadds, M. R., & Rapee, R. M. (1996). Family treatment of childhood anxiety: A controlled trial. *Journal of Consulting and Clinical Psychology, 64,* 333–342.

Beardslee, W. R., Versage, E., Wright, J., Salt, P., Rothberg, P., Drezner, K., & Gladstone, T. (1997). Examination of preventive interventions for families with depression: Evidence of change. *Developmental Psychopathology, 9,* 109–130.

Bickman, L. (1996). A continuum of care: More is not always better. *American Psychologist, 51,* 689–701.

Bickman, L. (1997). Resolving issues raised by the Fort Bragg evaluation. *American Psychologist, 52,* 562–565.

Borduin, C. M., Mann, B. J., Cone, L. T., Henggeler, S. W., Fucci, B. R., Blaske, D. M., & Williams, R. A. (1995). Multisystemic treatment of serious juvenile offenders: Long term prevention of criminality and violence. *Journal of Consulting and Clinical Psychology, 63,* 569–578.

Brandenberg, N., Friedman, R., & Silver, S. (1987). The epidemiology of childhood psychiatry disorders: Prevalence findings from recent studies. *Journal of the American Academy of Child and Adolescent Psychiatry, 29,* 76–83.

Brestan, E. V., & Eyeberg, S. M. (1998). Effective psychosocial treatments of conduct-disordered children and adolescents: 29 years, 82 studies, and 5,273 kids. *Journal of Clinical Child Psychology, 27,* 180–189.

Burns, B. J., & Friedman, R. M. (1990). Examining the research base for child mental health services and policy. *Journal of Mental Health Administration, 17,* 87–97.

Casey, R. J., & Berman, J. S. (1985). The outcome of psychotherapy with children. *Psychological Bulletin, 98,* 388–400.

Chamberlain, P., Patterson, G. R., Reid, J. B., Forgatch, M. S., & Kavanagh, K. (1984). Observations of client resistance. *Behavior Therapy, 15,* 144–155.

Cicchetti, D. (1984). The emergence of developmental psychopathology. *Child Development, 55,* 1–7.

Cicchetti, D., & Roth, S. T. (1998). The development of depression in children and adolescents. *American Psychologist, 53,* 221–241.

Clarke, G. N., Hawkins, W., Murphy, M., Sheeber, L. B., Lewinsohn, P. M., & Seeley, J. R. (1995). Targeted prevention of unipolar depressive disorder in an at-risk sample of high-school adolescents: A randomized trial of a group cognitive intervention. *Journal of the American Academy of Child and Adolescent Psychiatry, 34,* 312–321.

CMHS project develops performance indicators for managed behavioral health care. (1998). *National Mental Health Services Knowledge Exchange Network Bulletin, 1,* 1–3. Washington DC: Substance Abuse and Mental Health Services Administration (SAMHSA).

Cohen, P., Provet, A. G., & Jones, M. (1996). Prevalence of emotional and behavioral disorders during childhood and adolescence. In B. L. Levin & J. Petrila (Eds.), *Mental health services: A public health perspective* (pp. 193–209). New York: Oxford University Press.

Cornelius, D. S. (1994). Managed care and social work: Constructing a context and a response. *Social Work in Health Care, 20,* 47–63.

Cunningham, C. E. (1996). Improving availability, utilization, and cost efficacy of parent training programs for children with disruptive behavior disorders. In R. D. Peters & R. J. McMahon (Eds.), *Preventing childhood disorders, substance abuse, and delinquency* (pp. 144–160). Thousand Oaks, CA: Sage Publications.

Dadds, M. R., Schwartz, S., & Sanders, M. R. (1987). Marital discord and treatment outcome in behavioral family therapy for child conduct disorders. *Journal of Consulting and Clinical Psychology, 55,* 396–403.

De Shazer, S., & Berg, I. K. (1997). What works? Remarks on the research aspects of solution-focused brief therapy. *Journal of Family Therapy, 19,* 121–124.

Dishion, T. J., & Andrews, D. W. (1995). Preventing escalation in problem behaviors with high-risk young adolescents: Immediate and one-year outcomes. *Journal of Consulting and Clinical Psychology, 63,* 538–548.

Dishion, T. J., & Patterson, G. R. (1992). Age effects in parent training. *Behavior Therapy, 23,* 719–729.

Dodge, K. A., & Frame, C. M. (1982). Social cognitive biases and deficits in aggressive boys. *Child Development, 53,* 620–635.

Downey, G., & Coyne, J. (1990). Children of depressed parents: An integrative review. *Psychological Bulletin, 108,* 50–76.

Dumas, J. E., Blechman, E. A., & Prinz, R. J. (1994). Aggressive children and effective communication. *Aggressive Behavior,* 20, 347–358.

Dumas, J. E., & Wahler, R. G. (1983). Predictors of treatment outcome in parent training: Mother insularity and socioeconomic disadvantage. *Behavioral Assessment, 5,* 301–313.

Faenza, M. F., & Steel, E. (1999). Mental health care coverage for children and families. In T. P. Gullotta, R. L. Hampton, G. R. Adams, B. A. Ryan, & R. P. Weissberg (Eds.), *Children's health care: Issues for the year 2000 and beyond* (pp. 117–136). Thousand Oaks, CA: Sage Publications.

Fonagy, P., & Target, M. (1994). The efficacy of psychoanalysis for children with disruptive disorders. *Journal of the American Academy of Child and Adolescent Psychiatry, 33,* 45–55.

Gambrill, E. (1994). Social work research: Priorities and obstacles. *Research on Social Work Practice, 4,* 359–388.

Glisson, C., & Hemmelgarn, A. (1998). The effects of organizational climate and interorganizational coordination on the quality outcomes of children's service systems. *Child Abuse and Neglect, 22,* 401–421.

Gordon, D. A., Arbuthnot, J., Gustafsond, K. E., & McGreen, P. (1988). Home-based behavioral systems family therapy with disadvantaged juvenile delinquents. *American Journal of Family Therapy, 16,* 243–255.

Henggeler, S. W. (1994). A consensus: Conclusions of the APA task force report on innovative models of mental health service for children, adolescents, and their families. *Journal of Clinical Child Psychology, 23* (Suppl.), 3–6.

Henggeler, S. W., Melton, G. B., Brondino, M. J., Scherer, D. G., & Hanley, J. H. (1997). Multisystemic therapy with violent and chronic offenders and their families: The role for treatment fidelity in successful dissemination. *Journal of Consulting and Clinical Psychology, 65,* 821–833.

Henggeler, S. W., Melton, G. B., & Smith, L. A. (1992). Family preservation using multisystemic family therapy: An effective alternative to incarcerating serious juvenile offenders. *Journal of Consulting and Clinical Psychology, 60,* 953–961.

Henggeler, S. W., Schoenwald, S. K., Borduin, C. M., Rowland, M. D., & Cunningham, P. B. (1998). *Multisystemic treatment of antisocial behavior in children and adolescents.* New York: Guilford.

Henggeler, S. W., Schoenwald, S. K., & Munger, R. L. (1996). Families and therapists achieve outcomes: Systems of care mediate the process. *Journal of Child and Family Studies, 5,* 177–183.

Henggeler, S. W., Schoenwald, S. K., & Pickrel, S. G. (1995). Multisystemic therapy: Bridging the gap between university- and community-based treatment. *Journal of Consulting and Clinical Psychology, 63,* 709–717.

Henggeler, S. W., Schoenwald, S. K., Pickrel, S. G., Rowland, M. D., & Santos, A. B. (1994). The contribution of treatment outcome research to the reform of children's mental health service: Multisystemic therapy as an example. *The Journal of Mental Health Administration, 21,* 229–236.

Hoagwood, K. (1997). Interpreting nullity: The Fort Bragg experiment—a comparative success or failure? *American Psychologist, 52,* 546–550.

Hoagwood, K., Hibbs, E., Brent, D., & Jensen, P. (1995). Introduction to the special section: Efficacy and effectiveness in studies of child and adolescent psychotherapy. *Journal of Consulting and Clinical Psychology, 63,* 683–687.

Hoagwood, K., Jensen, P. S., Petti, T., & Burns, B. J. (1996). Outcomes of mental health care for children and adolescents: I. A comprehensive conceptual model. *Journal of the American Academy of Child and Adolescent Psychiatry, 35,* 1055–1063.

Ivanoff, A., & Stern, S. B. (1992). Self-management interventions in health and mental health settings: Evidence of maintenance and generalization. *Social Work Research and Abstracts, 28,* 32–38.

Kazdin, A. E. (1990). Childhood depression. *Journal of Child Psychology and Psychiatry, 31,* 121–160.

Kazdin, A. E. (1995). Scope of child and adolescent psychotherapy research: Limited sampling of dysfunctions, treatments, and client characteristics. *Journal of Clinical Child Psychology, 24,* 125–139.

Kazdin, A. E. (1993). Treatment of conduct disorder: Progress and directions in psychotherapy research. *Development and Psychopathology, 5,* 277–310.

Kazdin, A. E., Bass, D., Ayers, W. A., & Rodgers, A. (1990). Empirical and clinical focus of child and adolescent psychotherapy research. *Journal of Consulting and Clinical Psychology, 58,* 729–740.

Kazdin, A. E., & Kendall, P. C. (1998). Current progress and future plans for developing effective treatments: Comments and perspectives. *Journal of Clinical Child Psychology, 27,* 217–226.

Kazdin, A. E., Siegal, T. C., & Bass, D. (1992). Cognitive problem-solving skills training and parent management training in the treatment of antisocial behavior in children. *Journal of Consulting and Clinical Psychology, 60,* 733–747.

Kazdin, A. E., & Weisz, J. R. (1998). Identifying and developing empirically supported child and adolescent treatments. *Journal of Consulting and Clinical Psychology, 66,* 19–36.

Kendziora, K. T., & O'Leary, S. G. (1992). Dysfunctional parenting as a focus for prevention and treatment of child behaviour problems. In T. H. Ollendick & R. J. Prinz (Eds.), *Advances in child clinical psychology* (Vol. 15, pp. 175–206). New York: Plenum Press.

Klein, N. C., Alexander, J. F., & Parsons, B. V. (1977). Impact of family systems intervention on recidivism and sibling delinquency: A model of primary prevention and program evaluation. *Journal of Consulting and Clinical Psychology, 45,* 469–474.

Knitzer, J. (1982). *Unclaimed children: The failure of public responsibility to children and adolescents in need of mental health services.* Washington, DC: Children's Defense Fund.

Liddle, H. A., & Diamond, G. (1991). Adolescent substance abusers in family therapy: The critical initial phase of treatment. *Family Dynamics of Addiction Quarterly, 1,* 55–68.

Lourie, I. S., Howe, S. W., & Roebuck, L. L. (1997). Private sector managed care and children's mental health. In C. J. Liberton, K. Kutash, & R. M. Friedman (Eds.), *A system of care for children's mental health: Expanding the research base* (pp.47–54). Tampa, FL: Research and Training Center for Children's Mental Health.

Meyers, J. C. (1994). Financing strategies to support innovations in service delivery to children. *Journal of Clinical Child Psychology, 23* (Suppl.), 48–54.

Miller, B., & Farber, L. (1996). Delivery of mental health services in the changing health care system. *Professional Psychology: Research and Practice, 27,* 527–529.

Miller, G. E., & Prinz, R. J. (1990). Enhancement of social learning family interventions for child conduct disorder. *Psychological Bulletin, 108,* 291–307.

National Institute of Mental Health. (1990). National plan for research on child and adolescent mental disorders. (DHHS Publication No. ADM 90–1683). Rockville, MD: Author.

Ollendick, T. H., & King, N. J. (1998). Empirically supported treatments for children with phobic and anxiety disorders: Current status. *Journal of Clinical Child Psychology, 27,* 156–167.

Patterson, G. R., & Forgatch, M. (1985). Therapist behavior as a determinant for client noncompliance: A paradox for the behavior modifier. *Journal of Consulting and Clinical Psychology, 53,* 846–851.

Perloff, J. D. (1996). Medicaid managed care and urban poor people: Implications for social work. *Health and Social Work, 21,* 189–195.

Plant, R. W. (1999). The future of psychotherapy in a changing health care system. In T. P. Gullotta, R. L. Hampton, G. R. Adams, B. A. Ryan, & R. P. Weissberg (Eds.), *Children's health care: Issues for the year 2000 and beyond* (pp. 197–228). Thousand Oaks, CA: Sage Publications.

Prinz, R. J., Blechman, E. A., & Dumas, J. E. (1994). An evaluation of peer coping skills training for childhood aggression. *Journal of Clinical Child Psychology, 23,* 193–203.

Rubin, K. H., Bream, L. A., & Rose-Krasner, L. (1991). Social problem solving and aggression in childhood. In J. D. Pepler & K. H. Rubin (Eds.), *The development and treatment of childhood aggression* (pp. 219–248). Hillsdale, NJ: Erlbaum.

Ruffolo, M. C. (1998). Mental health service for children and adolescents. In J. B. W. Williams & K. Ell (Eds.), *Advances in mental health research: Implications for practice* (pp. 399–419). Washington, DC: NASW Press.

Russ, S. W. (1998). Psychodynamically based therapies. In T. H. Ollendick & M. Hersen (Eds.), *Handbook of child psychopathology* (pp. 537–556). New York: Plenum Press.

Saxe, L., & Cross, T. P. (1997). Interpreting the Fort Bragg children's mental health demonstration project. *American Psychologist, 52,* 553–556.

Saxe, L., Cross, T. P., & Silverman, N. (1988). Children's mental health: The gap between what we know and what we do. *American Psychologist, 43,* 800–807.

Scallet, L., Brach, C., & Steel, E. (1997). *Managed care: Challenges for children and family services.* Baltimore, MD: Annie E. Casey Foundation.

Schoenwald, S. K., & Henggeler, S. W. (in press). Services research and family based treatment. In H. Liddle, G. Diamond, R. Levant, J. Bray, & D. Santisteban (Eds.), *Family psychology intervention science.* Washington, DC: American Psychological Association.

Sechrest, L., & Walsh, M. (1997). Dogma or data. *American Psychologist, 52,* 536–540.

Shirk, S. R., & Russell, R. L. (1992). A reevaluation of estimates of child therapy effectiveness. *Journal of the American Academy of Child and Adolescent Psychiatry, 31,* 703–709.

Slaby, R. G., & Guerra, N. G. (1988). Cognitive mediators of aggression in adolescent offenders: 1. Assessment. *Developmental Psychology, 24,* 580–588.

Smith, C. A. & Stern, S. B. (1997). Delinquency and antisocial behavior: A review of family processes and intervention research. *Social Service Review, 71,* 382–420.

Spitzer, A., Webster-Stratton, C., & Hollinsworth, T. (1991). Coping with conduct-problem children: Parents gaining knowledge and control. *Journal of Clinical Child Psychology, 20,* 413–427.

Spivack, G., & Shure, M. B. (1982). The cognition of social adjustment: Interpersonal cognitive problem solving thinking. In B. B. Lahey & A. E. Kazdin (Eds.), *Advances in Clinical Psychology* (Vol. 5, pp. 323–372). New York: Plenum.

Stern, S. B. (1998). [Review of the book *Family-based services: A solution-focused approach*]. *Child and Adolescent Social Work Journal, 15,* 321–324.

Stern, S. B., & Smith, C. A. (1995). Family processes and delinquency in an ecological context. *Social Service Review, 69,* 703–731.

Stern, S. B., & Smith, C. A. (1999). Reciprocal relationships between antisocial behavior and parenting: Implications for delinquency intervention. *Families in Society, 80,* 169–181.

Stern, S. B., Smith, C. A., & Jang, S. J. (1999). Urban families and adolescent mental health. *Social Work Research, 23,* 15–27.

Strosahl, K. (1994). Entering the new frontier of managed mental health care: Gold mines and land mines. *Cognitive and Behavioral Practice, 1,* 5–23.

Stroul, B. A., & Friedman, R. M. (1986, rev. 1994). *A system of care for children and youth with severe emotional disturbance.* Washington, DC: Georgetown University Child Development Center.

Target, M., & Fonagy, P. (1997). Research on intensive psychotherapy with children and adolescents. *Psychotherapy, 6,* 39–51.

Taylor, T. K., & Biglan, A. (1998). Behavioral family interventions for improving child-rearing: A review of the literature for clinicians and policy makers. *Clinical Child and Family Psychology Review, 1,* 41–59.

Thyer, B. A. (1995). Effective psychosocial treatments for children: A selected review. *Early Child Development and Care, 106,* 137–147.

Tuma, J. M. (1989). Mental health service for children: The state of the art. *American Psychologist, 44,* 188–199.

Veeder, N. W., & Peebles-Wilkins, W. (1998). Research needs in managed behavioral health care. In J. B. W. Williams & K. Ell (Eds.), *Advances in mental health research: Implications for practice* (pp. 483–504). Washington, DC: NASW Press.

Wahler, R. G., Cartor, P. G., Fleischman, J., & Lambert, W. (1993). The impact of synthesis training and parent training with mothers of conduct-disordered children. *Journal of Abnormal Child Psychology, 21,* 425–440.

Webster-Stratton, C. (1990). Long-term follow-up of families with young conduct problem children: From preschool to grade school. *Journal of Clinical Child Psychology, 19,* 144–149.

Webster-Stratton, C., & Hammond, M. (1990). Predictors of treatment outcome in parent training for families with conduct problem children. *Behavior Therapy, 21,* 319–337.

Webster-Stratton, C., & Herbert, M. (1993). What really happens in parent training? *Behavior Modification, 17,* 405–456.

Webster-Stratton, C., & Herbert, M. (1994). *Troubled families, problem children—working with parents: A collaborative approach.* New York: Wiley.

Weiss, B., Catron, T., Harris, V., & Phung, T.M. (1999). The effectiveness of traditional child psychotherapy. *Journal of Consulting and Clinical Psychology, 67,* 82–94.

Weiss, B., & Weisz, J. R. (1995). Relative effectiveness of behavioral versus nonbehavioral child psychotherapy. *Journal of Consulting and Clinical Psychology, 63,* 317–320.

Weisz, J. R., Donenberg, G. R., Han, S. S., & Kauneckis, D. (1995). Child and adolescent psychotherapy outcomes in experiments versus clinics: Why the disparity? *Journal of Abnormal Psychology, 23,* 83–106.

Weisz, J. R., Donenberg, G. R., Han, S. S., & Weiss, B. (1995). Bridging the gap between laboratory and clinic in child and adolescent psychotherapy. *Journal of Consulting and Clinical Psychology, 63,* 688–701.

Weisz, J. R., Han, S. S., & Valeri, S. M. (1997). More of what? Issues raised by the Fort Bragg study. *American Psychologist, 52,* 541–545.

Weisz, J. R., Weiss, B., Alicke, M. D., & Klotz, M. L. (1987). Effectiveness of psychotherapy with children and adolescents: A meta-analysis for clinicians. *Journal of Consulting and Clinical Psychology, 55,* 542–549.

◆ CHAPTER 10 ◆

Facilitating the Enrollment of Elderly and Disabled Persons into Medicaid Managed Care

SUSAN M. CHANDLER

This chapter discusses the challenges faced and lessons learned when a state agency began planning for the enrollment of elderly and disabled people into a managed health care environment. The particular case study describes a state Medicaid agency's attempt to plan for the smooth transition of elderly and disabled people from their traditional fee-for-service medical system into privately managed care health plans under Medicaid contracts. The state agency had been anticipating this change since its inception of its Medicaid Managed Care Program. Phase I began in 1994 with the enrollment of the Aid to Dependent Children population and Phase II was expected to begin in 1997 with the aged, blind, and disabled populations. The agency wanted to ensure that:

1. There was sufficient information among the consumers about their choices so they could make well informed plan selections
2. There was sufficient inclusion of the target population in the planning efforts to ensure their active participation both in the program design and in the policy design
3. There was sufficient time to ensure that the medical provider networks were able to serve this population with continuous, high-quality medical care

THE HMO "MIRACLE" BEGINS TO FADE

It was becoming patently clear that many states had failed in their efforts to smoothly enroll consumers into managed care plans. The Health Care Financing Administration (HCFA), the federal agency that oversees Medicaid and Medicare, originally permitted each state a great amount of flexibility to enroll Medicaid-eligible persons into managed care. Early reports documented cost savings, high consumer satisfaction, and good qualitative outcomes (GAO, 1993; HCFA, 1993; GAO, 1995, National Governors' Association, 1996, Edinburg and Cottler, 1995). However, as more and more complaints were heard from both consumers and medical care providers (Rodwin, 1996), Congress and later the HCFA became more cautious about the benefits of managed care as the "solution" to the country's health care problems. Many states, as well as the U.S. Congress, began passing "patients' bill of rights" legislation, including measures that introduced more controls on managed care programs. The HCFA, as well as state insurance commissioners, began to more closely oversee managed care health plans. This Medicaid agency was cognizant of the many problems encountered by other states as they moved into managed care from fee-for-service plans. The approach attempted here was to employ a problem-*prevention* strategy. The agency initiated a plan that included facilitators and mediators to work with the target groups (i.e., the aged, blind, and disabled) to bring them into the change process.

GROWING COMPLAINTS ABOUT THE CURRENT HEALTH CARE INDUSTRY

In 1993, President Clinton attempted to reform the U.S. health care industry by using managed competition models. This effort, however, was scuttled without much serious congressional debate. The American Medical Association, along with the health insurance industry, launched a well-financed television advertising campaign that used a fictional couple named Harry and Louise. This couple raised the specter that Clinton's health care reform efforts were really a governmental take over of medical decision-making and raised fears among Americans that they would lose their ability to choose their own doctors or select their own insurance plan. The issue of "choice" is a strongly emotional issue among Americans and taps a deep vein of American values and beliefs. In reality, the health care policy problem in America is that there is no comprehensive, national health care policy or universal coverage. In fact, most Americans receive their health coverage based on the plan their employers choose for them and most employees are only covered with private insurance for as long as they are attached to the labor force. In 1998, over 40 million U.S. citizens had no health insurance at all. Nonetheless, the public's fear associated with any type of "national" health insurance system "reform" resulted in the Clinton initiative being defeated just as every other reform initiative has been defeated since President Roosevelt suggested that national health insurance should be a part of the Social Security Act in 1935.

The magnitude and breadth of these fears highlight the fact that complaints, disputes, and dissatisfaction with America's health care industry involve high stakes for everyone. Even before the recent explosion of managed care programs, most of the existing strategies for resolving consumers' problems with their health care providers were unsuccessful. Beckman et al. (1994) found that relationship issues were cited as a reason for 71% of all malpractice suits. Meschievitz (1994) suggested that malpractice litigation is extremely slow and complicated, prohibitively expensive, relatively inaccessible, and delivers only minimal patient satisfaction. James Reeves (1994) explained that understanding the physician-patient relationship is crucial to understanding how disputes developed and how they could best be resolved. He contends that from the patient's perspective, illness causes both intense physical and emotional suffering. Worries are often around how much discomfort there will be, when the ill person may return to a normal lifestyle, what the costs will be, and who will pay for the treatments. Patients place great trust in their physicians and believe that their doctor, with the help of technology, will fix their problem and cure the illness. The physician, on the other hand, knows that medicine is not perfect and that not all diseases are easily diagnosed or treatable. Physicians often believe, however, that they are in the best position to make decisions for their patients and patients cannot comprehend the complexities of the choices available. Physicians today bring to their work worries about managing the business, billing, insurance, personnel problems, and liability fears. These differing perspectives are rarely discussed or even fully understood by the doctors or the patients. As a result, the patient's subjective experience of the illness may seem to be ignored by the physician as he or she goes about the business of providing the best medical care available.

THE NEW COMPLEXITIES OF MANAGED CARE

Increased levels of complexities have now overlaid this situation with the new structures of managed care plans. Often, patients (now called "members") must communicate first with a primary care physician (often called a "gatekeeper") who has been incorporated into the health care plans and has the responsibility of monitoring and authorizing the use of health services. Gary Rosenberg (1998) states that managed care has resulted in a change in the benefits philosophy from an open-ended service benefit (e.g., fee-for-service) to negotiated payment mechanisms with utilization controls. The managed care entity, whether a public agency, lead agency or managed care organization (MCO), functions as the single point of entry to the service system. Managed care contracts generally require the contractor to provide, create, or purchase a specified, predefined package of services. If contractors need to purchase additional services beyond their capacity, they develop or subcontract with a network of other service providers. The member is guaranteed access to the benefit, but the organization or arrangement of how that benefit will be delivered is under the purview of the MCO. In the managed care environment, the primary care provider (PCP) is responsible for delivering or arranging for the delivery of all health services required by the covered person under the conditions of the contract. The PCP is typically responsible for approving and monitoring the provision of all services covered by the health plan to the member. Acting as a case manager, this primary care provider becomes the gatekeeper or single point of entry for patient access to health care services.

To simplify access to a continuum of services and ensure coordination of care, the plan may incorporate a broad range of general and specialty services within a network or organization of affiliated providers. To discourage and reduce unnecessary procedures or inappropriate service use, a member may be required to obtain prior approval or preauthorization for payment before admission to inpatient facilities, emergency rooms, or other high-cost or high-risk services.

MEDICAID MANAGED CARE

Prepaid health care plans were first developed under Medicaid contracts to improve access to and continuity of health care while controlling costs. Contracting with prepaid, fixed-fee managed care plans to deliver health care services to Medicaid beneficiaries first became an option for states in the 1960s. As federal and state Medicaid expenditures soared, states increasingly turned to managed care programs to help bring costs under control and expand access to health care for low-income families. By 1997, states had expanded prepaid managed care to cover more than 48 % of the Medicaid population (GAO, 1996). Most states felt comfortable moving welfare recipients into managed care environments. Most of these Medicaid beneficiaries were mothers and children who were relatively "inexpensive" to cover with medical insurance. Several states (Arizona, Tennessee, Oregon, Minnesota, and Michigan) enrolled their disabled populations into managed care plans along with their traditional welfare population groups. To date, only a few states have expanded their managed care initiatives to include acute care through nursing home–level care.

THE COMMON ELEMENTS OF MEDICAID MANAGED CARE

All prepaid managed care plans have two fundamental elements: a prospective capitated payment system and coordinated services. Generally, employers or the state will pay contracted health plans, such as HMOs, a monthly or capitated fee per enrollee to provide a range of medical services that are coordinated through primary care physicians. With a fixed prospective payment, this model attempts to create incentives for plans to provide preventive and primary care to ensure that only necessary medical services are provided. The second managed care element brings together an array of different services to ensure that an enrollee has access to needed care by linking individual beneficiaries with a single provider responsible for coordinating each member's health care needs (GAO/HEHS, 1996). Managed care programs have been severely criticized since these very incentives may be perverted to avoid spending money on the more vulnerable (and expensive) populations.

THE SPECIAL NEEDS OF THE DISABLED

Providing medical care for persons with disabilities is inherently challenging. As was evident in the early years of Medicare, the costs of providing health insurance to elderly and disabled citizens has outgrown all predictions. Medicaid eligibility groups the aged (those over sixty-five), blind persons, and persons with disabilities together into one category called the ABD categorically eligible. While these persons are grouped together for eligibility purposes, their needs and interests are quite different. Medicare will cover the ABD when the disability has been pronounced for over two years and there is little likelihood that a change will occur to return the person to an able-bodied status. However, with the tremendous technological improvements in health care, the elderly are living longer and for more time in a healthy status, while disabled persons may be quite young at the onset of the disability and have extensive medical needs for a very long duration. The younger disabled persons are also much more likely to want more independent living environments and community-based care, rather than long-term nursing homes or care home facilities that have been the traditional choice of frail elderly persons. Activist and rights groups for the disabled have also formed to insure that medical care is self-directed and responsive to their needs. An often ignored group lumped into the "disabled" category are the persons with serious mental illnesses. These people often have struggled for years to find a mental health professional and/or specific medications that match their particular needs. They and their advocates are quite reluctant to turn their care plans over to a new primary care provider under a new managed care network just because the state has begun contracting with managed care plans. Most of the ABD population feels strongly that the traditional fee-for-service system is appropriate for meeting their unique needs. Many disabled persons with complex medical or mental health needs have designed a unique network of medical providers—perhaps a cardiologist, an internist, a physiotherapist, and a social worker. They fear that enrolling in a managed care plan will result in the loss of a specialist who is familiar with their medical needs, and losing access to that physician is of great concern. While case coordination of a person's care (as is done in managed care environment) usually results in an improved array of services and less likelihood of negative prescription interactions, most consumers are content with their existing arrangement of health care and don't want to change.

CONSUMER PROTECTION

The rapidly changing health care market and growth of managed care has been able to offer more access to health care. Many consumers see some tangible benefits. Many managed care plans, in order to entice consumers to enroll in them, are offering special coverage. Home visits, extended hours, transportation, and "enabling services" such as bilingual health care providers are now being offered as benefits beyond the traditional benefit package. Managed care plans can eliminate incentives for overuse of services and reduce financial barriers to care by cutting or eliminating out-of pocket costs. Managed care plans have the potential to better coordinate services, monitor quality, assess the performance of providers and networks, and provide information to their members.

However, Rodwin (1996) cautions that managed care can also create problems for consumers. First, the reimbursement structure may create incentives to skimp on services since any expenditure for providing services reduces net profit. This is, however, balanced by the need of the corporation to attract consumers who have the choice to enroll elsewhere or disenroll. Contract monitoring done by state insurance commissioners, Medicaid/ Medicare, and HCFA are supposed to also serve as quality-assurance mechanisms. Managed care plans are often accused of restricting a member's choice, which would, in a fee-for-service system, act as an escape valve if providers were performing poorly. Since, in managed care, consumers must choose providers from selected panels or a network of providers, opting out is sometimes difficult and cumbersome, and many consumers are not aware of their options. Utilization reviews that limit access to specialists are also seen as a barrier for the member. Limiting "unnecessary" tests and access to more expensive but, from the plan's perspective, presumably unnecessary medical care may also lead to complaints, unhappiness, disputes, and consumer frustration.

Rodwin (1996) suggests there is a need to implement consumer protections in four areas. The necessary reforms include (1) increased information and options for consumers, (2) standards for quality and marketing, (3) oversight of managed care plans, and (4) due process rights for consumers who have been denied services.

State Medicaid programs have also seen the need for several of these reforms. HCFA now requires that each state demonstrate how information will be shared with consumers about each plan prior to enrolling. Each state Medicaid agency must approve all plan advertising and there are limits on the types and forms of advertising and marketing the health plans may utilize. HCFA requires extensive monitoring of the quality of care in each plan and data are sent to HCFA quarterly. Each state Medicaid plan must have a documented grievance system, dispute-resolution system, and appeal structure as a requirement for HCFA approval, and those data are sent to HCFA for review. Several states have opened ombuds offices designed to assist persons with problems enrolling in managed care plans as well as advocate for members as they seek the care they need.

There is still conflicting evidence on the impact of managed care plans for the poor and serious concerns about the ability of managed care to sufficiently meet the needs (Rowland et al., 1995). Many believe that the power differential between a poor welfare family and the managed care industry is clearly stacked against the poor. Designing independent dispute-resolution systems like an ombuds office may provide some protection that previously did not exist, but few believe managed care approaches will be able to solve the problem of the millions of uninsured and underinsured in America.

A CASE STUDY

This case study describes a participatory planning effort to *avoid* the commonly associated problems, conflicts, and grievances involved in enrolling persons into managed care plans. In 1994, this state implemented a new managed care health insurance program. The plan enrolled low-income individuals and families into one of five private health plans. The state paid each health plan a per-patient, per-month (i.e., capitated) rate for each member who enrolled in each plan. Each plan was required to cover, at a minimum, a standard set of health insurance benefits and services. Each plan could provide additional services such as extended hours, transportation assistance, etc., but the standard Medicaid package of benefits had to be provided to all eligible persons.

Some health plans such as Kaiser Permanente were managed care plans with a closed provider panel. This meant that enrollees were required to obtain all medical services through an established list of physicians. Other plans were structured like Blue Cross / Blue Shield plans with a broader choice of physicians. Each consumer could select the health plan of his or her choice. Different medical, dental, and behavioral health services were offered to all enrollees.

Three categories of persons were eligible. The largest number of persons eligible were those receiving welfare benefits (AFDC/TANF). A second category were those eligible for the state's general assistance program. These persons had a disability and were unable to work at least thirty hours a week, and were thus eligible for state-supported cash assistance and also automatically eligible for Medicaid benefits. The final group were those low-income families who were not Medicaid eligible but had been covered by a state-funded plan for the "gap group" of uninsured families. Approximately 120,000 people were expected to enroll in the new managed care plans during its first year. By 1996, 165,000 people had enrolled.

Medicaid-eligible persons who were aged, blind, or disabled (ABD) were not enrolled in Phase I of this initiative and remained in the traditional fee-for-service Medicaid program. Phase II was designed to enroll the ABD population at a later date.

The Participatory Planning Efforts

Various concerns had been raised about the lack of planning and consumer involvement in the start-up of Phase I. The Department of Human Services (DHS) decided to use a consumer-based participatory planning strategy to assist its planning of Phase II. The Department of Human Services (DHS) hired two faculty members to facilitate several focus groups, to provide consultation on the development of a grievance system for Phase II, and to conduct research on other states' initiatives. The focus groups were designed to learn about the Phase II consumers' concerns, hear from the advocate groups, and collect data from which to design a problem-resolution system during the enrollment process and after implementation. The facilitators' contract called for conducting focus groups composed of those who would be eligible for Phase II, advocates, and other interested persons to discuss how to plan for the implementation of Phase II. The DHS was interested in providing extensive information about the new program to all of the potentially eligible members and insure that the information being provided was clear, accurate, and consumer-friendly. Approximately 11,000 aged, blind, or disabled people who were Medicaid eligible would be *required* to enroll in one of the QUEST II managed care plans. Another 22,000 persons who were Medicaid *and* Medicare eligible would have the option of enrolling in a managed care plan or remaining in a fee-for-service health insurance system.

The facilitators were also asked to review other states' managed care initiatives and make suggestions for the design of a grievance process or problem-resolution plan for consumers as they transitioned into Phase II. The facilitators were also asked to assist in the development of a consumer handbook that would be designed and developed by consumers to explain the elements of the benefit package, the alternative plans, how the enrollment process would be implemented, and how to select the plan of their choice.

The purpose of the facilitated processes was to provide information to the state agency prior to the implementation of Phase II. The first enrollment process had been criticized widely by consumers, providers, and advocates, as well as by the State Legislature. Many felt the state had moved too quickly into the implementation of managed care and hadn't sufficiently informed consumers or the medical community about what the changes would entail. Others felt that there hadn't been sufficient consumer input into the planning processes prior to implementation. Some physicians complained that they had lost patients to other health plans and generally there was a great deal of confusion during the early days of the transition process. Nonetheless, over 100,000 persons did successfully select a health plan and were enrolled in the plan they chose. If a person did not select a plan, or did not respond to the mailed questionnaire, he or she was automatically assigned into a plan and then given the option to change the plan within the first thirty days of enrollment.

Medicaid Managed Care "Successes"

All states had similar start-up problems in enrolling members into managed care. And while there are still critics of mandatory enrollment into managed care, the data now show that there are significantly more people covered by health insurance than before (access has increased), that the quality of care has improved, and that the per-patient, per-month cost has significantly decreased. The requirement of budget neutrality has also been met. This means that the costs of managed care since 1994 are less than what the projected costs would have been with the fee-for-service model with this same population.

Nonetheless, this state's effort was to improve on its implementation for the next phase of enrollments and make a concerted effort to design an inclusive, participatory process *prior* to the implementation. The intent was that these activities would prevent repeating the commonly made mistake of government . . . providing too little information, too late.

Medicaid Waivers

In order for a state to change any Medicaid requirements, the state must apply to the federal government for a waiver and amend its state plan. If HCFA approves a state's modifications, the federal government will continue to support the program with matching federal funds. The waiver "waives" the state from implementing certain federal requirements. The purpose of a waiver is to conduct a research/demonstration pilot project and provide more flexibility to a state to design a new design. A crucial component of any waiver is the fact that although the state may redesign its program elements, all changes must result in "budget neutrality." The federal government will not add any funds to the new program; thus, the program changes cannot cost more than the projected expenditures of the original Medicaid program. While Phase I of this Medicaid waiver expanded access to health insurance to thousands more citizens (a 27% increase), it had to accomplish this increase through savings by using managed care approaches. States are free to expand Medicaid services with state dollars, but the federal government will participate only at the level of budget neutrality for all waiver programs.

Problems with the start-up of Phase I, such as the unexpectedly high number of enrollees, insufficient staff, inexperienced staff, and computer and information system problems all plagued the new Medicaid program and resulted in lukewarm community support for any expansion, such as enrolling disabled and elderly population groups. HCFA's enthusiasm for mandating managed care coverage also began to wane in the mid 1990s.

The DHS was cognizant of the different challenges associated with enrolling a new population of disabled persons into a managed care environment. These population groups have more complicated and complex medical needs and are by definition a significantly more medically fragile and vulnerable population than the Phase I enrollees.

The Stakeholders

The DHS made a concerted effort to include all the identified stakeholders into the focus group process. A technical advisory group (TAG) as well as an advisory board had already been established with the initiation of Phase I. A new Phase II TAG was organized with representatives from the medical community, disabled and elderly consumers and their advocate groups, the long-term-care associations (representing the nursing home industry), the Department of Health, the Nurses Association, the existing Phase I health plans, a medical supply company, the Center for Independent Living, the Alliance for the Mentally Ill, the Office of United Self Help, the Mental Health Association, the Association for Home Care Providers, the Executive Office on Aging, representatives of agencies concerned about health care for the homeless, the Developmental Disabilities Council (an attached agency to the Department of Health), the Healthcare Association (representing hospitals), and several other interested citizens. Separate TAGs were also organized around the topics of behavioral health, case management, quality assurance, eligibility, the aged, persons with HIV/AIDS, DD/MR, the homeless, personal care/habilitation and children with special needs. Extensive mailing lists were developed for each TAG, but due to an uncertain start date, it was becoming more and more difficult to keep people interested in coming to meetings and participating. Discussing program elements prior to approval by the federal government seemed pointless to many consumers and advocates. Many advocates grew frustrated with DHS when the agency couldn't answer specific questions about the new plan being designed since HCFA approval was required and not yet obtained. Thus, while the DHS wanted to structure groups to insure broad-based inclusion, participation withered away. (To date, HCFA has still not approved Phase II, although the DHS is expecting to implement the program in October 2000.)

The multiple TAGs and the increasing frustration of the committee members became even more complicated due to an external, unanticipated activity. While the TAGs were meeting with DHS staff and the focus group strategies were being designed, several state legislators called for a series of public hearings called "Phase II Roundtables." The Roundtable sessions were primarily attended by advocate groups such as the Legal Aid, the Developmental Disabilities Council, the Mental Health Association, AARP, and mental health consumer groups. At times, the medical establishment sent representatives the Health Plans, the AMA, or other physicians groups representing medical specialists. Individual disabled persons and other interested citizens attended intermittently. At times the group had over fifty participants; other times, only five people attended. Each time the Roundtable met, several new participants attended for the first time, making forward progress of the meetings difficult. At some meetings, people were hearing about Phase II for the first time while others had been at planning meetings for over two years. In addition, these forums were running parallel to the DHS focus group meetings and the TAG planning sessions.

Competing Conceptions

Even before the facilitators had a chance to report back to DHS on the focus group data, a "consensus" was emerging from the Roundtable that there was a need for an independent Phase II ombuds office that would serve in the capacity of client advocate. The DHS was initially opposed to such a piece of legislation prior to the completion of the facilitators' report. In addition, there was no legislative appropriation to fund such an office, nor had such a program been agreed to by the health plans already under contract with DHS. Six health plans had successfully won new Phase I contracts after competing in a Request for Proposals (RFP) process. These plans would also be required to enroll the Phase II population whenever HCFA approval was granted. Thus, the existing health plans had a tremendous stake in the design of the Phase II requirements. Nonetheless, the Roundtable decided to introduce legislation to mandate that the DHS design and implement a Phase II ombuds office. DHS resisted such legislation, arguing that the products of the facilitation had not yet been completed, and such a study would be extremely beneficial to any final implementation plan. As the weeks went by, an adversarial process was brewing. Issues were polarizing between the Roundtable participants demanding an ombuds office to advocate on behalf of the rights of the elderly and disabled populations, and the DHS suggesting that the problem-resolution process based on the outcomes of the focus groups be considered. The DHS had been considering implementing a problem resolution / mediation process to assist consumers with concerns surrounding Phase II enrollment, access to providers, and consumer satisfaction. The DHS had been discussing these ideas with the TAGs and the focus groups. A competing reality emerged when the legislators began considering making the ombuds office a prerequisite for their support of Phase II.

Other States' Experiences

The state of Oregon had implemented an ombuds program that was considered as the program closest to Model State Managed Care Legislation and supported by the Consumer Coalition for Quality Health Care. Oregon's Medicaid program had a strong consumer rights orientation and the state had funded consumer choice counselors to assist each disabled person to enroll in his or her managed care plan. The state of Oregon passed enabling legislation and funded an Office of the Ombuds prior to enrolling disabled or elderly people into their managed care plans. The Oregon legislation mandated that:

> An Ombuds shall serve as a patient's advocate whenever the patient or physician or other medical personnel serving the patient is reasonably concerned about access to, quality of or limitation on the care being provided by a health care provider.

The primary mission of the ombuds office in Oregon "is to act as a client's advocate." HCFA requires that all Medicaid managed care plans have a consumer grievance procedure in place. All Medicaid programs must review consumer complaints, document them, and send them to HCFA. Plans are monitored and evaluated using these data. However, the public debate quickly became polarized, with some advocating an ombuds office to advocate for consumers (supported by consumer and advocate groups) and others advocating a dispute resolution office that would mediate and resolve consumer issues (supported by DHS and the health plans).

Problem-Solving Systems in Health Care Disputes

Slaikeu (1989) suggests that there is a continuum of theoretical options for resolving any dispute. His continuum begins with avoidance that basically "leaves the decision to chance, with the hope that some random event or the passage of time will make the problem go away" (p. 396–397). Slaikeu then describes negotiation and mediation as procedures in which the final decision rests with the parties themselves. The difference is that in mediation there is a third party to structure talks and assist the parties in reaching agreements. Arbitration and litigation are both techniques that use a decision-maker of a higher authority, assuming the parties have been unable or unwilling to resolve the problem themselves. At the final end of Slaikeu's continuum is a unilateral power play in which one side has the power to force a solution on the other side and the power to implement the decision.

Currie (1998) contends that as physicians further consolidate their practices under the umbrella of managed care and as consumers become more vocal and assertive, health care administrators are becoming increasingly aware that customer satisfaction is a powerful key for success. Currie (1998) suggests that when disputes arise, it is in the best interest of managed care providers to respond efficiently and effectively by offering mediation. Mediation has the benefits of being a dispute-resolution system that is impartial, confidential, flexible, and focused on self-determination while at the same time promoting empowerment, recognition, and consideration of basic human needs. Mediation in health care settings may be the best arrangement to provide consumers with the best opportunity to feel heard, get their underlying questions and concerns addressed, let go of their anger, attain a sense of relief, and learn from the experience. Doctors too may have the best opportunity in mediation to decrease their defensiveness, feel heard, let go of their frustrations, attain a sense of relief, clear up presuppositions held by their patients, and learn. Galton (1994) contends that mediation works best when it is initiated early and used often. When used that way, the rates of success are quite high. Its focus is on cooperative learning. Brett et al. (1996) studied 449 cases of mediation conducted by four different types of mediation service providers. Her study found that the costs of mediation were less than arbitration (and litigation), it took less time, and was judged to be more satisfactory than arbitration.

Emerging Issues in Finding "Consensus"

Several interesting issues emerged in this state's planning efforts. Several of the consumer and advocate organizations questioned the facilitators' impartiality, confidentiality protections, who "owned" the process, who was really making decisions, and who had the power. Early on in the focus group process, members noted concerns that the facilitators were "from the university," "friends of the director," "did not understand the needs of the disabled," and, because they were being paid by DHS, would only report to DHS what DHS wanted to hear. Several focus group members expressed concerns that they could not really "tell it like it was" because it was dangerous to complain about DHS to DHS. Some even suggested that complaining might mean that they wouldn't get the health plan of their choice. The ownership of the facilitation became an issue and many members of the focus groups complained that "it was a one-way street," with information coming from the group, being screened and "censored" by the facilitators, and then reported to DHS.

Although the agency had hired the facilitators to gather information from consumers, there had not been sufficient discussion about the role of the focus groups with regard to the agency's final plan. Nor had there been any agreements as to the role that the focus groups would play in actual policy-level decisions or what feedback mechanisms would be used to show how their suggestions were being considered in relation to the final implementation plans. The attempt of the agency was to include potential consumers and increase their participation. In retrospect, this seems quite naãve. No structure for agreements between the agency and the focus groups had been promised and the power clearly remained with the agency. Unfortunately, this was not explicitly discussed with the facilitators and the agency prior to organizing of the focus groups. Their role became compartmentalized as the conduit of information rather than as facilitators between the groups and the agency.

Several crucial issues emerged:

- Who should participate?
- Did the advocates really represent those who would be enrolling?

- Could DHS get adequate information from the future enrollees for planning purposes?
- Could a state agency successfully hire consultants and facilitators who would be trusted by the consumers?
- Was there a single type of facilitation process that would best meet the needs of the consumers and DHS?
- Could the facilitators be "trusted" to protect the confidentiality of the participants but provide the agency with accurate information?
- Could the facilitators guarantee that the outcomes of the focus groups would be used by DHS?

Outcomes

The strategy was to include consumers, advocates, and interested persons in the design and implementation of Phase II. The planning process had been going on for several years and there were numerous community meetings and legislative hearings to inform the community about Phase II. However, since HCFA was asking more and more questions about the readiness of DHS to expand enrollment to aged, blind, and disabled groups, and there were ongoing negotiations about the budget neutrality formula that would be used, the planning phases became protracted and the actual plan itself kept changing. While the existing Phase I health plans were most concerned with the design of Phase II since they would be directly responsible for this new population, most of the interest and political energy was coming from the consumer and advocate groups. These groups were seeking inclusion in the decision-making processes prior to implementation. It was a concern at the DHS that a lot of negative publicity would contribute to a further delay of HCFA's approval, and thus successful inclusion and honest participation was an important goal.

Another DHS priority was to include the consumer and advocate groups in the design of a consumer benefits handbook, so it would be consumer-friendly, acceptable and appropriate to the needs of this special population. A final goal was to include these groups in the training of benefit counselors who would be hired to insure sensitivity with this new population group as well as assist them in making an appropriate choice of a health plan.

Data Collection

The facilitators asked focus groups members broad, open-ended questions like, What kind of person would you like as a benefit/choice counselor? What features would make a good grievance process? What are your concerns about enrolling in new health care plans? Many of the responses raised by the consumers related to their basic fears about managed care. Most wanted guarantees that their special array of doctors would remain available to them. Most expressed concerns that different doctors would be affiliated with different plans and they wouldn't know which one to choose. For example, the facilitators documented consumer concerns such as "We should restrict kickbacks to drug companies"; "Has the state saved any money yet?"; "The gap group won't qualify for insurance"; "I don't like the drug formulary on Medicaid"; and "Why do we have to change from fee-for-service?" This type of information had been gathered and heard many times before in the earlier TAGs and did not provide new or constructive information to the DHS planners. Unfortunately, the process also did not result in an outcome in which consumers felt that they were being included in a planning process. The parallel legislative forums continued to frustrate the participants when concrete answers weren't being provided by DHS and agreements couldn't be secured prior to the federal government's approval.

Conclusions

Many things were learned in this attempt to use facilitation to improve a state agency's planning process. It is clear that merely hiring facilitators to run focus groups with the hope that some product will help improve a planning process is unlikely to produce the desired result. One clear lesson learned is that a better description of the outcome desired is crucial before launching an information-gathering exercise. Much more time in front-end discussions are required.

SITUATION OR CONFLICT ANALYSIS?

The task of facilitators usually is to analyze the situation and the readiness of the group to proceed. However, in this case, the hiring agency, the Department of Human Services, was not entering into an agreement or process with a group but rather asking for information to assist the agency plan and guide implementation. The facilitators were not asked to analyze the DHS's or the focus group members' abilities or readiness to participate, nor did they suggest that they should do so. The facilitators responded to a request to assist a department in gathering information from consumer groups and did so under the terms of a narrowly defined contract.

The focus groups used the facilitators' skills in process design. Group norms were established and the groups expressed interest in meeting their goals of telling the department about their concerns, worries, and fears. However, an unresolved tension emerged between the facilitators' wish to meet the hiring agent's objectives and the needs of the group members. It became clear when the agency received updates about the groups' concerns that the issues being raised by the facilitators on behalf of the agency were not the priorities of the focus groups. The group members wanted more information from the agency about Phase II and had a different agenda from the agency's wish to design a problem-solving mechanism for future grievances. Perhaps the facilitators needed to be more involved with the agency by providing more intermediary feedback so the agency could have redesigned the participatory mechanisms to include more staff or provide more informational sessions to attempt to better explain the facilitators' role and task. Process design needs not only to include the members of the group being facilitated but also must examine the external roles and relationships of the direct funders and the influence of external communities' activities (such as legislative hearings or other round-tables). There must also be a process to redesign and reformat the processes when early warning signs of trouble are emerging.

It seems quite possible that a facilitation process may succeed but the overall task fail. For example, group members may feel validated in the moment, may actively participate in the group, empowered and believing they have participated in a honest dialog. However, even with the best intentions, the final product may, for a variety of external reasons, not resemble the group wishes.

CONCLUSIONS

This chapter discusses the attempt of one state agency to be responsive to the needs of people moving into managed care. The strategy design was to hire facilitators to work with focus groups, made up of consumers, that would shape the policy and program decisions for the transition plan. While some successes were achieved in terms of improved communication, increased understanding between the policy-makers and the consumers, overall, the powerful stakeholders (e.g., the agency and the legislators) controlled the definition of the problem and therefore what solutions were regarded as relevant. This case study demonstrates that consumer-based, participatory planning strategies, while laudable, have a difficult time being implemented. External sources of power, such as the federal or state/local government, limit the flexibility of even state agencies to design consumer-sensitive strategies. Dialog was short-circuited and polarized into positional debates. The focus groups were unable and eventually unwilling to continue dialoging with the state agency and legislation was passed to structure a solution based on another state's experience. It is not yet known if this approach will meet the needs of the aged, blind and disabled person who will be enrolling into managed care plans in the near future.

REFERENCES

Beckman, H.B. et al. (1994). The doctor-patient relationship and malpractice: Lessons learned from plaintiff disposition. *Archives of Internal Medicine, 154*(12), 1365–1370.

Brett, J. M. et al. (1996). The effectiveness of mediation: An independent analysis of cases handled by four major service providers. *Negotiation Journal, 12*(3), 259–269.

Butler, P. A. (1996). *Policy on reforming Medicaid.* (NGA. No. 6) Washington, DC: National Governor's Association.

Currie, C. M. (1998). Mediation and medical practice disputes. *Mediation Quarterly, 15*(3), 215–226.

Davis, K. et al. (1996). Choice matters: Enrollees' views of their health plan. *Health Affairs, 14(2),* 99–112.

Edinburg, G. A. & Cottler, J. M. (1995). Managed care. In R. L. Edwards (Ed-in-chief), *Encyclopedia of Social Work* (19th ed., Vol. 2, pp. 1635–1642). Washington, DC: NASW Press.

General Accounting Office. (1993). *Medicaid: States turn to managed care to improve access and control costs.* (GAO/HRD 93–46.) Washington, DC: Author

General Accounting Office. (1995, April). *Medicaid managed care: More competition and oversight would improve California's expansion plan.* (GAO/HEHS 95–87.) Washington, DC: Author

General Accounting Office. (1996, July). *Medicaid managed care: Serving the disabled challenges state programs.* (GAO/HEHS 96-136.) Washington, DC: Author

Galton, E. (1994). *Representing clients in mediation.* Dallas: Texas Lawyer Press.

Gray, B. (1989). *Collaborating: Finding common ground for multiparty problems.* San Francisco: Jossey-Bass Publishers

Herrman, M. S. (Ed.). (1994). *Resolving conflict: Strategies for local government.* Washington, DC: International City/County Management Association

Marcus, L. J. (1995). *Renegotiating health care: Resolving conflict to build collaboration.* San Francisco: Jossey-Bass Publishers

Meschievitz, C. S. (1994). Efficacious or precarious? Comments on the processing and resoution of medical malpractice claims in the U.S. *Annals of Health Law, 3,* 123–138.

Reeves, James W. (1994). ADR relieves pain of health care disputes. *Dispute Resolution Journal, 49*(3), 14–21.

Rodwin, M. A. (1996). Consumer protection and managed care: The need for organized consumers. *Health Affairs, 15*(3), 110–117.

Rowland, D., Rosenbaum, S., Simon, L., & Chait, E. (1995). *Medicaid and managed care: Lessons from the literature.* Washington, DC: Kaiser Commission on the Future of Medicaid.

Rosenberg, G. (1998). Social work in a health and mental health managed care environment. In G. Schamess & A. Lightburn (Eds.), *Humane managed care?* Washington, DC: NASW Press.

Slaikeu, K. A. (1989). Designing dispute resolution systems in the health care industry. *Negotiation Journal, 5*(4), 395–400.

Veeder, N. & Peebles-Wilkins, W. (1998). Research needs in managed behavioral health care. In G. Schamess & A. Lightburn (Eds.), *Humane managed care?* (pp. 483–504). Washington, DC: NASW Press.

◆ CHAPTER 11 ◆

Managed Care and the Severely Mentally Ill

Current Issues and Future Challenges

WES SHERA

Managed mental health care is a relatively recent phenomenon and it has unfolded in a variety of forms since the early 1980s (MacLeod, 1993). This chapter describes the evolution of managed mental health care and focuses on the challenges faced by social work in responding to these developments. Major areas of action needed to enhance social work's role in managed care are discussed and include the need to understand current knowledge and practice in managed care, both domestically and internationally; the importance of using efficacy and best-practices information to design systems of care; the need to promote cultural competence in the delivery of services; and the critical role of supporting consumer involvement in the design and monitoring of managed mental health care.

THE EVOLUTION OF MANAGED MENTAL HEALTH CARE

Gorski (1995) describes the evolution of managed care as moving through five distinct phases: utilization review and restricting access; managing benefit utilization; managing care with a primary emphasis on cost control; managing outcomes; and horizontal and vertical integration of managed care systems. A variety of organizational arrangements have emerged, some of the more common models include carve-out programs, the staff or clinic HMO, a hybrid model that includes the previous two plus a backup affiliate model of independent providers, EAP-based programs, and facility-based integrated delivery system programs (Geller, 1998). For social workers, the language associated with this paradigm shift has been new and somewhat foreign. Medical necessity, differential benefit packages, penetration rates, capitation contracts, cost offsets, carve-outs, cost bands, and report cards are but a few of the terms in the new lexicon (Shera, 1996).

Arizona, Massachusetts, Washington, Utah, Tennessee, and Oregon have been the major pioneers in managed mental health care in the United States and the Mental Health Program of the Western Interstate Commission for Health Education (WICHE) has attempted to capture their experiences by developing a set of "blueprints for managed care" (McGuirk, Keller & Croze, 1995). The managed care models used in each of these states were compared by mapping their overall system of care and reviewing each of the following core components: beneficiaries and enrollment process, benefit package, benefit management model, managed care technologies, provider participation, financing plan, contracting arrangements, and accountability requirements. The pictorial blueprints derived from this exercise are intended to provide guidance in describing and clarifying mental health system status; modeling state or local managed mental health care plans; designing regional, county, or community systems of care; explicating the role of state hospitals; designing information systems; conducting staffing analysis; and developing interactive blueprints (McGuirk, Keller & Croze, 1995).

While these blueprints, as a tool for designing coherent mental health systems, would appear to be a step in the right direction, some observers of managed care have suggested that we have moved to an even more chaotic system of care (Shera, 1996). Numerous criticisms regarding managed mental health care have been voiced. Difficulties include: unrealistic limits on the number of units of service; a reversion to a more medically driven model of care; lack of emphasis on community-based outreach and psychosocial rehabilitation; little reference to the efficacy of psychosocial interventions; inadequate evidence of cost-effectiveness; and the danger of lowest-bid providers (Berstein, 1994; Brickman et al., 1995; Corcoran & Vandiver, 1996; NASW, New York City Chapter, 1994; Stern, 1993; Woolsey, 1993).

In its report card on the managed care industry, the National Alliance for the Mentally Ill (NAMI) identifies a series of major problems including out-of-date guidelines for intervention with schizophrenia, the limits on hospital care, insufficient provision of PACT-type programs, insufficient use of new anti-psychotic medications, inadequate suicide response, inadequate involvement of consumers and families in planning and delivery of services, lack of serious efforts to systematically address outcomes, and lack of commitment to ensuring adequate housing and access to vocational rehabilitation services (Hall, Edgar & Flynn, 1997).

Based on a recent review of the performance of managed care, Mechanic (1999) observes that managed care can reduce costs, HMO's seek out and attract healthier enrollees, persons who are severely mentally ill are more typically in Medicaid and other government programs, and the capacity or willingness of HMOs to effectively serve the severely mentally ill is uncertain. Even though performance data on managed mental health care is very limited, Mechanic claims that its development provides an opportunity to define mental health needs more sharply and develop broader and more effectively integrated systems of mental health care, which includes attention to housing, rehabilitation, safety, and quality of life. Two major factors that are critical in determining whether managed mental health care programs control costs and improve access to quality care are (1) the time available to plan and implement the new system and (2) the degree to which oversight mechanisms are in place to monitor clinical, administrative, and financial performance (American Psychiatric Association, 1997).

MEETING THE CHALLENGE OF MANAGED CARE

Firstly, it is critical to stay abreast of developments in the field of managed mental health care (Minkoff & Pollack, 1997). Groups like WICHE, the Center for Mental Health Services, and the National Association of Mental Health, and journals such as *Behavioral Health Care Tomorrow, The Psychiatric Rehabilitation Journal,* and *Psychiatric Services* provide information on state-of-the-art developments. The managed-behavioral-healthcare list-serve on the internet is another excellent resource. Schools of social work must update their curricula and continuing education offerings to reflect the realities of the managed care revolution (Misrahi, 1993; Strom & Gingerich, 1993). Managed care systems will require practitioners to conceptualize their practice quite differently and clinical assessments, therapeutic interventions, and practice protocols will be significantly modified (Corcoran & Vandiver, 1996; Paulson, 1996). This enhanced knowledge and awareness should also be used to identify and act on policy initiatives and take legal action essential to furthering the greatest good for clients in these systems (NASW, New York City Chapter, 1994). Examples of these policy changes include insurance reforms, reform of Medicaid and Medicare, essential community provider's legislation, and accreditation procedures for utilization review firms (Manderscheid & Henderson, 1995). Numerous changes and improvements in these and other areas of managed care have resulted from legal action brought forward by a variety of stakeholders, including social workers (Corcoran & Vandiver, 1996; Durham, 1994).

In recent years many countries have embarked on various types of health and mental health reform. These reforms have in large part been driven by governments' concerns for cost-containment, which have, in turn, been driven by an increasing process of global marketization and the need to control national deficits. Mechanic and Rochefort (1996) observe that national health systems throughout the world experience a number of pressures in common related to demographic and epidemiological factors, developments in science technology, medical demand, and rising public expectations. They argue that these pressures are producing convergence in the objectives and outcomes of these systems in several key areas, including cost-containment, health promotion, expansion of access, primary health care, patient choice, and the linkage between health and social services. Some helpful work in the area of mental health systems includes Rochefort's (1992) comparison of the United States and Canada; Huxley's (1990) comparison of the United

States and England; Hollingsworth's (1992) analysis of mental health services in United States, Germany, and the United Kingdom; and Ramon and Mangen's (1994) cross-national comparison of community care.

A recent article by Shera, Aviram, Healy, and Ramon (in press) used a comparative policy framework to compare new developments in the mental health sector in Britain, Israel, Canada, and Australia. The framework used for this comparison focused on the defining characteristics of the society, legislative mandate, sectorial location (within or separate from the health sector), funding streams, organizing values of the system, locus of service delivery, service technologies, the role of social work, inter-professional dynamics, the role of consumers, and evaluation of outcomes at multiple levels.

In reviewing the experiences of these four countries, the authors identified several themes:

- In all four countries these reforms were primarily driven by concerns regarding cost-containment or cost-reduction.
- Market mechanisms have been introduced within the delivery of mental health services in most of the countries, but the evidence regarding efficacy is still not solid.
- The reforms in all countries espouse a progressive community-based philosophy of care but in most cases this is rhetorical—the real agenda is cost-containment, and there has been either very little or insufficient reallocation of resources to community care.
- In all countries they observed examples of deskilling and deprofessionalization, again driven by cost concerns.
- The mentally ill, in all of the countries reviewed, are a significantly marginalized group. Consumer/user groups however, particularly in Britain and Canada, have had significant impacts on reform efforts, including the design and delivery of services.
- In terms of inter-professional dynamics, medicine and psychiatry in particular are playing more significant roles; greater emphasis is also being placed on interprofessional teamwork in providing care, but sometimes at the cost of disciplinary identity.
- More emphasis is being placed on the need for families and the community to take an increased role in caring for persons with mental illness
- Public support for changes in mental health systems is not strong; political will is an extremely critical component in promoting change.
- More progressive legislation and service system improvements are critical; however, the translation and implementation of policies and plans into practice is not as effective as it should be.
- Systematic monitoring to document outcomes and improve performance is in its infancy.

The themes that emerged from this review of mental health reform are informative. The similarities and differences in the experiences of other countries can spur our thinking in terms of more adequately responding to the needs of our mentally ill citizens. Too often we become trapped in our own context and unable to generate alternate or innovative perspectives.

USING BEST-PRACTICES INFORMATION

Social workers have an enormous role to play in identifying and implementing those interventions that have demonstrated efficacy for the severely mentally ill. Bachrach (1993) has identified the nine essentials for successful rehabilitation of the severely mentally ill. These include:

1. Individualized treatments
2. Environmental adaptation
3. A focus on consumer strengths
4. An emphasis on restoring hope
5. Optimism about the consumer's vocational potential
6. A range of comprehensive services
7. Consumer involvement in the treatment process
8. Continuity of care
9. A therapeutic relationship between the consumer and caregiver

With this as a contextualizing set of principles, the social worker needs to carry out a holistic assessment of both individuals and target populations and identify those interventions and systems of care that have the best probability of achieving positive outcomes for consumers in a cost-effective manner (Jerell, Hu & Ridgely, 1994).

Recent studies have suggested that the long-term outcomes for the severely mentally ill are better than we have previously assumed (Harding & Zahniser, 1994; Harding, Zubin & Strauss, 1992) and that positive attitudes towards these persons are critical to developing working relationships in which helpers connect with the person behind the disorder (Shera & Delva-Tauiliili, 1996; Strauss, 1992).

Social workers can also use the opportunity that managed care provides to design new systems of service for the seriously mentally ill (NASW, New York City Chapter, 1994; Simmons, 1994; Vaccaro, Yong & Glynn, 1993). Social workers must draw on the latest efficacy information on the disorders involved and appropriate interventions (Jerrell, Hu & Ridgely, 1994; Vaccaro, Young & Glynn, 1993). A few of these include individual and family psychoeducation (Lefley & Wasow, 1994), supportive psychotherapy (Novalis, Rojcewicz & Peele, 1993), assertive community treatment (Santos, 1996), multiple family support groups (McFarlane, 1994), psychosocial rehabilitation (Bedall, 1994), social network intervention (Biegel, Tracy & Corvo, 1994), and self-help groups (Segel, Silverman & Temkin, 1993).

The National Mental Health Association recently announced a nationwide grassroots initiative to introduce tested and effective models of care to state and local government officials throughout the United States. This initiative, known as Partners in Care (Community Access to Recovery and Empowerment), is funded by grants from Eli Lilly and Company and Pfizer, Inc. (NAMH, 1998). These model programs include the following.

- *The Village Integrated Service Agency,* located in Long Beach, California, provides a coordinated, comprehensive range of services to persons with severe mental illness. Members are partners in service planning, empowerment and employment are emphasized, and financing is capitation-based. In terms of outcomes, less than 20% of the Village members required hospitalization over a three-year period. There were also significant improvements in the quality of members' living, work, and social lives (Chandler, Meisel, Hu, McGowen & Madison, 1998).
- *The ACCESS West Philly program* is an intensive case-management project and multi-service drop-in center working with persons who are homeless, mentally ill, and frequently addicted in the West Philadelphia community. A notable feature of this program is the Connections for Consumers in Crisis, an after-hours diversion center.
- *Consumer Connections* is a program sponsored by the Mental Health Association in New Jersey. It serves consumers of mental health services who are interested in employment in the field of human services. They have established a core training program to provide basic information and skills necessary to begin to work as a consumer provider. They also provide a job opportunity bank, continuing education and a support network.
- *Community Residences* in Arlington County, Virginia, provides services to culturally diverse mentally ill adults through a full continuum of residential and support services. Services provided are voluntary and noncoercive, easily accessible, culturally appropriate, and focus on recovery and promoting community inclusion. Residential services are provided in ten facilities throughout the county.
- *Fast Track to Employment* is a program of the Mental Health Association of New York City. The program uses both professional staff and trained consumer providers and offers comprehensive vocational assessment, job placement, and supportive services. Consumers are initially placed in paid internships and then move on to competitive employment. Throughout this process, the program provides ongoing support through peer support groups.
- *Schizophrenics Anonymous* is a self-help consumer-run support group in Michigan. The Mental Health Association of Michigan provides both financial and administrative support. Schizophrenics Anonymous offers fel-

lowship, positive support, and companionship as participants share their experiences in coping with schizophrenia. They have developed a tool that provides all of the necessary information needed to start a local group of Schizophrenics Anonymous.

In an effort to capture new developments in mental health reform and best practices across Canada, the Health Systems Research Unit of the Clarke Institute of Psychiatry in Toronto was commissioned by the Federal/Provincial/Territorial Advisory Network in Mental Health to carry out a critical, evidenced-based review of the current state of knowledge and a situational analysis of mental health reform policies, practices, and initiatives.

The project consisted of three phases, an evidence-based review of the current state of knowledge about best practices relevant to mental health reform, a situational analysis of mental health reform policies, practices, and initiatives in Canada, and the development of guidelines for the implementation of best practices across systems of care. The situational analysis included thirteen examples of best practices; four received intensive site visits and nine less intensive reviews. What emerged from these analyses was an important set of lessons about what facilitates mental health reform. The findings included the following:

- A clearly articulated philosophy and principles typically underlie the specific innovations that have been implemented.
- A wide range of stakeholders were meaningfully involved in the planning and operation of innovative programs.
- Political will is a special dimension of system change.
- Infrastructure support is another essential element with powerful consequences.
- It is possible to successfully reallocate funds and personnel from institutional to community care.
- When support extends beyond health services to involve agencies from other sectors, it becomes possible to better address the broad range of needs among those with severe mental illness.
- With concerted action, stigmatizing attitudes can be changed and resistance to change overcome.
- The enthusiasm and dedication of skilled program directors, staff, and volunteers is essential for making the programs work. (Health Systems Research Unit, Clarke Institute of Psychiatry, 1997, p.15)

The authors argue that best-practice checklists should be used as guidelines for mental health systems planning and assessment of performance. Regional service integration with authority to make changes is critical. They also feel that a separate, single funding envelope that combines funding streams for mental health services is essential. Explicit operational goals, performance indictors, and further research are also seen as pivotal in demonstrating the effectiveness of mental health services (Health Systems Research Unit, Clarke Institute of Psychiatry, 1997).

The Canadian Mental Health Association's national office is an important force in promoting a common set of principles through the diverse provincial and territorial mental health reform efforts, especially in encouraging formation of partnerships between mental health and other health and social service agencies and in emphasizing consumer involvement in planning, management, and evaluation of services and supports. In their recently released report, *Access: A Framework for a Community-Based Mental Health System,* they provide an organizing framework for the development of a continuous, integrated, and seamless mental health system. It is an approach that is person-centered, strengths-focused (Rapp, 1998), and embedded in a community resource base rather than professional services.

CULTURAL COMPETENCE

Managed care has forced practitioners to reflect on what are the essential skills needed to function effectively in the new health care environment. Schreter (1997) identifies six core skill sets: clinical care skills, clinical management skills, clinical knowledge, skills with special populations, administrative competence, and ethical care management. The skills within each of these areas recognize the need to be focused and realistic, use a variety of services, keep an emphasis on efficacy-based practice, work within administrative guidelines, and advocate for the patient's best interest.

What is notably absent in this discussion is the need to develop cultural competence in practice and in the delivery of mental health services. Increasing ethnic diversity is only one aspect of cultural difference. History in regards economic, social, and political status and beliefs, norms, and values are other important aspects of culture. In an effort to respond to the need for more culturally competent mental health services, the Western Interstate Commission on Health Education (WICHE) established four national panels to develop cultural competency standards in mental health services for four racial ethnic groups; African American, Asian American and Pacific Islander, Latino/Hispanic, and Native American/American Indian/Native Alaskan/Native Hawaiian (WICHE, 1997). The work completed by these panels includes a set of guiding principles, overall system and clinical standards with implementation guidelines, and a set of provider competencies. Each of the standards provided includes a precise definition, implementation guidelines, recommended performance indicators, and recommended outcomes. The state of California recently passed legislation to require that state departments include a cultural competence plan in their annual departmental plans. The plans must include performance indicators that form the basis of an annual progress report, which is subject to audit. This institutional approach to implementation has resulted in significant improvements in service delivery. Mental health providers are becoming much more aware that cultural competency is a critical component in providing effective mental health services.

SUPPORTING THE CONSUMER AGENDA

Social work, more than any other profession in the field of mental health, can and must support the involvement of consumers in the development of managed care (Cornelius, 1994). In the transition to managed care in the United States there has generally been little involvement of consumers; where it has happened is in locations where there was already an infrastructure of consumer involvement. This includes involvement in planning councils (PL 99-660), the inclusion of national organizations like NAMI, Protection and Advocacy Offices, state and national self-help groups and a variety of agency-based mechanisms for consumer input. We have also seen the growth of consumer-run services such as Mind Empowered in Portland (Nikkel, Smith & Edwards, 1992) and Mindstar in San Diego. Maximizing consumer involvement in managed mental health care reforms requires action on a number of fronts. Individualized capitation, flexible funding, more significant consumer participation in councils and commissions, consumer-run services, accreditation standards for consumer involvement in managed care, and innovative approaches for rural areas are only a few of the initiatives that will further consumer involvement in the reform agenda.

NAMI has published a managed care primer for families and consumers (Malloy, 1995) which covers basic concepts, alternative models, state experiences, and a checklist of ideal attributes of a system of managed care. Consumers have also organized the Consumer Managed Care Network (CMCN) as a vehicle for information and knowledge exchange on mental health managed care. At present, the National Association of State Mental Health Program Directors (NASMHPD) hosts the CMCN, which has memberships in over thirty-five States.

Social workers must work in partnerships with consumer groups to ensure that the consumer voice is heard and that systems of managed mental health care are as empowering as possible (Fisher, 1994). An example, mentioned earlier in the chapter, of a consumer-driven capitated approach is the Village in Long Beach, California. This innovative program merges capitation financing with state-of-the-art community support system policies and practice. Building on lessons from the program for assertive community treatment (PACT) in Madison, Wisconsin, and Rapp's strengths model of case management (Rapp, 1998), the Village provides a positive model of a consumer-guided outcome-focused managed care system (Goodrick, 1995). Professionals can work with consumers as partners in promoting the dissemination of best-practice information and by supporting the appropriate replication of consumer-driven initiatives such as those identified by NAMH in its new Partners in Care initiative.

CONCLUSION

In planning mental health initiatives, Wasyenki, Goering, and McNaugton (1992) take the view that the severely mentally ill should be a priority target; that the relative use of general hospital and psychiatric units and psychiatric hospitals should be clearly defined; that community support services should be expanded; and that continuity and integration of care should be emphasized. Working with co-morbidity and responding to the new consumerism are also pivotal challenges in improving mental health care. Scheyett (1997) argues that practitioners within managed care systems may need to shift their thinking and embrace a new approach, and identifies the following eight principles to inform this shift in thinking:

1. Use a strengths-based focus in your work.
2. Make sure your services are client- and family-driven.
3. Emphasize a long-term investment rather than a short-term perspective.
4. The goal of treatment is to maximize functioning and community tenure; service should focus on skill building, relapse prevention, and community support.
5. In order to help people become stable in the community in a cost-efficient manner, the focus should be on building internal capacity.
6. Treatment should focus specifically on high-risk clients and high-risk periods for clients.
7. To help people become stable in the community in a cost-efficient manner, the focus should be on developing natural supports in the community.
8. Families of people with serious mental illness need information about the illness, skill training in behavioral management, consultation, and emotional support.

Many of the best-practice approaches identified in this chapter incorporate several of these principles. They provide hope that significant positive changes can be achieved for this marginalized and often underserved population. Further research at the policy and program level should improve our understanding of how to more effectively meet the needs of those persons who are experiencing a severe mental illness. We can start by ensuring that we are abreast of current developments in managed care, use efficacy and best practice information to inform our practice, emphasize cultural competency, and work with consumers in collaborative partnerships to improve mental health policies and services.

REFERENCES

American Psychiatric Association. (1997). *Public mental health: A changing system in an era of managed care.* Washington, DC: American Psychiatric Press, Inc.

Bachrach, L. (1993). Continuity of care and approaches to case management for long-term mentally ill patients. *Hospital & Community Psychiatry, 44,* 465–468.

Bedall, J. (1994). Social skills training. In J. Bedoll (Ed.), *Psychological assessment and treatment of persons with severe mental disorders.* Washington, DC: Taylor and Francis.

Bernstein, C. (1994). Is managed care good for mental health clients? No. In S. Kirk and S. Einbinder (Eds.), *Controversial issues in mental health.* Needham Heights, MA: Allyn & Bacon.

Bickman, L., Guthie, P. R., Foster, E. M., Lambert, E. W., Summerfelt, W. T., Breda, C. S., & Hefinger, C. A. (1995). *Evaluating managed mental health services: The Fort Bragg experiment.* New York: Plenum.

Biegel, D., Tracy, E., & Corvo, K. (1994). Strengthening social networks: Intervention strategies for mental health case managers. *Health and Social Work, 19,* 206–216.

Chandler, D., Meisel, J., Hu, T., McGowen, M., & Madison, K. (1998). A capitated model for a cross-section of severely mentally ill clients: Hospitalization. *Community Mental Health Journal, 34*(1), 13–26.

Corcoran, K., & Vandiver, V. (1996). *Maneuvering the maze of managed care: Skills for mental health practitioners.* New York: The Free Press.

Cornelius, D. S. (1994). Managed care and social work: Constructing a context and a response. *Social Work in Health Care, 20,* 47–63.

Durham, M. L. (1994). Health care's greatest challenge: Providing services for people with severe mental illness in managed care. *Behavioral Sciences and the Law, 12,* 331–349.

Fisher, D. B. (1994). Health care reform based on an empowerment model of recovery by people with psychiatric disabilities. *Hospital & Community Psychiatry, 45,* 913–915.

Geller, J. L. (1998). Mental health services for the future: Managed care, unmanaged care, mismanaged care. In G. Schamess & A. Lightburn (Eds.), *Humane managed care* (pp. 36–50). Washington, DC: NASW Press.

Goodrick, D. (1995). Integrating values, resources, and strategies to achieve outcomes. *California Alliance for the Mentally Ill,* 4(2), 61–65.

Gorski, T. (1995). The evolution of managed care practices. *Treatment Today,* 10–12.

Hall, L., Edgar, E., & Flynn, L. (1997). *Stand and deliver: Action call to a failing industry, the NAMI managed care report card.* Arlington, VA: National Alliance for the Mentally Ill.

Harding, C. M., & Zahniser J. H. (1994). Empirical correction of seven myths about schizophrenia with implications for treatment. *Acta Psychiatrica Scandinavica, 90* (suppl. 384), 140–146.

Harding, C., Zubin, J., & Strauss, J. (1992). Chronicity in schizophrenia: Revisited. *British Journal of Psychiatry, 161,* (suppl. 18), 27–37.

Health Systems Research Unit, Clarke Institute of Psychiatry. (1997). *Best practices in mental health reform.* Ottawa: Minister of Public Works and Government Services, Canada.

Hollingsworth, E. J. (1992). The mentally ill: Falling through the cracks. *Journal of Health Politics, Policy & Law, 17,* 899–928.

Huxley, P. (1990). *Effective community mental health services*. Aldershot, U.K.: Avebury.

Jerrell, J., Hu, T., & Ridgely, M. S. (1994). Cost-effectiveness of substance disorder interventions for people with severe mental illness. *The Journal of Mental Health Administration, 21,* 283–297.

Lefley, H., & Wasow, M. (1994). *Helping families cope with mental illness*. Langhorne, PA: Harwood Academic Publishers.

MacLeod, G. K. (1993). An overview of managed health care. In R. R. Pongstredt (Ed.), *The managed care handbook* (pp. 3–11). Gaithersburg, MD: Aspen Press.

Malloy, M. (1995). *Mental illness and managed care: A primer for families and consumers*. Document prepared for the National Alliance for the Mentally Ill, Arlington, VA.

Manderscheid, R. W., & Henderson, M. J. (1995). Federal and State legislative and program directions for managed care: Implications for case management. Rockville, MD: Center for Mental Health Services, Department of Health and Human Services.

McFarland, B. H. (1994). Health maintenance organizations and persons with severe mental illness. *Community Mental Health Journal, 30,* 221–242.

McFarlane, W. R. (1994). Families, patients and clinicians as partners: Clinical strategies and research outcomes in single and multiple-family psychoeducation. In H. Lefly & M. Wasow (Eds.), *Helping families cope with mental illness*. Laughorne, PA: Harwood Academic Publishers, 195–222.

McGuirk, F. D., Keller, A. S., & Croze, C. (1995). *Blueprints for managed care: Mental healthcare concepts and structure*. Document published by the Mental Health Program of the Western Interstate Commission for Health Education, Boulder, CO.

Mechanic, D. (1999). *Mental health and social policy: The emergence of managed care*. Boston: Allyn and Bacon.

Mechanic, D., & Rochefort, D. A. (1996). Comparative medical systems. *Annual Review of Sociology, 22,* 239–270.

Minkoff, K., & Pollack, D. (Eds.). (1997). *Managed mental health care in the public sector: A survival manual*. Amsterdam: Harwood Academic Publishers.

Misrahi, T. (1993). Managed care and managed competition: A primer for social work. *Health & Social Work, 1,* 86–91.

National Mental Health Association. (1998). *Partners in care: Community, access, recovery, empowerment* [Information package]. Alexandria, VA: Author

Nikkel, R., Smith, G., & Edwards, D. (1992). A consumer-operated case management project. *Hospital and Community Psychiatry, 43,* 577–579.

Novalis, P., Rojcewicz, S., & Peele, R. (1993). *Clinical manual of supportive psychotherapy*. Washington, DC: American Psychiatric Press.

Paulson, R. (1996). Swimming with the sharks or walking in the Garden of Eden: Two versions of managed care and mental health practice. In P. Raffoul & C. McNeece (Eds.), *Future issues for social work practice*. Needham Heights, MA: Allyn & Bacon, 85–106.

Ramon, S., & Mangen, S. P. (1994). The continued care client: A European perspective [Special issue]. *International Journal of Social Psychiatry, 40,* 235–324.

Rapp, C. (1998). *The strengths model: Case management with people suffering from severe and persistent mental illness*. New York: Oxford University Press.

Rochefort, D. (1992). More lessons of a different kind: Canadian mental health policy in comparative perspective. *Hospital and Community Psychiatray, 43,* 1083–1090.

Santos, A. (1996). Assertive community treatment. In S. Soreff (Ed.), *The seriously and persistently mentally ill: The state-of-the-art treatment handbook* (pp. 411–430). Seattle: Hogrefe and Hober.

Schreter, R. K. (1997). Essential skills for managed behavioral health care. *Psychiatric Services, 48,* 653–658.

Scheyett, A. (1997). *Making the transition to managed behavioral healthcare: A guide for agencies and practitioners.* Milwaukee, WI: Families International, Inc.

Segal, S. P., Silverman, C., & Temkin. T. (1993). Empowerment and self-help agency practice for people with mental disabilities. *Social Work, 38,* 707–712.

Shera, W. (1996). Managed care and people with severe mental illness: Challenges and opportunities for social work. *Health and Social Work, 21,* 196–201.

Shera, W., Aviram, V., Healy, B., & Ramon, S. (in press). Mental health system reform: A multi-country comparison. *Health & Social Work.*

Shera, W., & Delva-Tauiliili, J. (1996). Changing MSW students' attitudes towards the severely mentally ill. *Community Mental Health Journal, 32,* 159–169.

Simmons, J. (1994). Community based care: The new health social work paradigm. *Social Work in Health Care, 20,* 35–46.

Stern, S. (1993). Managed care, brief treatment, and treatment integrity. *Psychotherapy, 30,* 162–175.

Strauss, J. (1992). The person—key to understanding mental illness: Towards a new dynamic psychiatry. *British Journal of Psychiatry, 161* (suppl. 18), 19–26.

Strom, K., & Gingerich, W. J. (1993). Educating students for the new market realities. *Journal of Social Work Education, 29,* 78–87.

Vaccaro, J., Young, A., & Glynn, S. (1993). Community-based care of individuals with schizophrenia. *Psychiatric Clinics of North America, 16,* 387–399.

Wasylenki, D., Goering, P., & MacNaughton, E. (1992). Planning mental health services: Current Canadian initiatives. *Canadian Journal of Psychiatry, 37,* 259–263.

Western Interstate Commission for Health Education. (1997). *Cultural competence standards in managed care: Mental health services for four underserved/underrepresented racial/ethnic groups.* Boulder, CO: Author.

Woolsey, S. L. (1993). Managed care and mental health: The silencing of a profession. *International Journal of Eating Disorders, 14,* 387–401.

◆ CHAPTER 12 ◆

Research Needs in the Managed Care of Substance-Abusing Patients

WILMA PEEBLES-WILKINS AND NANCY W. VEEDER

I. INTRODUCTION

Social work intervention with substance-abusing patients needs further study in the current health care delivery system, which focuses on cost-containment and short-term treatment approaches. In many instances, addicted patients need extended care and treatment. While to some extent health care delivery systems have accommodated this need by increasing the number of visits allowable for substance-abuse treatment, alcohol and drug addiction problems are so pervasive in our society that there is an ongoing need to examine the role of counseling professionals such as social workers. Cappocia (1998) asserts that, "substance abuse may well be our number one national health problem. It accounts for 25 percent of acute care hospital admissions; 60 percent to 80 percent of incarcerated populations in local and federal prisons; 50 percent of auto related deaths; and $200 billion plus in annual economic costs" (p. 3). Moreover, health care providers are faced with attempting to address the needs of a substance-abusing population in excess of 100 million who are covered by some form of managed health care system (Oss, 1994), and, for the most part, substance abuse and other behavioral health care services are provided as part of a managed care subcontract system to private vendors.

Behavioral health care and substance-abuse interventions have caused concern among health care professionals because of the pervasiveness and chronicity of addiction problems as well as the presence of mental illness in combination with addictive behavior. Emerging intervention approaches under managed care arrangements—such as brief treatment—are a source of debate among clinicians as well as researchers in the substance-abuse field. For example, some primary care or generalist physicians are expanding the traditional medical role of the doctor to include models of brief treatment of substance-abusing patients, especially those abusing alcohol. Given the traditional role of physicians, a better understanding of outcomes for abusing patients and the involvement of case management by other professionals are essential in models such as that of the physician counselor. While studies report the successful use of short-term psychotherapy with cocaine users (see Rounsaville, Gawin, & Kebler, 1985) and the work of Barnes and Samet (1997) suggests that brief treatment intervention with substance-abusing patients by generalist physicians yields effective patient outcomes, research studies that address these issues in a nonmedical, more long-term behavioral health care context, and research on drugs other than alcohol, will help expand our understanding of patient needs as well as help explicate more effective professional roles for social workers. We know, for example, that patients' substance-abuse problems often go undetected by primary care physicians and that primary care physicians lack both the skills and the inclination to intervene. Thus, it's crucial that social workers and other health care clinicians continue to research the prevention and treatment of substance abuse, as well as interdisciplinary needs.

This paper will present an overview of managed care systems and specifically address some current issues related to substance-abusing patients. It will also review existing research in the field (both methodological issues and findings), and will examine the research needed in the future to assess the traditional treatment of the substance-abusing patient and other prevention and treatment innovations to more effectively deal with the increasing social problem of alcohol and drug addiction.

II. MANAGED CARE SYSTEMS AND BEHAVIORAL HEALTH CARE ISSUES

Managed care systems have been characterized different depending on the focus of a given author. Definitions have focused on patient care as it relates to the practitioner (Alperin & Phillips, 1997; Corcoran & Vandiver, 1996; Goodman, Brown & Dietz, 1992; Winegar & Bistline, 1994), on health care as cost containment, and on utilization review and mechanisms of financing (Austed & Hoyt, 1992; Feldman, 1991; Hutchins, 1996). Understanding the implications of managed care for substance-abuse patients is perhaps best understood in the context of the definition by Winegar (1992): "Managed mental health care has as its focus the marshaling and coordinating of appropriate clinical and financial resources necessary for each client's care. Essentially managed care clients' needs are matched to appropriate treatment resources, and then the delivery and outcome of these resources are monitored" (p. 8). However, for the most part, nonmedical studies of managed care of substance abuse have focused on financing, and there is a dearth of nonmedical treatment outcome studies.

One of the main objectives of managed care has been to control costs of health care and to improve the efficiency of service across the entire set of services needed during illness. However, there are significant challenges in determining the effects of managed care on such indicators as cost, access, and outcomes. The difficulties stem from the wide range of managed care configurations currently available, such as multiple models of health maintenance organizations (HMOs) and preferred provider organizations (PPOs), the many variations of prepayment or capitation utilized, and the rapid development of new organizational and financing arrangements in managed care. The complexity in organizations and financing mechanisms make both comparison and generalization difficult.

Managed behavioral health care coverage is different from health care costs coverage in general. "Health maintenance organizations, preferred provider organizations, and point-of-service plans, the major variants of managed care, generally provide some coverage for mental health care within their broader benefit packages, but that coverage emphasizes acute care and, in general, is quite restrictive. Most managed-care plans do not cover chronic mental illness in their standard benefit packages. A typical benefit consists of a maximum of 20 outpatient visits and 30 hospital days a year. The services available within most managed-care plans are seen by mental health professionals as too limited for people with severe and persistent mental illness" (Iglehart, 1996, p. 131, from Mechanic, Schlesinger & McAlpine, 1995).

Feldman (1991) asserts that managed mental health may be, at best, an oxymoron, and at worst an exercise in futility. "At its best, managed mental health can improve quality, reduce inappropriate utilization, control costs and protect mental health and substance abuse benefits from a society that has not infrequently been inclined to reduce them. It can also protect individuals, most of whom have benefit limitations, from using up benefits on unnecessary care and then not having any left when care is truly needed. But at its worst, managed mental health can fall victim to greed, deprive people of services they really need, truncate the role of mental health providers and successfully cut costs but damage the quality of the clinician/patient relationship so central to the success of the therapeutic process" (p. xv). These issues are precisely those being discussed in the professional literature as well as the popular press and there are specific implications for patients who abuse substances or are dually diagnosed.

III. ISSUES IN THE MANAGED CARE OF SUBSTANCE ABUSE

Unique issues arise in the care of substance-abuse patients under managed care arrangements. Issues associated with carve-outs, costs, prevention and early detection, access for special populations, and ethical dilemmas for professionals are examples described below.

Carve-Outs

As noted earlier, the managed care of substance abuse includes a population exceeding 100 million. Substance-abusing individuals and others with diverse and complex mental health problems who require more than brief behavioral health care services may, in fact, receive "episodic, uncoordinated, and, therefore, inefficient" (Bachman, 1998, p.14) health care. This is a concern for the chronic and persistently mentally ill patient as well as the chronically addicted patient. Larsen, Samet, and McCarty (1997) define a managed care carve-out as one in which "an integrated plan (e.g. HMO) subcontracts to a managed behavioral health care organization for behavioral health services" (p. 1055). Bachman (1998) points out that carve-outs represent a curious dichotomy between the overall goal of managed care systems toward integration of services and the design of separated systems for mental health and substance-abuse services (behavioral health services).

By definition, carve-out systems (contrasted with "integrated" plans) mean a separate type of managed care system for health or behavioral health care services, to include special populations or diagnostic categories (Bachman, 1997). Essentially, "in a carve-out arrangement, a set of services or a population group is identified and is managed outside the mainstream managed care network that enrolls most members of the population. Carve-outs are commonly used by both Medicaid programs and private payers to provide behavioral health services . . . . Carve-out arrangements typically arise when a payer decides to require its insured population to enroll in capitated managed care plans" (Bachman, 1998, p.14). In such situations, adequate treatment for addicted patients who are poor is highly questionable.

Carve-outs are seemingly a two-way street arrangement: Managed care providers do not want these high-risk, potentially costly and long-term clients, and clients do not want behavioral health services provided by mainstream managed care providers, for fear of disrupting long-term pre-existing therapeutic relationships. Further, by definition, managed health and behavioral health care systems are interested in efficiency and a parsimonious approach to both the amount of services that can be received and the service length that is most often mandated. Substance-abusing clients, with their multitude of concomitant behavioral and physical health problems, are usually viewed by managed care systems as least amenable to brief, acute episodic encounters. Rather, these clients represent a very expensive long-term chronic health and behavioral health commitment, which is anathema to the "efficiency" axis of the managed health and behavioral health care equation (the other managed care axis is "effectiveness"). Primary care physicians may have caused physicians to become discouraged about treating addicted patients (Lewis, Ludden & McLellan, 1997). A recent research study of managed care carve-outs and Medicaid in Massachusetts found that requiring preauthorization to charge for substance-abuse counseling caused primary care and other physicians not to have the incentive to report substance-abuse diagnoses (Callahan et al., 1995). It is in this context that primary care or generalist physicians who are proponents of the success of brief treatment support this form of counseling by the doctor rather than a referral to subcontractors under managed care arrangements. (Barnes & Samet, 1997). The efficacy of this approach is the cause of some consternation since addictions issues such as relapse prevention, for example, may not be adequately addressed.

Proponents of carve-outs for behavioral health services argue several positives for the approach: providers participating in the carve-out have special behavioral health expertise and may have been the pre–managed care provider; behavioral health disorders, one of the chief among which is substance abuse, represent a substantial financial risk to capitated (set fee for set number of patients/clients) managed care systems; and a separate "account" for health and behavioral health services delivery obviates these specialized services getting lost amidst capitated mainstream managed care services delivery (Bachman, 1998, p. 14).

Costs

Excessive costs associated with health care have been a legitimate concern. In the realm of cost control, "which was always the primary concern of many of the policy elites anyway, the private sector has been quite successful. Health care spending was restrained without complicated governmental bureaucratic entities which American citizens found so unappealing" (Toner, 1996).

Managed care is a response to the failure of the health care system to maintain the goal of reasonable costs. The other major goals of the American public—to have universal health insurance so that health care is available and accessible when needed, and freedom to choose doctors and other health care professionals—are also essential. And equally important is the doctor's autonomy to choose appropriate treatment (Samuelson, 1996, p. 13).

According to Samuelson (1996), managed care thus far seems to have contained cost increases. Between 1965 and 1991, health spending rose to 8% of gross domestic product; in 1996, employers' health-care premiums rose less than 1%, whereas in 1991 the increase was 11.5%. In short, managed care's "triumph over 'fee-for-service' medicine has been stunning." This has come about largely through managed care's providing both insurance and health care simultaneously (Samuelson, 1996, p. 13).

Cost-effective procedures employed by managed care systems may include elimination of costly elective procedures; capitation; prospective utilization reviews to determine treatment necessity; diminution of medication waste; de-emphasis on research funding; more efficient and effective treatments for increasingly parsimonious costs; resources allocation for prevention; and privatization of Medicaid and other formerly not-for-profit and publicly funded categories and institutions such as hospitals, the penal system, and child welfare services.

Opponents generally criticize managed care for giving the public less than it needs. However, these generalizations may not pertain to behavioral health or substance-abuse treatment, special areas of health care services delivery that are less understood and valued by the public at large and its agents, such as managed care companies. Opponents also maintain that restrictions in service may be good for profits, but they are bad for patients. A classic exchange on this subject occurred in the *American Journal of Psychiatry* (1993) between Doctors B. S. Joseph and L. I. Sederer. Dr. Joseph, in responding to Sederer's article, stated that "neither hospitals or physicians can be seen to be 'above' the profit motive" (p. 1434). Dr. Sederer rejoined that doctors and hospitals can never disavow responsibility for patient care and clinical outcome. He asserted that proprietary managed care organizations make determinations on payment and, in so doing, disavow patient care and clinical outcome responsibility. "It is this difference which critically differentiates caregivers from cost containers" (p. 1434).

Detractors also question such cost-containment policies as: services monies being diverted to administrative costs (Christensen, 1995); lack of access to services by the most at-risk populations; services rationing, which is sometimes called "profit versus people" (D. B. Borenstein, 1990); and shift in control of finances from the provider-clinician to the corporation.

Prevention and Early Detection

Supporters of managed care point to improvements in health care and cost containment by means of preventive care emphasis and elimination of waste. For example, proponents argue, there are more immunizations and more screenings for breast cancer. There is far more early detection and outright prevention of disease. However, from the behavioral health care perspective and especially as related to substance-abuse treatment, it is not clear that there has been an increase in early detection.

The 1997 recommendations from the National Committee for Quality Assurance included standards for accrediting managed behavioral health care organizations that emphasized prevention. Prevention was noted as being an evolutionary process in managed behavioral health care. The NCQA recommendations conceptualized prevention activities in terms of what is usually thought of as a public health intervention model, which includes primary, secondary, and tertiary approaches to health care. For substance-abuse services, emphasis was placed on relapse-prevention support for patients. The implementation of relapse prevention in the context of evolving models such as brief interventions by generalist physicians and other clinicians raises concerns and it is not clear that any serious efforts to provide preventive services transpire in managed behavioral health care systems (Standards, p. 7). However, Lewis, Ludden, and McLellan (1997) note that research demonstrating the positive financial outcomes of substance-abuse prevention and treatment "has not had the desired impact on the way managed care organizations structure substance abuse prevention services (p. 3).

Perspectives similar to the NCQA recommendations in regard to substance-abuse prevention, treatment, and research have been raised in a variety of contexts by others in the field as well. For example, Cappocia (1998) notes:

> For better or worse, the substance abuse prevention and treatment field, almost 50 years old, still struggles for support, credibility and an opportunity to demonstrate what research has established—that treatment does work for alcohol- and other drug-dependent people. Despite its founding by a physician, the substance abuse field, in the self-help movement, is viewed by some as unscientific. Whether it is substance abuse treatment, prevention, or research, this topic is at the bottom of the status, funding, and priority food chain.

Similarly, other perspectives on the prevention of alcohol-related problems emphasize the need to employ a public health focus. A model with a heavier environmental focus in addition to individual patient-focused strategies is encouraged.

Access

Access to health and behavioral health services, particularly by known "at-risk" groups, is a problem in managed care systems. Concerns about the poor persist in spite of professional folklore that poor patients have better primary care service under managed care systems. Social workers, in particular, do not feel that they have equitable opportunities to provide service through managed care provider pools. Treatment for "pre-existing" health and behavioral health conditions is often denied by managed care companies. There is public outcry about the actual or potential neglect of the poor. This has come to a head with a variety of recent public hospital acquisitions and mergers by private health care corporations ("Questions About a Hospital Deal," editorial, *New York Times,* November 29, 1996; "The Future of a Medical Center," editorial, *Boston Globe,* November 11, 1996; "The Selling of a Hospital", Editorial, *Boston Globe,* November 21, 1996). There are currently no regulations that mandate the private corporations to serve the poor, a large part of whom were served by the previously public hospitals. Both costs and regulations are factors here. Access to care may be limited by the system of subcontracting for addictions services under managed care if case management and referral services are not effectively utilized because health care professionals such as social workers are not involved in the process or included as team members.

The *New York Times,* January 10, 1999 (p. 1), described a managed care rebellion by New York doctors who were dropping varied managed care plans. These doctors serve primarily upper middle class patients. Such situations raise continued concerns about the poor, who already have limited access to doctors.

Ethical and Other Professional Dilemmas

Ethical issues and dilemmas abound in the area of substance-abuse treatment. These dilemmas include treatment within the context of managed care systems as well as issues associated with professional ambiguity in working with the substance-abusing patient. There is a large body of descriptive issues-oriented literature in managed care addressing the ethical aspects of care (Chervenak & McCullough, 1995; Christensen, 1995; Emanuel, 1995; "Ethical Issues in Managed Care," 1995; Holleman, Edwards & Matson, 1994; Howe, 1995; Jecker & Pearlman, 1992; Morreim, 1995; Pellegrino, 1995; Sabin, 1994a; Sulmasy, 1995; Zoloth-Dorfman & Rubin, 1995). This literature highlights the variance between professional standards of care and the function and process of managed care systems.

Significant professional dilemmas, ethical and otherwise, arise for social workers. In the area of substance abuse, dilemmas include lack of interest in serving the poor and severely mentally ill (Schamess, 1996); lack of interest in serving the substance-abusing client, who is frequently a "dual-diagnosed" client; informed consent issues (Koppel, *Nightline,* November 8, 1996); nature of consumer freedom of choice; appeal provisions and sanctions available for poor treatment outcomes (NASW, 1994). Other dilemmas include the role of social workers with other health care professionals providing counseling services. These dilemmas suggest the need for more trans- or interdisciplinary work.

Social work as a profession has had particular difficulty dealing with substance-abusing clients. This difficulty has been linked to social work's marriage to the medical model in which the focus is on the addiction itself, which "directs exclusive attention to the presenting problem" (Rhodes & Johnson, 1996, p. 182). This myopic view of the substance-abuse problem, with all of its attendant environmental complexity, flies in the face of social work's avowed "systems" approach to individual, group, and community interventions, which stresses an understanding of the person in the environment. Over the past decade, this dichotomy in social work training and practice has been noted by several observers of social work practice in the field of substance abuse (Googins, 1984; Humphreys, 1985; Kagle, 1987; Rhodes & Johnson, 1996). Rhodes & Johnson (1996) further posit that blind acceptance of the medical model has contributed to the "reluctance of the profession to identify addiction as a problem appropriate for social work intervention," a view also shared by Alaszewski and Harrison (1992).

Rhodes & Johnson (1996) point out that social work's emphasis on an ecological model, which takes transactions with the environment as crucial causal and intervention variables, provides an opportunity for a much more comprehensive view of an addicted person's circumstances, which may include discrimination and deprivation issues such as sexism, poverty, racism, and homophobia, issues which are clearly intertwined with the complex issue of addiction. In sum, if substance abuse were a simple medical disease entity, then a medical solution would have long ago been found to this epidemic, similar to the medical solutions generated for polio, tuberculosis, and diabetes. In short, in medical settings dealing with substance abuse, social workers need to assert and promote the "unique perspective of social work [which] recognizes that interventions must be directed simultaneously at many relevant systems to improve social functioning" (Vayda & Bogo, 1991, p. 273).

Now the issue is drawn. There is a movement afoot to have substance abuse detection, treatment, and prevention carried out by primary care physicians. Larson et al. (1997) note that the primary care (or generalist) physician:

> May receive explicit expectations and incentives [from managed care organizations]. A common role is that of gatekeeper to specialty substance abuse care. It demands expanded involvement of the physician in managing substance abusers' symptoms and functioning to avoid relapse to substance use that may require hospitalization or lengthy treatment. Typically the physician gatekeeper is paid a monthly case management fee, and in risk-sharing models the physician groups have financial penalties or rewards based on utilization performance. Physicians have the most clinical discretion in this model but may feel extremely confined by the target utilization standards. Whatever the scenario and the form of managed care, the best practice involves significant interaction of primary care physicians, psychiatrists, and nonphysician addictions specialists. (p. 1063)

Noting the potential benefits in connecting substance-abuse treatment and primary care, these physicians go on to suggest that psychiatric liaison, expanded roles for physical intervention, case management, and a greater focus on prevention and treatment protocols could result in an improved service delivery.

Communication between the primary care physician and other professionals may be extremely difficult in a carve-out situation where psychiatrists, other nonphysician substance-abuse specialists, and other specialty behavioral health programs needed by the majority of substance-abusing clients are carved out into separate, largely impermeable systems. Further, the lack of substantive treatment knowledge about substance abuse on the part of the primary care physician, coupled with lack of at-the-worksite resources of time and expertise, may well precipitate quick decisions about the substance-abusing client in what is, by definition, a chronic and complex situation. Such quick "medical model" decisions based on a causal model of etiology and medical protocols for treatment may not assist recovery and may actually do harm. Such outcomes are implied by Barnes and

Samet (1997) when they suggest that primary care practitioners do brief interventions with substance-abusing clients. They assert that "brief interventions enable busy primary care practitioners to work effectively and efficiently with patients having problems related to the use of alcohol and other drugs" (p. 867). Before discussing the assertion, three operative words need to be dealt with here. The first word is "busy," which connotes a selection of anything "brief" not for diagnostic-intervention appropriateness, but simply because it is "brief." To the contrary, "research shows that there are some apparent trends in what works in substance abuse care. . . . The higher the number of visits patients get, the higher the rate of success" (Behan, 1998). Further, the phrase "effectively and efficiently" is the one adopted by managed care systems as both mission and operations statement.

Barnes and Samet observe that, "a brief intervention is a short counseling session focused on helping a person change a specific behavior . . . . The content of the intervention is tailored to the severity of the patient's substance abuse problem and to the patient's readiness to change behavior" (p. 867). Barnes and Samet, emphasizing brief intervention and motivational techniques, state further that "whatever the severity of the alcohol or drug problem, the physician needs to address the patient's readiness for change and help that patient move one stage at a time toward changing that behavior.

Two contrary points need to be made. First, the very nature of substance abuse cries out for treatment over time. This is the premise for nonprofessional interventions such as Alcoholics Anonymous (AA), which relies on a for-life support system, and professional interventions based on the premise that these are among the most difficult and intractable clients/patients to "motivate" toward changed behavior. The process of "motivation" in such chronic and complex situations takes much more time, support, and counseling than in a brief encounter suggested by Barnes and Samet in their strictly medical model of treatment in substance abuse situations.

The second point is that the studies reported by Barnes and Samet all rely on self-report as a primary measure of decrease in alcohol consumption. In the research methodological section discussion below, the obvious issues of unreliability and invalidity of self-report in alcohol- and drug-abuse situations will be discussed.

A major problem with primary care physicians offering brief treatment to their substance-abusing patients is of the type found in a recent study by Saitz, Mulvey, and Samet (1997a): "Almost one-half of the patients with an addiction serious enough to prompt a presentation for treatment perceived that they did not have primary care physicians. Most of the patients presenting for substance abuse treatment had been in an emergency department recently but most denied chronic or episodic medical illnesses" (p. 192). Further, "our findings are consistent with previous literature suggesting that alcohol- and other drug-abusing patients are not receiving adequate medical care . . . . The data presented help to characterize the magnitude and nature of the failure to link addicted persons with primary medical care. . . . If our results are generalizable, then substance abuse treatment sites are not being successfully utilized to initiate primary care linkage efforts" (p. 193).

Saitz et al. (1997b), in a study of 3,253 patients, found that "forty-five percent of patients with substance abuse serious enough to prompt a presentation for treatment stated that the physician who cared for them was unaware of their substance abuse . . . .Even among substance abusing patients requesting addiction treatment, many perceive that their physicians do not recognize their substance abuse" (p. 344). Training of primary care physicians in crucial diagnostic and treatment aspects of substance abuse at the operational level has been suggested, as has the integration of primary health care with behavioral health care in managed care systems at the policy level (Lewis, Ludden & McLellan, 1997). However, this argument suggests the need for better physician training in the area of substance abuse identification and at the same time casts doubts on the ability of primary care doctors to succeed using brief interventions. National policy, programmatic, and research debates in the area of substance abuse must include a dialogue between medical professionals, who define issues within the narrow lens of the medical model of etiology and treatment, and professionals such as social workers, whose training includes an inclusive lens encompassing those environmental, ecological, cultural, psychological, and social factors that are crucial to prevention, problem definition, and intervention in substance abuse.

Additional social work competencies include interdisciplinary collaboration and other collaborative relationships, including with clients, policymakers, and legislators; consumer participation; advanced case management (Billig & Levinson, 1989; Johnson & Rubin, 1983); group work; community building, to include community practice and knowledge about community self-sufficiency (Weil, 1996); joint micro-macro assignments and field-training opportunities; coalition-building; prevention; physical health and its impact on emotional well-being; management for change (strategic management); information technology; marketing; and advocacy, particularly in relation to the severely mentally ill and substance-abusing populations (Cornelius, 1994; Peebles-Wilkins & Veeder, 1996; Veeder & Peebles-Wilkins, 1998).

Interdisciplinary collaboration is essential in the complex area of substance abuse. "Managed care has mandated the collaborative model of professional, interdisciplinary interaction to better serve health and behavioral health consumer groups (Hawkins, Veeder & Pearce, 1997). Interdisciplinary collaboration is seen as focal in the delivery of managed care substance-abuse services because managed care systems stress coordination and interdisciplinary services delivery based on complex, jointly derived service-delivery protocols and outcome evaluations in complex situations such as substance abuse, which need a variety of professional interventions (Saltz & Schaefer, 1996). The subcontracting or carve-out arrangements used for substance-abusing patients suggests as well the need for interprofessional activities that include case management approaches among health care professionals.

IV. EXISTING RESEARCH IN MANAGED CARE OF SUBSTANCE-ABUSE PATIENTS

Substantial research has been done on health care financing of substance abuse under managed care systems. While there is a dearth of nonmedical patient outcome studies , it should be noted that there have been a considerable number of medical outcomes studies in the area of substance abuse, particularly in relation to alcohol abuse. In this section, general methodological research issues are discussed and existing needs assessment, outcome, and practice studies are described.

Methodological Issues in Research in the Managed Care of Substance-Abuse Patients

A 1997 book by Bryant, Windle, and West discusses research methodological issues in alcohol- and substance-abuse research, with an emphasis on prevention research into "the development of a strong knowledge base for identification of risk and protective factors as well as the design, evaluation, and dissemination of interventions" (Bryant, West & Windle, 1997, p. xviii). The research methodological issues include measurement issues such as selection of optimal number and spacing of measurement occasions (Sher & Wood, 1997; Windle, 1997); statistical tests appropriate to non–statistically independent data (Kreft, 1997; Velicer & Colby, 1997); alternate statistical models (Collins et al., 1997; Foss, 1997; Manning, 1997; Windle, 1997); measurement error (Collins et al., 1997; Velicer & Colby, 1997; Windle, 1997); comparisons of measurement across different gender, ethnic, and language groups (Widaman & Reise, 1997); complex multi-component programs (West & Aiken, 1997); and individual studies vis-à-vis meta-analytic findings based on an entire research literature (Bangert-Drowns, Wells-Parker & Chevillard, 1997).

Needs Assessments

A major drug abuser needs assessment was undertaken in Rhode Island (McAuliffe et al., 1991). This study took 70.3% (5,176 persons) of the eligible households in the sample and obtained drug abuse needs assessment data.

Outcome Studies

Two excellent overview articles examine the state of the art in outcome research in the area of managed mental health care and substance-abuse patient outcomes in particular (Mechanic, Schlesinger & McAlpine, 1995; Wells et al., 1995). Mechanic, Schlesinger, and McAlpine suggest that outcome research on managed mental health/substance abuse has produced "some plausible, although less than firm, conclusions" (p. 43). These conclusions include:

- The application of managed care to the treatment of mental illness and substance abuse can produce a substantial reduction in cost.
- Managed care programs have the potential to improve and apply standards of appropriate treatment in areas where practice variations are large and where there is substantial potential for unnecessary or unduly expensive treatment.
- Managed care may be applied to the treatment of mental illness and substance abuse in ways that are not sensitive to the special characteristics that distinguish these conditions from other health needs.
- Managed care can be used as a strategy for selecting from a flexible set of benefits those services that best meet patients' needs in a cost-effective way or simply as a technique for reducing costs, with little sensitivity to quality of care.
- On the more negative side, in the absence of contrary information, there is some indication that managed care is operating as a rationing system and not as a means of achieving a more appropriate balance of inpatient and outpatient services (pp. 44–46).

An outcome evaluation comparing the effectiveness, safety, and costs of outpatient (n = 87) and inpatient (n = 77) detoxification from alcohol concluded that outpatient medical detoxification is an effective, safe, and low-cost treatment for patients with mild to moderate symptoms of alcohol withdrawal (Hayashida et al., 1989). A recent study (Westhuis et al., 1998) undertaken with 120,775 soldiers in the U.S. Army, addressed three issues: (1) whether there is a requirement for gender-specific substance-abuse treatment approaches for men and women, (2) if women and men can be efficaciously treated in an integrated non-gender-specific program, and (3) what the predictors of success in an employee assistance program are. Findings indicated that women were more successful in the program than men; that treatment combinations using group, Alcoholics Anonymous, and an educational focus were the most successful for both men and women; and that length of time in treatment had no impact on treatment success for women and only minimal impact for men.

Practice Studies

Several studies of practice with substance-abusing clients have been reported. In a study of perceived physician unawareness of serious substance abuse among 3,253 patients, 45% of patients with substance abuse serious enough to prompt a presentation for treatment stated that the physician who cared for them was unaware of their substance abuse. An even more disturbing finding was that even among substance-abusing patients requesting treatment for addiction, many perceived that their physicians do not recognize their substance abuse (Saitz, Mulvey, Plough & Samet, 1997). As noted in the section on professional dilemmas, these results, while providing evidence for the need for physician competencies in substance abuse, at the same time casts doubts on the reliability of short-term treatment by primary care physicians. Another study of 575 managers' beliefs about substance abuse found that respondents rejected the idea that substance abuse was a disease caused by heredity or other biological factors. Rather, they espoused and endorsed the view that substance abuse stemmed from psychosocial factors (Burke & Clapp, 1997).

One study reported a decrease in cost of care, stabilized client behaviors, and improved agency functioning in an innovative collaboration project among mental health, alcohol and drug treatment, corrections, forensic, and social and housing agencies uniting to provide more effective services at lower cost (Buckley & Bigelow, 1992).

Public service practice in substance abuse, such as that under Medicaid, has shown a status quo or minimal increase in quality and access under managed care (Beinecke et al., 1996). In another study conducted by a group from the Florence Heller School at Brandeis, which evaluated the managed care Medicaid program in Massachusetts, it was found that mental health expenditures were reduced by $47 million, or 22% of levels predicted without managed care (Callahan et al., 1995). In addition, no overall decrease in access to care or quality of care was found. Reduced lengths-of-stay, lower prices, and fewer inpatient admissions were the major factors. These findings were thought to give some support for the usefulness of a managed care program for mental health and substance-abuse services, and its applicability to high-risk populations.

In a five-year follow-up to the Callahan study (Beinecke & Keane, 1997), a survey of fifty-eight mental health providers' perceptions of program viability indicated that during the five years since the Callahan study had been implemented, costs had been much less than what the original study had predicted. Providers also felt that during the period quality, access, aftercare planning, and service integration had improved. However, the major negatives had to do with the most intractable groups of mentally ill substance abusers. "The issues that providers are most concerned about have changed little since the Brandeis study. They include treatment of persons with dual diagnoses of substance abuse and mental health . . . [and] linkages of mental health/substance abuse care with primary medical care" (p. 2). One of the strongest recommendations of this study is "to improve linkages between state agencies, referrals among providers, and between primary care and mental health / substance abuse providers" (p. 3).

In another Medicaid recipient study in Hennepin County (Minneapolis), Minnesota, it was found that those mentally ill/substance-abusing patients in prepaid health plans showed little difference from those in fee-for-service situations, findings which supported "efforts to expand the use of prepaid health plans to meet the needs of non-institutionalized chronically mentally ill Medicaid beneficiaries" (Moscovice et al., 1993, p. 75).

Several recent discussions of instrument design geared to assessing the degree of substance abuse among clients have been instructive. For example, Faul and Hudson (1997) report the reliability and validity of the Index of Drug Involvement (IDI), and Harvard-Pilgrim managed care provider has developed an index for substance use assessment.

V. FUTURE RESEARCH NEEDS IN THE MANAGED CARE OF SUBSTANCE-ABUSE PATIENTS

Managed care of substance-abuse patients research need areas will be listed under the National Institutes of Mental Health categories of *cost effectiveness* and *services delivery efficacy*.

Cost Effectiveness

- Is managed care cost effective? With whom? With which treatments and for what duration? Services provided by which profession or nonprofessional?
- How do various payment approaches affect the provision of care?
- Comparison of for-profit and not-for-profit delivery systems on cost effectiveness indicators
- Comparison of for-profit and not-for-profit delivery systems in relation to actual and proportions of expenditures on services versus administration
- Immediate versus long-term cost benefits of managed care systems

Services Delivery Efficacy

Needs Assessments

- Services needed by specific target groups
- Professional competencies needed for behavioral health care practice with addictive disorders

Assessment, Diagnostic, and Outcome (to Include Follow-Up) Measurement Instrument Development Needs

- Initial protocols (care pathways) and goals as outcome evaluation benchmarks (Dorwart, 1990)
- Other outcome tool development (Harvard-Pilgrim Mental Health Patient Assessment Tool; Judge Baker Cultural Competency; Berkman, 1996 etc.)
- Case recording for quality assurance (Corcoran & Gingerich, 1994)

Access and Rationing

- Which groups have and do not have access to behavioral health care services, and why?
- Rationing of services: for whom and under which circumstances?
- Market research to target underserved groups and increase access and utilization

Services Delivery Outcome Evaluations

- Application to addictive disorders; the measuring of benefits and outcomes; effectiveness of managed behavioral health interventions (Hargreaves & Shumway, 1989; Mirin & Namerow, 1991)
- Comparison of for-profit and not-for-profit delivery systems on services delivery efficacy indicators

Comparative Studies of Different Interventions

- Will persons with chronic mental illness and chronic addictive disorders receive an adequate share of Medicaid funding when managed care becomes the chief mechanism of funding in the formerly public sector?
- Comparisons of how various lower-cost treatments are affecting the mental health and other patient quality-of-life factors
- Comparisons of different professionals delivering different services
- Assessments of effectiveness of interdisciplinary teams versus solo interventions
- Effects of managed care policies
- Short- versus longer-term interventions with the more chronic addictive disorders and chronic mental ill
- Intensive treatment versus periodic interventions; missed therapeutic sessions versus spaced sessions for various types of problems
- Comparison of service outcomes between two groups of addictive disorder consumers, one in a managed behavioral health plan and the other group not in a managed care plan (outcomes in relation to such factors as readmissions, functional levels, maintenance in the community)
- Follow-up studies to determine goal-attainment maintenance as well as consumer satisfaction (consumer satisfaction does not necessarily co-vary with desirable clinical outcome)
- Are treatment outcomes improving or declining as a result of use of nonphysician providers in companies' networks
- Provider decision-making (Gottlieb, 1989)

Professional Social Work Education and Practice

- Social workers who are taking leadership roles in defining, developing, and studying managed care operations

- Advanced case management versus less skilled interventions outcomes
- The viability of community-building
- Preventive interventions viability
- Strengths/competency approaches to assessment and intervention versus psychodynamic approaches
- Has the advent of managed behavioral health care stifled the development of new drugs and other clinical improvements for the mental illness and addictive disorders?

VI. CONCLUSION

Much more research needs to be done to insure both cost-effectiveness and services-delivery efficacy. Primary care physicians may be a starting point for brief interventions, but existing studies suggest the need for interdisciplinary teamwork. Noting the need for internal as well as external evaluation strategies, Wells et al. (1995) suggest that we need to build on existing studies "to examine the effects of utilization review, precertification, provider selection, 'case management,' and 'clinical consultation,' among other managed care activities, on the quality of care and outcomes in mental health. While doing so, we will undoubtedly observe conflicting results, especially in the initial phases of less rigorously designed research, but we will be building an information base and theory that will more broadly inform the national policy and research agendas" (p. 72).

Mechanic (1995) suggests that in the future the following mental health care research issues that are applicable to addictive disorders be addressed: (1) establish the consequences for quality of care when external management reduces inpatient care or overall service use; (2) better link evaluation methods to a conceptual framework for how managed care shapes the delivery of services and the nature of the patient-provider relationship; (3) identify the negative effects of managed care; (4) develop a more comprehensive set of measures for both outcomes and process than have been used in past research; (5) develop longitudinal study designs and measures; and, (6) evaluate the ways managed care affects mental health care (pp. 45–50).

Shore and Beigel (1996) observe that "the challenges to all mental health professionals are to prepare themselves to assume responsibility for population-based practice without losing concern for the care of individual patients and to strike a balance between individual professional responsibility and corporate accountability, both of which will be demanded by patients and funding sources. The challenges to the definition of illness, professional ethics, the allocation of professional resources, and professional accountability brought by the emergence of managed behavioral health care will not disappear and must be resolved by professionals and managed behavioral health care companies working together to craft new forms of professional practice" (p. 118).

Multiple approaches to effectively treating substance abuse are indicated. These challenges in the field of managed care of substance abuse patients must be met with the assistance of empirical data so that the best of the past is reformulated into the best current and future managed behavioral health care services-delivery packages which maximally combine cost-effectiveness and services-delivery efficacy. Keeping in mind the admonition of Wells et al. (1995), "We must ask the right questions concerning the effects of managed care, based on knowledges of what it is and how its components are likely to affect patients" (p. 72). We must, therefore, renew a commitment to evaluate every aspect of managed care, from services delivered and their outcomes, to administrative issues, to ethical concerns, to policies generated and implemented, to protocol-proprietorship and other legal issues, and to the viability of managed care approaches compared with other approaches in the treatment of substance-abuse patients.

REFERENCES

I. Introduction

Barnes, H., & Samet, J. (1997) Brief intervention with substance-abusing patients. In J. Samet, P. O'Connor, & M. Stein (Eds.), *The Medical Clinics of North America, 81*(4), 867–879. Philadelphia: W.B. Saunders Company.

Cappocia, V. (1998). Substance abuse: Dispelling the myth. In *The view* (p. 3). Waltham, MA: The Florence Heller School for Advanced Studies in Social Welfare.

Oss, M. (1993). Managed behavioral health market share in the United States. *Behavioral Health Industry News, 7*(1), 10.

Rounsaville, B.J. Gawin, F., & Kebler, H. (1985). Interpersonal psychotherapy adapted for ambulatory cocaine abusers. *American Journal of Drug and Alcohol Abuse, 11,* 171–191.

II. Managed Care Systems and Behavioral Health Care Issues

Alperin, R. M., & Phillips, D. G. (1997). *The impact of managed care on the practice of psychotherapy: Innovation, implementation, and controversy.* New York: Bruner/Mazel.

Anders, G. (1996). *Health against wealth: HMOs and the breakdown of medical trust.* Boston: Houghton Mifflin.

Austed, M. F., & Hoyt, C. S. (1992). The managed care movement and the future of psychotherapy. *Psychotherapy, 29,* 109–113.

Battle over managed care rules expected to intensify (1996, November 24). *The Boston Sunday Globe,* p. 12.

Bernstein, C. A. (1994). Is managed care good for mental health clients? No. In S. A. Kirk & S. D. Enbinder (Eds.), *Controversial issues in mental health* (pp. 245–251). Boston: Allyn and Bacon.

Corcoran, K. (1994). Is managed care good for mental health clients? Yes. In S. A. Kirk & S. D. Enbinder (Eds.), *Controversial issues in mental health* (pp. 240–245). Boston: Allyn and Bacon.

Corcoran, K., & Vandiver, V. (1996). *Maneuvering the maze of managed care: Skills for mental health practitioners*. New York: The Free Press.

Cornelius, D. S. (1994). Managed care and social work: Constructing a context and a response. *Social Work in Health Care, 20*(1), 47–63.

Feldman, S. (1992). *Managed mental health services*. Springfield, IL: Charles C. Thomas.

Freeman, M. A., & Trabin, T. (1994). *Managed behavioral healthcare: History, models, key issues, and future course.* Chicago: Behavioral Health Alliance.

Goodman, M., Brown, J., & Dietz, P. (1992). *Managing managed care*. Washington, DC: American Psychiatric Press.

Gordon, S. (1996, October 13). Is research being 'managed' out of existence? *Boston Globe,* pp. D1, D2.

Hutchins, J. (1996). Managing managed care for families. *Empowering Families, 5*(2), 1, 6–7.

Iglehart, J. K. (1996). Health policy report: Managed care and mental health. *The New England Journal of Medicine, 334*(2), 131–135.

Joseph, B. S. (1993). Cost containment and the profit motive. *American Journal of Psychiatry, 150*(9), 1432–1433.

Leadholm, B. A., & Kerzner, J. P. (1995). Public managed care: Comprehensive community support in Massachusetts. *Administration and Policy in Mental Health, 22*(5), 543–552.

Mechanic, D., Schlesinger, M., & McAlpine, D. D. (1995). Management of mental health and substance abuse services: State of the art and early results. *Milbank Quarterly, 73*(1), 19–55.

Minkoff, K. (1994). Community mental health in the nineties: Public sector managed care. *Community Mental Health Journal, 30*(4), 317–321.

Questions about a hospital deal [Editorial]. (1996, November 29). *New York Times,* p. 22.

Rowland, D., Rosenbaum, S., Simon, L., & Chait, E. (1995). *Medicaid and managed care: Lessons from the literature. A report of the Kaiser Commission on the Future of Medicaid*. Washington, DC: The Kaiser Commission on the Future of Medicaid.

Samuelson, R. J. (1996, November 24). Mismanaged care [Review of the book *Health against wealth*]. *New York Times,* Review of Books, p. 13.

Sederer, L. I. (1992). Judicial and legislative response to cost containment. *American Journal of Psychiatry, 149(8*), 1157–1161.

Sederer, L. I. (1993). Dr. Sederer replies. *American Journal of Psychiatry, 150*(9), 1434.

Shera, W. (1996). Managed care and people with severe mental illness: Challenges and opportunities for social work. *Health and Social Work, 21*(3), 196–201.

Shore, M. F., & Beigel, A. (1996). *New England Journal of Medicine,* 334(2), 116–118.

Winegar, N. (1992). *The clinician's guide to managed mental health care*. New York: Haworth.

Winegar, N., & Bistline, J. (1994). *Marketing mental health services to managed care*. New York: Haworth.

III. Issues in the Managed Care of Substance Abuse Patients

Alaszewski, A., & Harrison, L. (1992). Alcohol and social work: A literature review. *British Journal of Social Work, 22,* 331–343.

Bachman, S. S. (1998). Managed mental health care for elders: The role of the carve-out. *The Public Policy and Aging Report, 9*(1), 14–16.

Bachman, S. S., Burwell, B. O., Albers, L. A., Herz, L., & Jackson, M. E. (1997).

Medicaid carve-outs: Policy and programmatic considerations. Princeton, NJ: Center for Health Care Strategies, Inc.

Barnes, H. N., & Samet, J. H. (1997). Brief interventions with substance-abusing patients. In J. Samet, P. O'Connor, & M. Stein (Eds.), *Medical Clinics of North America, 81*(4), 867–879. Philadelphia: W.B. Saunders Company.

Billig, N. S. & Levinson, C. (1989). Social work students as case managers: A model of service delivery and training. *Hospital and Community Psychiatry, 40*(4), 411–413.

Callahan, J. J., Shepard, D. S., Beinecke, R. H., Larson, M. J., & Cavanaugh, D. (1995). Mental health/substance abuse treatment in managed care: The Massachusetts Medicaid experience. *Health Affairs, 14*(3), 173–184.

Cappocia, V. (1998). Substance abuse: Dispelling the myth. In *The view* (p. 3). Waltham, MA: The Florence Heller School for Advanced Studies in Social Welfare.

Chervenak, F. A., & McCullough, L. B. (1995). The threat of the new managed care practice to patients' autonomy. *The Journal of Clinical Ethics, 6*(4), 320–323.

Christensen, K. T. (1995). Ethically important distinctions among managed care organizations. *Journal of Law, Medicine, and Ethics, 23,* 223–229.

Cornelius, D. S. (1994). Managed care and social work: Constructing a context and a response. *Social Work in Health Care, 20*(1), 47–63.

Emanuel, E. J. (1995). Medical ethics in the era of managed care: The need for institutional structures instead of principles for individual cases. *The Journal of Clinical Ethics, 6*(4), 335–338.

Council on Ethical and Judicial Affairs,

American Medical Association. (1995). Ethical issues in managed care. *Journal of the American Medical Association, 273*(4), 330–335.

Googins, B. (1984). Avoidance of the alcoholic client. *Social Work, 29,* 161–166.

Hawkins, J. W., Veeder, N. W., & Pearce, C. W. (1997). *Nurse–social worker collaboration in managed care: A model of community case managemen*t. New York: Springer Publishing Company.

Holleman, W. L., Edwards, D. C., & Matson, C. C. (1994). Obligations of physicians to patients and third-party payers. *The Journal of Clinical Ethics, 5*(2), 113–120.

Howe, E. G. (1995). Managed care: "New moves," moral uncertainty, and a radical attitude. *The Journal of Clinical Ethics, 6*(4), 290–305.

Humphreys, N. (1985). Social workers: Roles in alcohol and drug abuse services. *Alcohol and Health Research World, 9,* 28–29.

Jecker, N. S., & Pearlman, R. A. (1992). An ethical framework for rationing health care. *The Journal of Medicine and Philosophy, 17,* 79–96.

Johnson, P. J., & Rubin, A. (1983). Case management in mental health: A social work domain? *Social Work, 28,* 49–55.

Kagle, J. (1987). Secondary prevention of substance abuse. *Social Work, 32,* 446–448.

Koppel, T. (1996, November 8). Mental health care privacy and managed care. [Transcript]. *Nightline.* ABC Television, pp. 1–5.

Larson, M. J., Samet, J. H., & McCarty, D. (1997). Managed care of substance abuse disorders. Implications for generalist physicians. *Medical Clinics of North America,* 81(4), 1053–1069.

Lewis, D. C., Ludden, J. M., & McLellan, A. T. (1997). Training primary care physicians to recognize and treat substance abuse. *National Health Policy Forum,* No. 706, Washington, DC: The George Washington University, 1–10.

Morreim, E. H. (1995). Lifestyles of the risky and infamous: From managed care to managed lives. *Hastings Center Report, 25*(6), 5–12.

NASW code of ethics. (1996). Washington, DC: National Association of Social Workers.

Peebles-Wilkins, W., & Veeder, N. W. (1996). *Research needs in managed behavioral health care in Massachusetts* (NIMH Technical Paper).

Pellegrino, E. D. (1995). Interests, obligations, and justice: Some notes toward an ethic of managed care. *The Journal of Clinical Ethics, 6*(4), 312–317.

Rhodes, R., & Johnson, A. D. (1996). Social work and substance-abuse treatment: A challenge for the profession. *Families in Society, 2,* 182–185.

Sabin, J. E. (1994). A credo for ethical managed care in mental health practice. *Hospital and Community Psychiatry, 45*(9), 859–860, 869.

Saitz, R., Mulvey, K. P., & Samet, J. H. (1997a). The substance-abusing patient and primary care: Linkage via the addiction treatment system. *Substance Abuse, 18*(4), 187–195.

Saitz, R., Mulvey, K. P., Plough, A., & Samet, J. H. (1997b). Physicians unawareness of serious substance abuse. *American Journal of Drug Alcohol Abuse, 23*(3), 343–354.

Saltz, C. C., & Schaefer, T. (1996). Interdisciplinary teams in health care: Integration of family caregivers. *Social Work in Health Care, 22*(3), 59–70.

Schamess, G. (1996). Who profits and who benefits from managed mental health care? *Smith College Studies in Social Work, 66*(3), 209–220.

Schamess, G., & Lightburn, A. (1998). *Humane managed care.* Bethesda, MD: NASW Press.

Sulmasy, D. P. (1995). Managed care and the new medical paternalism. *The Journal of Clinical Ethics, 6*(4), 324–326.

Toner, R. (1996, November 24). Harry and Louise were right, sort of. *New York Times,* section 4, pp. 1, 3.

Vayda, E., & Bogo, M. (1991). A teaching model to unite classroom and field. *Journal of Social Work Education, 27,* 271–278.

Veeder, N. W., & Peebles-Wilkins, W. (1998). Research needs in managed behavioral health care. In G. Schamess & A. Lightburn, *Humane managed care.* Bethesda, MD: NASW Press.

Weil, M. O. (1996). Community building: Building community practice. *Social Work, 41*(5), 481–499.

Zoloth-Dorfman, L., & Rubin, S. (1995). The patient as commodity: Managed care and the question of ethics. *The Journal of Clinical Ethics, 6*(4), 339–357.

IV. Existing Research in Managed Care of Substance Abuse Patients

Bangert-Drowns, R. L., Wells-Parker, E., & Chevillard, I. (1997). Asessing the methodological quality of research in narrative reviews and meta-analyses. In K. J. Bryant, M. Windle & S. G. Wells. *The science of prevention: Methodological advances from alcohol and substance abuse research.* Washington, DC: American Psychological Association.

Beinecke, R. H., & Keane, R. J. (1997). *Mental health providers assessment of the Massachusetts managed mental health/substance abuse abuse program: Year Five.* Boston: Suffolk University, Department of Public Management.

Beinecke, R. H., Callahan, J. J., Shepard, D. S., Cavanaugh, D. A., & Larson, M. J. (1996). The Massachusetts mental health/substance abuse managed care program: The providers' view. *Administration and Policy in Mental Health, 23*(5), 379–391.

Bryant, K. J., West, S. G., & Windle, M. (1997). Overview of new methodological developments in prevention research: Alcohol and substance abuse. In K. J. Bryant, M. Windle, & S. G. West, *The science of prevention: Methodological advances from alcohol and substance abuse research.* Washington, DC: American Psychological Association.

Bryant, K. J., Windle, M., & West, S. G. (1997). *The science of prevention: Methodological advances from alcohol and substance abuse research.* Washington, DC: American Psychological Association.

Buckley, R., & Bigelow, D. A. (1992). The multi-service network: Reaching the unserved multi-problem individual. *Community Mental Health Journal, 28*(1), 43–50.

Burke, A. C., & Clapp, J. D. (1997). Ideology and social work practice in substance abuse settings. *Social Work, 42*(6), 552–562.

Callahan, J. J., Shepard, D. S., Beinecke, R. H., Larson, M. J., & Cavanaugh, D. (1995). Mental health/substance abuse treatment in managed care: The Massachusetts Medicaid experience. *Health Affairs, 14*(3), 173–184.

Collins, L. M., Graham, J. W., Rousculp, S. S., & Hansen, W. B. (1997). Heavy caffeine use and the beginning of the substance abuse onset process: An illustration of latent transition analysis. In K. J. Bryant, M. Windle, & S. G. West. *The science of prevention: Methodological advances from alcohol and substance abuse research.* Washington, DC: American Psychological Association.

Drake, R. E., Becker, D. R., Biesanz, J. C., Torrey, W. C., McHugo, G. J., & Wyzik, P. F. (1994). Rehabilitative day treatment vs. supported employment: I. Vocational outcomes. *Community Mental Health Journal, 30*(5), 519–532.

Faul, A. C., & Hudson, W. W. (1997). The index of drug involvement: A partial validation. *Social Work, 42*(6), 565–572.

Foss, M. A. (1997). Practical power analysis for substance abuse health services research. In K. J. Bryant, M. Windle, & S. G. West, *The science of prevention: Methodological advances from alcohol and substance abuse research.* Washington, DC: American Psychological Association.

Hayashida, M., Alterman, A. I., McLellan, A. T., O'Brien, C. P., Purtill, B. A., Volpicelli, J. R., Raphaelson, A. H., & Hall, C. P. (1989). Comparative effectiveness and costs of inpatient and outpatient detoxification of patients with mild-to-moderate alcohol withdrawal syndrome. *New England Journal of Medicine, 320*(6), 358–365.

Kreft, I. G. G. (1997). The interactive effect of alcohol prevention programs in high school classes: An illustration of item homogeneity scaling and multilevel analysis techniques. In K. J. Bryant, M. Windle, & S. G. West, *The science of prevention. Methodological Advances from alcohol and substance abuse research.* Washington, DC: American Psychological Association.

Manning, W. G. (1997). Alternative econometric models of alcohol demand. In K. J. Bryant, M. Windle, & S. G. West, *The science of prevention: Methodological advances from alcohol and substance abuse research*. Washington, DC: American Psychological Association.

McAuliffe, W. E., Breer, P., Ahmadifar, N. W., & Spino, C. (1991). Assessment of drug abuser treatment needs in Rhode Island. *American Journal of Public Health, 81*(3), 365–371.

Mechanic D., Schlesinger, M., & McAlpine, D. D. (1995). Management of mental health and substance abuse services: State of the art and early results. *The Milbank Quarterly, 73*(1), 19–55.

Moscovice, I., Lurie, N., Christianson, J., Finch, M., Popkin, M., & Akhtar, M. R. (1993). Access and use of health services by chronically mentally ill Medicaid beneficiaries. *Health Care Financing Review, 14*(4), 75–87.

Sher, K. J., & Wood, P. K. (1997). Methodological issues in conducting prospective research on alcohol-related behavior: A report from the field. In K. J. Bryant, M. Windle, & S. G. West, *The science of prevention: Methodological advances from alcohol and substance abuse research*. Washington, DC: American Psychological Association.

Velicer, W. F., & Colby, S. M. (1997). Time series analysis for prevention and treatment research. In K. J. Bryant, M. Windle, & S. G. West. *The science of prevention: Methodological advances from alcohol and substance abuse research*. Washington, DC: American Psychological Association.

Wells, K. B., Astrachan, B. M., Tischler, G. L., & Unutzer, J. (1995). Issues and approaches in evaluating managed mental health care. *The Milbank Quarterly, 73*(1), 57–75.

West, S. G., & Aiken, L. S. (1997). Toward understanding individual effects in multicomponent prevention programs: Design and analysis strategies. In K. J. Bryant, M. Windle, & S. G. West, *The science of prevention: Methodological advances from alcohol and substance abuse research*. Washington, DC: American Psychological Association.

Westhuis, D. J., Hayashi, R., Hart, L., Cousert, D., & Spinks, M. (1998). Evaluating treatment issues in a military drug and alcohol treatment program. *Research on Social Work Practice, 8*(5), 501–519.

Widaman, K. F., & Reise, S. P. (1997). Exploring the measurement invariance of psychological instruments: Applications in the substance use domain. In K. J. Bryant, M. Windle, & W. G. West, *The science of prevention: Methodological advances from alcohol and drug abuse research*. Washington, DC: American Psychological Association.

Windle, M. (1997). Alternative latent-variable approaches to modeling change in adolescent alcohol involvement. In K. J. Bryant, M. Windle, & S. G. West, *The science of prevention: Methodological advances from alcohol and substance abuse research*. Washington, DC: American Psychological Association.

V. Future Research Needs in the Managed Care of Substance Abuse

Clarke, G. N. (1995). Improving the transition from basic efficacy research to effectiveness studies: Methodological issues and procedures. *Journal of Consulting and Clinical Psychology, 63*(5), 718–723.

Dorwart, R. A. (1990). Managed mental health care: Myths and realities in the 1990s. *Hospital and Community Psychiatry, 41*(10), 1087–1091.

Gottlieb, G. L. (1989). Diversity, uncertainty, and variations in practice: The behaviors and clinical decisionmaking of mental health care providers. In C. A. Taube, D. Mechanic, & A. A. Hohmann, *The future of mental health services research* (pp. 225–251). Rockville, MD: U. S. Department of Health and Human Services.

Hargreaves, W. A., & Shumway, M. (1989). Effectiveness of services for the severely mentally ill. In C. A. Taube, D. Mechanic, & A. A. Hohmann, *The future of mental health services research* (pp. 253–283). Rockville, MD: U. S. Department of Health and Human Services.

Mirin, S. M., & Namerow, M. J. (1991). Why study treatment outcome? *Hospital and Community Psychiatry, 42*(10), 1007–1013.

◆ CONCLUSION

Managing the Change in Health and Behavioral Health Care

Issues discussed in this book are not isolated, anemic academic concepts. Every one of these issues has been recently and tragically realized in an HMO disaster of the first order.

The completion of the first draft of this book coincided with the largest managed health and behavioral health care organization in Massachusetts, Harvard Community Health Plan (HCHP), going into state receivership, owing $280 million in payments to providers. This corporation, a not-for-profit managed care organization, covered 1.1 million people, including 30% of the mental health market. Other large managed care insurers in the region are expected to follow in this massive managed care debacle. Such crises are not limited to the New England region; Kaiser-Permanente in California faced massive shortfalls of approximately $300 million this year as well.

The major reason for the receivership and precarious status of HCHP is, ironically, the failure to contain costs, one of two basic criteria, along with delivery of quality services, of all managed health and behavioral health corporations, whether for-profit or not-for-profit. Other more specific reasons for the crisis are a reliance on the low-bid wars of the marketplace; failure, because of the need to bid low on enrollment, drug costs, and physician and other provider reimbursements, to charge enough in drug costs and premiums to employers to cover costs, much less to make profits; gross overpayment of administrative staffs; decentralized and unreliable record-keeping systems and data gathering; and failure to keep consumers' service needs in the forefront of activities. In short, the system self-destructed because of more and more money being spent on marketing and attempted cost-containments and less and less on care.

A former editor of the *New England Journal of Medicine* observed in the *Boston Globe* that, "Harvard Pilgrim is a victim of a marketplace that emphasizes price over quality" (Dr. Arnold Relman, in Kuttner, January 9, 2000, p. A12). The *Globe* article describes the dramatic managed care dilemmas highlighted in the Harvard Pilgrim receivership, issues and dilemmas discussed in every chapter in this book: "Indeed, the ideal of managed care in the constructive sense as practiced by Harvard Community Health Plan, is too expensive for today's cost-conscious marketplace. . . . Instead of having one large pool, in which the premiums paid by the well subsidize the medical care of the sick, insurance companies following market principles seek to avoid insuring or treating sick people. It is a sign of the sickness of the system that relatively ethical plans go under" (Kuttner, January 9, 2000, p. A12).

Managed health and behavioral health care in some form or another will be with us from now on. The purpose of this book has been to lay out ways to better manage the inevitable change that managed health and behavioral health care systems have, and will, provide to their many stakeholders, corporations, government, providers, and consumers. The following sections outline what is needed to manage managed care in the near and long future in the areas of needed policies, programs, and research.

POLICY

Over 45 million people are uninsured as of the advent of the year 2000. The number grows daily. To the previous list of at-risk and vulnerable individuals—such as the poor, substance abusers, unemployed, homeless, elderly, disabled, children, minorities of color, and the mentally ill—is now added new categories of those at-risk: the underemployed, those employed by small companies unable to purchase group insurance for employees, those with pre-existing conditions which render them incapable of being insured or reinsured, and those increasingly responsible for the physical and financial care of the elderly. The continuity of care available to the currently insured can vanish overnight, as the receivership of Harvard Pilgrim described above attests.

Most Americans want health and behavioral health security, which means universal, affordable, accessible, and uninterrupted coverage throughout the life span. In order to achieve this, the following policy issues must be dealt with at both the federal and state levels, and by the public and private sectors:

- *Publicly Managed Health and Behavioral Health Insurance.* One strong consumer-provider opinion, repeatedly expressed in opinion polls and state and local referenda across the country, is to return health and behavioral health care services from a commodity in the marketplace status, which is currently the case, to an essential social good status. Desperately needed is some form of public safety-net program for the growing number of at-risk un- and underinsured people.

  Many observers have documented cost savings that could be achieved through a single insurance pool, administered by one public agency, which would collect all of the money now spent on private health insurance or medical care directly and then pay bills incurred by all citizens. This so-called single-payer system would save enough, advocates project, to finance coverage for all of those uninsured currently and in the future (savings of 10% of the total cost of health care last year are estimated).

Advocates for such a system assert that more benefits for the same dollars would accrue, coverage would be wider than now allowed, drugs would cost less, and there would be increased access to home-care services. Most important, consumers could choose their own health care providers, and health care providers would not be pressured to deny necessary tests and treatments, or prematurely eject patients from the hospital. Among the stated drawbacks for such a publicly run health care system is that public systems have difficulty setting priorities and rationing care. Such issues would have to be addressed by a variety of oversight features, to include inputs from all stakeholders in the delivery of health care, which would be built in from the inception of such a system.

The crucial issue in such a system, given an aging population and escalating technology costs, would be judicious management in an arena where the public, rather than private insurers, providers, and employers, has the final word about quantity, costs, and, most important, quality of health and behavioral health services (Early & Gordon, January 11, 2000, p. A15).

- *Cost of Care.* The cost of basic preventive and primary health and behavioral health care must be affordable, either by direct payment, insurance, or federal and state subsidization to all citizens from cradle to grave.
- *Access to Care.* All citizens must have equal access to preventive and primary health care.
- *Parity of Behavioral Health Services Reimbursement.* Mental health services must have parity of payment with other health services. One in five Americans has a mental disorder in any given year. Currently, only twenty-eight states have partial—not necessarily full—parity in payments for mental health services.
- *Mental Health Services Must Be Integrated with Other Health Services.* Mental health services should not be "carved out" of health services delivery packages but should be offered, at parity with all other health services, as a primary care package.

PROGRAMS AND SERVICES DELIVERY

The major programmatic issue in health and behavioral health services delivery is lack of utilization of all health and behavioral health services, but particularly preventive services such as early screening and detection. Those persons already at high risk for poor outcomes on any number of health and sociodemographic risk factors form a disproportionately high number of those who underutilize services, thus compounding their risk status. Programs, services, and professional education, therefore, must be designed in a manner that increases the likelihood of risk reduction through increased and appropriate services utilization.

- Design services sufficient in breadth, complexity, and cultural relevance to ameliorate both acute and chronic illnesses, particularly among special-needs and at-risk groups.
- Deliver services in a flexible, culturally relevant manner in the community, utilizing a multidisciplinary team model.
- Case management, or care management, must be the advanced psychosocial and educational intervention mode in managed care; care management combines sophisticated understanding of health and mental health needs with complex systemic understanding of ethnic and cultural diversity, disability and welfare benefits, housing, psychosocial prevention and rehabilitation, sheltered and competitive work programs, and legal and criminal justice system issues.
- Programs and services must be designed with non-market ethical issues in mind.
- Professional education programs in medicine, nursing, and social work must focus on managing managed care and delivering those services that are consonant with the training of the particular professional group, rather than on carrying out the market stance of health insurers.

RESEARCH

The greatest need in the delivery of managed care services is the availability of reliable and valid data bases in relation to consumer need, services delivered, and outcomes studies.

- Experiments are needed in different managed care services-delivery modalities. Initially, when the current system of managed care was implemented across states, there should have been studies of health care financing models in terms of cost, quality of outcomes, and access efficiency. A series of experimental designs to test a variety of care delivery models should have been fielded in all 50 states. Unfortunately, these studies were not implemented. However, there is every reason to recommend that controlled experiments be designed and implemented in the future.
- Consumer need must be assessed across ethnic and cultural groups and health and mental health diagnostic categories. Currently there are insufficient data to assess the pervasiveness of problems, the types of services being delivered and by whom, and the utilization rates among need areas.

- Quality-of-life outcomes must be assessed—with which populations, with which services-delivery modalities, for what length of time, at what cost. Also needed are comparisons of various models for integrating versus carving-out services; such comparisons are limited and confounded by complex variables of quality, provider incentive, workload, and skill level. Whatever the outcomes criteria are, they must not be limited to consumer satisfaction, but must include hard data such as medical and psychiatric diagnosis, treatment protocols and outcomes; best-practices research.
- Cross-cultural studies must be designed to answer questions such as, Are there differences in cost in providing services to people of color and other vulnerable and at-risk groups? If so, which factors explain these differences? Are there utilization differences, differences in types of successful and unsuccessful programs and services, and differences in professional training needed for these at-risk groups?
- Research on the place of preventive services in managed care must assess whether the potential for freeing of financial resources for preventive services in managed care systems has, in fact, been realized, and if so, with what empirical results.
- Research on the value of interdisciplinary practice must empirically examine assertions of improvements in both cost-efficiency and quality of services-delivery outcomes through interdisciplinary collaborative service-delivery arrangements.

The current chaos in the managed care approach to health and mental health services-delivery may well provide an opportunity to redress the balance between the currently dysfunctional and unsuccessful overemphasis on cost, products, and the marketplace and underemphasis on consumers, particularly those at medical and mental health risk. The redress of this imbalance will require careful and united simultaneous action on the policy, programmatic, and research fronts in the future delivery of health and behavioral health care services to the entire population.

REFERENCES

Early, S., & Gordon, S. (2000, January 11) Amid HMO crisis, Bay State can make health history. *Boston Globe*, A12.

Kuttner, R. (2000, January 9) Harvard Pilgrim's error. *Boston Globe*, A15.

◆ MANAGED CARE GLOSSARY

BBA: Balanced Budget Act.

CAHPS: Consumer Assessment of Health Plans Survey.

Capitation: Physician is paid a per-member, per-month fee regardless of whether the patient uses the service. Shifts focus of practice from patient-provider to population-provider.

Carve-outs: Separate management of a particular service such as mental health, through an organization or network of providers that functions independently of the medical provider network (common carve-outs are substance abuse and pharmaceuticals); contrasting system to carve-outs is generalist physician as gatekeeper to specialized mental health services.

Case management: Services which include medical compliance, home-based patient management, utilization management, risk management, service coordination; continuity management, utilized extensively with high-risk, high-cost medical conditions.

Clinical practice guidelines/critical pathways/practice protocols/clinical pathways: Standardized intervention and treatment protocols designed to insure timely and appropriate care; standards of care.

CMCN: Consumer managed care network.

Cost Shifting: To provider (salary cuts, salary increases) and consumer (home care, private financing).

CPI: Consumer price index.

DRGS: Diagnostic related groups; groupings of health care consumers into similar diagnostic categories for efficiencies of cost in delivery of services.

EDI: Electronic data interchange.

Fee-for-service: A method of paying for health care services in which the provider diagnoses the ailment, prescribes the treatment, and determines the length of care and the fees; each unit of service is billed to the consumer, insurer, or employer; financial risk is carried almost exclusively by the insurer and the employer is responsible for payment of premiums; based on fees paid for private physicians; system of payment for services which was supplanted by managed care.

Gatekeeper: Refers to primary care case management where all health and behavioral health care from providers other than the primary care physician must be authorized by the primary care physician; predominant feature of all HMOs.

GDP: Gross domestic product.

HCFA: Health Care Financing Administration.

HEDIS: Health Care Employer Data and Information Set.

HMO: Health maintenance organization.

IPA: Independent-practice-association-model Health Maintenance Organization (HMO).

Managed care: A comprehensive system of health and behavioral health services that aims to combine cost-efficiency with services-delivery effectiveness.

MCO: Managed care organization.

Medicaid: Federal program finances long-term care for elders.

Medical management: Achieved through such processes as physician profiling and peer review; specialty and emergency referral authorization; hospital precertification; clinical practice standardization; and physician incentives. Employed by payers and health systems to ensure delivery of medical services by the most appropriate provider at the lowest appropriate level of care and at the lowest cost.

Medicare: Federal program financing acute care for elders.

MLR: Medical loss ratio; the percentage of each premium dollar that is expended on administrative overhead versus direct medical care.

NCQA: National Commission on Quality Assurance; establishes standards of accreditation for managed care organizations.

Non-market values: Found in fee-for-service and government programs such as Medicaid: entitlement, choice, participation, autonomy, unlimited access, rights, and information sharing; managed care systems are dominated by market values.

OAA: Older Americans Act; combines with Medicaid and various state-funded programs to finance long-term care for elders.

PACE (Program for All-Inclusive Care for the Elderly): A new capitated benefit that combines Medicare and Medicaid Funds to provide acute and long-term health care services for older patients who are eligible for nursing home care.

Patient Dumping: Removing patients from health insurance rosters, frequently due to pre-existing conditions or at-risk status.

Physician profiling: Creating effective and professionally acceptable mechanisms for communicating utilization, referral, and cost information to physician groups throughout the network.

POS: Point of service.

PPMCs: Physician practice management companies.

PPO: Preferred provider organization.

Pre-existing conditions: Conditions, such as in hypertension and diabetes, which managed care wishes to avoid insuring due to high actual or potential treatment costs.

Risk Adjustments: Identification of financial risk factors within a given population; to adjust capitation fees based on those risk factors.

Risk pools: Distributes financial risk among a group of providers.

Segmentation: Categorization of individuals and groups within a market or population based on some key identifiable characteristic: age, gender, religion, social class, type of employment, place of employment, education, neighborhood, race, ethnicity, or marital status; the aim of segmentation is to reach the most profitable and least costly markets, penetrate them, and sell the goods and services designed for this market; correspondingly, the intent is to avoid investments in markets that have less potential for profit or a higher probability of increased demands and costs.

S/HMO: Social health maintenance organization; involves an integration of acute care and long-term care for the elderly on a capitation basis.

Selective Contracting: Contracting on the basis of consumer demographics, such as contracting with providers of services to healthy clients.

Utilization management: Using gatekeeping and preauthorization for certain referrals or tests; profiling of utilization patterns; clinical practice guidelines.

Utilization review: A process through which insurers and providers monitor and regulate level of care, length of stay, and service utilization in ambulatory, emergency, and acute care settings.

Withholds: Percentage of fee-for-service payments that are withheld during a set period of service and are returned to the provider based on his/her practice patterns. The percentage of the "withhold" that is returned to the provider is based on the costs he/she generates. Provider is penalized for costly practices.

◆ INDEX